CHRISTIANITY DIVIDED

Protestant and Roman Catholic
Theological Issues

CHRISTIANITY DIVIDED

Protestant and Roman Catholic
Theological Issues

edited by
DANIEL J. CALLAHAN
HEIKO A. OBERMAN
DANIEL J. O'HANLON, S.J.

SHEED AND WARD — NEW YORK

© SHEED AND WARD, INC., 1961

LIBRARY OF CONGRESS CATALOG CARD NUMBER 61–11789

For that portion of the book written by Catholic theologians: *Nihil obstat,* John R. Ready, *Censor Librorum,* June 27, 1961; *Imprimatur,* ✠ Robert F. Joyce, Bishop of Burlington, June 28, 1961.

MANUFACTURED IN THE UNITED STATES OF AMERICA

Contents

Introduction

THE rapid growth of concern over Christian disunity which began
with the end of World War II has surely been one of the most remarkable spiritual events of our times. In Europe, it was the war itself and
the shared suffering of all Christians which made the evil of division
and separation so apparent. In America, spared such direct suffering,
the emergence of a more fully pluralistic society has brought home to
many a sharp sense of the spiritual losses that inevitably trail in the
wake of religious differences. It has become apparent that Christian disunity is nothing less than an offense to our common Lord, a
blight on the Spirit, and a scandal to the world.

The response to this scandal has taken many forms. From the
Protestant side the World Council of Churches has led the way in the
quest for unity. For Roman Catholicism the search for unity has taken
varied directions, the most prominent perhaps being the establishment of a number of European centers (and several in America)
devoted to the study of Protestantism and the Orthodox Churches.
Apart, however, from the more formal efforts, numerous individual
scholars have dedicated much of their work to sympathetic studies of
differing theological systems and forms of Christian life. A number of
periodicals devoted exclusively to ecumenical questions has provided
still another source of stimulation.

Most importantly, it was recognized from the outset in Europe
that only the direct encounter of Christian with Christian could pre-
pare the ground in which the seed of charity might grow into the tree
of unity. Of immediate importance, however, was the possibility of
frank exchanges of theological comments and criticisms which such
encounters afforded. Once the climate of good will was firmly established, it was possible to take up once again so many of the issues
which had not been openly discussed at close quarters since the years
of the Reformation. Although proceeding somewhat more slowly,

the situation in America and England has developed in a fashion similar to that on the Continent.

In venturing to publish the collection of articles which follows we are frankly hopeful that the atmosphere of discussion in America and England is sufficiently healthy to allow us to take a direct plunge into some key theological problems. There are good grounds for such a hope. First of all, it is a simple fact that there are now a considerable number of groups of Roman Catholic and Protestant theologians and clergy which meet frequently to discuss fundamental ecumenical matters. Secondly, more and more of the theologically educated laity are becoming absorbed in questions of Christian unity and disunity. Thirdly, the astounding proliferation of books and articles on this subject suggests a growing body of Christians deeply disturbed about their separation from one another. Yet so far most of the published material has centered on very general matters—the sources of disunity, the positions of the Churches toward one another, sweeping theological evaluations, and so on. We believe the time is ripe to advance beyond the level of generalities to more specific questions; the very fruitful results of the broad discussions impel us forward.

Our purpose, then, can be stated quite directly. We want to make available to a wider audience some significant works by important theologians in critical areas of ecumenical discussion. Our aim has been to present these works in such a way that it will be possible for the reader to note pertinent areas of agreement and disagreement between Protestant and Roman Catholic; and to note as well differences of interest and emphasis. This latter point is important. For we soon came to discover that it was often quite impossible to match the discussions perfectly: what is of crucial concern for one communion may be of minor importance at a given moment in history for another. Finally, we hope that this collection may prove useful for some of the increasing number of study groups, seminary and university courses and seminars springing up here and abroad.

Now it should be said that, as hopeful as the state of our discussion appears to be, a return to genuine theological conversation runs many risks. It is all too easy to open old wounds and exacerbate old differences. It is one thing to talk of good will and the need for "dialogue." It is quite another to be able to listen with charity to views we may consider false or even a fundamental betrayal of the Christian faith. This risk seems to us unavoidable. The possibility of an increase of ill will rather than a decrease is the price that must be paid if frankness and honesty are to be the rule governing our conversation with one another.

The other danger, of course, that discussion entails is that of raising false hopes and encouraging illusory dreams. Some indeed may feel that the very fact of mutual interest and exchange is the first step toward doctrinal compromise and theological indifferentism. There seems to us little basis for such worries. The experience of the Continental talks provides good evidence that a frank exchange of views in an atmosphere of Christian charity leads neither to increased hostility nor doctrinal compromise. There is no reason to believe the same will not be true in this country. Indeed, our courage to be frank with one another will provide the best protection against any temptation to weaken fundamental positions in the name of unity. So too it will be our mutual respect which will provide the best protection against a new birth of rancor and recrimination which could spring from this frankness. Too frequently in the past doubts about the very integrity and motives of one another have poisoned the beginnings of a fruitful encounter. There is not—need we add—any certain way of forestalling this kind of cynicism other than to listen, and listen patiently, to the human being who speaks to us.

We are neither romantic nor cynical about the value of the kind of direct confrontation this collection exhibits. To expect that a mere airing of differences, an open presentation of one's thoughts and aspirations, will lead to ultimate reunion is sheer naïveté if not madness. But a belief that such confrontations are mere exercises in futility has little to commend it: that assumes the equally naïve, if not arrogant, view that we know all that we need to know about the other. However modest one's expectations may be, we are convinced that even the slightest possibility of an increase of understanding and insight makes the attempt fully worth the efforts and the risks.

What can one hope from the kind of airing of old questions we present here? We can surely hope that we will, here and there, learn something new about one another: not only what we were thinking fifty or three hundred years ago but what we think today. We can hope that the very restating of old positions will, on occasion, reveal emphases and shadings often missed in past statements. We can be quite certain that the simple fact of saying the same thing again (when that is necessary) from time to time, in different ages by different people to different listeners, will produce different reactions, different possibilities of response. We can surely hope that, at the very least, we may show each other that our respective commitments are the fruit of a genuinely Christian commitment and concern.

To be more specific, we think that many of the selections in this book will reveal new directions and emphases in Roman Catholicism and Protestantism which are not nearly as well known as they deserve to be. It may, for instance, surprise many Roman Catholics to learn that there is a lively interest today within Protestantism in the problem of Tradition. Many Protestants will doubtless be surprised to discover that Roman Catholic theologians have a lively awareness of the dangers of a sheerly mechanistic theory of the sacraments. Even when, as it often turns out, we are dimly aware that new wine is being poured, we will still need to see for ourselves just what this means in specific settings. Inevitably there will be some unpleasant surprises as well. These have their place also in any honest encounter.

Now that we have stated our purposes and our hopes, it will be well to provide some idea of our principles of selection. What we immediately discovered, when we first conceived this collection, was that the very choice of topics and authors was in itself something of an ecumenical problem. Is it actually possible to reduce the areas of theological difference to a few basic ones? Is there such a thing as "the" ecumenical problem from which all others stem? Which theologians can be said to be "representative" in their churches? Or is the *non*representative theologian the one who ought to be of interest and concern since he may be the one who will shape future trends? These and many other questions troubled us. We cannot attempt here to discuss these matters in detail. We can only set down the decisions we made and briefly note our reasoning in coming to them.

The first consideration that influenced our choice of topics was our belief that *theological* differences are most important and *theological* problems are most central. No one can doubt that cultural differences, historical events, social and political upheavals, and questions of Christian life and conduct have been a tremendous force in shaping both the content and direction of our disunity. But in the end our theological perspectives will determine our understanding of Christianity: it is on these perspectives that we have chosen to concentrate our efforts.

The second consideration influencing our choice of topics was our decision that the areas of discussion should be ones which have been of traditional significance and which, by general agreement, remain significant. We are well aware that other topics than those we have chosen might have fitted these specifications. Natural law, the relationship of faith and reason, the role of the layman, the source of Christian authority, apostolic succession, the integrity of conscience: all of these topics have loomed large at one time or another. We would by no means want to suggest that they are not important.

One particularly vexing question was whether the book should be given over to one topic only or, at the other extreme, the greatest possible number. In settling on five topics we sought to strike a mean between the assumption that all the differences between Roman Catholicism and Protestantism are reducible to one (the meaning of the Church or justification or faith and reason or authority, etc.) or that in every conceivable particular there are radical differences. The trouble with adopting what might be called the "single issue" view is that each age since the Reformation has had a somewhat different conception of just what this issue might be. Justification was put forward most frequently in the sixteenth century; the development of doctrine in the nineteenth; the nature of the Church in the middle of our own century. The "single issue" approach is further complicated by the fact that Protestants and Roman Catholics have rarely been able to agree about what the most basic and determinative difference between them is. In settling, finally, on *Scripture and Tradition, the Bible: Hermeneutics, the Church, the Sacraments,* and *Justification,* we believe we have sufficiently met our initial requirements of traditional significance and contemporary relevance.

If the choice of topics was a difficult one, the choice of authors and articles posed even more complicated puzzles. Our first condition was that the selections should be of a length adequate to insure a reasonably full treatment and a reasonably good glimpse of the process of theological thought. We wanted the reader to see not only *what* our chosen theologians think but, of equal importance, *how* they think. Hence we sought to avoid formal statements, confessions, and pronouncements. Our main consideration was that the selection be of value in an ecumenical context, either by being clear restatements in some detail of traditional positions or by being suggestive of new trends and developments within the Protestant and Roman Catholic communities. It was the latter aim which led us to undertake to make available material not easily accessible even to an interested clergy and laity. In many instances this meant that translations were necessary. This was especially true in our choice of the articles by Fathers Schillebeeckx, Geiselmann, and Küng, all of whom are very influential in Europe but are practically unknown in English-speaking countries. And although the writings of Doctors van Ruler and Thurian are somewhat known among theologians in this country, their increasing influence moved us to translate and reprint some of the results of their work.

We should make it clear, however, that we do not claim that the theologians we have chosen or the viewpoints they express are "representative"—especially if by that one means holding positions which all other theologians of their respective Churches would fully accept. In some instances this is true and in others not. We do believe, nonetheless, that the men who speak here are important and influential: they are men who are listened to within their own Churches and whose voices cannot be ignored.

Many important theologians are, naturally enough, not represented in this book and many important Churches are not represented at all. Most notably, we have included no Anglican theologians, no French Roman Catholics, and no American Protestant theologians. One major reason for these omissions is that the writings of these men are for the most part easily available and well known; and that includes the large group of French Roman Catholic theologians who have done important ecumenical work, most of whom have had some of their articles and books translated.

We have tried in one way to balance the scales by taking account of such omissions in our choice of "Selected Readings" appended to each article. We have attempted in these "Selected Readings" to provide a twofold balance: a balance between introductory and advanced works and a balance between varying schools of thought on the topic in question. Our annotations are intended to make these differences clear.

There is one omission in the book which requires a special note. At first we had hoped to be able to include at least one article by an Orthodox theologian. We quickly found that to limit ourselves to just one article would inevitably seem arbitrary and peripheral, and would fail to do justice to the important position of the Orthodox Churches. An obvious complication too was the fact that the Orthodox Churches stand in different relationships with Protestantism and Roman Catholicism—relationships which could scarcely be made clear without greatly expanding the size of our book. In the end, it seemed apparent to us that nothing short of a full collection of Orthodox writings would be satisfactory or sufficient.

As a final note, it would be appropriate to indicate the respective duties undertaken by each of the three coeditors. The choice of the Protestant articles and the writing of the introductions to those articles were the responsibility of Rev. Dr. Heiko A. Oberman. Rev. Daniel J. O'Hanlon, S.J., performed the same task for the Roman Catholic selections. The general direction and final preparation of the collection was the responsibility of Daniel J. Callahan. At all times, however, and especially in the preliminary stages, we worked closely together and freely discussed our views until we reached agreement.

We would like to take this opportunity to express our appreciation to the numerous people who have assisted us, either with their advice or their time and, in some cases, both. A special word of thanks is due our translators, many of whom undertook their work amidst already crowded schedules. To David Willis, Teaching Fellow in the Church History Department of the Harvard Divinity School, Helmut Koester, Associate Professor of New Testament Studies, Harvard Divinity School, and Mrs. Sidney deS. Callahan, goes our gratitude for their assistance in the preparation of the final manuscript.

DANIEL J. CALLAHAN
HEIKO A. OBERMAN
DANIEL J. O'HANLON, S.J.

CHRISTIANITY DIVIDED

Protestant and Roman Catholic
Theological Issues

PART ONE

Scripture and Tradition

The Protestant Position

The Roman Catholic Position

INTRODUCTION:

THE PROTESTANT VIEW OF
SCRIPTURE AND TRADITION

THE respective conceptions of the relation between Scripture and Tradition are widely held to constitute the most decisive and fundamental issue at stake between Roman Catholicism and Reformation. It is therefore not unexpected that this problem has been chosen as the subject matter of the first section. At the same time, its very importance makes a separate treatment of the relation of Scripture and Tradition seem artificial since it is impossible to deal with the doctrine of justification and the sacraments—and especially with biblical hermeneutics and the doctrine of the Church—without being decisively influenced by one's understanding of the relation between Scripture and Tradition. That is why the other contributions all deal to some extent with this issue and why much of what is said in this introduction applies equally to the other Protestant sections, especially the following two.

There is also a second, though less conspicuous, reason for giving priority to the problem of the sources of the Christian faith: in this area there are some hopeful signs of interconfessional cross-currents. Yet old fronts still stand and it would be unrealistic even to think in terms of an imminent agreement.

Viewed from the Reformation tradition, the functional equality of Scripture and Tradition as codified by the Council of Trent has proved to undermine the authority of Holy Scripture. While the Fathers of Trent thought of the Tradition only in terms of a materially secondary source of the Christian faith, they still shared the medieval conviction that Holy Scripture contained all that is necessary for salvation. Much of the dogmatization of post-apostolic developments, such as the declarations of the Immaculate Conception (1854) and of the Bodily Assumption (1950) of the Virgin Mary, is widely explained by Mariologists as being based on extrascriptural data and on the present self-understanding of the Roman Catholic Church, designated as "the living Tradition."

The principle of *sola scriptura* was used by the Reformers to disclose the nonbiblical accretions of scholastic philosophical theology. That same principle still provides the present generation of children of the Reformation with the standard according to which every development in the Church's self-understanding has to be tested. In the Reformation formula "Scripture alone," the word "alone" retains its original function of safeguarding the primacy of Holy Scripture in the Church's life and thought; in itself this would lead us to think only in terms of Scripture *or* Tradition.

Developments in the understanding of the first word "Scripture," however, have brought about a new openness for an appreciation of *the organic unity of Scripture and Tradition.* This development can best be understood as one of the fruits of biblical criticism. The seventeenth century's attitude of protest against the increasing Roman Catholic emphasis on the authority of Tradition led to a regrettable identification of Revelation with Inspiration, of God's redeeming action in Jesus Christ with the formation of Holy Scripture. When we take the vague term "fundamentalism" to refer to the movement characterized by this identification, our time can be said to have witnessed a rediscovery of the nonfundamentalistic scriptural principle of the major Reformers. In this respect, the chains of a negative protest attitude, typical of one kind of post-Reformation thought, have been shaken off.

The primacy and normative authority of Holy Scripture are now seen to be not contained in Scripture itself but in the Word who became flesh. Revelation is increasingly understood, once again, not as a body of revealed truths which the Church is bound to hold, but as the work *and* person of Jesus Christ. Holy Scripture witnesses to this event and points, therefore, beyond itself. As a *primary* witness, its authority is a derived one. Scripture is also the primary witness in such a way that it has priority over other forms of witness but does not exclude these other forms of witness which are dependent upon it.

Here we touch upon another area where progress has been made in Protestant thought in recent years. Scripture is recognized to be the codification of oral traditions and to mark the *beginning* (Scripture is also the "primary" witness in this sense) of post-apostolic tradition. In this way, again, we can legitimately speak about the organic unity of Scripture and Tradition. One of the most exciting tasks for the theologian today is to express the full catholicity of the Christian faith by interrelating the two elements, Scripture-or-Tradition and Scripture-and-Tradition, and to do so by acknowledging at the same time the connection and distinction between the apostolic tradition and the post-apostolic tradition.

The following article by Professor Oscar Cullmann has been chosen because it is representative of the new developments we have described and because its impact is felt in almost every important study of this subject. In choosing Professor Cullmann's article to represent contemporary Protestant thought on Scripture and Tradition, we do not mean to imply that fundamentalism as we have defined it has disappeared, nor does our choice imply that Professor Cullmann's study will not have to be more fully absorbed on the level of many local congregations. But in this essay we have before us a position which is both a reflection of contemporary theology and a shaper of that theology.

Oscar Cullmann was born in Strasbourg, Germany, in 1902. From 1927 to 1938 he taught at the University of Strasbourg where he was, successively, Professor of New Testament and Professor of Early Church History. At present he is, simultaneously, Professor of New Testament and Early Church History (since 1938) at the University of Basel, Switzerland, and, since 1949, Professor of the Study of Early Christianity at the Sorbonne. He has written a number of important books, among them *Peter: Disciple, Apostle, Martyr; Christ and Time;* and *A Message to Protestants and Catholics*. He was, with Maximilian Roesle, O.S.B., the coeditor of the important ecumenical collection, *Begegnung der Christen,* from which two of the selections in this volume are taken.

1

SCRIPTURE AND TRADITION

OSCAR CULLMANN

THE SIGNIFICANCE OF THE UNIQUENESS
OF THE APOSTOLATE

THE problem of the relationship between Scripture and Tradition is in the first place a problem of the theological relationship between the apostolic period and the period of the Church. All the other questions depend on the solution that we give to this problem. The alternatives—co-ordination or subordination of Tradition to Scripture—derive from the question of knowing how we must understand the fact that the period of the Church is the continuation and unfolding of the apostolic period. For we must note right away that this fact is capable of divergent interpretations. That is why agreement on the mere fact that the Church continues the work of Christ on earth does not necessarily imply agreement on the relationship between Scripture and Tradition. Thus in my thesis developed in *Christ and Time* as well as in my studies on the sacraments in the New Testament I came considerably nearer to the "Catholic" point of view. In fact I would affirm very strongly that *through the Church* the history of salvation is continued on earth. I believe that we find this idea throughout the New Testament, and I should even consider it the key for the understanding of the Johannine Gospel. I would maintain, moreover, that the sacraments, Baptism and Eucharist, take the place in the Church of the miracles performed by Jesus Christ in the period of the Incarnation. And yet I am going to show in the following pages that I subordinate Tradition to Scripture. Vice versa, certain "Catholic" expositions of the unique role played by the period of the Apostles in the story of Revelation seem to come curiously near to the "Protestant" point of view. And yet their authors resolutely co-

7

ordinate Scripture and Tradition and set them side by side. This means that there is a need to define exactly the temporal relationship of which we have spoken.

The time within which the history of salvation is unfolded includes the past, the present, and the future. But it has a center which serves as a vantage point, a norm, for the whole stretch of this history, and this center is constituted by what we call the period of direct Revelation, or the period of the Incarnation. It consists of the years from the birth of Christ to the death of the last Apostle, that is to say the death of the last eyewitness who saw the risen Jesus and who received, either from the incarnate Jesus or the risen Christ, the direct and unique order to bear witness to what he had seen and heard. This witness can be either oral or written.

All the particular segments of total time derive their meaning from these few years which are the years of the Revelation. If we want to assign to them a date in accordance with secular chronology, we can only do so approximately, because we do not know the exact date of the birth of Christ or of the death of the last Apostle. We can say, however, that they are the years which run from about the year 1 to the year 70 or 80 of our era, without these being taken as exact limits—all the less so in that the written witness of certain Apostles was fixed only after their death.

If we consider the Christian faith from the point of view of time, we should say that the scandal of the Christian faith is to believe that these few years, which for secular history have no more and no less significance than other periods of history, are the center and the norm of the totality of time. This is a scandal of which our usual manner of reckoning the years from the year 1, which is supposed to be the year of Christ's birth, can be considered as a symbol. It is only from the starting point of the events of these central years that faith sees the history of salvation unfolding in two directions, backwards and forwards, within secular history. It is only in the light of these years that it speaks of the history of a chosen people which moves toward the Incarnation of Christ. It is only in the light of these years that it awaits a fulfillment of all things linked with a return of Christ, and it is above all in the light of these years that it believes, in the present time, in a Church-body of Christ by which the Lord exerts His contemporary rule over the universe.

The problem of Scripture and Tradition concerns the place which we assign to the period of the Church with reference to the period of the Incarnation. This period of the Church is part of the history of salvation. We would deliberately underline this over against a narrow Protestant position which does not assign to the period of the Church any value *sui generis* in the history of salvation, and which recognizes no other possibility of being a Christian than that which consists in living in the past time of the Incarnation of Jesus Christ and of the Apostles. This is to fail to recognize that the Christ reigns now and that the Church is the center of His universal reign.

But this affirmation is not enough. Like every other period in the history of salvation, the period of the Church must be defined and determined from the center. Just as the past appears to us as the period of the preparation (the "Old" Testament), and the future as that of the final fulfillment, so the period of the Church is the *intermediate* period. Intermediate: for the decisive event has already taken place, but the final fulfillment is yet to come. The miracles of the years 1–70 continue to happen, and yet neither the absolute of the central period nor the absolute of the fulfilment is realized: a period essentially intermediate. The Church shares in this intermediate character. It is indeed the body of Christ, resurrection-body, but being composed of us sinners, still sinners, it is not just simply the resurrection-body. It remains at the same time a terrestrial body which can not only be crucified, but which shares in the imperfections of all terrestrial bodies.

This is to say that the period of the Church is a prolongation of the central period, but that it is not the central period: it is a prolongation of the period of the incarnate Christ, but it is not the period of the incarnate Christ and of His apostolic eyewitnesses. The Church is built upon the foundation of the Apostles. She will continue to be built upon this foundation as long as she exists, but at the present period she can no longer produce Apostles.

In fact, the Apostolate is by definition a unique function which cannot be prolonged. According to Acts 1:22, the Apostle is a unique, because direct, witness of the Resurrection. Moreover, he has received a direct order from the incarnate or risen Christ. On the model of the Jewish *shaliach* he is "as him that sent him." He cannot transmit to others his completely unique mission. After having discharged it, he gives it back to Him who has confided it to him: the Christ. That is why in the New Testament the Apostles alone fulfil exactly the functions which are those of Christ Himself. The missionary command that Jesus gave them in Matthew 10:7 ff. corresponds exactly to the mission which in His reply to John the Baptist (Mt 11:6) Jesus assigns to His own person as Messiah, to heal the sick, to cast out demons, to raise the dead, to preach the good news. That is why the New Testament attributes the same images as are applied to Jesus to the Apostles: "rocks," and the corresponding images of "foundation," "pillars." Never are these images used to designate the bishop.[1]

The function of bishop which is transmitted is essentially different from that of Apostle which cannot be transmitted. The Apostles institute bishops, but they cannot delegate to them their function which cannot be renewed. The bishops succeed the Apostles, but on a completely different level. They succeed them, but precisely not as Apostles but as bishops, also an important function for the Church, but clearly distinct. The Apostles did not institute other Apostles but bishops. That is to say that the Apostolate does not belong to the period of the Church but to that of the Incarnation of Christ.

The Apostolate consists in the witness given to Christ. It is true that the Church also gives witness to Christ. But she can no longer give that direct witness which characterizes the witness of the Apostles. Her witness is a *derived* witness because it no longer rests on the direct Revelation which was the privilege of the Apostle alone —the *eye*-witness.

The Epistle to the Galatians makes the clearest, the most explicit, distinction between the preaching of the Apostle and the preaching of those who depend on the Apostles (Gal 1:1–12 ff.). The Apostle alone has received the Gospel *di apokalypseōs* (Gal 1:12) and not *di anthropou* (Gal 1:1–12)—by direct Revelation without human intermediary. The Apostle Paul agrees with his Judaizing opponents on this point: an Apostle is one who has been called by Christ *with-*

out the intermediary office of another; in other words, outside the succession of a tradition. The Judaizers reproached Paul precisely on this point of having received the Gospel by the intermediary office of other men and refused him, for this reason, the title of Apostle. Paul denies the fact stoutly, but he implicitly acknowledges that in fact he would not be an Apostle if he had not received the Gospel in a *direct* way from Christ.

To affirm like this the unique character of the Revelation given to the Apostles is not to deny the value of all post-apostolic tradition, but it is to bring it clearly down to the level of a human fact, even although the Holy Spirit can reveal Himself also through this agency. I have shown elsewhere that there is an apostolic tradition, and this is identified with the Kyrios Himself.[2] The Apostles compare their witnesses; for the richness of the Revelation demands a plurality of apostolic witnesses, as it demands a plurality of written Gospels, and they transmit to one another their unique and apostolic witnesses. This is a tradition, a *paradosis* which does not fall under the condemnation which Jesus pronounces with regard to the *paradosis* in general. There is one normative tradition: that of the Apostles considered in its diversity as a unity.

No writing of the New Testament emphasizes so much as the Johannine Gospel the fact of the prolongation of the work of Christ incarnate in the Church of believers. It is the very object of this book to set forth this continuation. But it is precisely this Gospel which distinguishes clearly between the continuation by the Apostles which is part of the central period and the continuation by the post-apostolic Church. The high-priestly prayer (chapter 17) establishes this line of descent: Christ—the Apostles—the post-apostolic Church. The members of the last are designated there as those who *believe because of the word of the Apostles* (Jn 17:12).

I have already said that the uniqueness of the Apostolate is emphasized, forcibly emphasized, by Catholic theology, but it seems to me that at the decisive moment it does not draw the necessary conclusions. For if one thinks through this important idea of the uniqueness of the Apostolate, one necessarily gets to the point of making an essential difference, also from the point of view of the Revelation, between *the foundation of the Church,* which took place in the period of the Apostles, and the *post-apostolic Church,* which is no longer that of the Apostles but of the bishops. There is consequently a difference between apostolic tradition and ecclesiastical tradition, the first being the foundation of the second, which excludes the co-ordination of the two.

If the apostolic tradition ought to be considered as the norm of the Revelation for all time, the question arises, How can we make alive for us this witness which God has consented, for the salvation of the world, to grant to the Apostles at a period which we call the mid-point, the center of time? The Catholic Church replies: by the apostolic succession, by the infallible teaching office of the Church, by means of the ulterior, post-apostolic tradition. Thus the objective Revelation of God would come to us (1) by means of the Apostles, (2) by means of the ecclesiastical tradition which would make explicit the witness of the Apostles. But is the *uniqueness* of the Aposto-late a guarantee of any such thing? It rests, as we have seen, on the immediate character of the Revelation granted to the Apostles, on the fact that it did not come to them through any intermediary: *alla di apokalypseōs Iēsou Christou* (Gal 1:12). The Apostle cannot therefore have any successor who could replace him in the role of bearer of the Revelation for future generations, but he must con-tinue *himself* to fulfil his function in the Church of today: *in* the Church, not *by* the Church, but *by his word, dia tou logou* (Jn 17:12); in other words, by his writings.

The oral and written word of the Apostles is, of course, not iden-tical with the objective Revelation, with the divine Word itself, since human language—spoken and written—partakes of our weak-ness and consequently cannot be an adequate vehicle for the Word pronounced by the omnipotent God. But it is only by this means which is accessible to us that God can address us, and He has chosen the Apostles in order that it might be through their *witness* that the good news is transmitted to us. In order that *other* human elements should not penetrate this witness the Apostolate has pre-cisely this character of uniqueness which can be safeguarded for us only by the *writings* of the Apostles. These writings maintain on the one hand the uniqueness of their mission, and on the other hand they ensure the direct action of the Apostles upon us, the men of the twentieth century.

Since it has thus pleased God to *restrict* the transmission of the Gospel of Christ to this one category of the contemporaries of Jesus, in order to *reduce to a minimum* its deformation by the human element, should the Church not do everything in her turn to respect this reservation? We shall see that the Church of the second century has in fact understood this necessity in creating the Canon of the New Testament and in taking care to admit only the writings of which she could actually guarantee the *apostolic* origin.

The fixing of the Revelation that God accorded to the Apostles —eyewitnesses—took place at the very period which we have called the mid-point of time, the center of the history of salvation. No word pronounced or written later by other men belonging to the Church of Christ ought to be placed alongside the apostolic writings which, if they have not all been edited by the Apostles themselves, nevertheless all claim to be the immediate expression of their eyewitness.

The written witness of the Apostles is for us the living element which continually sets us anew face to face with Christ. If we realize the magnitude of this miracle—the *unique* ministry of the Apostles who lived at the time of the Incarnation actualized among us, in the twentieth century, not by ourselves or certain of our contemporaries, but by these Apostles themselves, men of the first century—we can no longer speak of the dead letter of the Bible. Yet this presupposes that we share of the faith of the first Christians that the Apostles are not writers like other authors of antiquity, but men set apart by God for the execution of His plan of salvation by their witness, first oral, then written.

The Scriptural principle is therefore not, as one might believe, a simple application of the scientific principle which the Renaissance stressed: the necessity of resorting to the sources in order to study and understand an historical phenomenon. On the contrary, it is based on faith in this essential fact of the history of salvation—the setting apart, at the moment of the Incarnation, of the Apostles as unique instruments of the Revelation of God in Jesus Christ. But it is true that through the natural consequences which it implies for theological method the Scriptural principle meets the scientific motto

—back to the sources. This is the meeting ground of historical science and Protestant theology.

If we believe with the first Christians that the divine institution of the Apostolate has had, in the economy of salvation, this sense of transmitting the Revelation of God in Christ in an *immediate* way (that is, by eliminating all other intermediaries, an evitable source of deformation), we ought to respect God's plan by reserving to the Apostolate this same function in our Church of today. The real presence of the Apostles in the Church of all periods is given to us in the New Testament. But we shall find it precisely insofar as we seek direct contact with these witnesses, eliminating in our turn the intermediaries.

Does this mean that the Church in which we are set by Baptism is not for us the place where the Holy Spirit is at work? This conclusion would be contrary to the faith attested by all the New Testament writings. On the contrary, according to this faith, the Holy Spirit who had previously been reserved for certain men of God became accessible after Pentecost to the whole community of believers. We must reckon seriously with this conviction of primitive Christianity. It implies that the work of the incarnated Christ is carried on in His Church; the history of salvation continues. There is no chasm between the Ascension of Christ and His Return. The Johannine Gospel was written to show that in leaving the world the Christ has not abandoned the world. The Holy Spirit is at work in it. There are still miracles of faith, as in the period of the Incarnation, as in the period of Jesus and the Apostles. And the great miracle of the redemptive death and the resurrection of Christ is given to the Church in the sacraments of Baptism and Holy Communion.

We could go even further. Inspiration through the Holy Spirit continues also in the sense that the *Paraklete* is the Spirit of Truth. There will still be Revelation. And yet the high-priestly prayer makes a clear distinction between the Apostles and those who believe "because of their word." Perhaps it is for this reason that the Johannine Gospel reports a special effusion of the Holy Spirit which took place before that spoken of in the Book of the Acts, on Easter day itself, and which was experienced by the Apostles only (20:22). The revelation of the Word of God continues in the Church, but it will no longer be a *norm*, a *criterion*, as is the Revelation granted to the Apostles. The Church will examine every later revelation but will always take as criterion precisely this norm of the apostolic witness. The Church will therefore not be a superior tribunal able to decree what must be added to this norm. *God speaks to the Church today through the witness of the Apostles.* As long as there shall be a Church this witness of the Apostles will be a *sufficient norm.*

The apostolic witness has a double role: it engenders inspiration and acts as its controller, since in all inspiration there is a risk of other spirits putting themselves in the place of the Holy Spirit. Thus the Church will have the right and the duty to proclaim whatever, examined in the light of the apostolic norm, appears to her as a Revelation. In this way an ecclesiastical tradition is elaborated. It will have great value for the Church, and Protestantism is wrong in underestimating this in principle. In any case, it recognizes it in fact by giving a large place in its teaching to the writings of the theologians of the sixteenth century and even to the decisions of the early Councils. But whatever the respect owed by the Church to the tradition, and the importance attaching to it in the elaboration and understanding of Christian doctrine, it can never assume the same value as the apostolic tradition; it can never itself become a norm. A norm is a norm precisely because it cannot be expanded. We must not confuse *Revelation* and *criterion of Revelation.*

In practice the institution of the Apostolate, which is unique in the divine history of salvation, seems to us to be devalued by the infallible teaching office of the Catholic Church. The uniqueness of the Apostolate is annulled by this teaching norm. The period of the Apostles and the period of the Church are confused. It is true that the Catholic Church claims to *interpret,* only to explicate the apostolic witness by its decisions which constitute the tradition. But when the ecclesiastical interpretation assumes the same normative value *for all periods* as the apostolic norm itself, does the affirmation that there is only interpretation not become a fiction? Is it not the characteristic of a true interpretation not to have the same definite character as is possessed by the norm itself? Certainly we must always consult the interpretations of the norm which have been given in order to understand it, but we must always be ready to revise them, and even to abandon them, by setting oneself precisely before the norm itself; this is to say, precisely by eliminating the screen of later interpretation.

Moreover, has the Catholic Church not tended to abandon, if not in theory certainly in fact, the fiction that tradition equals interpretation of Scripture, when in justifying the dogma proclaimed in 1950 it does not waste time giving a Scriptural foundation, but relies on the *consensus* of the Church, as if collective inspiration in the Church has no longer any need at all to be controlled by the apostolic witness; as if it were sufficient to control it by the infallible teaching office of the Pope?

None the less, Catholic theology will always oppose the affirmation of the superiority of Scripture to Tradition by the argument that the Scripture *needs to be interpreted*. We willingly concede this necessity. For, as we have already said, the Apostles used the imperfect instrument of human language, and moreover languages and forms of thought that are no longer ours. We are likewise of the opinion that the Church ought to take more seriously than is the case in the Protestant Churches the teaching office, the duty of pronouncing as Church in matters of exegesis. She ought to take up a position regarding any interpretation proposed by the exegetes, and she ought to pray for the help of the Holy Spirit when exercising this teaching office. She ought to translate the Biblical message into the language of today. But in doing this, she ought to know that she is fulfilling her duty for her period, and that she is not doing a work which, like that of the eyewitnesses, binds all the future centuries of the period of the Church, so that future generations will be bound by her decisions in the same way as they are bound by Scripture. Former decisions of the Church will serve as guides to the exegetes, but not as norms, not as criteria.

Even when there is the inspiration of the Holy Spirit in every interpretation of the Scripture there is a human element. I repeat that there is also this human element in the apostolic writings themselves, which are already a transposing of the divine Word into human language. But behind them there are the Apostles, the eyewitnesses. The human element is here reduced to an *inevitable minimum inherent in the very notion of a divine Revelation to man*. If, on the other hand, we set between Scripture and ourselves as a norm the total collection of official interpretations given in all past centuries by the Church, then errors which are insignificant when considered singly, are amplified by virtue of a development which no tradition transmitted by men who are not eyewitnesses can escape. The chronological question necessarily comes into play here: this is why the period of the Church cannot be normative as is the period of the *foundation* of the Church.

Otherwise our interpretation would risk coming under the condemnation pronounced by Jesus on the *tradition* (Mk 7:9): "Ye reject the commandment of God, that ye may keep your own tradition." The interpretation which the rabbinic tradition has given to the commandment to honor father and mother was considered also to be faithful to the divine Word, to shed light on a written commandment which was not clear in itself, and yet Jesus recommends here, as in the antitheses of the Sermon on the Mount, the necessity of returning to the Word itself to get from it the divine intention without going through the intermediacy of a traditional interpretation.

But is this not to miss the fact that everything has been changed by the coming of Christ, by the existence of the Church of Christ? Is it not a blasphemy thus to assimilate the tradition of the rabbis and the tradition of the Church? With this objection we come back to our starting point: the distinction which can be drawn between the period of the Incarnation and the period of the Church. For to make this distinction amounts exactly to saying that there is tradition *and* tradition within the Christian field. There is an apostolic tradition which is a norm because it rests upon eyewitnesses chosen by God, and there is a post-apostolic tradition which is a valuable help for the understanding of the divine Word, precisely on condition that we do not consider it as a norm. While accepting humbly the *exegetical directives* of the Church and its teachers we must remain ready to set ourselves face to face with the tradition of the Apostles, as the Apostles themselves were face to face with the divine Revelation itself (Gal 2:12), without the intermediacy of any interpretation.

It is true that the same Holy Spirit who inspired the Apostles is at work in the Church, and the Church is the place where Christ manifests His presence. "Quench not the Spirit," says St. Paul to the Thessalonians, but he knows too that other spirits are at work in the Church itself. That is why he adds: "Prove all things; hold fast that which is good." To say that inspiration needs to be controlled is not to deny it. But we add: to say that the teaching office of the Church needs to be controlled is not to deny it: it must be controlled by the word of the Apostles.

THE SIGNIFICANCE OF THE FIXING
OF THE CANON BY THE CHURCH
OF THE SECOND CENTURY

To determine the connexion between Scripture and Tradition we began, in the preceding exposition, from the very foundation of the Christian Church, that is to say from the period which we call the central period in the history of salvation, the period of Jesus and His Apostles. Thus we have interrogated the New Testament about our problem and we have found that the idea of the Apostolate, or more exactly of the uniqueness of the Apostolate, has forced us to give the answer which we have thought must be given. By centering all our argumentation on this idea of Apostolate we have been considering so far only the New Testament as Scripture, that is to say the direct witness of the Apostles to the fundamental facts of the work of the incarnate Christ and their own acts.

Now we are about to deal with the question from the starting-point of the history of the primitive Church, and we are going to find out if this will confirm our results. If we have just been looking for the answer to our problem in Scripture, we are now going to look for it, as it were, in the tradition. Here we shall insist on the fact that *the infant Church itself made the distinction between apostolic tradition and ecclesiastical tradition,* subordinating the latter clearly to the former.

Catholic theology, in order to combat the thesis of the superiority of Scripture, lays much stress upon the fact that Tradition is anterior to Scripture. This is a fact that no one will think of denying, provided however that one notes that it is a question of priority of the *apostolic* tradition. But if one can demonstrate that the Church herself recognized an essential difference between the tradition before and the tradition after the establishment of the Canon, the fact of the priority of the oral apostolic tradition over its fixation in writing will prove nothing about the tradition as such. We shall speak about the origin of the first Christian writings, then about the origin of the Canon.

In fact, of course, the oral tradition of the Apostles precedes the first apostolic writings. The oral tradition prior to the first writings was certainly quantitatively richer than the written tradition. But we must ask what is the significance of the fact that the Apostles, or the mouthpieces who served them as secretaries, at a given moment took up the pen to give this tradition a written form. This is a fact of the very greatest importance *for the history of salvation*. Its meaning cannot be other than that of having delimited the oral tradition of the Apostles, so as to make of the apostolic witness in this form a definitive *norm* for the Church, at the moment when she was going to expand into the whole world and had to be built up until the Kingdom of God itself was established. If one admits that the oral tradition of the Apostles had been confided as a deposit to the Church in order that she might, in the course of centuries, draw from it elements which are not to be found in the apostolic writings, then the fact of the coming into being of writings which have for authors men whom the Church calls "sacred authors" is completely minimized. The writings of the Apostles are devalued to the point of becoming instruments which are useful indeed but in no way indispensable. In actual fact the theory of "secret," not written, traditions of the Apostles was elaborated by the Gnostics, and the Church herself drew attention to the consequent danger.

If on the other hand the written fixation of the witness of the Apostles is one of the *essential facts of the Incarnation*, we have the right and the duty to assimilate apostolic tradition and New Testament writings, and to distinguish both from the post-apostolic, post-canonical tradition. We shall see that the rule of faith which was transmitted in oral form has, however, been accepted as norm alongside of Scripture only because it has been considered as having been *fixed by the Apostles*.

But did the primitive Church herself really distinguish between apostolic and post-apostolic tradition? This is the moment to speak about the establishment of the Canon by the Church of the second century. We are in complete agreement with Catholic theology when it insists on the fact that *the Church herself* made the Canon. We even find in this fact the supreme argument for our demonstration. The fixing of the Christian Canon of Scripture signifies precisely that *the Church herself*, at a given moment, traced a clear and firm line of demarcation between the period of the Apostles and the period of the Church, between the time of foundation and the time of construction, between the apostolic community and the Church of the bishops, in other words between apostolic tradition and ecclesiastical tradition. If this was not the significance of the formation of the Canon, the event would be meaningless.

In fact, we must recall the situation that led the Church to conceive the *idea* of a Canon. About the year 150 there is still an oral tradition. We know this from Papias who wrote an exegesis of the words of Jesus. He tells us himself that he used as a basis the "viva vox" (*phōnē zōsa*) and that he attributed more importance to it than to the writings. But from him we have not only this declaration of principle: he has left us some examples of the oral tradition such as he found it, and these examples show us well what we ought to think of an oral tradition about the year 150! It has an entirely legendary character. We can be persuaded of this by examining the story that Papias reports about Joseph Barsabbas, the unsuccessful candidate, according to Acts 1:23 ff., for the post of twelfth disciple, vacant as a result of Judas' treason. Above all we must mention the obscene and completely legendary account of the death of Judas Iscariot himself.

About 150, on the one hand, one is relatively near to the apostolic period, but on the other hand, one is yet by this time too far away for the living tradition still to offer in itself the least guarantee of authenticity. The oral traditions which Papias echoes arose in the Church and were transmitted by the Church. For outside the Church no one had any interest in describing in such crude colors the death of the traitor. Papias was therefore deluding himself when he considered the "viva vox" as more valuable than the written books. The oral tradition had a normative value in the period of the Apostles, the eyewitnesses, but no longer in 150 after it had passed from one mouth to another.

The traditions reported by Papias are not the only ones. From the same period we have the first apocryphal Gospels which made a collection of other oral traditions. It will suffice to read these Gospels, one of which tells of the infant Jesus manufacturing living sparrows, carrying water in His smock, miraculously killing comrades who were troubling Him; or else to read the numerous apocryphal Acts, in order to realize that the tradition, in the Church, no longer offered any guarantee of veracity, even when it claimed a chain of succession. For all these traditions were justified by the establishment of chains going back to the Apostles. Papias himself also makes this claim when he says that he got his information from people who had been in contact with the Apostles. The teaching office of the Church in itself did not suffice to preserve the purity of the Gospel.

By establishing the *principle* of a Canon the Church recognized in this very act that *from that moment* the tradition was no longer a criterion of truth. She drew a line under the apostolic tradition. She declared implicitly that from that moment every subsequent tradition must be submitted to the *control* of the apostolic tradition. In other terms, she declared: here is the tradition which *constituted* the Church, which imposed itself on her.[3] Certainly she did not intend by this to put an end to the continued evolution of the tradition. But by what we might call an *act of humility* she submitted all subsequent tradition to be elaborated by herself to the superior criterion of the apostolic tradition, codified in the Holy Scriptures. To establish a Canon is equivalent to recognizing: henceforth our ecclesiastical tradition needs to be controlled; with the help of the Holy Spirit it will be controlled by the apostolic tradition fixed in writing; for we are getting to the point where we are too distant from the period of the Apostles to be able to guard the purity of the tradition *without a written norm recognized as superior,* too distant to prevent slight legendary deformations creeping in, and thus being transmitted and amplified. But at the same time this signified also that the tradition that was to be considered alone apostolic had to be *delimited;* for all the Gnostics boasted of secret traditions, unwritten, that claimed

to be apostolic. To fix a Canon was to say: henceforth we renounce
the right to consider as a norm other traditions that are not fixed
by the Apostles in writing. Of course there may be certain other
authentic apostolic traditions, but take as the apostolic *norm* only
what is written in these books, since it has been demonstrated that
by admitting oral traditions not written by the Apostles as norms we
are losing the criterion for judging the validity of the claim to
apostolicity made by the many traditions in circulation. To say that
the writing brought together in a Canon should be considered as
norm was to say that they should be considered as *sufficient*. The
teaching office of the Church was not abdicated by this final act of
fixing the Canon, but its future activity was made to depend on a
norm that was superior.

By fixing a Canon the Church of the second century did not only
take up a position with regard to the difficulties that arose at that
particular time, especially with regard to Gnosticism. *She took a
decision that committed the whole future of the Church.* She did
not fix a norm for others; she fixed a norm *for herself,* and she committed the Church for all future centuries to this norm. In doing
this she did not deprive the Church of her teaching office. But she
gave to this teaching office its exact character: it will be truly the
teaching office of the Church in so far as its starting point is the act
of submission to the ecclesiastical norm of the Canon. Its efficacity
derives from this submission. The Holy Spirit will be at work in this
very submission. *Within this framework* the Revelation will continue to be granted to the Church.

Is it legitimate to attribute such a primordial importance in the
history of salvation to this act of fixing the Canon? Does this not
mean attributing an exceptional dignity to the Church of the second
century which conceived this idea of a Canon? We must recognize
that this was in fact a decisive moment for the history of the Church.
On the one hand, about the year 150 they were still near enough to
the period of the Apostles to be able, with the help of the Holy
Spirit, to make the selection among the oral and written traditions;
on the other hand, the shocking multiplication of Gnostic and
legendary traditions had made the Church ripe for this *act of
humility* which is indicated by the submission of *all* later inspiration

to a norm. At no other moment in the period of the Church could the fixing of the Canon have been undertaken. It is at this very moment that God granted to the Church the grace of recognizing the difference between the period of the Incarnation and the period of the Church. Only the clear distinction between these two periods enables the Church to preserve the sublime consciousness of having her own place, her own time, in the history of salvation. And she has it precisely in so far as she recognizes that the period of Jesus and of the Apostles is the mid-point of all time and gives its significance to every period, including the period of the Church.

But the Canon fixed by the Church of the second century does not contain only the books of the Apostles, but also the Old Testament. We must say, right away, that the Old Testament was admitted only because it was understood that the period of the Incarnation is the mid-point of time, the mid-point in the history of salvation which has its beginning before the Incarnation and is prolonged beyond it. The Old Testament was received into the Canon in the capacity of witness to that part of the history of salvation which prepared for the Incarnation. It is in this way that Jesus and the Apostles understood the history of Israel. Thus the Church was faithful *to the Apostles* themselves in admitting the Old Testament into the *apostolic norm* which is the Canon.

Here an objection must be raised: since the history of the people of God in the Old Testament thus acquires a normative character, why should it not be the same for the people of God in the New Testament, i.e., the Church? Does this not grant a privileged position to the period of preparation for the Incarnation as compared with the period of the unfolding of the Incarnation which is the period of the Church?

The objection is perfectly legitimate.[4] But here again we must consider the fixing of the Canon as an element in the history of salvation itself. To fix this *norm* certainly did not mean, as many Protestants think, that the history of salvation was to be henceforth halted until the moment of the Return of Christ, so that we should have nothing else to do than to mark time. We must even say quite boldly that the people of the New Testament are, on the contrary, in a privileged position as compared with that of the Old, since they already live in the new aeon even although the final fulfilment is still to come.

And yet this period of the Church, in spite of all the graces bestowed upon it, especially in the sacraments, in spite of all its privileges, cannot be *norm, for it is not completed,* as the preparation for the Incarnation of Christ in the history of the people of Israel was completed by the time of the Apostles. In creating a norm the Church did not desire to be her own norm since she had established precisely the fact that *without a superior written norm her teaching office could not preserve the pure apostolic tradition.* While remaining conscious of her high mission of representing the Body of Christ on earth in the present period, that is to say the highest mission that exists, she understood that she could not accomplish this mission except by submitting herself to the norm of the apostolic Canon. If the fixing of the Canon had been carried through by the Church with the tacit presupposition that the teaching office of the Church, that is the *subsequent* traditions, should be set alongside this Canon with an *equal normative authority,* then one could no longer see the reason for her creation of the Canon. If after as well as before its constitution the teaching office of the Church continued to be a *supreme* norm of equal value, the Church could by herself alone always judge afresh as a last resort as to the conformity of the teaching of her scholars with the apostolic tradition. In this case the fixing of a Canon would have been superfluous. It makes sense only if the Church from that moment exercises her teaching office in submission to this supreme norm, and always returning afresh to this norm. We could even risk the paradoxical statement that the teaching office of the Church at least approaches real infallibility in so far as through submission to the Canon it abandons all *claim* to infallibility; that the tradition created by the Church assumes a real value for the understanding of the divine Revelation insofar as it does not claim to be an indispensable screen by placing itself between the Bible and the reader.

There is however the rule of faith. But is it not important that the idea of giving it a normative authority was conceived *at the same time* as that of giving a normative authority to the Canon, that is to say about the middle of the second century? By misunderstanding the significance of certain declarations of the Fathers of the second century we have the habit of opposing (too much) rule of faith and Canon, as if the former constituted the continuous tradition of the Church, alongside of the writings of the Apostles. In fact, the definitive fixing of the *apostolic rule of faith corresponded exactly to the same need* of codifying the apostolic tradition as did the canonization of the apostolic *writings.* We do not have on the one hand the Apostles' Creed, and on the other their writings. The two form henceforth one block of apostolic tradition over against the post-apostolic tradition. The *apostolic* rule of faith is the very tradition of which the Fathers of the second century speak. What is important is not that it was first of all transmitted by oral methods, but the conviction that its text has been *fixed*—just as was that of the canonical books of the New Testament—by the Apostles. According to the conviction of the Church of the second century it is not a question of a secret or implicit tradition, but of a text already fixed in the period of the Apostles, as were their writings.

The Credo was a kind of apostolic résumé of the books of the New Testament—as it were a rule of apostolic interpretation of all the very different books. The multiplicity of apostolic writings made necessary a short résumé of the truths that are common to them for the different needs of the Church.[5] In order to be the norm of interpretation this Credo itself must be *apostolic.* Of course there were still fluctuations, on the subject of the precise and definitive text, but in the main lines the different affirmations were already contained in the symbols of the middle of the second century, and, above all, the principle of the norm of an apostolic rule of faith was admitted at that point. The attribution of each phrase to one of the twelve Apostles is a legend. But what is true is that the basis of the developed symbols is formed by the oldest of the shorter formulae whose text was fixed in the *apostolic* age, traces of which we have found in the New Testament.

The role of *future* Credos of the Church as they were elaborated by the councils is quite different. Certainly they are also necessary in the sense that they are designed to define a position over against the problems of their period, the heresies of the day. They are necessary, and at every period the Church ought to elaborate a Credo.

But never can these subsequent confessions assume the value of a symbol attributed to the Apostles: never can they become norms for all time. Here again we must repeat what we have said about the post-apostolic traditions of the Church. They have a very great importance in that they can guide our understanding of the apostolic Revelation, but they are not, as the *Apostles'* Creed seems to be, a kind of last page to be added to the New Testament.

Thus we arrive at the conclusion that the difference we have established between apostolic tradition and post-apostolic tradition is not arbitrary, but that it is *the difference which the Church, at the decisive moment, in the second century, herself made by formulating the principle of an apostolic Canon and an apostolic résumé.*

We could find an intrinsic confirmation of all that precedes in the evolution of patristics. For a long time it has been noted that, apart from the letters of Ignatius, the writings of the *so-called* apostolic Fathers (which in reality do not precisely belong any longer to the apostolic age but to the beginning of the second century) —the First Epistle of Clement, the Homily assigned to Clement, the Epistle of Barnabas, the Shepherd of Hermas, the Epistle of Poly-carp—in spite of the theological interest they possess, are at a considerable distance from the thought of the New Testament, and in a large measure fall back into a moralism which ignores the notion of grace, the redemptive death of Christ which is so central for the apostolic theology. It has also been noted that the Fathers of the Church who wrote after 150—Irenaeus, Tertullian—although chronologically more remote from the New Testament than the authors of the first half of the century, understood infinitely better the essence of the Gospel. This fact appears paradoxical but it is perfectly explained by this most important action of codification of the apostolic tradition in a Canon, henceforward the superior norm of all tradition. The Fathers of the first half of the century wrote at a period when the writings of the New Testament already existed but without being vested with canonical authority, that is to say, without being set apart. Therefore they did not have at their disposal a norm, and on the other hand they were too far distant already from the period of the Apostles to be able to draw directly on the eyewitness source. The encounters of Polycarp and Papias with apostolic personages could no longer guarantee a pure transmission of authentic traditions: the fragments that have been preserved of their literary work are proof.

On the other hand, after (*c.* 150) contact with the apostolic age had been re-established thanks to the constitution of the Canon, this process of elimination of all impure elements, sources of deformation began. Thus it is confirmed that by submitting all subsequent tradition to the Canon, the Church once and for all saved its apostolic basis. She permitted her members to hear, thanks to this Canon, continually afresh and for all centuries to come the authentic word of the Apostles, a privilege which no oral tradition, passing through Polycarp or Papias, could any longer have assured them.

We have said that the Scriptures need to be interpreted. The Church ought to feel herself responsible for this interpretation. She ought to declare herself, when that is necessary, over against certain Biblical explanations proposed by her teachers or independent scholars of her time. But her responsibility in this case consists, as we have seen, precisely in pronouncing judgment in humble submission to the apostolic norm of the Canon. This implies two things: (1) that she does not impose on future generations the obligation to take as a starting point and as a norm of their interpretation of the same text the decision that she believes it necessary to take, but that she remains conscious of the superiority of Scripture, the immediate witness of the divine Revelation, to the interpretation which she herself feels compelled to give, and which cannot be other than a derived witness in which the human element has a greater share; (2) that she herself takes her decision by confronting the Biblical text itself, trusting in the internal witness of the Holy Spirit, and having recourse to the tradition only as a secondary source, a guide which can give us light precisely on condition that we do not set it above the word of the Apostles, and that we are ready, when necessary, to break loose from it.

Do we not continually experience afresh a kind of liberation when, after having read a quantity of commentaries, however good they may have been, we read the Biblical Word itself, forcing ourselves to forget the very things we have read in the commentaries, with the healthy *naïveté* of the catechumen seeking to hear the Apostles speak of what they have seen and heard? Certainly the Bible needs to be interpreted. For their authors were men of their time and therefore it contains inevitable imperfections, inherent in any human word which is seeking to translate the divine Word. But is it not to lack faith when we base ourselves on the human character of the Revelation transmitted by the Apostles in order to claim that we are no longer capable of hearing their witness without passing through a long chain of intermediaries in which the human element incidentally plays a greater part because these are not eyewitnesses like the Apostles? Certainly we ought to undertake the reading of the Biblical Word with the philological knowledge that we have acquired, and we ought to give certain directives to the common man who does not have them at his disposal. But in order that the exegete, like the common man, should become capable of hearing, in this twentieth century, the very voice of the Apostles, he must be certain (and communicate this certainty to others) that the eyewitnesses, while expressing themselves in the language of their time, are still able to speak to us in a *direct* manner, precisely when we are ready to confront their word with this faith in the Holy Spirit who is able to dispense with intermediaries.

Is the gulf which separates Catholic doctrine and Protestant doctrine on this point unbridgeable? Perhaps in what concerns the theory. In practice the two attitudes have come curiously near to one another. We have said that Protestants have always recognized a tradition as guide—the decisions of the first councils and the writings of the Reformers. But for some time now the interest of Protestant theology has been turning, more than in the past, also to the study of patristics. Thus we are beginning to understand on the Protestant side what an immense treasure there is in the work of the Fathers of the Church, and we have begun to break away from that strange conception of Church history and Christian thought which supposed that between the second and the sixteenth centuries there was, with the exception of certain sects, a complete eclipse of the Gospel.

Vice versa, we are seeing today a Catholic interest in the reading and study of the Bible such as perhaps no preceding period has known. The work of Père Lagrange, to name only one; the encyclical

Divino afflante Spiritu; the extraordinary energy of the Biblical Institute at Rome and the Biblical School of the Dominicans in Jerusalem; the publication of the excellent edition of the *Sainte Bible,* known as the Jerusalem Bible; do these not prove that the most valuable Catholic contributions to the understanding of the Bible are due, in spite of the theory of tradition, to a *direct, immediate* contact with the Biblical text, even in its original language? And the "Catholic variations" in the appreciation of certain exegetical problems—I am thinking for instance of the famous "Johannine colon"—are these revisions of previous judgments not a proof that on many occasions the Catholic Church has known how to set Scripture above her tradition?

In mentioning these *rapprochements* that can be noted on the practical level, we are not trying to minimize the great divergence of doctrine which nevertheless exists. But we think that they ought to incite us to discuss the old theoretical problems of "Scripture and Tradition" without any polemical intention, with an absolute frankness and sincerity which can only profit from the dialogue of Christian confessions.

EDITOR'S NOTE

After the publication of the above article, a series of reactions appeared, of which one by Père Jean Daniélou was so significant that it led in turn to a further clarification by Oscar Cullmann. It is at Professor Cullmann's request that we bring the discussion up to date.[6]

Professor Cullmann describes Père Daniélou's response as one "in which strongly opposing my arguments, he preserves throughout an admirable spirit of scientific objectivity. Although his arguments do not all seem to me to have the same force, most of his objections are interesting and instructive and, in my opinion, are a contribution to progress in the debate."

Without presenting a detailed reproduction of the argumentation of Père Daniélou, we should like at least to indicate in what general direction the discussion developed by pointing in a few words to three elements in it.

(1) Not only Père Daniélou but Roman Catholics in general find it difficult to understand how books, i.e., Holy Scripture, can confront us with Christ without the infallible teaching office of the Church where the Holy Spirit unfolds the implications of Tradition. Professor Cullmann answered that "in the New Testament the Kyrios *Christ is present in the tradition of the apostles and therefore also in this tradition as fixed in the written documents. The believer holds that these documents are not simply historical records (although they are that), but that the Holy Spirit confronts the believing reader directly with Christ."*[7]

(2) How can one—so reads a second objection by Père Daniélou —hold the ongoing and present activity of God in the sacraments and deny the same ongoing and present activity in the teaching office of the Church? Cullmann answers this by pointing out that as regards revelation there is a fundamental difference between the Apostles and the post-apostolic church. The Roman Catholic Church also rejects post-apostolic revelation. As regards the sacraments, however, it should be acknowledged that they are an actualization of the Work of Christ in apostolic times and *now in exactly the same fashion. The sacraments and the teaching authority of the Church should therefore not be placed on the same level.*[8]

(3) According to a third objection, the distinction between the "time of the Incarnation" and the "time of the Church" would imply that the people of the Old Covenant would hold a privileged position compared with the people of the New Covenant, since the Old Testament containing the history of Israel has canonical authority while to the history of the Church such an authority is denied.[9]

This third argumentation is, according to Cullmann, the result of the erroneous assumption that there is in the Old Testament an infallible teaching office. The early Church accepted the Old Testament

as part of the normative history of salvation through Christ, in the same way as that of several New Testament books. The Church saw in the

Old Testament, the activity of the spirit and it is for this reason that the primitive confessions of faith lay stress on his speaking through the prophets. This means that for the Church the Old Testament is canonical only insofar as it is explicitly oriented toward the New; in other words because the time of the Incarnation is regarded as normative for the time which preceded it, and as the criterion by which it is to be understood.

Thus the apostolic writings are the norm not only of the post-apostolic, but of the pre-apostolic period.[10]

NOTES

This article appeared originally in the *Scottish Journal of Theology*, Vol. 6 (1953), and was translated by the Rev. D. H. C. Read, B.D. This is a sequel to " 'Kyrios' as Designation for the Oral Tradition concerning Jesus," *Scottish Journal of Theology*, Vol. 3 (1950), pp. 180 ff. It is reprinted here with the kind permission of the editor and of Professor Cullmann.

1. Cf. Oscar Cullmann, *Petrus*, reviewed by Canon S. L. Greenslade, in *Scottish Journal of Theology*, Vol. 6 (1953), p. 203 ff.
2. *Scottish Journal of Theology*, Vol. 3 (1950), pp. 180 ff.
3. The point is strongly underlined by H. Diem, *Das Problem des Schriftkanons* (*Theol. Studien*), 1951.
4. It has been formulated in oral discussion with Père Daniélou.
5. See Oscar Cullmann, *The Earliest Christian Confessions* (London: Lutterworth Press, 1949).
6. Cf. Jean Daniélou, "Réponse à Oscar Cullmann," *Dieu Vivant*, Vol. 24, pp. 107 ff. and Professor Cullmann's answer in text and footnotes of the chapter entitled "The Tradition," in his *The Early Church* (London: S. C. M. Press, 1956), pp. 59 ff.
7. Cullmann, *op. cit.*, p. 81.
8. Daniélou, *op. cit.*, p. 114; Cullmann, *op. cit.*, p. 83.
9. Daniélou, *op. cit.*, pp. 111 ff.
10. Cullmann, *op. cit.*, pp. 93 ff.

SELECTED READINGS

1. Barth, Karl, *Church Dogmatics*, Vol. I, Pt. 2, trans. by G. T. Thomson and Harold Knight. Edinburgh: T. and T. Clark, 1956; Chap. 3, "Holy

Scripture," pp. 455–740. This theologian's most thoroughly expressed views on authority and freedom in the Church; valuable also for the important exegetical and historical excursus. See also Barth's interesting treatment of the *paradosis* of Jesus and the function of *paradosis* in the Church: *Church Dogmatics*, Vol. II, Pt. 2, trans. by G. W. Bromiley, *et al.* Edinburgh: T. and T. Clark, 1957, pp. 458–506.

2. Boisset, Jean, Goguel, M., *et al., Le problème biblique dans de protestantisme.* Paris: Presses Universitaire de France, 1955. A volume of essays on this problem by some of the more important scholars of the French Protestant community, representing a wide variety of views on the historic character of revelation to which the biblical documents testify.

3. Brunner, Emil, *Dogmatics*, Vol. I, trans. by Olive Wyon. Philadelphia: Westminster Press, 1950; "Prolegomena," and "Appendix to Prolegomena," pp. 3–113. This influential thinker's statement of the basis and task of dogmatics.

4. Brunner, Peter, *Schrift und Tradition,* Berlin: Lutherisches Verlaghaus, 1951. A significant part of this author's participation in a Roman Catholic and Evangelical ecumenical study circle.

5. Fairweather, E. R., "Scripture in Tradition," *Canadian Journal of Theology*, Vol. 5 (January 1959), pp. 7–14, and "Faith and Tradition," *Canadian Journal of Theology*, Vol. 3 (April 1957), pp. 79–86. Interesting as examples of the re-examination of the question of Tradition from an Anglican viewpoint.

6. Flew, R. Newton, and Davies, Rupert E., eds., *The Catholicity of Protestantism.* Philadelphia: Muhlenberg Press, 1950. A volume prepared by thirteen English Free Church theologians and pastors for discussions with the Church of England; a foreword by the Archbishop of Canterbury.

7. Grant, Robert M., *The Bible in the Church.* New York: Macmillan Co., 1948. A critical history of biblical interpretation.

8. Hök, G., "Holy Spirit and Tradition," *Scottish Journal of Theology,* Vol. 10 (December 1957), pp. 389–398.

9. Jenkins, Daniel, *Tradition, Freedom and the Spirit.* Philadelphia: Westminster Press, n.d. An important consideration of the work of the Holy Spirit in relation to tradition broadly understood; by a foremost representative of those Congregationalists who are creatively re-examining their heritage.

10. Outler, Albert C., *The Christian Tradition and the Unity We Seek.* New York: Oxford University Press, 1957. A Methodist examines, in the Richard Lectures, the relation between a particular understanding of Scripture and Tradition and the ecumenical movement.

11. Reid, J. K. S., *The Authority of Scripture: A Study in the Reformation and Post-Reformation Understanding of the Bible.* London: Methuen and Co., Ltd., 1957. Brings to bear on contemporary discussions of Scripture and Tradition the historical backgrounds implied in the positions of representa-

tives of the Reformation, the Counter Reformation and the so-called Protestant Orthodoxy.

12. Tillich, Paul, "The Problem of the Theological Method," *The Journal of Religion,* Vol. 27 (January 1947), pp. 16–26. A supplement to the concise references to the problems related to Scripture and Tradition, in this theologian's *Systematic Theology,* Vol. I (Chicago: University of Chicago Press), pp. 34–52, 83–86.

13. Turner, H. E. W., *The Pattern of Christian Truth.* London: A. R. Mowbray & Co., Ltd., 1954. While the entire volume is of interest as an examination of the norms and manner of theological reflection in the patristic period, the final chapter presents the author's conclusions about the proper relation between Scripture, Tradition, and reason.

14. Hodgson, Leonard, *et al., On the Authority of the Bible.* London: S.P.C.K., 1960.

15. Richardson, A., and Schweitzer, W. W., eds., *Biblical Authority for Today.* Philadelphia: Westminster Press, 1951. A World Council of Churches Symposium on the biblical authority for the Churches' social and political message today; a wide variety of theological views are represented.

INTRODUCTION:

THE ROMAN CATHOLIC VIEW OF
SCRIPTURE AND TRADITION

ONE of the most interesting discussions now going on among Catholic theologians, especially in Germany, centers around the problem of the relation between Scripture and Tradition. This discussion is especially significant for the theological dialogue between Catholics and Protestants because it touches on an issue which in one way or another involves almost all of the other issues, and most particularly the question of the nature of the Church. Is the Church subordinate to the Word of God? Is the Word of God subordinate to Tradition in the Church? Or does some other relationship exist between Church, Tradition, and Scripture?

The Council of Trent had said that the truth of the gospel which Christ himself had proclaimed and commanded the apostles to preach to every creature was contained in written books and unwritten traditions. Trent went on to say that it accepted and revered both the Sacred Scriptures and these Traditions which had come down to us from the apostles. What did Trent mean by this? Did it mean that the revelation which God made to man in Jesus Christ has come down to us through two separate sources, one of them written and one of them oral, in such a way that part of this revelation is contained in one of these sources and part of it is contained in the other? Or did Trent respect the classical view that Scripture contains all revealed truths, and that the Church's faith, which includes apostolic traditions, interprets it?

Most of the theologians of the Counter Reformation interpreted Trent in the first way, namely, that Scripture was a partial source of faith, complemented by Tradition. Some of them saw Tradition as

35

a partial source, a supplementary appendix to Scripture, but an appendix which became more important than Scripture itself. Some even considered Tradition to be complete, to contain the whole of Christian doctrine, without any help from the written word. It is interesting to note that during this period the Anglican divines remained closer to the theology of the Catholic eras, patristic and medieval, than did most Catholic Counter Reformation controversialists.

In recent years, concern has grown among some Catholic theologians over what they consider to be a misreading by post-Tridentine theologians of the decree of Trent on Scripture and Tradition. They draw attention especially to the long debate which took place at the Council in 1546 during the two months between February 8 and April 8. A first draft of the decree had declared that the truth of the gospel was contained partly in written books and partly in unwritten traditions. But this draft immediately met sharp opposition, led by Pietro Bertano, Bishop of Fano. Angelo Bonucci, the General of the Servites, flatly contradicted the opinion that the gospel is no more than partly in Scripture. He asserted that *all* evangelical truth was in Scripture and that it was wrong to say that it was only *partly* in Scripture. At the last minute before the promulgation of the decree Bonucci's point was accepted. The gospel was not described as residing partly in the Scriptures, partly in traditions. It was said to be contained in the Scriptures *and* in the traditions. The contention of Bonucci, Bertano, and others that "all is contained in Scripture" was not contradicted by the final decision of the Council.

In the contemporary Catholic discussion the opinion that all the truths of salvation are contained in Scripture and that Tradition is their living interpretation is defended by G. H. Tavard, B. Bartmann, A. Müller, K. Rahner, M. Schmaus, G. de Broglie, H. Küng, P. Lengsfeld, O. Semmelroth, B. van Leeuwen, Y. Congar, J. Ratzinger, L. Scheffczyk, and others. Among those who have opposed this view are H. Lennerz, J. Beumer, M. Bévenot.

But the principal name associated with the discussion is that of the author of the following article, Josef Rupert Geiselmann, who has been Professor of Dogmatic Theology on the Catholic theological faculty of the University of Tübingen since 1934. He has given fresh vigor to the tradition of the Catholic Tübingen school, partly through his studies on his most renowned predecessor in the school, Johann Adam Möhler, and even more in recent years by his studies on Tradition which have sparked the contemporary Catholic discussion. The following article is the first of Professor Geiselmann's writings on Scripture and Tradition to be translated into English.

2

SCRIPTURE, TRADITION, AND THE CHURCH: AN ECUMENICAL PROBLEM

JOSEF RUPERT GEISELMANN

A *Festschrift* concerned primarily with things ecumenical offers a rightful place to the problem of the relations between Scripture, Tradition, and the Church. Indeed, it is safe to go a step further and to assert that this is one of the problems fundamental to the ecumenical dialogue. The problem is topical enough. The walls which have so long separated the confessions and which harm all theology are now largely razed. Once again we ask questions of one another. We listen to one another; we come together at conferences. Such is the case not only in Germany; similar things are happening in Belgium, France, the Netherlands, and England. In all these interconfessional conversations there arises sooner or later the question of Scripture and Tradition. The background of this curious fact throws sudden light on the fact itself: our present intellectual situation has changed greatly.[1]

Of course one would have to be far gone in utopian optimism to believe that the new insights and knowledge concerning our very problem will begin their triumphal march unobstructed.

OBSTACLES TO THE NEW KNOWLEDGE

We are going to treat the problem of Scripture, Tradition, and the Church purely from the Catholic point of view. But precisely in that context there are strong psychological and theological obstacles to the new developments. Such obstacles must be treated prudently

39

and considerately. The author can speak only of conditions in German Catholicism. Its catechetical practice has been for centuries to teach children that the gospel of Jesus Christ is brought down to us partly in Holy Scripture, partly in oral Tradition. The catechisms of Saint Peter Canisius with their "partly-partly" have been the basis of instruction. In view of the authority which Canisius enjoyed as a catechist it is not surprising that this "partly-partly" has survived in the catechisms of German dioceses based on Canisius, up to the most recent past. Thus the catechism of the Archdiocese of Cologne read as late as 1915: "By tradition we mean those truths which the apostles preached but did not write down." And even in 1924, in the advance edition of the preliminary draft of the uniform catechism[2] published with ecclesiastical approbation we read: "Other divine revelations (i.e., other than those recorded in Holy Scripture) were only preached by the apostles and faithfully handed down in the Church. They are called tradition or inherited teachings."[3] The situation has, if anything, been worsened by a very unhappy formulation in the new uniform catechism, a formulation in danger of contradicting the decision of the Council of Trent.[4] In the new catechism of the Archdiocese of Vienna the "partly-partly" has, it is true, disappeared and been replaced by an "and" faithful to the wording of the Council of Trent. Still, one may legitimately doubt that this will bring about a new situation in catechetical practice. On the contrary, there are reasons for thinking that the new "and" will continue to be generally explained in the traditional sense of "partly-partly," just as long ago Melchior Cano read his preconceived "partly-partly" into the decision of the Council of Trent about Holy Scripture and Tradition almost immediately after the pronouncement of that Council. All indications are that a long and patient retraining of our zealous catechists will be necessary to introduce the new insights into catechetical practice.[5]

But the difficulties are not only catechetical. We confront the same difficulties in the field of theology. For Canisius maintained the *partim-partim* not only in his purely catechetical works, but also in those passages of the *Summa doctrinae christianae* (1566–1592), written after the Council of Trent, in which he deals with dogmatic Tradition. There he takes the Apostles' Creed and Holy Scripture as the sources (*fontes*) of our faith, from which sources one can derive what is to be believed. The question whether a Christian need believe only the contents of the Apostles' Creed is answered by the great Jesuit theologian with four requirements to be met by the Christian. The third of these is: "Here it is a question of what is deduced as necessary conclusion partly from the articles of the Creed and partly from the Scriptures, both taken as divine sources."[6] Here the Apostles' Creed is taken to represent Tradition.[7] But in this Canisius was preceded by another, no less important theologian who had a much greater influence on the theological definition of Tradition: Melchior Cano with his *Loci theologici*. Albert Lang has been able to show that the first ten books of the twelve making up the *Loci* were written from 1543 to 1550.[8] Hence the third book, "De traditionibus apostolicis," was probably written shortly before or after 1546; around the time, therefore, when the fourth session of the Council of Trent, on April 8, 1546, formulated its decrees about Scripture and Tradition.[9] Cano, however, decidedly maintains the *partim-partim*. For this purpose he cites—like John Fisher and Johannes Eck—the first chapter of the *De ecclesiastica hierarchia* of the Pseudo-Dionysius in the translation of Ambrosius Traversari, called Camaldulensis, who renders the Greek "both . . . and" by *partim-partim*.[10] After the extensive quotation from the Pseudo-Dionysius, Cano continues by saying that, having thus laid the foundation, it remains to be shown and proven that the apostles passed on the teachings of the gospel partly in writing and partly also orally.[11] Cano adduces the (alleged) witnesses to this *partim-partim;* in other words, he wants to bring the proof of Tradition for his *partim-partim*. He comes to the conclusion that one cannot deny "That not all of the doctrine of the faith was handed on in writing, but part of it was handed on by the Apostles orally."[12] With this definition of the matter he shows himself to be a true disciple of nominalist theology. Having thus stated his view of the relation between Scripture and Tradition, Cano in Chapter 6 finally strains the decision of the fourth session of the Council of Trent to prove his *partim-partim*. The manner in which he does it is more than characteristic. He approaches that decision with a categorical and a priori *partim-partim* and reads that *partim-partim* into the decision of the Council by quoting it in such a way that it proves his *partim-partim*.[13] For Cano does not quote the decision of the Council verbatim; he gives the content in an abridged form. Precisely his omission throws decisive light on the fact that he reads the decision of the Council with the eyes of a theologian completely caught up in the *partim-partim*. He leaves out the decisive thought that Christ has given the apostles the mission of announcing to all creatures the good tidings which He Himself made public with His own mouth, as *the* source (*fons*) of all truth of salvation and morality. Yet here it is explicit that the apostolic word proclaimed by a living voice (*das lebendig verkündigte apostolische Wort*) is the form in which the gospel of Christ is to speak to us; which means that the apostolic kerygma, the apostolic *paradosis,* transmits the gospel in its entirety. This fundamental idea, which alone makes intelligible the subsequent passage concerning Holy Scripture and unwritten Tradition, is left out by Cano. He quotes the conciliar decision as follows: "The sacred Council of Trent, observing that the saving Truth and moral teaching of the Gospel is continued in written books and unwritten traditions of Christ himself. . . ."[14] That completed the two-source theory. From then on one could speak of Scripture and Tradition as the two sources of revelation which divide between themselves the transmission of the gospel. The textbooks of dogmatics and of fundamental theology did just that very extensively, with the intention of explaining the decisions of the Council of Trent.[15]

Not Canisius, then, but Melchior Cano was the first to begin the merry-go-round of those who called on the Council of Trent as the star witness for the *partim-partim*.[16] In view of the powerful influence which his *Loci theologici* exercises to this day, one can understand how Canisius, Bellarmine, and post-Tridentine theology in general almost universally interpreted the Tridentine decision until well into the nineteenth century, in the sense of the *partim-partim,* although we now know, since the publication of the acts of the Council, that it knowingly excluded its own initial *partim-partim* from the definitive formulation of the decree.[17]

So it is understandable that in the nineteenth century very few theologians professed the sufficiency of the content of Holy Scripture and few opposed the *partim-partim* view, which had become the *opinio communis* (general opinion). As far as the author of this study could determine, Dobmayer-Senestrey was the first to maintain again the view of the sufficiency of the content of Holy Scripture. This dogmatic theologian remarks against the Walenburg brothers and the Bishop of Belley, Jean-Pierre Camus (1583–1652), that it is not *de fide* that some dogmatic traditions exist which are mere *orales:* "This much seems to be certain, that the Council of Trent did not decide whether there are propositions of faith which are not at all contained in Scripture or deducible from it; suffice it that there are *traditiones hermeneuticas.*"[18] The same view was, furthermore, held by Newman, who retained his Anglican conviction "that the whole Christian Faith is contained in Scripture" even after his conversion,[19] apparently because of the influence of William Palmer.[20] Johann Adam Möhler and Johann Kuhn, both of Tübingen, held the same view.

THE COUNCIL OF TRENT ON THE RELATION OF SCRIPTURE AND TRADITION

Before we can approach our task of clarifying the relations of Scripture, Tradition, and the Church, the foundation for our theology must be firmly laid. That foundation is the decision of the Council of Trent in the fourth session, April 8, 1546. What did the magisterium of the Church decide there on the relation of Scripture and Tradition? As previously stated, the *opinio communis* of theologians immediately after the Tridentinum was determined by the influence of the *Loci theologici* of Melchior Cano, by the catechisms and theological writings of Canisius, and the *Controversies* of Bellarmine, which say that the Council decided the relation of Scripture and Tradition in the sense of "partly-partly." Is that possible? In any case, the magisterial decision of the Council has had a curious fate. And it would not be surprising if, in view of this fact, one or another were to express a kind of uncertainty and unrest. Some words which Johann Adam Möhler wrote in the introduction to his *Symbolik* may contribute to a clarification of our problem. The post-Tridentine interpretation of the Council's decision is a *theological discussion* of the dogma, not the dogma itself. Precisely for that reason it would be very foolish to confuse it with the teaching of the Church itself. A certain conception of a dogma or any kind of conception may be fairly universal even for some time without becoming an integral part of the dogma or becoming dogma itself. Such conceptions are ever-changing, individual forms of a universal reality; they may have served this or that person or also a particular age to master the universal by way of reflection and speculation. They may also be more or less true; but on this score the Church remains silent because it lacks the foundation in tradition which would enable her to make a decision; instead, the Church leaves it entirely to theological criticism to judge the truth of such conceptions.[21]

Curiously enough, it was Anglican theology which first expressed doubts whether the decision of the Council of Trent had to be understood in that way. These doubts were voiced by the Anglican theologian William Palmer in his *Treatise on the Church of Christ*.[22] There he states that the Council of Trent by no means sanctioned the view that the Holy Scripture contains only a part of revelation, the other part being contained in oral Tradition. Rather, he said, the decree of the Council comes much closer to the teachings of the sixth Anglican Article, according to which Holy Scripture contains everything necessary for salvation; and the similarity of this Anglican doctrine with the Tridentine decree is much greater than the teaching of the Roman theologians would have it. He said that the Fathers of the Council were well acquainted with the question disputed at the time, whether the truths of faith were contained only partly (*ex parte*) in Holy Scripture. But, he continued, they did not mean to decide that question to the effect that Christian doctrine is contained *ex parte* in Holy Scriptures, *ex parte* in Tradition. They declared, rather, according to Palmer, the general proposition that the truth and discipline of the gospel are contained in the written books and in unwritten traditions. He said this was not disputed by the Anglican Church, and that it was also the view of very many Roman theologians. To this J. Perrone remarks: it remains unknown where Palmer got the information that there was, at the time of the Council of Trent, a controversy as to whether there are articles of faith certified only by Tradition, and that the Council did not mean to decide this controversy.

On this point the Acts of the Council as well as the histories of it by Sarpi and Pallavicini are silent.[23] The publication of the Acts of the Council by the Görres-Gesellschaft has, however, proved the Anglican theologian right. Did he have special information? There is little likelihood of it, since Perrone would have had to have access to it just as well. Was it an intuition of genius?

Very recently the Anglican theologian Edward C. Rich—now converted—took a similar position:

When the Council of Trent decreed that the truth and discipline of the Christian religion "are contained in written books and in unwritten traditions," it would *seem* to make "traditions" an authority independent of holy scripture. But this is not a necessary deduction. At any rate whatever Roman Catholic *practice* may have been, it is arguable that this is a false deduction from *official* Roman teaching. . . . The VIth Anglican Article "Of the Sufficiency of Scripture," "is possibly patient of a (Roman) Catholic interpretation," according to a Roman Catholic theologian.[24] Certain it is that the Anglican appeal is not incompatible with the Tridentine decree if we enquire closely into the official teaching of the Roman Church. The real problem, which constitutes the heart of the controversy, then and now, as between the Roman and Anglican doctrines of authority, is that of the Teaching Authority or Interpretation of Faith. This is the question of the *magisterium*.[25]

Rich's conception has not, however, found unanimous approval among Anglican theologians. It does have the merit, nevertheless, of having started a discussion of the problem. While E. C. Rich considers the Roman Catholic view of the relation of Holy Scripture and Tradition similar to the Anglican view, F. W. Dillistone has opposed to Rich's *Spiritual Authority in the Church of England* a co-operative volume, by various authors, entitled *Scripture and Tradition*.[26] The essay which concerns us is that of F. J. Taylor on "Scripture and Tradition in the Anglican Reformation."[27] Taylor is much more critical of the Roman Catholic view of the relation of Scripture and Tradition than E. C. Rich. The latter thinks that the sixth Anglican Article on the sufficiency of the content of Scripture admits of an interpretation in the Roman Catholic sense and that the real problem lies in the magisterium of the Church, i.e., in the authoritative explanation of Scripture and Tradition. Taylor, on the other hand, thinks that such an interpretation of the sixth Anglican Article is out of the question because, although it does not explicitly deal with the proceedings of the Council of Trent, it was, nevertheless, formulated with conscious reference to the decision of the Council.[28]

But surely that is to say that if the sixth Anglican Article stresses the sufficiency of content so much with reference to the Council of Trent, the assumption is that the Council did not proclaim such a sufficiency of content. If, like E. C. Rich, one interprets the view of the Council to be that the entire faith is contained in Holy Scripture and is simultaneously represented by oral Tradition, then indeed there is only a small difference of principle between the Anglican and Roman Catholic conceptions. However, the words of the Council seem to say, and have generally been interpreted by Roman authors to say, that written and unwritten Tradition is an independent and equally important source next to Holy Scripture for the preservation of the faith. They seem to say that if Holy Scripture is not looked upon as an inherently sufficient and ultimate arbiter, but if it must share that function with unwritten Tradition, then it follows that there must be some authority able to decide which traditions meet the requirements established in the decree of the Council. If this premise is accepted, then, continues Taylor, it is difficult to doubt the conclusion that such an authority can be found only in the Papacy. He says that the concept of Tradition maintained by the Fathers of the Council was based on the mediation (by oral means since the first days of the Church) of *a few teachings* and practical exercises ordained by Christ or by the apostles, guided by the Holy Spirit. If that be the case, one may reasonably demand that such traditions identify themselves by the necessary historical evidence. However, says Taylor, few traditions added to the substance of faith by the authorities of the Roman Church were subjected to such testing or would have passed such examination had they been subjected to it. According to Taylor the consequence has been—thus diverging from the aforementioned wording of the Tridentine decree—that the written tradition of Holy Scripture, generally accepted in the Church since the earliest centuries, was subordinated to the unwritten traditions which, in the Roman community, were accepted solely on the authority of papal promulgation. In the words of Lord Acton, "tradition was required to produce what it had not preserved."[29] Taylor says that this violent change in the concept of Tradition, contrary to its historical meaning, became apparent toward the end of the sixteenth century in the writings of the great theological controversialist, Cardinal Bellarmine:

When the universal Church embraces as a dogma of the faith something which is not found in holy Scripture, we must say that it is held from a tradition of the apostles. When the universal Church observes some practice which no one could appoint save God, but which is nevertheless nowhere found in Scripture, we must say that it is a tradition from Christ and his apostles.[30]

The meaning of this passage, Taylor continues, is that from now on it is in the power of the Papacy to add something, as necessary for salvation, to the faith of the Church if it is considered necessary; and to do this by simply asserting that the addition is in fact not an addition but was implicitly contained from the beginning in the ensemble for the sake of the maintenance of faith. This introduced a frightening uncertainty into the idea of maintaining the faith. Cranmer drew this conclusion when in his *Confutation of Unwritten Verities* he observed:

If there were any word of God besides the Scripture, we could never be certain of God's word. If the Church and the Christian faith did not stay itself upon the word of God certain, as upon a sure and strong foundation, no man could know whether he had a right faith and whether he were in the true Church of Christ or in the Synagogue of Satan. If we be bound to believe certain things delivered from the apostles by word of mouth only, without writing, as they would make us believe (but what those things be no man can tell) it should hereof follow that we are bound to believe we wot not what.[31]

What exactly, then, was actually decided by the Council of Trent about doctrine concerning the relation of Scripture and Tradition? We may now answer: neither the sufficiency of content of Holy Scripture was proclaimed, nor was the relation of Scripture and Tradition decided in the sense of "partly-partly." One cannot emphasize enough that nothing, absolutely nothing, was decided at

the Council of Trent concerning the relation of Scripture and
Tradition. Unfortunately, it is impossible to document that here
in detail.[32] Suffice it to say that it had been planned from the beginning of the Council to define the relation of Scripture and unwritten
Tradition by "partly-partly." In the general meeting of theologians
on February 12, 1546, Cardinal del Monte said: "This (revelation)
given to us by the Church partly from the Scripture of the Old and
New Testaments, partly from simply being handed on by tradi-
tion."[33] One may infer from this that it was, at first, the intention of
Rome to fix the relation of Scripture and Tradition in this sense.
Thus also the preliminary draft of the decree of March 22, 1546:
"That this truth is contained partly in written books, partly in unwritten traditions."[34] This text was still before the session of April
1, 1546, and had the consent of an overwhelming majority of the
Fathers of the Council. Only two of them, the learned General of the
Servites, Bonucci, and the Bishop of Chioggia, Jacob Nachianti, well
versed in the Bible, protested energetically against this *partim-
partim*. Six days later, in the decisive session of April 8, there sud-
denly appears a modified text. The *partim-partim* has disappeared
and been replaced by *"et."* The records of the Council leave us, unfortunately, entirely in the dark about the events which moved the
committee charged with the editing of the text to make this decisive
change. With this *"et"* the Council avoided a decision about the
relation of Scripture and Tradition; for, in view of the two conflicting
theological positions represented at the Council, the question was
deemed not yet ripe for decision.[35]

SCRIPTURE AND TRADITION IN THE
COMPREHENSIVE CATHOLIC VIEW

The task before us is to attain a truly Catholic, all-embracing view
of the relation of Scripture and Tradition. To begin with, we note
that such a view is irreconcilable with the kind of mechanistic
division of two sources of Scripture and Tradition put forth by
post-Tridentine theology with its *partim-partim*.[36] To put it more
clearly, the latter view is un-Catholic. God is no plumber who, so to
speak, provides the Church with running water, letting the word of

God flow out of two sources of faith, Scripture and Tradition, as out of two water taps marked hot and cold.[37] Such a view conflicts with the *kath' holon* by which the Church stands and falls. If *kath' holon* means "containing in a single part the reality of the whole," as Aristotle says,[38] then the relation of Scripture and Tradition can be defined in a Catholic way only if both Scripture and Tradition mediate for us the entire gospel, though each does so differently.

Furthermore, it is necessary to bring this question out of the ghetto into which it has strayed because of the purely anti-Reformation view of the matter. The Council of Trent made its decision with a view to the Reformation antithesis of *sola scriptura* and with a view to the assertion that purely human traditions are irrelevant, if not actually harmful, to faith and morals.[39] In opposition thereto the Council determined in principle that there are, in the Church, traditions at once divine and apostolic, without going into the question—in spite of repeated demands by Fathers of the Council —precisely which traditions are, in the concrete, to be considered as such. That decision of principle is all we have up to the present. For although the Vatican Council went beyond the Council of Trent in the matter of Holy Scripture by explaining its inspiration, the Vatican Council accepted the decision of the Council of Trent concerning Tradition with only unessential modifications.[40] The dialectic of the Council of Trent, however, is determined by a clearly circumscribed antithesis. It follows that only a particular, clearly limited, aspect of the comprehensive problem of Scripture and Tradition is brought into view; the teaching office of the Church did not deal with the entire question in all its broadness. "Anti-Reformation" is far from being a synonym for "Catholic." It is necessary, therefore, to look at the problem of Scripture and Tradition in an all-embracing Catholic light, just as H. Küng recently did with respect to justification[41] and as August Deneffe attempted to do with respect to Tradition.[42]

Nevertheless, the Council of Trent points the way to a truly Catholic comprehension of Scripture and Tradition. That comprehension lies in viewing Scripture and unwritten Tradition from the point of view of the gospel of Jesus the Christ, which gospel has been proclaimed to us in the apostolic kerygma as the (sole) source of all truth of salvation and morality.[43] From that point of view one may define Scripture and Tradition only as the different modes of existence within the Church of the gospel of Jesus Christ.

The task of viewing the relation of Scripture and Tradition in its all-embracing, Catholic sense can be solved only by placing Scripture and Tradition in the setting which embraces both, the Church. For "Church, gospel and tradition always stand or fall together."[44] This takes us squarely into the heart of the problem which today dominates our concern with the nature of Holy Scripture. Möhler's organic view, unfortunately, had almost no effect during the nineteenth century. One may call the period behind us that of the isolated consideration of Scripture, Tradition, and the Church; that period is now over in all Christian denominations. The period of isolating is ended. It belongs to the past. The fault for that isolated view lies, for one thing, with the extreme theory of inspiration held by Lutheran orthodoxy at the end of the sixteenth century and during the seventeenth. That theory of inspiration turned Holy Scripture into a wandering body which had lost its bearings or, if you will, into a meteorite fallen from the sky, without relation to the life of the Church.[45] This criticism includes, however, the way in which Catholic theology treated inspired Scripture during the nineteenth century. Where did that theology show the essential reference of Holy Scripture to the Church? And the theology of "partly Scripture, partly oral Tradition" led automatically to a view of Scripture and Tradition as separate problems, each of them to be considered and theologically solved by itself. Hence many will find utterly strange what Karl Rahner says in his most recent work *Über die Schriftinspiration:* "God wills Scripture and wills to be himself its cause; he posits both because, and to the degree that, he wills to be himself acting and effective as the cause of the Church."[46] I say this may sound utterly strange. For as L. Bouyer remarks, "What is most surprising is that these theories about inspiration [of Lutheran orthodoxy, with the consequent isolating of Scripture] came during the nineteenth century to carve their way even into certain manuals of Catholic theology."[47] The inevitable counterattack against that extreme theory of inspiration was not able to rescue Holy Scripture from its isolation; on the contrary, the counterattack only pushed Holy Scripture into an even deeper isolation. For the inspiration of Holy Scripture was abandoned; it was treated as a purely human, historic document. Scripture becomes the Bible, i.e., "a collection of ancient religious documents."[48] No doubt research by literary criticism and by the history of religion has given us an understanding of this book which we will not again do without. Theology cannot, without harm to itself, ignore the fact that "Scripture as such is, to begin with, a document of the past and is, therefore, subject to historical criticism as the generally accepted approach to documents of the past."[49] Still, to take Holy Scripture—the inspired word of God—out of the context of all human (historical, religious, and intellectual) movements is no less one-sided that to evaluate it only as a bible, i.e., as a collection of ancient religious documents and therefore purely as a human, historical religious document to be put in the context of intellectual, linguistic, and religious history. One must do both; and that is to say that the document is to be viewed from a double point of view. It is both bible and Holy Scripture.[50] These are two different things. Something may be scriptural and unscriptural, or biblical and unbiblical. One is a value judgment, the other a judgment of fact. The former is a theological statement, the latter one of critical interpretation. "The statement 'biblical-unbiblical' and the evaluation 'scriptural-unscriptural' belong to universes of discourse qualitatively different. The same object is examined in two specifically different respects: as bible, from the point of view of a collection of ancient religious documents; as Scripture, from the point of view of a challenging call to contemporary man. In both cases we deal not with partial aspects but with views of the whole. The same complex of literature is, as a monument of the past, the bible; and, as a determining power in the present, Scripture."[51] As we are examining the problem of Scripture and Tradition from the dogmatic point of view, we are concerned with that body of literature only insofar as it is Holy Scripture.

THE ORGANIC CONNECTION OF
HOLY SCRIPTURE WITH TRADITION
AND THE CHURCH

How difficult it is to attain a right understanding of the Word of
God in Holy Scripture is forcefully indicated by the two extreme
positions which today confront one another in this field. On the
one hand, we have the existential interpretation of the word of
God, as expressed in the actualistic view of the revealing Word which
characterizes the theology of Bultmann. On this view the revealing
Word is limited to the present existential fact (the "*Dass*") of God's
challenging call and of man's being addressed in his personal center;
this present existential fact is to help man, through his obedience in
faith, to existence (*Existenz*), i.e., to his proper personal fulfillment.
Revelation—in the sense of uncovering an event of salvation tran-
scending natural human horizons—is banished into the realm of
myth. On the other hand, there is the concept of revelation which
sees it as a gift by God of a bonus of truths. This view divorces the
inseparable unity of the revealing God and his revelation, of God
who speaks to man by revelation and God who challenges man to
decision. One can only emphasize the words of O. Semmelroth: "This
view reduces the importance of the *manner* in which these truths
were made accessible to the mind. The fact that *God* has revealed
them to us seems important only as a means of taking possession
of these truths. This view easily comes to emphasize things in a
way not entirely corresponding to God's plan of salvation."[52] On
this view the truths of revelation appear as independent realities
which man has at his disposal. Holy Scripture becomes a textbook
containing truths, much as a mathematical textbook contains the
theorems of Pythagoras. Holy Scripture is degraded to *instrumentum
doctrinae* (a means of transmitting doctrine).

Our last sentence already brings up the second difficulty which
makes it so difficult for us in the West to enter the world of Holy
Scripture, if it does not actually bar it to us. I shall leave it to the
Anglican (and meanwhile converted) theologian E. C. Rich to express this difficulty:

It is not easy for us in the West to get into the frame of mind by which we can approach the Bible in this way [i.e., in its own spirit—translator]. By long custom inherited from the days of scholasticism our minds have been dominated by rational concepts; and for us moderns this generally means scientific concepts. We fail to build up our rational knowledge into the whole context of "truth." Consequently we have got into the habit of treating the Bible as a quarry from which we may dig out proofs to substantiate our theological presuppositions. But this is not the reason why the Bible was written for our learning. The Church did not put its *imprimatur* upon these particular documents to provide us with evidence for argument but to build us up into the Faith which she proclaims; and she points us to the Scriptures not to "prove" her doctrine but to tell us how it became known to her. The Church went out into the world proclaiming the Gospel. This Proclamation concerned Jesus of Nazareth who was declared to be the Son of God with power. And this Revelation was made known by His coming in the likeness of human flesh, in which flesh He died and rose again and ascended and then sent the gift of the Spirit upon His Church which is His Body. These are the "facts of the Gospel" which are "according to the Scriptures." They are embodied in the *paradosis* or tradition of this living Society and they concern everyman; because, by reason of these facts "God calls upon men everywhere to repent and believe the Gospel." It is therefore impossible to separate the Bible from the Church's life and worship without doing violence to each. It tends to depersonalize both the Church and the Scriptures.[53]

Thus this Anglican theologian has chosen the best way to formulate a criticism of that view of Holy Scripture which looks upon it as a collection of doctrines. Holy Scripture is that too, of course. The New Testament itself calls the gospel a doctrine, *didachē* (Rom 16:17, Acts 2:42, *didaschalia* (Rom 12:7; pastoral letters, *passim*). To preach the word of God is also paraphrased with *didaschein* (2 Thes 2:15; Col 2:7; Eph 4:21; 1 Tim 4:11; Acts 5:42, 18:11, 28:31). The announcer of the word of God may also be honored by the title of teacher (*didaschalos*) (1 Ti 2:7; 2 Ti 1:11). "The gospel, then, is also a teaching. This must, therefore, mean that it is an *instructive* communicating of facts and events of salvation, or instructive interpretation of the Holy Scripture of the Old Testament.

Again, the notion of "teaching" points out that the gospel may be present in a fixed tradition, as the expression *hygiainousa didaschalion* (2 Tim 4:5 *et al.*) already suggests. Naturally the gospel is not primarily such 'teaching' but only secondarily so."[54]

The Anglican theologian points out that when we deal with the content of Holy Scripture we are dealing with the gospel, proclaimed by the Church, of Jesus of Nazareth, the Son of God who came to us in the likeness of human flesh. We are also dealing with the saving events of his death, resurrection, ascension, and his gift of the Holy Spirit to his Church, which is incorporated into the *paradosis* of the Church, that living community which is his body. Thus Holy Scripture, Tradition, and the life and divine service of the Church become a living unity which suffers no dividing. To divide it would amount to robbing the Bible and the Church of their personal character.

Thus, proceeding from the gospel of salvation of Jesus the Christ and Son of God, we arrive at a new evaluation of the Word of Holy Scripture. That Word is, essentially, the good tidings of Jesus the Christ, proclaimed by the Church. And, in connection with this, a second problem necessarily arises: the living connection between Scripture and Tradition. How do we reach this solution?

THE WORD OF HOLY SCRIPTURE,
THE RECORDED KERYGMA OF THE
CHURCH IN APOSTOLIC TIMES

Whenever the question weighing on us about the "historical" Jesus is answered in such a way as to divorce the Jesus of history from the Christ of faith, criticism is led from the so-called historical picture of Jesus, elaborated from the sources of Holy Scripture, to the problem of the specific character of our Gospel reports. Thus the separation of the historical Jesus from the myth of Christ in the *Leben Jesu* by David Friedrich Strauss led the then young New Testament exegete, J. E. Kuhn, who was later to become a famous dogmatic theologian at Tübingen, to ask about the specific character of the Gospel reports and about the concept of history implicit in them. He realized that the Gospels are not at all interested in the life (*bios*) of Jesus, i.e., in an historical report in the usual historical sense. Rather, they are concerned with history in a most particular sense; history as the story of salvation (*Heilsgeschichte*). Kuhn drew the conclusion that if one approaches the Gospels as historical sources in the usual sense in order to obtain a picture of the historical Jesus, one lacks the instruments necessary for the task; and that the resulting so-called historical Jesus is a product of the imagination insofar as it separates the alleged historical Jesus from the mythical Christ. What the Gospels are concerned with is not mere history in the usual sense, but the history of salvation; hence, what the Holy Scripture is concerned with cannot be a mere historical record. It can only be the tidings of Jesus the Christ; in other words, kerygma.[55] Holy Scripture is the *paradosis* of the apostolic kerygma, become writing. Nor does Kuhn leave any doubt about the historicity of the words and deeds reported of Jesus. After World War I theology was in a similar position when Albert Schweitzer's *The Quest of the Historical Jesus*[56] reduced the liberal life-of-Jesus theology to the absurd.

Today it is no longer possible for anyone to write a life of Jesus. This is now the result, surprising but hardly disputed, of researches which for almost two hundred years expended extraordinary and by no means fruitless labor on an attempt to depict and represent the life of the historical Jesus, free of all "retouching" by dogma or doctrine. At the end of this research into the life of Jesus there comes the recognition of its own failure. To that research Albert Schweitzer, in his classic *The Quest of the Historical Jesus*, erected a monument and at the same time delivered its funeral oration.[57]

Today it is emphasized, in contrast to the life-of-Jesus theology, that Holy Scripture is not a report about the history of Jesus but a gospel, the kerygma of salvation in Jesus Christ. The kerygmatic nature of the Gospel and of the New Testament writings generally is now recognized. At the same time research into the history of the forms, genre, traditions, and liturgy which lay behind New Testament documents has taught us that the New Testament is the written deposit of the living *paradosis* of the primitive Church. This, too, is gospel,

not only the spoken word of the apostles but also the written; not only the spontaneous word, but also the word modified by oral and written transmission; not only the *viva vox*, but also tradition, the word which has entered tradition and is there preserved. . . . One should remember that these letters employ much formulated *kerygma* especially in homologies (creeds), hymns and liturgical sayings [*Kultesprüche*] (1 Cor 15:1 ff., 11:23 ff.; Phil 2:15 ff.; Eph 5:14; 1 Ti 3:16; 1 Peter 3:20 ff., 3:18 f., 3:20). In the sense of formulated *kerygma, paradosis* is explicitly mentioned, *e.g.,* in Rom 6:19; 1 Cor 11:2 and 23; 1 Thes 4:1; 2 Thes 2:15, 3:6. This, too, is gospel (cf. Gal 1:9) which is received. In such traditions, too, one "receives" the Christ (Col 2:6). The gospel does indeed not lose its character if its living word is crystallized in a particular form.[58]

Once the kerygmatic nature of our Gospels is grasped, it is concluded that the Easter faith of the Church just begun is not simply the bearer, but actually gave its present form to the gospel written in the Bible. That is to say that Christian faith is faith in the risen *Kyrios:* for this faith the historical Jesus, his words and deeds, have no more constitutive significance.[59] Hence in Bultmann's theology the historicity of the kerygma of Christ hangs from a thin thread insofar as the kerygma is connected to the historical event of the crucifixion of Jesus of Nazareth. Thus the extreme kerygmatic interpretation of our Gospels was in so great a danger of falling into a "Christological docetism and gnosticism" that a reaction was inevitable. The extreme kerygmatic interpretation of the New Testament raised anew the very question which that kerygmatic theology had attacked: the question of the historical Jesus.[60] This has led, in the most recent past, to an important correction of the purely kerygmatic view of our Gospels. It is now said that they "combine in a peculiarly intense way a *report* of Jesus Christ with a simultaneous profession of faith in him, a *witnessing* by the community believing in him with a *narrative of his history*."[61] This modifies essentially the picture of the *paradosis* of the apostolic Church written down in the New Testament. It does not merely hand on the faith of the Church in the risen and ascended Lord; nor does it heighten and idealize everything that happened before Easter by the transfiguring light of the Easter faith; it also reports what the historical Jesus preached and did. However, in the Gospels this "account of Jesus Christ" is not a wooden repetition of what Jesus preached and did. This account is *paradosis;* that is to say, it puts the words of Jesus into the changing situation of the apostolic Church so as to make the formerly spoken word of Jesus into the ever-present, living word of the Lord. Thus the word of Jesus undergoes in the *paradosis* variations conditioned by new situations. It would be wrong to explain these transformations which the words of Jesus had to submit to, by the laws governing popular transmission of oral tradition, which transforms, elaborates, or deletes. The *paradosis* of the apostolic Church preserves the word of Jesus "but does not guard it with an archivist's piety, nor is it handed on like the sayings of famous rabbis and provided with interpretations. Indeed one may put it as follows: tradition does not actually repeat and hand on his formerly spoken word at all; it *is* His word today. Only from this point of view can one understand the manifold modifications of his word in tradition."[62] Still, these variations conditioned by the situation do not make it impossible to make an approximate reconstruction of the word once spoken by Jesus. To take a single example, Luke reports Jesus' parable of the meal to the effect that the rich man, after his acquaintances have refused the invitation, sends out his servants a second and third time; the second time to the poor, lame, and crippled in the city, the third time to those by the hedges outside the city. Here the third mission is a modification of the Lord's parable, conditioned by the new situation; the modification serves to illustrate the progress of the mission of the Church from Israel to the pagan world.[63] This modification of the saying of Jesus is in accord with the basic conception of the Gospel according to Luke. In the Gospel according to Matthew, however, Jesus considers himself sent only to the lost sheep of the house of Israel (Mt 15:24); he cannot make a statement of this kind. Hence he sends the servants out only twice; and no doubt Matthew's version of the parable is closer to its original wording by Jesus (Mt 22:1–14).

THE SUFFICIENCY OF HOLY SCRIPTURE

We have clarified the organic connection of Holy Scripture with
the apostolic Tradition and with the apostolic Church, and have
realized that its content is the written apostolic *paradosis,* i.e., the
preaching (*Verkündigung*) of the faith, the liturgy, the sacramental
rites, and in general the life of the apostolic Church. We may, therefore, now raise the question of the sufficiency of the content of Holy
Scripture. Does the New Testament contain all, or only a part, of
what God has in these latter days spoken through one who is his
son (Heb 1:1)? If Holy Scripture is not a book telling us only the
revealed truths of faith and the moral commandments, but if its
main purpose is, rather, to announce to us our salvation in Jesus the
Christ and make it present to us in the world,[64] then perhaps it is
possible to clear up this problem. The mystery of Jesus the Christ,
the salvation of the world, is central to Holy Scripture. But this is
an event which took place in our very midst; and that historical
event is an organic whole of which the scriptural *paradosis,* already
fixed in form and formulae, and the homologies, hymns, and liturgical sayings are only the radiations, the concrete external forms in
the life of the apostolic Church. Furthermore, Holy Scripture does
not stand in isolation but is always connected with the living Tradition which preceded it, accompanies it, and which is not replaced
by the determination of the canon of Scripture. We can also observe
—already in Holy Scripture—how this living *paradosis* puts the
words and sayings of Jesus into the changing situation and by so doing also interprets them. For all these reasons it is out of the question
that Holy Scripture should give us only fragments of the gospel of
Jesus the Christ, the rest being given to us by Tradition. On the contrary, there are good reasons for assuming that the apostolic kerygma
recorded in Holy Scripture announces to us the whole mystery of
Jesus Christ, supposing that Holy Scripture is read in the context
of the Church, i.e., as a part of the Church and therefore in the
light of the commentary furnished by the life of the Church, its
liturgical practice, and the conduct of the Christian community in
morals and discipline.[65] Given these suppositions, we may speak
of a sufficiency of the content of Holy Scripture. By maintaining

that sufficiency we breach the solid wall of the *partim-partim* theology which extends from the days of Cano to the present. But we are not alone in our view. The earliest pioneers came in the nineteenth century: Dobmayer-Senestrey, Möhler, Newman, and J. E. Kuhn. They are now joined by leading theologians of all countries. Suffice it to mention only August Deneffe, Karl Rahner, Otto Karrer, P. A. Liégé, O.P., M. Chenu, O.P., J. Daniélou, S.J., and in England Henry St. John, O.P., and Sebastian Bullough, O.P. O. Semmelroth is in sympathy with this view. J. Ratzinger also defends it.[66] A. M. Dubarle, O.P., especially maintains the sufficiency of the content of Holy Scripture. In his treatise on *Les fondements bibliques du titre marial de nouvelle Ève* he remarks:

The Catholic need not lessen the role played by the preaching of the living word as a necessary means of conveying religious truth or as a rule to give definite form to the assent of the believer. He can think that all objective revelation is contained in the Scriptures, although in different ways, and in some cases in a form which is no more than implicit.[67]

For this Dubarle invokes Newman.[68] In a review of I. Seynaeve, *Cardinal Newman's Doctrine of Holy Scripture* (1954), he defends his opinion that Newman maintained the sufficiency of the content of Holy Scripture. He claims that Newman's statement that the Word of God, written and unwritten, constitutes revelation in its entirety does not mean, as Seynaeve thinks, that the unwritten word contains truths lacking in the written. And he says that Newman's statement of 1851 that a certain number of doctrines was bequeathed by the apostles not in writing but alive in the spirit (*Geist*) of the faithful does not exclude the implicit inclusion of these doctrines in the books of the Old Testament. He maintains that it cannot be proved that Newman's view of this matter changed between his Anglican and Catholic periods. In his Anglican period Newman thought that all revealed truth was contained in Holy Scripture, though not obvious and easily accessible without the help of Tradition. This view, continues Dubarle, he did not change in his Catholic period. At that time, too, he considered Tradition an indispensable means for the transmission of the word of God.

Tradition has an authority of its own. That does not prevent him, though, from assuming that the entire revelation of God is contained in Holy Scripture, even though this revelation be not always obvious.[69] In his introduction to Holy Scripture, A. M. Dubarle has systematically presented and established this view of the relatively complete rendition of the revealed word of God in Holy Scripture, a view briefly suggested and more indirectly expressed in his critical reviews. Revelation is knowledge of the gift of God which is to be presented to us in the new life by means of our rebirth. Revelation is an organic whole. The concepts and propositions in which it is expressed can never reproduce it exhaustively. Hence they are not truths independent of one another nor without relation to their living, comprehensive possession by the Church. Thus there is reason for assuming that in this revelation every expression that has any content at all must show, at least in germ, everything which is virtually contained in it and a connection with all doctrines which reflect that revelation. It is, therefore, entirely improbable that the collection of biblical writings, extending over more than a millennium and so varied in their themes and aspirations [*preoccupations*], should be entirely silent on an essential point of the divine message, Tradition alone informing us of it. . . . One may, then, think that not all aspects of divine revelation are brought out equally by Holy Scripture. But it is unthinkable that there should be certain revealed truths without any connection with the Holy Books.[70]

Research into the history of the forms, genre, and traditions which lay behind the books of the New Testament has enabled us to see that the Holy Scriptures of the New Testament are the written form of a preceding, living *paradosis* of the apostolic Church.[71] That insight makes obvious the primacy of *paradosis,* the proclamation through the Word, over the written Tradition. It makes equally obvious the interplay of very flexible relations between these two poles of Christian life, which have been set in contrast to one another like black and white in theological controversies for centuries.[72] Today Protestant theology is also beginning to recognize the connection between Scripture and Tradition;[73] this has led to the fact that competent quarters now oppose that heritage of the Reformation, "the widespread anti-tradition sentiment," as E. Kinder calls it, with its pre-

conceived notion of an essential conflict between Scripture and Tradition. The same men also oppose the principle of *sola scriptura*.
Thus E. Kinder, a Lutheran theologian competent in this matter,
notes:

Protestant thought is moving away from the compulsions growing out
of the presumed consequences of an assumed "Reformation Principle,"
and leaving behind humanist, baroque-scholastic, exaggeratedly spiritual
or strongly anti-Catholic modes of thought. Certain formal "Protestant
traditions" are clearly seen to be a loosely assorted collection, involving
conclusions arrived at too hastily and demanding closer examination.
To the degree that these developments are taking place, and also because of many impartial, unprejudiced exegetical and historical researches, many Protestant theologians today look at the relation of
Scripture and tradition more impartially and objectively. They are becoming more and more convinced that it is no longer possible to consider that relation as contradictory purely on principle and without
making the necessary distinctions. They are gaining a new feeling for,
and a new comprehension of, genuine traditions of the Church, which
are evoked by the gospel as a force in history and are of theological
significance because of the gospel. This may also be due to the fact that,
contrary to religious individualism, we have learned to see the spiritual
reality of the Church more clearly, and to value it more strongly in
theology.[74]

At any rate, the new understanding of Holy Scripture, dawning
simultaneously on Catholics and Protestants alike, has torn down
the walls which separated them for centuries; a basis has been created
on which conversation between the denominations is possible.[75] Of
course we stand only at the beginning; it would be too optimistic to
think that in these fundamental questions theologians from the
various denominations will be able to attain a consensus in the near
future.[76] The authoritative interpretation of Holy Scripture by the
teaching office of the Church, the explanation of Scripture "in accordance with that meaning which the Church has always held and now
holds,"[77] the "development" of the data of Holy Scripture in the historical process of their interpretation through centuries—these are
some of the problems answered differently by Catholics and Protestants. Although, as far as development of Scriptural content is con-

cerned, Max Lackmann most recently comes very close to the Catholic view, if he does not actually join it, in saying that "Catholic faith
cannot be read in simple and rational manner in Scripture . . . though
it is confirmed by Scripture if one lives and believes with the Church.
If something is found in the Church which is not confirmed by Holy
Scripture, it is *eo ipso* not of the Catholic faith." The reason is said to
be that "The Catholic doctrinal decisions required from time to time
in the history of the Church prove their divine legitimacy not at all
merely by being formally or substantively identical with the written
word. For in these doctrinal decisions the life and work of Christ
develop in an historical process and under the particular conditions
and requirements of the people of God, led through the 'desert' by
the Holy Spirit. Though the life and work of Christ are documented
in a unique and binding way by the word of Scripture, they create new
concepts for themselves and reveal new relationships of the content
of revelation not explicitly found in Scripture in those words."[78] This
development, then, takes place more explicitly in the Tradition of
the Church.

Translated by John Tashjean

NOTES

This article appeared originally as "Schrift-Tradition-Kirche, ein ökumen-
isches Problem," in *Begegnung der Christen,* published jointly by Evangelisches Verlagswerk, Stuttgart, and Verlag Josef Knecht, Frankfurt am Main,
1959, and edited by Maximilian Roesle, O.S.B., and Oscar Cullmann. It is
translated and reprinted here with the kind permission of the author and
publishers. *Begegnung der Christen* was published as a *Festschrift* dedicated to
the distinguished German Catholic theologian, Dr. Otto Karrer, on his
seventieth birthday. It contains articles by sixteen Catholic and sixteen Protestant theologians.

1. For the history of ideas in the background of the reviving interest in the
problem of Tradition, cf. my essay on Tradition in *Fragen der Theologie
heute* (Einsiedeln: Benziger Verlag, 1958[2]), pp. 71–75.
2. This uniform catechism appeared in 1925; it was only a preliminary step
toward the present internationally famous German Catechism, an English

translation of which, entitled *A Catholic Catechism*, was published by Herder and Herder in 1957. Cf. also J. A. Jungmann, *Handing on the Faith* (New York: Herder and Herder, 1957), pp. 120–123. [Ed. note]

3. August Deneffe, *Der Traditionsbegriff* (Münster i. W.: Aschendorffsche Verlagsbuchhandlung, 1931), pp. 127 ff.

4. Cf. also "Schrift und Tradition," *Herderkorrespondenz*, Vol. 13 (1959), p. 350.

5. In this matter France is a good deal more advanced. Two leading Dominican theologians (Liégé and Dubarle) maintain the sufficiency of Holy Scripture in *Initiation Théologique*, Vol. I³ (1955), a publication of Les Éditions du Cerf, addressed to sisterhoods and the laity.

6. "Huc illa pertinent, quae partim ex symboli articulis, partim ex scripturis velut divinis fontibus necessario deducuntur." [Editors' note: The English translation of this quotation which appears in the text, and all such translations from the Latin which appear in further footnotes, are by the editors.]

7. Cf. my "Das Konzil von Trient über das Verhältnis der Heiligen Schrift und der nichtgeschriebenen Traditionen," in Michael Schmaus, ed., *Die mündliche Überlieferung* (Munich: Max-Hueber-Verlag, 1957), p. 173. I shall reply elsewhere to the criticism of this position by Johann Beumer in *Scholastik* (1959), pp. 20–22.

8. Albert Lang, "Die Loci theologici des Melchior Cano und die Methode des dogmatischen Beweises," in *Münchener Studien zur historischen Theologie*, Vol. VI (1925), p. 18. Most recently Lang fixed the date of the genesis of the *Loci* after 1546: *Lexikon für Theologie und Kirche*, Vol. II (1958²), p. 908.

9. Cf. my "Das Konzil von Trient" etc., *op. cit.*, p. 147.

10. Cf. *ibid.*, pp. 140–147, for the history of translations of the first chapter of the *De ecclesiastica hierarchia* of the Pseudo-Dionysius.

11. "Apostolos evangelii doctrinam partim scripto, partim etiam verbo tradidisse." *Loc. theol.*, III c. 3.

12. "Fidei doctrinam non scripto totam, sed ex parte verbo ab Apostolis esse traditam." *Ibid.*

13. E. Ortigues judges Cano's procedure more harshly: Cano gives "un texte du decret, qui est tout simplement faux," in "La tradition de l'Évangile dans l'Église d'après la doctrine catholique," *Foi et Vie* (1951), pp. 317–321. Cf. C. Moeller, "Tradition et oecuménisme," *Irénikon*, Vol. 25 (1952), p. 345.

14. "Sacrosancta Tridentina Synodus prospiciens veritatem Evangelii salutarem et morum doctrinam contineri in libris scriptis et sine scripto traditionibus ipsius Christi. . . ."

15. Moeller, *op. cit.*, p. 346.

16. My "Das Konzil von Trient," *op. cit.*, p. 170, should be corrected accordingly. However, it should be noted that the *Loci theologici* first appeared only in 1563.

17. C. Moeller judges the effects on theological controversy as follows: "Il

suffit de rappeler l'influence de Cano sur la controverse postérieure pour mesurer l'importance d'une pareille erreur; petite, à l'origine, elle creusera un fossé de plus en plus profond entre catholiques et réformés." At the same time Moeller draws attention to the value of positive theology (with its documentary research) for the ecumenical movement. Moeller, *op. cit.*, p. 344, n. 3.

18. *Systema theolog. cathol.*, Vol. IV (1811), Para. 57, p. 95. Dobmayer here follows the concept of Tradition of Vincent of Lérins.

19. O. Karrer, "Der Streit der Konfessionen," in Hans Asmussen and Otto Karrer, eds., *Trennung und Einung* (Stuttgart: Evangelisches Verlagswerk, 1956), p. 48. Cf. also, Karrer, "Apostolische Nachfolge und Primat," in *Fragen der Theologie heute*, p. 186.

20. In the later editions of his *An Essay on the Development of Christian Doctrine* Newman added the following remark to Part II, Chap. 7, Para. 4: "A recent writer (Palmer) goes further, and maintains that it is not determined by the Council of Trent whether the whole of Revelation is in Scripture or not: 'The Synod declares that the Christian truth and discipline are contained in written books and unwritten traditions. They were well aware that the controversy then was whether the Christian doctrine was only *in part* contained in Scripture. But they did not dare to frame their decree openly in accordance with the modern Romish view; they did not venture to affirm, as they might easily have done, that the Christian verity was contained "*partly* in written books, and *partly* in unwritten traditions"'." William Palmer, *A Treatise on the Church of Christ*, Vol. 2, p. 15. See *Difficulties of Anglicans*, Vol. 2, pp. 11–12. Newman, *An Essay on the Development of Christian Doctrine*, ed. by Chas. F. Harrold (New York: Longmans, Green, 1949), p. 316, n. 15.

21. Johann Adam Möhler, *Symbolik*. Einführung und Text herausgegeben von J. R. Geiselmann (Cologne: Jakob Hegner, 1958), Vol. I, p. 26. It is true that Möhler does not make this statement with reference to the decision of the Council of Trent, but his words fit our subject admirably. [English trans. of *Symbolik* under the title of *Symbolism*, New York, 1869—Ed. note]

22. London, 1838, Vol. 2, Part III, Chap. 1.

23. *Praelectiones theologicae*, Vol. 9 (Rome, 1843), pp. 257 ff. Perrone himself definitely maintains the *partim-partim*.

24. He is referring to Sebastian Bullough, O.P., "Relation of Scripture and Tradition," in *Tradition and Scripture, Eastern Churches Quarterly*, Conference between Catholics, Orthodox, and Anglicans, Vol. VII (1947), Supplementary Issue, p. 29.

25. Edward C. Rich, *Spiritual Authority in the Church of England* (London: Longmans, Green, 1953), pp. 27 ff. Italics by Rich.

26. Greenwich, Conn.: The Seabury Press, 1955.

27. *Ibid.*, pp. 83–85.

28. Newman contested that (even before his conversion). Cf. his *Apologia*

pro vita sua (1865). America Press edition, New York: 1942, pp. 104–110, esp. pp. 108–110.

29. *History of Liberty,* p. 513.

30. *De Verbo Dei,* Bk. IV, Chap. IX; as given by F. J. Taylor [Ed. note.]

31. *Miscellaneous Writings and Letters* (P.S.), p. 52; quoted by Taylor, *op. cit.,* p. 86. [Up to this point the author is restating the views of Taylor. Ed. note]

32. May the author refer to his "Das Konzil von Trient über das Verhältnis der Heiligen Schrift und der nichtgeschriebenen Traditionen. Sein Missverständnis in der nachtridentinischen Theologie und die Überwindung dieses Missverständnisses," in Schmaus, *op. cit.,* pp. 121–206. Cf. also Ortigues, "Écriture et Traditions apostoliques au Concile du Trente," *Recherches des Sciences Religieuses,* Vol. 36 (1949), pp. 271–299, and "La Tradition de l'Évangile dans l'Église d'après la doctrine catholique," *op. cit.,* pp. 304–322. This interpretation of the Council of Trent is agreeable to the [Anglo-] Catholic theologian H. Edward Symonds, C.R., who came to the following conclusion in his address on "The Patristic Doctrine of the Relation of Scripture and Tradition" at a round-table discussion between four Dominicans and four Anglican theologians of the Mitfield Community in July 1946: "It would seem therefore that the Sufficiency of Scripture as containing all necessary doctrine is taught by the *consensus Patrum* [consensus of the Fathers]. This in no sense detracts from the function of the Church of proclaiming and indeed defining all saving truth. It means that the Church never claims to add new truths to the final revelation given by Our Lord to his Apostles, and has at the time of forming the Canon of the New Testament (and in accepting that of the Old) decided that the truth handed down in the Tradition is in fact embodied in the writings of the Apostles and Evangelists. Consequently the Council of Trent is at one with the Fathers in treating both sources of doctrine *pari reverentia* [with equal reverence], but to teach that there are doctrines *de fide* which cannot be found in, or based on Holy Scripture, is to go beyond the teaching of both the Fathers and of the great reforming Council." Rich, *op. cit.,* p. 133. For the complete text of the address, see H. Edward Symonds, C.R., "The Patristic Doctrine of the Relation of Scripture and Tradition," *Eastern Churches Quarterly,* Vol. VII (1947), Supplementary Issue, pp. 59–70. [Rich, *op. cit.,* p. 133, refers to Fr. Symonds' paper as "written of course from the Anglican point of view." Translator's note.] Simultaneously and independently of me, A. M. Dubarle expressed the same view in a book review of J. Seynaeve, *Cardinal Newman's Doctrine on Holy Scripture* (1953): "Il est utile d'insister ici, car les discussions contemporains sur la tradition entre catholiques et protestants font état parfois de notions trop floues. On semble considérer parfois, du côté protestant, comme la doctrine catholique l'affirmation que la tradition ecclésiastique ajoute au capital des vérités transmis par les apôtres; ceci, en réalité, serait directement contraire à une déclaration expresse du concile

du Vatican (Session IV, chap. 4; *Denzinger* no. 1836). Ou l'on considère, des deux côtés, comme la doctrine catholique l'affirmation qu'il y a dans la tradition orale (apostolique, puis ecclésiastique) des vérités non contenues dans les Écritures; ceci, en réalité, est une doctrine que le concile de Trente a volontairement et consciemment évité de définir, et qui n'est pas tenue par certain théologiens catholiques, dont Newman." *Revue des Sciences Philosophiques et Théologiques,* Vol. 39 (January 1955), p. 73, n. 3. Similarly, Dubarle in "Introduction a l'Écriture Sainte," in *Initiation Théologique,* Vol. I (1955), p. 80. O. Karrer repeatedly agrees with this view: "Der Streit der Konfessionen," in Asmussen and Karrer, *op. cit.,* pp. 48 ff; *Fragen der Theologie heute* (1957), p. 186.

33. "Hanc (revelationem) nobis traditam ab ecclesia partim ex scripturis, quae sunt in veteri et novo testamento, partim etiam ex simplici traditione per manus." *Concilium Tridentinum,* Diariorum, actorum, epistularum, tractatuum nova collectio (Freiburg: Görres-Gesellschaft, 1911), Vol. V, p. 7, ll. 34–36; p. 31, ll. 25–26.

34. "Hanc veritatem partim contineri in libris scriptis, partim in sine scripto traditionibus." *Loc. cit.,* Vol. V, pp. 31, 25.

35. Cf. my "Das Konzil von Trient," *op. cit.,* p. 163. This has been criticized by H. Lennerz and J. Beumer. There is, however, no need to change the views expressed in that publication, as shall be shown elsewhere. Cf. H. Lennerz, "Scriptura Sacra?" *Gregorianum* (1959), pp. 38–53. J. Beumer, "Die Frage nach Schrift und Tradition nach Robert Bellarmin," *Scholastik* (1959), pp. 1–22; "Katholisches und protestantisches Schriftprinzip im Urteil des Trienter Konzils," *Scholastik* (1959), pp. 249–258.

36. On that theology and the overcoming of it, see my "Das Konzil von Trient," *op. cit.,* pp. 123–206.

37. This metaphor is used by C. Moeller, *Irénikon* (1952), p. 346.

38. *Metaphysics,* Vol. V, p. 26. Cf. Ernst Finke, "Die katholische Wahrheit im Neuen Testament," in Max Lackmann *et al.,* eds., *Katholische Reformation,* (Stuttgart: Schwabenverlag, 1958), pp. 150 f.

39. J. N. Bakhuizen van der Brink criticizes the fact that one looks in vain for anything under the heading of "human traditions" (*Menschensatzungen*) in the *Bekenntnisschrift der evangelisch-lutherischen Kirche* (Göttingen, 1956[3]); and that the word itself gives the impression that the concept of Tradition in the Church has no truly theological meaning, standing only for purely human institutions. Of course it is well known that many customs in the Church are of purely human origin. This fact, recognized by all, does not entitle us to say that that is all there is to it and that there is here no longer any truly theological problem. The Reformed theologian Bakhuizen is concerned with this problem in his examination of the concept of Tradition in the Church of Christian antiquity (Irenaeus, Tertullian, Cyprian, and Minucius Felix). He comes to the conclusion that they all know of divine

Tradition: "En interprétant chez les pères le terme: tradition autant que possible par: revelation, nous comprendrons mieux la foi et la vie de l'Église primitive." That Tradition may not be ignored if one studies Church history and dogmatic history as a real theologian, lest one be lost in chaos and end in skepticism. J. N. Bakhuizen van den Brink, "La tradition dans l'Église primitive et au XVI⁰ siècle," *Revue d'Histoire et de Philosophie Religieuses,* Vol. 36 (1956), pp. 270–281; cf. also "Traditio in de Reformatie en het Katholicisme in de zestiende eeuw.," *Mededelingen der Kon. Nederl. Academie van Wetenschapen,* N.R. XV, afd. Letterkunde (1952), p. 41. On this cf. also E. Flessemann Van Leer, "Tradition and Scripture in the Early Church," *Van Gorcums Theolog. Bibliothēk* (Nr. 26 Ossen, 1954).

40. Nor do the pronouncements of the magisterium since the Vatican Council go any farther, except that the more recent pronouncements prefer the term *divina traditio* [divine Tradition] to *sine scripto traditiones* [unwritten traditions]. Such is also the view of C. Baumgartner, "Tradition et magistère," *Recherches des Sciences Religieuses,* Vol. 41 (1953), pp. 165, 166, 168. G. Filograssi speaks of "leggermente modificandolo" (modifying it slightly) in "La Tradizione divinoapostolica e il magisterio ecclesiastico," *Civiltà Cattolica,* Vol. CII (July 1951), p. 141. Similarly in "Tradizione divinoapostolica e Magisterio della Chiesa," *Gregorianum,* Vol. 33 (1952), p. 138.

41. Hans Küng, *Rechtfertigung* (Einsiedeln: Johannes Verlag, 1957).

42. *Der Traditionsbegriff* (Münster i. W., 1938).

43. Heinrich Denzinger, *Enchiridion Symbolorum,* 28th ed., ed. by C. Rahner (1952), p. 783.

44. J. A. Möhler, *Die Einheit der Kirche,* ed. by J. R. Geiselmann (Cologne: J. Hegner, 1957), p. 80.

45. L. Bouyer, *The Spirit and Forms of Protestantism* (Westminster, Md.: Newman Press, 1956), pp. 121–122.

46. *Über die Schriftinspiration* (Freiburg: Verlag Herder, 1958), p. 58.

47. Bouyer, *op. cit.,* p. 121.

48. G. Gloege, "Bibel III dogmatisch," in *Religion in Geschichte und Gegenwart,* Vol. I³ (1957), p. 1142.

49. Ernst Käsemann, "Neutestamentliche Fragen von Heute," *Zeitschrift für Theologie und Kirche,* Vol. 54 (1957), p. 7.

50. In Catholic theology there are two schools of thought about the task of exegesis. One would restrict exegesis to the purely literary and historical interpretation of the inspired texts; the other demands "integral" exegesis, which necessarily includes biblical theology. Still, "integral" exegesis remains based on philological and historical interpretation. The representatives of integral exegesis maintain, however, that literary exegesis must have for its aim the investigation of the meaning intended by God in the scriptural statements; which, they say, leads necessarily to biblical theology. In contrast with integral exegesis they give the name of philological exegesis to that

method which restricts itself to historical and critical research. Cf. C. Moeller, "Bible et oecuménisme," *Irénikon,* Vol. 23 (1950), pp. 170 f.

51. G. Gloege, *op. cit.,* p. 1142. O. Semmelroth also considers this distinction useful for the Catholic understanding of Scripture: "Die Heilige Schrift als Glaubensquelle," *Stimmen der Zeit,* Vol. 61 (1958), p. 49.

52. Semmelroth, *op. cit.,* p. 46.

53. Rich, *Spiritual Authority in the Church of England,* p. 118.

54. Heinrich Schlier, *Wort Gottes. Eine neutestamentliche Besinnung* (Rothenfelser Reihe, ed. by H. Kahlefeld; Würzburg: Werkbund Verlag, 1958), p. 39. This was precisely the observation which the young exegete at Giessen, Joh. Ev. Kuhn, made in his controversy with David Friedrich Strauss. J. R. Geiselmann, *Die lebendige Überlieferung als Norm des christlichen Glaubens* (Freiburg: Herder, 1959), pp. 7–47.

55. J. R. Geiselmann, "Der Glaube an Jesus Christus—Mythos oder Geschichte?" *Theologische Quartalschrift* (1949), pp. 257–277, 418–439. Cf. also Kuhn's teaching about Tradition: J. R. Geiselmann, *Die Lebendige Überlieferung als Norm des christlichen Glaubens, loc. cit.*

56. Third ed., London, 1956.

57. Günther Bornkamm, *Jesus von Nazareth* (1956), p. 11. Cf. also E. Käsemann, "Neutestamentliche Fragen von Heute," *op. cit.,* pp. 11 ff.

58. H. Schlier, *op. cit.,* pp. 40 f.

59. E. Käsemann, "Das Problem des historischen Jesus," *Zeitschrift fur Theologie und Kirche* (1954), pp. 125 f. Bultmann has drawn the consequences. The "historical" Jesus is relegated to the world of late Judaism; Jesus was no "Christian" but a Jew. *Das Urchristentum in Rahmen der Antiken Religionen* (Zurich: Artemis-Verlag, 1949), p. 78. [Eng. trans.: *Primitive Christianity in its Contemporary Setting* (New York: Meridian Books, 1956)]. In his work on Jesus, Bultmann concerns himself only with the earliest layer of the primitive Christian gospel; a precise distinction is no longer made between the preaching of Jesus and the kerygma of the community. In Bultmann's theology of the New Testament the gospel of Jesus is no longer the object, but only the presupposition. E. Käsemann, *loc. cit.*

60. Bornkamm, *op. cit.,* p. 12.

61. E. Käsemann, *op. cit.,* pp. 125, 153; Peter Biehl, "Zur Frage nach dem historischen Jesus," *Theologische Rundschau* (neue Folge, 1957), pp. 54–76; Ernst Fuchs, "Glaube und Geschichte im Blick auf die Frage nach dem historischen Jesus," *ibid.,* pp. 117–156.

62. Bornkamm, *op. cit.,* p. 15.

63. Cf. also Bornkamm, *op. cit.,* p. 16.

64. That is the meaning of the New Testament *kataggellein tou thanaton tou kyriou* and *tou Christou kataggellein* (1 Cor 11:6; and Phil 1:17; Col 1:28). It means to proclaim the death of the Lord and thereby to make him, the proclaimed, present; to proclaim Christ and have him present by and in the

proclamation. Heinrich Schlier, *op. cit.*, p. 43. According to Schlier the apostolic kerygma also contains reports and communication. "But such communications do not exhaust the preaching of the gospel; indeed, they are not even the characteristic thing which happens when it is preached. The peculiar genitive cases of *ho logos* or *to euaggelion* draw our attention to this fact. What is, for instance, the actual meaning of *euaggelion tēs dozēs tou Christou* (2 Cor 4:4)? Does it mean only a message reporting the glory of Christ? Does *logon zōês epechontes* (Phil 2:16) mean only that one should cling to the word which speaks of life? Does *ho logos tēs sōtērias tautēs* (Acts 13:26) mean only the word which tells of that salvation? What of the *logos tēs katallagês* (2 Cor 5:19) which God 'set up' as the other act of salvation next to the cross? Is that only a word which makes reconciliation known? Is 'the word of the cross' (1 Cor 1:18) only a word teaching us about the cross? How could that word be 'a power (*dynamis*) of God for those who are saved'? Does an imparting of knowledge save in the Pauline sense, and is a proposition about the cross a means of divine power? Is knowledge power here, too? Such an interpretation of the genitives in these contexts seems in itself very improbable. To translate them as indicated is possible only if one follows the habit of assuming without examination that a word is primarily a 'means of communication.' But what authority is there for saying that that was the view of St. Paul or St. Luke or the New Testament as a whole?" H. Schlier, *op. cit.*, pp. 41 ff.

65. Cf. P. A. Liégé, O.P., *Initiation Théologique*, Vol. I[3] (1959), p. 28.

66. O. Semmelroth, *op. cit.*, pp. 42–44. J. Ratzinger, "Offenbarung, Schrift, Überlieferung," *Trierer Zeitschrift*, Vol. 67 (1958), pp. 13–27.

67. *Mélanges Jules Lebreton* I, *Recherches des Sciences Religieuses*, Vol. 39, (1951), pp. 50 ff.

68. J. H. Newman, *Via Media* (London, 1877), Vol. I, Chapt. 11, pp. 288 ff.; *An Essay on the Development of Christian Doctrine* (London, 1878), Chap. 7, Para. 4, nr. 4, pp. 339–342; *Difficulties of Anglicans*, Vol. II, pp. 11–13. Cf. also A. M. Dubarle in *Revue des Sciences Philosophiques et Théologiques*, Vol. 39 (1955), p. 73, n. 3.

69. *Revue des Sciences Philosophiques et Théologiques* (1955), pp. 72 ff. On this question cf. Günter Beiner, "Die Lehre von der Tradition nach John Henry Newman" (Tübingen dissertation in theology; typewritten, 1959), pp. 330–332.

70. "Introduction à l'Écriture Sainte," *Initiation Théologique* (Les sources de la théologie), Vol. I (1955[3]), pp. 48–94.

71. This was recently put very clearly by the Lutheran theologian Ernest Finke: "Jesus took the amazing risk of not writing down any of his words. His saving word was to go into the world through the thinking and living experience of the Church. In this manner the New Testament word was already born as 'tradition,' faithfully preserved by the receiver and yet transformed by his situation. This 'tradition' is an essential part of the

mystery of worship, i. e., of the act by which Christ, his word and his work are rendered present. It is combined with the act by which he is made sacramentally present which requires also external tradition, the authoritative form given to the ministry and to the patterns of divine worship. God created in that tradition an indispensable dialectic (*Gegenüber*) between apostolic and all later times. The former time is the hour of birth of the Church, in which God created, through the apostles and the earliest Church, the permanently valid form of the word of His Son in the New Testament, as well as the basic structure of the ministry and divine worship. This dialectic between the hour of birth and later time, between Scripture and tradition, expresses concretely the dialectic between Christ and His Church. The Church has been continually exposed to the danger that this may stop being a genuine dialectic. Holy Scripture became, more and more, material in evidence for the theoretical construction of ecclesiastical doctrine. The weight of tradition and logical deduction crowded out the risk of listening with constantly renewed attention to the voice of the Good Shepherd in Scripture. The Reformation was a powerful reaction against that, seeking to give back to Holy Scripture its proper weight. But, as was explained earlier, even in the Reformed churches Scripture is accorded only partial significance (unconsciously so in most cases). How is this to be explained? Perhaps it is because, next to the word of God in Holy Scripture, tradition was thought of only as 'human opinion.' Such a view contradicted not only Scripture, which knows of the continuing word of the prophets of the new covenant (Eph 2:20; 4:11) as well as of the conclusive word of the apostles. Such a view also made absolute one's own understanding of Scripture vis-à-vis all preceding 'tradition,' i.e., the faithful handing-on of the word in a revised form conditioned by our situation. The fullness of Scripture enters the thinking, living and shaping of the Church only if one also takes seriously the fullness of tradition—in spite of its possible and actual mistaken developments—because of the divinely ordained connection of tradition with Scripture." E. Finke, "Die Katholische Wahrheit im Neuen Testament," in Lackmann, *et al., op. cit.,* pp. 167 ff.

72. C. Moeller, "Bible et oecuménisme," *op. cit.,* p. 166.

73. Evidence of Protestant theology on this point prior to 1957 has been collated in my "Das Konzil von Trient," *op. cit.,* pp. 125 ff., and in the critical edition of Möhler's *Einheit der Kirche* (1957), pp. 596 ff.

74. Ernst Kinder, "Schrift und Tradition," in Hans Asmussen and Wilhelm Stählin, eds., *Die Katholizität der Kirche* (Stuttgart: Evangelisches Verlagswerk, 1957), pp. 11, 27 ff.

75. E. Kinder, *op. cit.,* p. 30, agrees.

76. Cf. also I. N. Bakhuizen van den Brink, *op. cit.,* pp. 280 ff.

77. "Secundum eum sensum, quem semper tenuit ac tenet ecclesia."

78. Max Lackmann, "Ruf der evangelischen Christenheit zur katholischen Erfüllung," in Lackmann, *et al., op. cit.,* pp. 90 ff.

SELECTED READINGS

1. Bévenot, Maurice, S.J., "Tradition, Church and Dogma," *Heythrop Journal,* Vol. 1 (1960), pp. 34–37. Criticizes Geiselmann's interpretation of Trent, but suspends judgment until Geiselmann's projected three-volume work on Tradition appears.

2. Burghardt, Walter J., S.J., "The Catholic Concept of Tradition," *Theology Digest,* Vol. 1 (1953) pp. 81–87. Digested from *Proceedings of the Catholic Theological Society of America (1951),* pp. 42–76. Stresses the role of the Church.

3. Daniélou, Jean, S.J., "Écriture et Tradition dans le dialogue entre chrétiens séparés," *Documentation Catholique,* Vol. 54 (1957), pp. 283–294. Daniélou had carried on a discussion with Cullmann on the problem of Tradition. Cf. pp. 29 ff. above.

4. Davis, Charles, "The Living Word," *Worship,* Vol. 32 (1958), pp. 518–531. The liturgy of the Church provides a living synthesis of Scripture and Tradition.

5. Dejaifve, G., S.J., "Scripture, Tradition and the Church," *Theology Digest,* Vol. 6 (1958), pp. 67–72. By a Belgian theologian who has a wide acquaintance with Protestant theology.

6. Dubarle, A. M., "Écriture et Tradition. À propos de publications protestantes récentes," *Istina,* Vol. 3 (1956), pp. 399–416; Vol. 4 (1957), pp. 113–128. Critical examinations of Diem, Cullmann, Grass, and the papers of the 1953 *Evangelical Fellowship of Theological Literature,* which dealt with Scripture and Tradition. The doctrine of the Assumption is examined in the second article.

7. Geiselmann, Josef Rupert, "Scripture and Tradition in Catholic Theology," *Theology Digest,* Vol. 6 (1958), pp. 73–78. Digested from an article in *Una Sancta,* Vol. 11 (1956), pp. 131–150, which is found in full French translation in *Istina,* Vol. 5 (1958), pp. 197–214.

—*Die lebendige Überlieferung als Norm des christlichen Glaubens (Die Tradition in der neueren Theologie,* Vol. III). Freiburg: Herder, 1959, 369 pp.

—"Die Tradition," in J. Feiner, J. Trütsch, and F. Böckle, eds., *Fragen der Theologie heute* (Einsiedeln: Benziger, 1957), pp. 69–108.

—"Das Konzil von Trient über das Verhältnes der Heiligen Schrift und der nichtgeschriebenen Tradition," in M. Schmaus, ed., *Die mündliche Überlieferung. Beiträge zum Begriff der Tradition,* (Munich: Max Hüber, 1957), pp. 123–206.

8. Jedin, Hubert, *Geschichte der Konzil von Trient,* Vol. II. Freiburg: Herder, 1957. Full bibliography (up to 1957) of studies on the background of the Tridentine decree on Scripture and Tradition (pp. 455–456).

9. Lengsfeld, Peter, *Überlieferung. Tradition und Schrift in der evangelischen und katholischen Theologie der Gegenwart.* Paderborn: Bonifacius-Druckerei,

1960. 263 pp. Concentrates on Tradition in the New Testament and on contemporary Protestant developments. Extensive bibliography.

10. Moeller, C., "Tradition et oecuménisme," *Irénikon*, Vol. 25 (1952), pp. 337–370. The living link between Scripture and Tradition which united revelation and the Church is the person of Jesus Christ.

11. Murphy, John L., *The Notion of Tradition in John Driedo*. Milwaukee: Marquette University Press, 1959. 321 pp. Studies the teaching of an influential pre-Tridentine theologian who taught at Louvain from 1512 to 1536.

12. Tavard, George H., *Holy Writ or Holy Church. The Crisis of the Protestant Reformation*. New York: Harper and Bros., 1959. 250 pp. A scholarly historical study which concentrates on the fifteenth and sixteenth centuries.

13. Vawter, Bruce, *The Bible in the Church*. New York: Sheed and Ward, 1958. A brief and readable explanation of the relation of the Bible to the Church.

INTRODUCTION:

THE PROTESTANT VIEW OF
THE BIBLE: HERMENEUTICS

JUST as "eschatology" was the reigning catchword in theological circles for a long, long time, "hermeneutics" is increasingly the password to the circle of those who have "arrived" theologically. Although the term "hermeneutics" is broad and fluid, it can be said to refer to the art or methodology of interpretation, whereas the closely related term "exegesis" refers to the application of hermeneutical principles in the actual exposition of a text.

A large portion of the total theological enterprise hinges on the so-called hermeneutical problem. That problem, which is not a new one, has been faced by the Church for centuries, but it has become sharpened and demands urgent attention in our time because of at least three interrelated developments of major significance. (1) Persistent analysis has disclosed a biblical eschatology in many respects alien to the eschatology of later Christianity. This has made clear the danger of applying to New Testament material the presuppositions of a later period. (2) Along with advances made in historical studies, biblical history has increasingly come to be viewed as the interpretive witness to God's activities in space and time rather than as the mere chronicling of events. One of the great contributions of Form Criticism has been to call our attention again to the kerygmatic character of New Testament writing. (3) The scientific revolution has accentuated the unmistakable hiatus existing between the world views assumed and lived by first-century and twentieth-century men.

These factors have served to locate the so-called hermeneutical problem squarely at the exciting and difficult spot where faithfulness to the apostolic witness and relevant translation of that witness cross. Here, as in the problem of Scripture and Tradition, we meet one of the more important points of the ecumenical discussions, How is the first apostolic message to be actualized and translated in such a way that it becomes again the kerygma for the present generation? Indeed, the history of the Church can be seen as the ongoing effort to translate Holy Scripture and to make the gospel contemporaneous. It unfolds under the abiding tension of a dual freedom: the freedom obediently to conform to the apostolic witness, and the freedom creatively to translate that witness for the experiences and thought patterns of successive generations. This is a task of freedom because it is the Holy Spirit who leads the Church into new responses to the unique historic revelation in Christ.

Implied in what has been said is that the task of interpretation can never (and in this, contemporary Protestant thought accurately reflects the heritage of the Reformation) be considered complete in official Church decreta nor even in the doctor's study. The hermeneutical task has its completion and fulfillment when Scripture becomes meaningful in a saving way as the Word is rightly proclaimed and rightly heard. One can say that Roman Catholicism and the Reformation are fully agreed that valid interpretation of Scripture takes place only within the Holy Catholic Church. But it is important to note that valid biblical interpretation is centralized in the Roman communion in the *teaching office,* the magisterium. The Reformation, while never minimizing the importance of confessions and doctors in the life of the Church, holds the preaching office to be the primary organ for valid interpretation. That organ functions within the congregation of the faithful, who as believers share a common priesthood. Here, as the Word is expounded by one whom God and the congregation has called to that special task and as the Word is heard, it becomes, by the work of the Holy Spirit, true and vivifying. The responsibility for the proper proclamation of the Word rests not with any one person or order but with the whole Church. Therefore, the locating of valid interpretation in the corporate life of the worshipping community guards against shallow individualism and subjectivism.

When one turns from a consideration of the *organ* and *localization* to the *foundation* of valid biblical interpretation, two currents of contemporary Protestant theological reflection deserve special mention. The first, the so-called "dialectical" or "neo-orthodox" theology, most often associated with the names of Karl Barth and Emil Brunner, stresses the *obedience* part of the two-fold hermeneutical task and emphasizes the *givenness* of that to which existential response is made by the believer. It is felt that the content of the kerygma, the Word, Jesus Christ himself, gives to the text and to the interpreter the manner of interpretation appropriate to Holy Scripture; from this scriptural interpretation we learn about the interpretation of nonscriptural literary works. The second current is that which issues from the demythologizing program of Rudolf Bultmann, in which the primary interest is in the *adaptive* character of the kerygma and its existential *appropriation* by him to whom the kerygma is addressed. Here the rules of biblical hermeneutics are derived from the method of interpretation applicable to nonbiblical literary material, and texts which describe the acts of God have to be interpreted according to the implied self-understanding of man.

The author of the first article, Ernst Fuchs, is, together with Gerhard Ebeling, one of the most original scholars in this important area of contemporary theology. Though indebted to Karl Barth, he can more precisely be called a disciple of Rudolf Bultmann and Martin Heidegger. Other articles of this scholar may be more representative for his independent contribution as far as the underlying systematic principles are concerned, but this article has been chosen as an example of the way some aspects of the hermeneutical problem are related to the preaching task of the Church in our time.

The second article, by Professor Arnold A. van Ruler, analyzes the validity of development in the reception of the kerygma. This gives Van Ruler's article the advantage of informing the larger issue of Scripture and Tradition with the motivating principles behind the modern hermeneutical quest. Though not yet sufficiently known in the English-speaking world, on the Continent Professor van Ruler is increasingly regarded as providing a third option alongside the two contemporary theological currents mentioned above.

Ernst Fuchs was born in 1903. He has been a Privat-dozent at the University of Tübingen and Professor of New Testament in the Kirchliche Hochschule in Berlin, and he has just been appointed in the same field as Professor at Marburg. He is the author of a number of books including *Hermeneutik*.

Arnold Albert van Ruler was born in Holland in 1908 and received his theological education at the University of Groningen. He is a minister of the Reformed Church in Holland. Since 1947 Doctor van Ruler has been Professor of Dogmatics, Christian Ethics, and Church Polity at the University of Utrecht. Professor van Ruler took an active part in the reorganization of the Dutch Church after the chaotic war years.

3

THE TASK OF NEW TESTAMENT SCHOLARSHIP FOR THE CHURCH'S PROCLAMATION TODAY

ERNST FUCHS

THE Church's proclamation is the Good News about Jesus Christ, the Son of God, Our Lord, and as such the good news about the Word of God. This Word summons us out of a world condemned by the wrath of God in order that we, as a community of believers in this world, may no longer live for ourselves but for him who died and rose for us, and that we thus bear witness to man who is condemned to death that God has revealed grace and peace. The proclamation of the Church is addressed to all men. It seizes man at the point of that responsibility which God has imposed upon him by calling him into life. It confronts him with the wrath of God, because man has violated life which is the grace of God. It discloses to him the severity of the divine wrath by indicating the consequences which man's irresponsibility has brought upon the world—for God is not mocked (cf. Gal 6:7). Finally, the proclamation shows man the way to grace and peace by bidding him to believe that he overcomes God's wrath and its consequences (i.e., a world given over to death), if he allows himself to be told that God's will encounters him anew in Jesus, so that he receives a life purified from sin and death through love. The person who *allows himself to be told* this has gained a new existence within the community of believers which is the fellowship of those who love, for he has encountered Jesus the Lord.

The *response* to the Church's proclamation indicates at the same time its essential content: Jesus is the Christ, the Son of God, Our Lord. In her confession the Church repeats what she has heard from

God. The Church's proclamation derives from the will of God and makes its appeal to the will of man. Therefore, the confession of the Christian community must make clear what it intends by believing that it represents the will of God in the world today. The Christian community which has heard the Word of God determines in its confession what falls under the divine judgment as the guilt of the world *today* and what is able to give grace and peace as the love of the world *today*. It is not as though Jesus had been Lord in some other way in other times! However, by challenging man to confession of faith in Jesus today, the Church's proclamation translates God's Word for the man of today.

The Church's proclamation includes, therefore, a *whence* and a *whither*. Let us define this whence and whither somewhat more precisely, in order to understand with greater clarity *what it is* in the Church's proclamation seen as the Word of God that requires translation. If the Church's proclamation results, as it were, in the confession of the Christian community—but the confession at the same time constitutes the indication of the essential content of the proclamation—it can indeed be said that the proclamation advances from confession to confession. In fact, together with the proclamation of Jesus (fragmentarily transmitted), the so-called kerygmatic fragments (e.g., Rom 1:3 f., etc.) constitute the oldest passages of the New Testament. Furthermore, Paul indicates in Rom 10:9 f. how he has translated this kerygma (= *regula fidei*). It would be wrong, however, to understand everything between Rom 1 and Rom 10 simply as a translation of one confession into another. Rather, Paul as an apostle vouches for the truth of his proclamation *himself* by unfolding it as the revelation of God, as Rom 1–3 already indicates. In exactly the same way Jesus himself, in his proclamation, unfolds the revelation of God, and he by no means confines himself to making an appearance, e.g., as an exorcist or a man of love. However, there is a difficulty involved here. Unmistakably, even Jesus starts from a given confession, that is, from the confession of the Parousia of the Son of Man (cf. Lk 12:8 f.: "Everyone who confesses me before men, the Son of Man will also confess before the angels of God," etc.). Thus, the succession of confessions seems to extend back into an untraceable past. That, however, is precisely what is not the case. For what is essentially new is this: that at least Paul (but even the primitive Palestinian church before him), after the death of Jesus, clung to the encounter with Jesus. This is seen in the fact that the apostles (in the restricted sense of the word) appealed to the encounter with Jesus as an encounter with the Risen One (1 Cor 15:1–11, etc.). A very old confessional formula (Acts 2:36) says that God has made him both Lord and King, "this Jesus whom you crucified." Paul, previously a zealous champion of his "ancestral traditions" (Gal 1:14), reflects upon what this implies for him. He concludes that this act of God implies the preaching of the Cross (1 Cor 1:18 ff.). In this preaching one overcomes his "old man" by trusting in this Lord (1 Cor 1:31), that is, by honoring through faith in Jesus the fact that God has decided in favor of grace (Phil 3:2–11). This is the grace granted to those who recognize in the death of Jesus God's judgment on the world (Rom 10:4, Gal 6:14), because they see that in Jesus the aeon of love willed by God has begun (1 Cor 10:11). God's revelation is therefore a word which places us simultaneously *before* the wrath of God and *after* the beginning of his grace (cf. 1 Thes 1:10 and 2 Cor 6:2 ff.; Gal 4:4–7). It does this in such a way, however, that we are asked whether we can acknowledge with Jesus the justice of God's wrath, since we see God on our side in Jesus (Lk 12:8 ff.; 18:9–14; cf. Jn 3:18). If we can make this acknowledgement, we shall also experience Jesus' glorious power over the condemned world (2 Cor 4:11). The new way of salvation is self-surrender in favor of love (Gal 5:5 ff.), the surrender which loves neighbors and in which man knows himself to be loved in that he surrenders himself to the legitimate claims of the justice which is embraced by love (Gal 6:2; Col 1:24; Mt 22:34–40). If we do this we have at the same time peace with God (Rom 5:1). Thus it is precisely Jesus in the flesh who is the way to God for us (1 Jn 4:2) and through whom life is given us anew (2 Cor 5:17).

This means, however, that the Church's proclamation derives not from a confession but from the *revelation* of God, for its content is Jesus himself. The confession of the Church, which begins with Easter, is a word *about* Jesus and thus determines that the Church's proclamation proclaims nothing other than precisely Jesus.

Without this confession one would not have begun with preaching, because it was necessary first of all to respond to God's act. *That which* the proclamation proclaims, however, is God's act itself, Jesus. There is, then, a first confession of the Church with which the apostles initially responded to God's act. From the very beginning, however, this confession was in need of renewal because the Church proclaims not herself, not her confession, but God's act which calls for a new response at any given time. Consequently, the Church's proclamation derives from Jesus and leads through confession to Jesus—*from* Jesus, insofar as through the act of God he himself is the content of the Church's proclamation; *to* Jesus, because he wants, through the proclamation, to become our Lord whom we confess.

The *history* of the Church of Jesus Christ does not begin with the confession of Jesus: It is rather the Church itself that begins here. The history of the Church begins with the New Testament. To be sure, the confession of the Church precedes, for instance, the letters of Paul or the Gospels. But these letters and Gospels contain more than just confessions of Jesus; they contain the basic proclamation about Jesus Christ in the way that the first witnesses and their disciples, i.e., the first preachers, proclaimed Jesus. This proclamation in the New Testament is founded upon the confession because it holds to the act of God as its content. If the response to this act had not become confession, the proclamation could not even have begun. The content of the proclamation, however, is the act of God itself, i.e., Jesus. For this very reason the proclamation in the New Testament can reproduce Jesus' own proclamation because it belongs to Jesus. Nevertheless, it does not do this without making clear that God's act was disclosed only on the basis of the Resurrection of Jesus. Therefore, the reproduction of the proclamation of Jesus is determined by the understanding which the significance of Jesus, as made known through Easter, bestowed upon his own proclamation. *God's act is the historical fact which is called Jesus,* because this is what he is (cf. Mk 9:7 as an Easter logion). This fact and the confession relating to it are deposited in the New Testament. Jesus "is written," as faith and love "is written." What faith and love are, however, is determined from the fact which is called Jesus. Let us choose for the proclamation itself the word "witness," in order to distinguish it from the concept of confession. In these terms the proclamation of the Church has the primary task of translating for the man of today the witness of Jesus to which the New Testament witnesses. This must be done in such a way that the confession of Jesus occurs as a response when and where God wills it (*Confessio Augustana* V), i.e., if it has been rightly heard. This is to be done above all in preaching (Lk 10:16), but through deed as well (Jn 12:34 ff.). A deed is not inferior to preaching as a translator of the New Testament.

Since witness to Jesus *and* confession of him occur side by side in the New Testament, the content of the Church's proclamation, in the special sense of preaching, can be discussed from two approaches, from the New Testament witness and from confession. The translation of the New Testament witness is repeatedly accomplished. Such translations are embraced by the constantly new formulation of confessions which shows us how the Fathers have understood the New Testament. The comparison of these confessions will constitute a self-analysis on the part of the Church in regard to the correctness of her understanding of Jesus. Such a self-analysis is carried on in dogmatic theology (which takes its starting point in the Credo). New Testament scholarship, however, has a different task. It provides the text for preaching, inasmuch as it is precisely preaching which has the task of translating for the man of today the New Testament witness to Jesus; the task, that is, of proclaiming Jesus to him. In this connection the question (which properly belongs to New Testament scholarship) concerning the Old Testament witness to Jesus may be left out of consideration (cf. Mt 5:21–48; 1 Pt 2:9 ff.). It is not the task of New Testament scholarship itself, however, to develop into preaching. Furthermore, just as surely as preaching cannot dispense with the self-analysis of the Church in regard to the fidelity of her confession (and thus needs dogmatic theology), it is equally in need of practical theology, which deals with the problem of how the man of today can relevantly be addressed in the light of the New Testament witness. To be sure, it is the preacher himself who makes the actual decision about his preaching because he alone faces, in the name of God, the congregation to which he preaches. New Testament scholarship provides him simply with the *text of the sermon,* the witness to Jesus which is written in the New Testament.

Of course, the preacher should not preach the New Testament; rather, he ought to proclaim Jesus. It is therefore necessary that he realize that as a preacher he stands in the continuity of an historical tradition which, to be sure, has always given him the text, but by no means the text alone. It has given him at the same time an abundance of facts, ideas, truths and errors, prejudices and genuine deposits of faith. As a theologian, he has had an opportunity to become conscious of the state of affairs of the living tradition in the history of the Church. Therefore, to provide the preacher with the text for preaching does not mean merely to place in his hands a text of the New Testament which is literally as accurate as possible. Far beyond this, it means to make possible for him the historical understanding of this historical document. New Testament scholarship, in accordance with the object of its investigation, the New Testament, is a *positive historical science.* It does not relieve the preacher of the responsibility to witness to Jesus, although, corresponding to the nature of its object, it shares instructively in this witness if indeed it properly interprets the New Testament. Rather, New Testament scholarship supplies the preacher with the text by attempting to make the text so transparent for him that he can translate the New Testament. "Translation" is here to be understood in the sense of perceptive repetition in the language of the man of today, though, to be sure, within the concrete situation of preaching.

Therefore, as far as *method* is concerned, New Testament scholarship, whether one likes it or not, must include textual history and textual criticism, linguistics, history of literature, and history of religion, in order to provide the means for a theological interpretation. These means are indispensable for a complete translation and explanation and thus for an understanding of the New Testament. It is not our task to proclaim, let us say, Martin Luther, but Jesus as the New Testament witnesses to him. Jesus himself is the Word of God. The New Testament, however, is a human word, even though it is filled with the Spirit of the first witnesses. As an historical document, it speaks in the language of men of the distant past with whom we cannot converse as easily as, for instance, we can converse with

Martin Luther (and it is difficult enough even to converse with Luther). Indeed, Jesus himself spoke a language totally different from ours. But God has made this language of Jesus and his apostles important for us by revealing Jesus as his Word (Jn 1:14). Accordingly, obedience to the Word of God demands that we study this language of Jesus and his witnesses to the limit of our ability and that we familiarize ourselves with the world in which they lived and worked.

Yet *historical distance* from the New Testament is not only a disadvantage; it is to an even greater extent a distinct advantage. As we become aware of the distance which separates us from this document, our own seemingly obvious relation to the subject matter, to Jesus himself, becomes problematic for us. Without a stimulus from the outside no one becomes aware of his prejudices. Usually we are unlikely to give the biblical words, which have long since been familiar to us, the meaning which they once had; instead, we give them the meaning which our own tradition has transmitted to us. What was perhaps a correct interpretation and translation some time ago may be wrong today because our very language is subject to a change of meaning with the coming and going of men and their history. If the point in question is to understand, say, what death means in the New Testament, then we need an over-all view of what death meant at that time, what it meant later, and what it means today. For, as language changes, the subject matter of language changes with it. The question whether I understand death as a friend or an enemy, as a natural occurrence or an historical phenomenon, is not irrelevant for the interpretation. And we should not presume that we freely control our understanding of death. Many die without ever having really understood anything about death. How much more difficult, then, will be the understanding of what the New Testament calls life. Measured against tradition, which immediately thrusts upon the preacher a settled interpretation of his text, New Testament scholarship may well be designated the theological *conscience* of the preacher.

The conscience can terrify men. Thus, New Testament scholarship also terrified our preachers when they learned that they had hitherto regarded as revelation what is, in reality, no more than an obsolete mythological world view or world understanding. It is to the credit of the history of religions school (Gunkel, Wrede, Bousset, Heitmüller, to name only a few; also the philologists, e.g., Reitzenstein, H. H. Schaeder, should not be forgotten) that it clarified for us the character of the world of religious conceptions in the New Testament and thus made clear the distance which separates the New Testament from the world of modern man. What if the empty tomb, the miracles of the Lord, the virgin birth, the apocalyptic conception of the Parousia, the hope for the rapture of the Church (1 Thes 4:17), the Ascension, the outpouring of the Holy Spirit—what if all these were more or less mythological conceptions bound to a mythological world *understanding* which had to give way to our modern world *view?* A world *view* which, in spite of all the difficulties in physics with the measurement co-ordinates, is conceived in mathematical terms and is, to that extent, a demythologized world view. Is there anything left? Well, since the understanding of the doctrine of justification had already been lost, of course nothing would be left from the antiquated conceptual world of our preachers. For after all nothing was there in the first place. But surely Jesus is there? By all means. New Testament scholarship, as a matter of fact, has learned anew to ask the question concerning Jesus more seriously than it has been done in theology for centuries. We can now learn from R. Bultmann what happens if a mythological fact is mistaken for an historical fact as so often in the New Testament. There really is a critical question of existence with regard to faith. Therefore, we have to say: the failure, especially that of the clergy, in the Church controversy of the Nazi period was a failure of their cryptomythological understanding of existence which was no match for the hard reality of the Nazi criminals. A high-ranking Church leader was commended not for his witness as a preacher but chiefly for his personal courage. In the same way, Niemöller's witness to Christ was discredited as being an overcharge arising from the stormy nature of the man. The real issue was seen much more clearly by the cynical Gestapo officer who said to the chairman of the Barmen Synod: "Now I should like to see for once who has more power, the police or that fictitious Christ in whom you believe!" That is precisely the issue: the *power* of Jesus. If this power stems from God, it cannot be dependent on a mythological world *view*. For it is man who produces the world *view* himself.

What service can New Testament scholarship perform for us today at a time when we as theologians and pastors have the task of clearing away the debris even of our Christianity? If it remains true to its task, it performs for us the indispensable service of depriving us of the sinful naïveté of our self-understanding. It does this by forcing us, through the exegetical demonstration of our historical distance from the New Testament, to face the *question concerning our own self-understanding*. This is the same theological task as that assumed by the fourth Gospel over against its own tradition and by Paul particularly over against the Jews. The Jews were hiding behind their Torah mythology and believed that they could thereby escape the judgment of God. To be sure, they not infrequently did this with a bad conscience, as is shown by the discussions concerning the sufficient merit of the righteous. They possessed as little real certainty of salvation as our champions of new observances who take refuge in liturgical ceremony. How does Paul confront them? He lays bare to them the righteous universality of the divine judgment by showing them that they have already failed themselves in their own existence. They have done this, beginning from a presumptuous *petitio principii,* by basing their security on that which must clearly be judged by God, that is, their works (Rom 1–4). Paul thus definitely undertook something like a demythologization of the Law. There is apparently an essential connection between a mythological world *understanding* and righteousness by works. Whether Paul proceeded consistently in this matter is another question. Among us, however, the message of grace and peace with God has been turned into a mythology of eternal tranquillity into which one senses his way, with solemnity, through participation in ceremonies. We shall have to learn from the New Testament that every self-tranquilization is the enemy of loving self-surrender since self-tranquilization veils our vision of the true need of our neighbor; the need that is, which cries to God for justice and help. Therefore, we are left especially to a new interpretation of the ethics of Jesus. For this we may very well receive an adequate preparation from Paul. Then we will perhaps learn again what, according to the will of God, is to be called righteousness on earth—a strange righteousness, indeed. It is capable of actually setting us free for what is right.

Therefore, with regard to the Church's proclamation today, the special task of New Testament scholarship is the confrontation of a traditional, but no longer vital, pseudo-Christian self-understanding, which paralyzes the preachers, with the self-understanding of the New Testament which is called in question by the witness of Jesus. To put it concretely, the task is the *critique of the religious self-affirmation in the New Testament*. Precisely in this way New Testament scholarship is a theological discipline which, in the service of the Church's proclamation, today makes explicit the revelation which is witnessed to in the New Testament. New Testament scholarship thus continues that which, in the horizon of the Old Testament, of Judaism, and the pagan *conception* of the world (e.g., Gnosticism), the theology of the "Apostles" of Jesus set out to do.

Translated by Eugene Peters

NOTES

A translation of "Die Aufgabe der neutestamentlichen Wissenschaft für die kirchliche Verkündigung heute," by Ernst Fuchs, which appeared originally in *Zur Frage nach dem historischen Jesus* (Tübingen: J. C. B. Mohr [Paul Siebeck], 1960, pp. 55–65). It is translated and reprinted here by the kind permission of the publisher.

4

THE EVOLUTION OF DOGMA

A. A. VAN RULER

IT IS crystal clear that there is evolution in the sense of movement and change. To see this one has only to look for a moment to the reality of history which is mysterious in so many of its aspects. The discovery of evolution in history—that is, the discovery of history— was a far more radical one than the discovery of evolution in nature. Troeltsch in particular wrestled all of his life with the problems engendered by this discovery. Of particular importance is the fact that all values and norms in becoming individual historical phenomena are made relative. At the same time, however, they become absolute because they cannot be repeated in their very uniqueness. This historizing is carried to the ultimate and to the most central of all things: the articulate expression of salvation—the very things of God, so to say, the dogma. For it appears there is an evolution of dogma also. Dogma has not always been the very same: it too goes through a process of change. Has it then perhaps become relative? Can it still be dogma in that case?

In 1845 Newman wrote his book *An Essay on the Development of Christian Doctrine*. This was no less than fourteen years before the year which we celebrate here [the date of the publication of Darwin's *Origin of Species,* 1859. Ed. note]. In this respect Christianity has not lagged behind the times. As a matter of fact, even in the Continental Protestant theology of the nineteenth century one discovers, against the backdrop of romanticism and idealism, the conception of the evolutionary character of truth—or at least of the knowledge of truth. Initially, this was the case particularly in the instance of Hegel's way of thinking. With Hegel, the history of doctrine came into being

89

as a theological discipline. It took the place of a theology determined by controversy and by apologetical concerns. In the Netherlands we can even witness how dogmatics became, by civil law, separated from the history of doctrine. The former then was in danger of becoming like a fish squirming out of the water of historical relativity on the beach of absolute truth.

In any case, Protestant theology had taken the way of least resistance and the general opinion was that dogma became invalid once its historical nature was discovered. Roman Catholic theology showed greater wisdom and maturity in this respect. It commenced to reflect on the problem which now has arisen, How could one understand the historical character of dogma while recognizing its revealed content? In recent decades Roman Catholic theology has dealt with this question in a rather thorough manner. One has the feeling that the crisis of Modernism has been overcome. The dialectical or scholastic solutions to the problem no longer seem adequate. The search is now for other, more dynamic and vital, and particularly also, supernaturally structured, solutions.

It is not my intention to report on the various ways in which the Roman Catholic theologians have struggled with the problem. That would carry us too far afield, firstly, because of the divergencies of the various solutions, and secondly, because of the rather complex character of each of these solutions. Besides, our Roman Catholic brethren start from certain presuppositions which are, and not without reason, rather alien to us. I am thinking particularly of the scheme of nature and supernature and of the concentration of infallibility in the teaching authority of the office. For that reason it seems more fruitful to me to attempt to deal with this problem independently. I do this to some extent against the backdrop of the Roman Catholic problematic. I intend to scrutinize the presuppositions with which one can and must operate in the consideration of this problem.

Let us take a closer look at the problem. How great a problem arises if one discovers the evolution and the historical nature of dogma? As I see it, one has to give a threefold answer to this question. The evolution of dogma is, in the first place, a problem because of the fact that revelation was completed in Jesus Christ. This is indeed the basic theme of the New Testament: God has at last spoken through His Son and in Him He has expressed Himself. This theme is characteristic of almost the whole of Christianity: it points to one man, one name, one historical fact. In Jesus Christ God has given His definitive revelation since He has given Himself.

As far as I can see, this is the theological significance of the problem. On one hand, one sees the historical development of dogma, but, on the other, it is taken seriously that the Christian faith is historically anchored. Thus although anchored in history on one certain historical fact, one is, so to speak, adrift, taking one's course on the stream of history, thinking and speaking about this historical fact and the salvation given with it.

This paradoxical understanding of the problem becomes somewhat more complicated when one realizes that one does not say enough by stating the completeness of the revelation in Jesus Christ. We can enter into this revelation only by means of the witness of the evangelists and the apostles. Therefore, we have to qualify the original formulation with the following one: the completeness of the revelation in apostolic time. This accent immediately appeals to theologians of the Reformed tradition, since it underlines the unique significance of the Bible, of the canonical Holy Scripture, and particularly the New Testament.

Having said this, we introduce a new factor. The revelation in Jesus Christ is reality, act, life, presence of God. But the witness of the evangelists and the apostles was expressed in words. Consequently the revelation became something articulated. In this process definitions were born. What value and how much authority do these words have? They are words of revelation. How then is this original apostolic witness related to the words of later dogma?

If one really adheres to the completeness of the revelation in the apostolic era, is not one, then, forced to conclude to the concept of an identity of content of later dogma with the original witness? This leads us to a second answer to the question why the evolution of dogma raises a problem for us at all. The question at stake is whether and how we can prove that we still are the selfsame Church. This is a peculiar problem, and a very important variation of the whole ecumenical concern of the Church. As a rule we think about the question of unity and identity of the Church in terms of space, insofar as it per-

tains to the whole inhabited world today. However, in the problem of
the evolution of dogma a different notion arises. We have to consider
the unity and identity of the Church in the dimension of time. The
ecumenical movement in the ordinary sense of the word encounters
this problem in many areas, both in relation to the confession and in
relation to the office, church order, liturgy, and discipline. Even when
considering the ecumenical problem from the missionary and apostolic side one runs into this question. One notices this immediately in
formulating the question as to how we can prove that we still are
the apostolic Church today so many centuries after the apostles.
One can never separate the actual and eschatologically orientated
apostolate from the original apostolate. Besides, one cannot simply
pass over those figures who stand out during the centuries between
then and now. There is at least a *successio apostolicae doctrinae*
(apostolic doctrinal succession). Or better: everything points to
such a succession. The question is, Is there *really* one?

This then, in the third place, is a very urgent matter in view of
the fact that the Church—by which is meant Christendom—understands itself as that body to which God has given great promises and
great tasks. The Church is the people of God, the body of Christ,
the temple of the Holy Spirit. It is the task of the Church to mediate
salvation, to pronounce truth, to hold the keys of the heavenly
kingdom. The Church is entrusted to the infallible leadership of the
Holy Spirit. In her the authority of divine salvation and divine
truth is embodied in the world. The Church is the bride of Christ
and she is consequently in a very special situation. That is to say,
the Church is not purely human and cannot, roughly speaking, err.
In her dogma the Church cannot and should not substantially de-
viate from the apostolic witness.

Related to this insight is another one. Dogma, since it is an expression of the redeeming truth and reality, has soteriological significance. Man and the world can as little do without dogma in their
individual as in their communal existence. This brings up still another very important aspect of the problem of the evolution of
dogma, How could people have done without dogma prior to the
time in which it was formulated? How could these people have been
in the state of salvation? How could they have possibly entered

into that state? These questions are all the more urgent if one
realizes that salvation in the sense of *beatitudo* (beatitude) consists in *gaudium de veritate* (joy of truth). Besides, there is the
question, How could they have served God? Serving God is active
existence in the categories of truth. Is it conceivable that the Church
did not always have the whole truth? And is it not a fact that the
Church erred for centuries, at least when considered from the viewpoint of the later fixation of dogma? Was it possible to have a purely
Trinitarian life and thought previous to A.D. 381 and a purely
Christological life and thought before 451 and a purely predes-
tinarian life and thought before 1619? How should one see all these
things in the light of the fact that the Church is the bride of Christ
and that the joy of truth is essential for salvation and for the
service of God?

The question is whether one can prove strictly, *historically* speaking, that the Church of all ages always believed the same as far as
the heart of the matter is concerned. No one would say that. Can one
then perhaps arrive at this conclusion *dialectically*—by seeing that
the evolution of dogma is nothing but a development of that which
was logically implicit in dogma? Can one say that the Church from
the beginning contained the whole truth in an implicit manner?
Drawing this conclusion, one should argue the unity and identity
of the Church in the dimension of time by forging a chain of logical
development connecting the Church of today with that of the apostolic witness. However, many Roman Catholic theologians are no
longer satisfied with this dialectical solution of the problem. They
take a third road, the so-called *theological* way. Once again some
basic conceptions of Möhler and Newman become relevant. In a
nutshell, one can summarize what is at stake in this third way by
saying that the Church's possession of truth is primarily a supernatural matter—in accordance with the nature of the Church and
in accordance with the nature of the created reality which is embraced
by the order of grace. The revelation completed in Jesus Christ and in
the apostolic era is thus more than a communication of doctrine. It
is rather a revelation that creation shares in the reality of the life
of God. The apostles and the Church after the apostles have always

been focussed on this total reality given in revelation by an intuition of the whole of being. In fact, all knowledge arises only from the enduring contact between Spirit and earthly reality. All knowledge must be integrated in the total person, in his heart and in his life. Truth must be practised in a supernaturally new life; only thus will it be known. Besides, there are other factors than these.

One must remember that all knowledge is communal and consequently must be integrated in the total life of the community. Seen from this angle, one can say that the evolution of dogma is somewhat of a retardation: the whole truth and full knowledge have been given from the very beginning, but they could not break out into full ripeness due to the retarding process of the growth of the community. Wherever truth and knowledge break forth, this happens in logical formulations. Therefore, we must distinguish between the word which is spoken and the reality which it intends to express. The continuity which is real in the Church of the ages cannot be understood therefore by historico-critical reason, nor by logical reason, because the whole process is centrally governed by supernatural factors. One can be sure, however, that there is such a continuity because the teaching authority which in the last instance defines dogma is itself of a mystical and supernatural character.

As I said before, I do not intend to consider in detail the Roman Catholic solution to this problem. I merely indicate that the third solution just mentioned reminds us of expressions like: we confess our faith today *"in communion with* the confession of the fathers" and "the confession of the ages does not matter, but *the religion* which has been expressed in it." By means of these terms the Reformed Church in the Netherlands tries to master the problem of the authority of the Confession in Church life.

What then can one say dogmatically about these questions? I do not claim to have an answer, but a few relevant considerations can be introduced.

In the first place, there is the metaphor of the egg of the cuckoo. The *depositum fidei* (deposit of faith) is like an egg of the cuckoo laid in the nest of the Church by the apostles. Is it possible to accept such a metaphor when applied to dogma? No doubt something has been deposited, namely, the contingent deed of God in Christ. Besides, there is the apostolic witness. But the question is, Can one say that the dogma has been deposited by God in Christ and in the apostolic witness? Or is perhaps the definition of dogma specifically the work of the Church, of man, standing over against God and yet being a partner of God? Even in that case the formulation of dogma has a divine origin. The relationship of God and man seen in biblical and Christian perspective is then such that God does not *deposit* the dogma among men but that God *evokes* if from men. God invites man to express what he understands the deed of God to be and what he thinks about it. The prototype of this invitation is contained in the question of Jesus, "Who do the people say that I am?" (Lk 9:18).

The possibility of God inviting man to formulate dogma has deep roots. In the Reformed tradition the deepest root is the thesis that the *imago dei* (image of God) even if it is understood as *similitudo* (similarity) is not supernatural but natural. This would also mean that there are no mysteries in God which by definition exceed the capacity of the created human reason. The being and the counsel, or at least the acts of God, are within reach of the human reason, if we may put it this way. This can be said at least about the *sana ratio* (sane reason). But the question is, however, to what extent the *sana ratio* reappears again in the reason which is illuminated by revelation.

If there is some truth in what we have said, one could conclude that the formulation of dogma is essentially the work of the *ratio christiana* (Christian reason) and of the consciousness of the faith of the Church, and not a gift of God in Christ.

One could even go one step further. The formulation of dogma is a projection of the reality of revelation, of salvation, and of redeemed existence into the field of thought. This projection always takes place in a specific culture and by means of the structures of thought of this culture. One might say that the urge to make this projection, the basic need to think through such things, is of a cultural nature. Perhaps even dogma has an element of luxury and play in the same sense in which all culture as such is essentially the play of man with the material world. The main concern of Christian

faith is redeemed life, but this concern is mirrored in human consciousness. But one should not go too far in this direction. The
very insight that dogma is necessary for the protection of preaching
means that dogma is to be taken more seriously. Besides, why would
not this reflection in the consciousness be at the same time the *scopus*
(goal) of God in His revelation? Dogma is really also a participation
of thought and speech in the reality of revelation. Moreover, thinking and speaking are basic characteristics of man even in his encounter with God.

But what do we say then about the relationship between the apostolic witness and ecclesiastical dogma? Is the thesis of the Reformed
tradition perhaps wrong when it insists that dogma must be scriptural and that the Word alone creates the dogma? To this I would
answer in the first place that there are doctrinal elements in the
apostolic witness, but, secondly, that it would be an irreparable
confusion if one were to overlook the distinction between the apostolic witness and the gospel story on the one hand and the proclamation of doctrine and the definition of dogma on the other. These
two categories are wholly different from one another. Indeed, the
Word creates dogma, but it does so by evoking it from redeemed
existence in its thinking activity.

By conceiving in this way the relationship between Holy Scripture and the Church, one allows more room for the evolution of
dogma even if one insists on the thesis that revelation was completed
in the apostolic era. In this case a greater emphasis is placed on the
original character of the Church and her Tradition as over against
Holy Scripture. It seems to me that this greater allowance for the
independence of the Church and her Tradition is characteristic of
the Reformed viewpoint in comparison with that of the Roman
Catholic Church. Holy Scripture is a wholly unique but not the sole
and only thing that counts in the realm of God. The Scriptures are
the source, but the source is not the same as the brook. The Scriptures
are the norm, but the norm is not the matter itself. The brook or the
matter we are talking about here is ourselves.

We must state the question somewhat more broadly and more
deeply. This is my second consideration. We are not dealing merely

with the relationship between Holy Scripture and the Church; rather, we are speaking about the relationship of Christology and pneumatology.

It makes a great deal of difference whether one approaches dogma and all the other things connected with the Church solely from the standpoint of the Incarnation of the Logos or whether one sees it primarily in the context of the Spirit. If one wants only to reckon with the Incarnation of the Logos, then, if we may put it this way, the whole truth is contained in the reality of revelation. The truth is then a bar of gold which still has to be minted. As soon as one begins to sees these things in pneumatological perspective, they look somewhat different. In a purely Trinitarian way of thinking the Holy Spirit is the third person and not a repetition of, but rather truly other than, the eternal Son. Applied to the mystery of salvation, this means that the outpouring of the Holy Spirit must be understood as a truly new manifestation and a truly new act of God when compared with the Incarnation.

Imagine now—and this is quite feasible to do—that the Church in all the aspects and dimensions of her reality, even in matters of the formulation of dogma, should be seen in the context of the Holy Spirit which is poured out and which lives in the Church, the heart of man, and in the redeemed cultures of nations, rather than against the backdrop of the Incarnation of the Logos! This would mean that one can no longer be satisfied with the concept of the total reality of Christ always totally present and conceived of as a continuum in space and time proceeding uninterruptedly and directly from God. Things do not proceed from God in this continuous, full, and pure manner. There is a gap between Christology and pneumatology. This metaphor of gap is characteristic of the whole of pneumatology. Why? Because there is always a jump from one moment to the next in the Spirit. This is the element of the freedom of the Spirit. And above all it is characteristic of the Holy Spirit that he puts man over against God, as his partner, especially over against God in Christ. The Spirit is the leap from God to man and vice versa.

If one one sees the formulation of dogma as the work of the Church within the framework of the work of the Spirit as we previously characterized it, one can understand theologically that there is evolution of dogma and why there is. We would even be inclined to conclude, to use the image once more, that the Spirit is intent on using these leaps in their various forms in the evolution of dogma.

I now come to my third consideration. It is typical of the Spirit to use man. The whole outpouring of the Spirit and his indwelling in man is accomplished for the sake of man in his temporality, his isolation, and guilt. Salvation must be mediated. This means that on the one hand salvation must be given and on the other hand applied. This application means that man becomes part of the body of Christ and that Christ takes form in the human. There is always this twofold relationship in the Spirit: Christ and man and man and Christ. One may go so far as to say that man gains self-understanding in and through the work of the Spirit—the self-understanding of being saved in Christ and also of being elected from eternity and for eternity.

From what we have said here we derive three points which could be of great importance for the understanding of dogma and its evolution. In the first place, the heart of the revelation of salvation of God in Christ must be sought in the atonement of guilt. This atonement certainly should not be lightly confused with the proclamation of dogma. The former is still something quite different from the sharing of life, even of supernatural life. Atonement of guilt is a category of its own. It comes to man as a creative and redeeming message. From this message originates the new life and from the reflection upon this message the dogma arises. And yet in itself this atonement is a mystery and a message. This leads to a second viewpoint: the good news as a message for sinners was there even before the dogma. In this good news man encounters God himself. Man consequently was always saved and has always served God even without dogma. This means, in the third place, that we must put a heavy accent on preaching as the only form of the mediation of salvation. Preaching, the living voice of the gospel, is a category of its own. In preaching, God himself comes to us in the reality of His historical presence. The preaching more than the teaching of the formulation of dogma is the heart of the *potestas docendi* (power of teaching). One could ask whether the dogma itself should be understood as the preaching

of the Church in the world? The question also arises whether the
dogma could perhaps be the content of the preaching? It seems generally accepted that the dogma is the framework of preaching and
consequently helps and protects it. Still, the preaching itself, which is
given from the whole Scripture in the context of the fullness of life, is
a category completely of its own. Preaching alone creates the presence
of salvation and of God in Christ in the present time. Of course the
preaching of historical revelation has a dimension of knowledge
about historical facts as deeds of God in the real world. It is also
essentially evoking in man a confession of faith. This too is the
work of the Holy Spirit. This very confession which is primarily a
confession of sin and of grace crystallizes into a dogma. One could
go so far as to say that this reflection of salvation in the consciousness of man belongs to the *scopus* (goal) of preaching and the revelation. In this respect dogma and the sacraments are on one level.
The sacrament is also beyond preaching and believing.

At any rate, if the dogma is a reaction to the *viva vox evangelii*
(living voice of the gospel), it is not hard to see that this reaction
changes in the course of the centuries. Firstly, it changes because
the dogma is reaction to the *living* voice of the gospel and, secondly,
because it is *reaction,* reaction in ever-changing generations and in
ever-changing cultures. Again, from this it follows then that there
is a place for the evolution of dogma.

My fourth consideration is meant to give a considerable elaboration of a particular point from my third consideration. In the latter
we spoke about man in his individuality and his temporality. Man
is grasped by the Spirit and used; this means with his knowledge of
his eternal election and with his certainty of eternal salvation. These
considerations do not come to the fore in the Christological perspective because the individual man is other than Jesus Christ; man is
not the same as the mediator. And yet because of the Spirit man
is added to the mediator. This event is a new moment or rather a
complex of new moments which are added to the historical revelation in Jesus Christ.

My fifth consideration consists of a question. Are there perhaps
still other creative elements in the work of the Spirit? This problem

takes the form of a series of questions. They are, in short, as follows. Must we understand Tradition really only as an explication, development, illumination, or growth? Can one really defend the viewpoint that there is only a continuum, a continuous development from God in Christ leading to the end of time and to the ends of the earth? What then is the role of the various forms of human thought in which the revelation is being projected? Is it not so that we have to draw a parallel between the dogma on one side and, for instance, architecture, the liturgy, church order, spirituality, discipline (in the sense of style of living), and perhaps also the cultural community on the other side? In all these various fields we see a thousandfold change. There is for instance not a single Christian European form of piety which is truly identical with the piety of, for instance, the Psalmists. Besides, does it not make good sense to hope that the dogma outside of Europe in the so-called younger Churches will take completely new forms because it will be fed there from the sources of Asian speculation and the vitality of Africa? Is not what we do with this revelation and the form which Christ takes in us more important than the revelation itself? Is man not of the most central importance in the final analysis? Basically, history does not mean Christ but man and the Kingdom of God in man. Does this not mean that the demons are not merely cast out but that they are subdued, or, in other words, that the pagan world somehow will be integrated into the Kingdom of God? In view of these things, is it possible that no new things and no new truths and no new realities are being revealed? Is it not precisely one of the secrets of history that it is being wholly renewed over and over again in an incomprehensible spontaneity and creativity? Should not perhaps all Christian confessions blossom out into a philosophy of history? All these questions suggest an unlimited range for the concept of the evolution of dogma. This evolution embraces constantly renewed integration of new elements which arise in the historical process.

My sixth consideration deals with the heart of the matter. Is the Incarnation, is Jesus Christ, actually the definitive reality given in revelation? One cannot deny that He is just that. The New Testament expresses this clearly enough and the whole tradition of

Christianity witnesses to this fact very strongly. The question is, however, in what sense is He the definitive revealed reality given in revelation? Is Jesus Christ the definitive revelation in the sense that He is the highest revelation of God in the world and that this is the crucial one, so that all the arrows of God's acts are pointed toward Jesus Christ? In this case the purpose of man and the world would be that they become incorporated in Jesus Christ to find their ulti-mate destiny, and their essence in God and in the participation in His trinitarian life. Or is Jesus Christ the definitive reality given in revelation in this sense, that He is the most profound revelation of God in the world, as it were the very last emergency measure of God which finally establishes and anchors once and for all the things which God intends, with the understanding that this act of God is really only a beginning? In this case all arrows are pointed away from Jesus Christ and He is being considered the means and we the goal. Accepting this alternative, man and the world find their destiny and essence really in themselves, namely, insofar as they are the realm of God.

We must be extremely careful when employing the idea that rev-elation is complete. That we have to be careful we see illustrated in the following example: the reverse side of the idea that revelation was completed in the apostolic era is that the same actually only started in the apostolic period. What do we do with the Old Testa-ment in that case? Israel had practically no dogma and certainly no Christian dogma. And yet the Israelites could be saved and could serve God as we in the Reformed tradition believe. Should we then perhaps understand the Old Testament allegorically? Does this mean that only we can understand the Old Testament fully? Or should we accept the alternative that God truly came under the Old Covenant and that the Old Testament in its literal sense is the fully canonical Word of God? In that case we cannot hold that revelation only began in the apostolic era. This leads to a greater reservation to-ward the idea that God's revelation was completed in the Incarnation and contained in it and that God is revealed exhaustively in Christ. The Christian God is not only "in Christ."

Starting from another angle, we come to the same conclusion. The

work of the Spirit is not merely *illuminatio* (illumination), application, and incorporation. There is also an element of perfection and
realization. The Spirit perfects and realizes in us the salvation which
is given in Christ. In this process Christ gains something. He receives
something, namely, a human form in a thousandfold manner. This
fact adds to the concept of Tradition an essential eschatological
focus. Tradition is not purely a matter of the past. Tradition is
equally a matter of the future. Time is not yet completed and dogma
shares this incompleteness of time. On the Dutch scene Isaac Da
Costa (1790–1860) and J. H. Gunning (1824–1905) in particular
have stressed this aspect and drew conclusions from it for the problem
of the authority of the Confession.

My last consideration is concerned with infallibility. Christian
thinking is necessarily concerned with this category because the
pretensions of the Christian faith are great. The Church is really the
bride of Christ. There is a real revelation of God in the world. The
true God can be known and can be served. The created reality can
be experienced purely. All these moments are contained in the
promise of infallibility.

But how should we understand infallibility? It is wrong to isolate
infallibility in one moment of the Church, in the office, the teaching
authority, or even and primarily in the pope. It is equally wrong to
concentrate infallibility wholly in the infallible Holy Scriptures. The
root of either of those one-sided emphases is, as I see it, that infallibility is one-sidely considered from a Christological point of view.
Christologically speaking, one must indeed understand infallibility in
the sense of something that cannot be questioned since we are thinking about God's being in Christ. *Enhypostasis* demands infallibility
in this straight sense. But it is not enough to limit one's Christian
thought to the Christological point of view. One must think in terms
of the Trinity and consequently pneumatologically. As a matter of
fact, infallibility is above all a characteristic of the Holy Spirit and
His work. But it is also essential for the Spirit that He use man. He
works in the ways of man to such an extent that man must give an
account of his work even insofar as it is the work of the Spirit or

God's work. As in Christ, it is a matter of not being able to doubt of God; in the Spirit it is a matter of the possibility of doubting of man. Pneumatologically speaking, the relationship between God and man is not one of an *enhypostasis* but one of inhabitation. Consequently, infallibility in a pneumatological sense does not exclude fallibility but includes the same. It is for this reason that the evolution of dogma can take the form of the reformation in that necessary, serious, yes, terrible sense, which we witnessed in the sixteenth century. Such a reformation is then fully a moment in the Catholic tradition.

The Reformation is not a revolution and one should not exaggerate the eschatological focus of the evolution of dogma. For we are not only directed toward the future. Were that so, the meaning of history would fall away. The Christian is also looking toward the past. All knowledge is a matter of community, not in the least in the dimension of time. Previous generations made their contributions. We ourselves are merely links in the chain of generations. The Spirit connects the future with the past and vice versa. For this reason I cannot see how one can posit the distinction between traditional and experimental as a contradiction. All experiments are cases of reordering tradition and they in turn create new tradition. The evolution of dogma, as all evolution, is a careful navigation along a course of a thousand and one failures. One never starts *ab ovo*. Only now and then can one leap. Only to God is the whole of time from the beginning to its consummation, and with all its unity and comprehensiveness, the revelation of His image and the establishment of His kingdom. As human beings we have to stand in this whole in a particular spot in the present. This means that we consume the past and anticipate the future. The dogmatical labors of the Church and of theological science, when seen from the viewpoint of the evolution of dogma, can be compared with the card player. The card player has in mind at each particular moment in the game all that has taken place before. The dogmatical labors of the Church and of theological science can also be compared with the chess player who while making his individual moves sees through the whole of the game yet to be played. It is obvious that these metaphors suggest a great task for the Church and theology. But in view of this great task the infallible guidance of the Spirit has been promised to us.

Translated by Tjaard Hommes

NOTES

This article originally appeared in Dutch under the title "De Evolutie Van Het Dogma" and was included in the collection *De Evolutieleer Na Honderd Jaar*, pp. 16–30, published by De Erven F. Bohn N. V., Haarlem, in 1959, and is translated here with their kind permission.

SELECTED READINGS

1. Barth, Karl, *Church Dogmatics*, Vol. I, Pt. 2, trans. by G. T. Thomson and Harold Knight. Edinburgh: T. and T. Clark, 1956, pp. 462–472, 719–740; *Kirchliche Dogmatik*, Vol. III, Pt. 4. Zürich: Evangelischen Verlag A. G. Zollikon, 1951, pp. viii–x; "Preface to the Second Edition," *The Epistle to the Romans*, trans. from the 6th ed. by E. C. Hoskyns. London: Oxford University Press, 1933, pp. 2–15. In these three places Barth is defining his hermeneutics in confronting other hermeneutical possibilities; this historical context is necessary to a balanced understanding of Barth's hermeneutics.

2. Bartsch, H. W., ed., *Kerygma and Myth*, trans. by Reginald H. Fuller. London: S.P.C.K., 1953. A theological debate with contributions by R. Bultmann, E. Lohmeyer, J. Schniewind, G. Schumann, H. Thielicke, and Austin Farrer.

3. Blackman, E. C., "The Task of Exegesis," in W. D. Davies and I. Daube, eds., *Background of the New Testament* [Festschrift for Dodd] (Cambridge: Cambridge University Press, 1951), pp. 3–26. *Biblical Interpretation: The Old Difficulties and the New Opportunities*. London: Independent Press, Ltd., 1957. The book is designed to make clearer an alternative to the fundamentalist's and to modern criticism's interpretation of the Bible.

4. Bornkamm, Günther, *Jesus of Nazareth*, trans. by Irene and Fraser McLuskey with James M. Robinson. New York: Harper and Bros., 1960. An important part of "the new quest for the historical Jesus" (cf. James M. Robinson, *A New Quest of the Historical Jesus*, Studies in Biblical Theology, No. 25. Naperville, Ill.: Alec R. Allenson, Inc., 1959). This study was made,

significantly enough, by one of Bultmann's students in an attempt to define the Person behind the kerygma.

5. Bultmann, Rudolf, "The Problem of Hermeneutics," in *Essays,* trans. by C. C. Greig. London: S.C.M. Press, 1955, pp. 234–261. Bultmann describes his own analysis of the hermeneutical problem with special reference to the hermeneutics of Schleiermacher and Dilthey.

6. Diem, Hermann, *Grundfragen der biblischen Hermeneutik* (Theologische Existenz heute, #24). Munich: Chr. Kaiser Verlag, 1950. In this short paper Diem addresses himself to the problem raised for the Church by Bultmann's theology and attempts to reorient the discussion of that theology.

7. Farrer, Austin, "Typology," *Expository Times,* Vol. 67 (1956), pp. 228–231. See *A Study in Mark* (Westminster: Dacre Press, 1951) for Farrer's hermeneutics at work with New Testament material.

8. Fuchs, Ernst, *Zum hermeneutischen Problem in der Theologie. Gesammelte Aufsätze,* Band I. Tübingen: J. C. B. Mohr, 1959.

9. Grant, F. C., "Guiding Principles for the Interpretation of the Bible," in A. Richardson and W. W. Schweitzer, eds., *Biblical Authority for Today.* Philadelphia: Westminster Press, 1951, pp. 240–243.

10. McClelland, J. C., "Mythology and Theological Language," *Scottish Journal of Theology,* Vol. 11 (March 1958), pp. 13–21.

11. Niebuhr, Richard R., *The Resurrection and Historical Reason.* New York: Charles Scribner's Sons, 1957. "An attempt to understand the connection between the Biblical proclamation of the resurrection of Jesus Christ and the order of theological thought."

12. Piper, Otto, "Principles of New Testament Interpretation," *Theology Today,* Vol. 3 (July 1946), pp. 192–204.

13. "Problems in Biblical Hermeneutics," *Journal of Biblical Literature,* Vol. 77 (1958), pp. 18–38. A symposium including "Preface to Hermeneutics" by James Muilenberg, "The Problem of Faith and History in Biblical Interpretation" by J. C. Rylaarsdam, and "Implications of Form-Criticism and Tradition-Criticism for Biblical Interpretation" by Krister Stendahl.

14. Van Ruler, A. A., *Die Christliche Kirche und das Alte Testament.* Munich: Chr. Kaiser Verlag, 1955.

15. Von Rad, G., "Typologische Auslegung des Alten Testaments," *Evangelische Theologie,* Vol. 12 (1952), pp. 17–33.

16. Wright, G. Ernest, "Interpreting the Old Testament," *Theology Today,* Vol. 3 (July 1946), pp. 176–191. See also Wright's *The God Who Acts,* Studies in Biblical Theology No. 8. London: S.C.M. Press, 1952.

INTRODUCTION:

THE ROMAN CATHOLIC VIEW OF THE BIBLE

IN NO area of Catholic scholarship is the recovery from the "siege mentality" more striking today than in the field of biblical studies. This is all the more noteworthy, since fifty years ago there was no area of scholarship in which this attitude had been more in evidence. The stages in this reversal of attitude deserve our attention.

The Catholic Modernist crisis of the turn of the century was produced from two principal ingredients: a highly trained corps of hard-working, mainly German, Protestant biblical scholars, generally liberals with a deep suspicion of dogmatic theology and a phenomenal store of erudition; and a body of mainly Latin Catholic theologians who were simply not equipped with the historical, archaeological, and philological scholarship which advances in biblical studies demanded. This was an explosive mixture, and it inevitably produced the Modernist crisis. During those steamy years there were Catholic biblical scholars so fiercely conservative that they clung to outdated human opinions as doggedly as they clung to the basic dogmas of the Catholic faith.

Naturally they felt their conservatism vindicated when they saw Catholics like Loisy, who were fascinated by the liberal exegetes, reinterpreting the faith in which they had been reared in almost purely symbolic terms.

But besides the fundamentalist conservatives and the all-out liberals, there was another group of Catholic scholars typified by the Dominican Père Lagrange, founder of the *École biblique* and the *Revue biblique,* whose voice may have sounded rather faint at the time, and who had to endure the suspicions and attacks of ultra-

conservatives, but who were eventually vindicated in the encyclical
of 1943, *Divino afflante Spiritu,* the Magna Charta of modern Catholic biblical studies.

What made this possible was that during the period between the
two world wars, the two ingredients mentioned above had taken on
quite a different flavor. After the first World War the confident
liberalism which had been such a prominent feature of Protestant
exegesis declined. The revival of interest among Protestant exegetes
and theologians in the Word of God as revelation, of which Barth
became the center and symbol, helped to allay the suspicions of conservative Catholic scholars. And the quiet labor of Catholic biblical
scholars, which had been pretty much of an underground stream
during the hectic, suspicious Modernist years, began to remedy the
scientific unpreparedness which had formerly prevailed.

But it was only with the publication of *Divino afflante Spiritu* in
1943 that the kind of biblical scholarship which Père Lagrange had
symbolized was cleared of the last vestiges of suspicion and whole-
heartedly recommended. The modern Catholic biblical movement
had come of age.

In recent years the growing desire of the faithful to understand
the religious message of the Bible, the basic book of their faith, has
put pressure on Catholic exegetes to satisfy that need, and now even
in the United States, which is still behind France and Germany in
this respect, first-class examples of biblical *haute vulgarisation* are
beginning to multiply. The following article of Father Stanley is an
example of this work.

But much remains to be done, and the direction in which that
work is moving is toward syntheses in biblical theology; partial
syntheses to begin with, a Pauline synthesis, for instance, or a
Johannine synthesis, of New Testament theology, for instance, or
Old Testament theology. The thorny problem which will have to be
met here is the problem of somehow remaining faithfully within the
greatly varied biblical categories of thought, as the methods of
biblical theology demand, and yet eventually building a *unified*
theological synthesis of the *whole* Bible.

The following article of Father David M. Stanley, S.J., shows
the influences at work which are typical of modern Catholic biblical

studies. Father Stanley is a Canadian Jesuit, who received the rarely given doctoral degree from the Pontifical Biblical Institute in Rome in 1952 with a dissertation on "Christ's Resurrection in Pauline Soteriology." In February 1961, after teaching New Testament exegesis for a decade at the Jesuit theologate in Toronto, he began a three-year appointment as Associate Professor of New Testament Theology at the School of Religion of the State University of Iowa. His numerous articles have appeared in *Verbum Domini, Sciences Ecclésiastiques, Theological Studies, Worship,* and the *Catholic Biblical Quarterly.* He is a member of the Canadian Society of Biblical Studies.

5

THE GOSPELS AS SALVATION HISTORY

DAVID MICHAEL STANLEY, S. J.

FOR some time now, it appears, a new breeze has been blowing in the domain of Catholic biblical studies. "The breeze blows wherever it pleases," St. John informs us; and the breeze, which for well over a decade has sprung up to revivify Catholic scholarly endeavor, has been felt in almost every branch of scriptural research. Biblical inspiration and inerrancy, the Mosaic authorship of the Pentateuch, the "prehistory" of the first eleven chapters of Genesis, all exemplify the type of question which has received quite new solutions. Among the problems that have undergone a reorientation in New Testament studies, that of the historical character of the Gospels has enjoyed a certain pre-eminence. Catholic exegetes are now permitted to voice opinions upon this difficult question which fifty, even twenty-five, years ago would have caused considerable concern, if not explicit censure.[1]

While the professional student of Scripture rejoices at the new impetus thus given his work through the present-day liberal attitude of the magisterium, he is also conscious that, on the part of some within the Church, there has already been a reaction to many of the views he now feels free to express. He would be foolish indeed to ignore the fact that a certain malaise has manifested itself on the part of some theologians. They are not quite so sure as their biblical colleagues that the effects of the twentieth-century scriptural renaissance can be called progress. There are undoubtedly some who feel, even though perhaps they do not express their fears too openly, that the old ghost of Modernism, which Pius X was thought to have laid

111

within the household of the faith, has staged a reappearance, this time as a poltergeist. As John L. McKenzie recently observed, "At the present writing, fifteen years after the publication of the encyclical [*Divino afflante Spiritu*], opposition to creative biblical scholarship speaks only in whispers, and it no longer inhibits original work which goes beyond commonly accepted theological opinion."[2]

The publicity which this divergence of views on scriptural interpretation among Catholics has received in our day may indeed serve a useful purpose, if it convinces non-Catholic scholars that, on "many, very important questions," to cite a phrase of Pius XII, there is room in Catholic scholarship for freedom of opinion about the meaning of biblical passages, that there is not, in other words, a "party line" which all are obliged to follow unthinkingly.

Nowhere, perhaps, is this difference of viewpoint so strikingly exemplified as it is with regard to the exegetes' new conception of what has always been known as the "historicity" of the Gospels. Even some of those who have come to recognize the validity of certain principles of Form Criticism, when they are applied to the Old Testament books, hesitate to permit these same principles to operate in the study of the Gospels. The truth is, of course, that if these principles have real, universal validity, then it ought to be not only possible but necessary to apply them (due regard being had for the variety that obtains in biblical historical narrative) no less in the New than in the Old Testament.

Let me say at once, on the other hand, that there is some reasonableness in this somewhat conservative attitude. It is only too obvious, for instance, that between the antiquity and folkloric character of many oral traditions incorporated in the Old Testament and the relatively short-lived and well-substantiated oral traditions forming the basis of the written Gospels, there is a vast and easily discernible difference. Anyone can surely see that there were no human eyewitnesses to the creation. By contrast, the evangelists could have found a not inconsiderable number of serious-minded, sincere men to testify to the sayings and doings of Jesus of Nazareth. That they actually succeeded in doing so has been convincingly demonstrated by C. H. Dodd in his *History and the Gospel*.[3]

We do not wish to minimize this attitude of reserve which, though rarely vocal, is certainly present in some Catholic minds. It is based really upon a fear that, because certain familiar props have been pulled out from under the structure of Catholic apologetics by the new methods, the whole edifice is in danger of collapse. I find no difficulty in granting that such a fear (undoubtedly unfounded, as I believe) has been partly caused by a few of the Catholic exegetes themselves. It is most regrettable that occasionally the Scripture scholar has, in the exuberance of his new-found freedom, displayed an entirely too negative attitude in approaching the question of the Gospels' historical character. Fr. Thomas Worden, editor of the English Catholic periodical *Scripture,* gives a balanced and penetrating criticism of such a regrettable outlook in his article, "Is Scripture to Remain the Cinderella of Catholic Theology?"[4]

Certainly what is needed, if the work of demolition of certain outmoded solutions to scriptural difficulties is to be helpful, is the stressing of those positive values which are to be found in the explanations which modern biblical science is capable of offering and must offer. The New Testament critic must shoulder his new responsibility of developing a much-needed New Testament biblical theology.

FUNDAMENTALISM

Still, when we speak of the need of delicacy and prudence in promoting the new Catholic approach to Gospel criticism, we do not mean to suggest that the biblical scholar can take refuge in a conservatism which borders upon obscurantism. J. Cambier describes the proper approach to the subject in a paper read at the Louvain biblical week a few years ago, "Historicité des évangiles synoptiques et Formgeschichte":[5]

The judicious, nuanced application of this literary method . . . for the study of the synoptic Gospels demands that we admit the existence of certain liberties which the evangelists have taken with history in the critical and modern sense of that word. We feel that, both for a more balanced understanding of the sacred history, and also to assist the seminary student or the educated Catholic to avoid an unnecessary lapse into scepticism, we must attempt to provide them with a clearer insight into the problem.

More recently, this sane, very Catholic attitude has been serenely
expressed by Fr. L. Alonso-Schökel, professor at the Pontifical Biblical Institute. I refer to his trenchant review of an Old Testament
Introduction, whose author, to say the least, has not moved with the
times. "The author," Alonso-Schökel said,

appears to feel that progress consists solely, or at least principally, in
the fact that those opinions which he is pleased to call "traditional"
should receive confirmation. He is doubtless convinced that he is serving
the Church more faithfully by teaching safer doctrine. Actually, the
more rigid opinion is not always the safer one. Pupils formed according
to the spirit of this book will approach their priestly work armed with
the arguments which it contains. They will propose them to the faithful, among whom will be educated, intelligent laymen, who will be
told that these opinions, thanks to such arguments, form part of the
faith. Will not their own belief be endangered, or at least, will they not
be afflicted with doubts, which might easily have been avoided?[6]

As splendid examples of modern Catholic work on the Gospels, I
might mention here the commentaries in the *Bible de Jérusalem* on
St. Matthew and St. John by P. Benoit and D. Mollat, respectively.
The remarks of my colleague, R. A. F. MacKenzie, in a review of
several Old Testament fascicles in this same collection, apply also to
these New Testament studies. "These Catholic scholars, free of polemical preoccupations, are going about their own proper work,
in the calm assurance that they are carrying on the centuries-old
exegetical tradition of the Church, and that, in the light of faith, they
can safely and profitably use modern discoveries, to achieve that
fuller understanding of Sacred Scripture which the Holy See hopes
and expects of them."[7]

Opposed to such a serene and scholarly spirit of inquiry is an attitude, which, while more characteristic of certain Protestant students of the Bible, is also operative in the thinking of not a few
Catholics. I mean, of course, biblical fundamentalism. Fundamentalism's adherents have been chiefly found amongst certain non-Catholic sects, for the very good reason that Bible reading has been more
commonly practiced by them than by Catholics. In addition, the
fundamentalist viewpoint has developed partly as a corollary of the
Protestant dogma of "private interpretation," partly as a repudiation

by sincere (and often uneducated) Christians of that "historicism" to which nineteenth-century Protestant rationalism lent its patronage. Historicism, which, applied to the Gospels, was known as the "quest of the historical Jesus," never won any support in Catholic scholarship. "The revolt against historicism and the demand for a biblical theology in the Protestant churches has had a parallel in the Catholic Church. Here there was no revolt against historicism, because there never had been any historicism against which to revolt. But there was a stout affirmation of the 'historical character' of the Bible without any attention whatever to the study of literary forms. The purely defensive and almost entirely controversial scholarship of the era of the siege mentality had by 1943 proved its sterility beyond all question."[8]

John L. McKenzie has defined fundamentalism as "the crass literal interpretation of the Bible without regard for literary forms and literary background."[9] Indeed, it consists essentially of a conscious and deliberate "literal-mindedness" in accepting the affirmations of biblical writers without regard to the idiom, the context, or the literary form through which they are expressed. I used the terms "conscious" and "deliberate" in order to exclude the simple faithful who, despite an unconsciously ingenuous attitude toward much in the Bible, do reach *the real message* of the sacred text. The fault inherent in fundamentalism is the result of a misguided determination to cling to a superficial meaning of the Bible at all costs—even the cost of real understanding. A form of anti-intellectualism, it is quite out of harmony with that spirit of religious inquiry (*fides quaerens rationem*) [faith seeking understanding] which the Catholic Church has always sought to encourage in the faithful, and which is the ideal and the guiding principle of Catholic theology.

One pernicious effect of the fundamentalist mentality is to expose the Scriptures to serious misunderstanding and even ridicule by those who do not possess Christian faith. It can, moreover, create a harmful dichotomy between faith and reason amongst Christians in whom a well-developed literary or scientific education is combined with religious instruction that is uncritical and intellectually deficient.

Indeed, fundamentalism has been known to lead to a kind of "illuminism." I am thinking of the injudicious attack by an Italian priest, Dolindo Ruotolo, made in 1941 upon Catholic biblical scholarship through a pamphlet which had to be censured by the Biblical Commission. In his tract, *Un gravissimo pericolo per la Chiesa e per le anime: il sistema critico-scientifico nello studio e nell'interpretazione della Sacra Scrittura, le sue deviazioni funeste e le sue aberrazioni,* Ruotolo, or "Dain Cohenel" (as he signed himself), advocated giving free rein to the Spirit for a proper comprehension of the Bible, "as though," to cite the Church's official condemnation of his ideas, "all were in personal communion with the divine Wisdom and received from the Holy Spirit special personal illumination...."[10]

DIVINO AFFLANTE SPIRITU

In his encyclical of 1943, *On Biblical Studies and the Opportune Means of Promoting Them,"* Pius XII "unequivocally repudiated fundamentalism in Catholic exegesis."[11] This statement of John L. McKenzie requires some amplification, since the fundamentalist attitude had, over all too long a period, become firmly entrenched in Catholic thinking. And this was particularly true where the Gospels were concerned. Accordingly, it may not be out of place here to recall briefly those directives of Pius XII which provide norms for the desirable, indeed necessary, Catholic approach to Gospel studies.

Pius lays down two principles of paramount importance, which run directly counter to the fundamentalist position: (1) "the supreme law of interpretation is that by which we discover and determine what the writer meant to say";[12] (2) there are only very few texts of the Bible, "whose meaning has been declared by the Church's authority, nor are those more numerous about which there is a unanimous opinion of the holy Fathers."[13] It may be helpful to examine the scope of these two norms, which are applicable to the study of the Gospels, in greater detail.

How, in the opinion of Pius XII, does one determine the sacred writer's meaning? "Let the interpreter therefore use every care, and take advantage of every indication provided by the most recent research, in an endeavour to discern the distinctive genius of the sacred writer, his condition in life, the age in which he lived, the written or oral sources he may have used, and the literary forms he employed. He will thus be able better to discover who the sacred writer was and what he meant by what he wrote."[14] The Pope's insistence upon the human character of the Bible is noteworthy. Also to be noted is his repeated emphasis upon the primacy of what he calls the *sensus litteralis*.

In fact, in his encyclical *Humani generis* the Pope added a further important nuance. "Indeed, it is useless for them [certain writers whose attitude the Pope condemns] to speak of the human meaning of the sacred books, under which their divine meaning, the only one in their opinion which is infallible, lies hidden."[15] "And moreover, the *sensus litteralis* of Holy Writ and its exposition, which has been elaborated by so many and such great exegetes under the eye of the Church, must, according to their erroneous views, give way to a new exegesis which they call symbolic or spiritual."[16] In commenting on this papal document, Gustave Lambert observed: "The encyclical *Divino afflante Spiritu* had however insisted with all the clarity that could be desired upon the *only meaning* which is found *everywhere* in Scripture: *the literal sense*. This literal sense, which is also *the theological sense* of the sacred texts, is that which was known and willed *conjointly* by the principal author, God, and by the intelligent, free, instrumental cause, the human hagiographer. . . . The hagiographer by writing in a human fashion, has expressed a divine way of thinking."[17]

Divino afflante Spiritu makes it abundantly clear that belief in God's primary authorship of the sacred books must not be misunderstood, so that, for instance, we attempt implausible "harmonizations" of various Gospel accounts of the same episode, forcing them to agree where they actually differ in details. We shall cite here two examples of such a mentality.

While the Synoptics agree in placing Jesus' cleansing of the Temple at the close of his public life, indeed in its last week (Mt 21: 12–13; Mk 11: 15–17, where it occurs the day *after* Jesus' messianic entry into Jerusalem; Lk 19: 45–46), Jn 2: 13–22 employs the episode as the inaugural act of Jesus' Jerusalem ministry. There are various ways of explaining these variations. The Synoptic writers, who depict Jesus' public life as chiefly a Galilean ministry, bring him to Jerusalem only in the last ten days before his death. John, on the other hand, whose Gospel might be considered a kind of commentary on the saying found in Lk 13:34 and parallels, may well be following the chronological order. But in any event, the postulating of two cleansings of the Temple is nothing but a refusal to explain the difficulty, a refusal to understand what the sacred writers are attempting to tell us.

The second example concerns the two stories of Judas' death (Mt 27: 3–10; Acts 1:18–19), which differ categorically on three important details. Did Judas commit suicide (Mt), or die of some mysterious accident or disease (Acts)? Did the Sanhedrin purchase the "potter's field" (Mt), or did Judas himself buy it as a farm (Acts)? Whose blood led to the naming of the area Haceldama, Jesus' (Mt) or Judas' (Acts)? It seems unreasonable to deny the fact that two quite independent traditions of how a bad man came to a bad end have been preserved in the New Testament. Nor does any ingenious harmonizing, like that of the Vulgate for Acts 1:18, "*suspensus crepuit medius*" [and being hanged burst asunder in the midst— Douay], really resolve the difficulty.

The proper method of handling these questions, we are told by Pius XII, entails careful research into the inspired author's background and culture, as well as his manner of writing (sources used, literary forms employed). We must not allow ourselves to overlook the profound differences separating our modern, Occidental point of view from that of the ancient Near East. "Frequently the literal sense is not so obvious in the words and writings of ancient oriental authors as it is with the writers of today"[18]—an admirable example of papal understatement. A good illustration of what is meant here is provided by Mt 23:9: "And do not call anyone on earth your father. Only one is your Father, and he is in heaven." This text, which causes some people to have scruples about addressing a Catholic priest as "Father," probably is a warning to the disciples not to imitate the scribes and Pharisees in their pretensions. These delighted in assuming high-sounding titles and assimilating themselves to "the Fathers," i.e., the patriarchs and other famous forebears of Israel.

If, then, we are to grasp the mind of authors of an age so remote and of a culture so alien to our own, it is not enough to study the rules of grammar and philology which govern their languages. We must invoke the aid of history, archaeology, ethnology, and even psychology. "For what they [the sacred writers] intended to signify by their words is not determined only by the laws of grammar or philology, nor merely by the context; it is absolutely necessary for the interpreter to go back in spirit to those remote centuries of the East, and make proper use of the aids afforded by history, archaeology, ethnology, and other sciences, in order to discover what literary forms the writers of that early age intended to use, and did in fact employ."[19] As examples of studies of the psychological differences between the Western and the biblical mentalities, we might cite the book of Gregory Dix, *Jew and Greek,*[20] or the article by Célestin Charlier, "Méthode historique et lecture spirituelle des écritures."[21]

The importance which Pius XII attached to the study of the literary types surviving in Near Eastern literary remains for mastering the thought of the sacred writers is worthy of our attention.

For to express what they had in mind the ancients of the East did not always use the same forms and expressions as we use today; they used those which were current among the people of their own time and place; and what these were the exegete cannot determine *a priori,* but only from a careful study of ancient oriental literature. This study has been pursued during the past few decades with greater care and industry than formerly, and has made us better acquainted with the literary forms used in those ancient times, whether in poetical descriptions, or in the formulation of rules and laws of conduct, or in the narration of historical facts and events.[22]

As regards the variety of historical writing to be found in the Bible, the interpreter must constantly bear in mind "the special purpose, the religious purpose of biblical history." As we shall return to a consideration of this remark when we discuss the special character of the Gospels as salvation history, it may not be out of place to cite the Pope's remarks in full. "This same study has now also clearly demonstrated the unique pre-eminence among all the ancient nations of the East which the people of Israel enjoyed in historical writing, both in regard to the antiquity of the events recorded and to the accuracy with which they are related—a circumstance, of course, which is explained by the charisma of divine inspiration and by the special purpose, the religious purpose, of biblical history."[23]

Speaking more generally of the great riches of biblical literary forms, Pius XII states that "the sacred books need not exclude any of the forms of expression which were commonly used in human speech by the ancient peoples, especially of the East, to convey their meaning, so long as they are in no way incompatible with God's sanctity and truth."[24] Thus, that ingenuous apriorism habitually found in the fundamentalist interpretation of the Bible is effectively ruled out. The exegete "must ask himself how far the form of expression or literary idiom employed by the sacred writer may contribute to the true and genuine interpretation."[25]

The second basic principle of Catholic hermeneutics, namely, that only a tiny sector of the many affirmations in the Bible has received any authoritative interpretation, has been called "perhaps the most important statement of the encyclical."[26] The Pope asserts that the Catholic exegete must be given full liberty in his search for solutions to "many important questions," which admit of free discussion within the limits of orthodoxy. Not infrequently we meet the tendency on the part of some Catholics to cling doggedly to what they imagine to be the "traditional" interpretation of a scriptural passage. They sincerely feel that in this way they are being most orthodox, when in point of fact there is no such tradition, I mean, theologically significant tradition, existing. To cite one example of this sort of thing, S. Lyonnet[27] has pointed out in his interpretation of the Pentecostal "gift of tongues," which he claims is a form of mystical or ecstatic prayer, that the rather commonly accepted view (that it was a gift of speaking foreign languages in a miraculous way) was based upon the demonstrably erroneous view that the charism was given for preaching. As he ably shows, it was a question not of preaching but of prayer.

This is but one instance of the vast quantity of "unfinished business" which Pius XII urges the Scripture scholar to deal with courageously. "This state of things must in no wise daunt the Catholic interpreter; prompted by a practical and ardent love of his science, and sincerely devoted to Holy Mother Church, he must grapple perseveringly with the problems so far unsolved . . . to find an explanation which will be faithfully consonant with the teaching of the Church, particularly with the traditional doctrine of the inerrancy of Scripture, while being at the same time in due conformity with the certain conclusions of profane sciences."[28]

Another point clarified by this papal directive is the concept of "private interpretation." Provided it does not conflict with Catholic doctrine, any explanation of the great bulk of scriptural texts is as good or bad as the reasons given for it, and this holds good equally for the majority of the patristic opinions or those given by theologians, however ancient, as for the suggestions of modern exegetes. Indeed, today's biblical scholar may quite conceivably provide a far more satisfactory explanation of a scriptural difficulty than his predecessors.[29] Moreover, he is, through *Divino afflante Spiritu,* informed that this is the direction in which his duty lies, while those who differ are warned by Pius XII not to employ the term "new," as if it were a stigma.

And let all other children of the Church bear in mind that the efforts of these valiant labourers in the vineyard of the Lord are to be judged not only with fairness and justice, but also with the greatest charity; they are to avoid that somewhat indiscreet zeal which considers everything new to be for that very reason a fit object for attack or suspicion. Let them remember above all that the rules and laws laid down by the Church are concerned with the doctrines of faith and morals; and that among the many matters set forth in the legal, historical, sapiential, and prophetical books of the Bible there are only a few whose sense has been declared by the authority of the Church, and that there are equally few concerning which the opinion of the holy Fathers is unanimous. There consequently remain many matters, and important matters, in the exposition and explanation of which the sagacity and ingenuity of Catholic interpreters can and ought to be freely exercised. . . .[30]

With the insights provided by these hermeneutical norms, we must now examine what is meant by the historical character of our Gospels.

HISTORICAL CHARACTER
OF THE GOSPEL NARRATIVES

The modern concept of history goes back ultimately to the Greeks, who classed it among the arts under the patronage of the muse Clio. "The concept of history," as Erich Dinkler has remarked, "has been given to us by Greek science and to this very day is employed by us in a Greek sense. From Thucydides to Toynbee the common and connecting assumption has been that history is a rational, intelligible continuity, an integrated nexus or concatenation, operating in a unified world, capable of investigation and illumination by historical method."[31]

In our day, inasmuch as it is the product of the historical method, history is classed as a social science. However, the writing of history remains an art, involving, as it inevitably does, the *selection* and *interpretation* in some literary form of the "remembered past."[32]

More basically, history in the modern sense of that word is to be identified with the ancient Greeks' view of it, because the intelligibility sought by the contemporary as by the classical historian is a *human* intelligibility. Both share the conviction that there is a pattern discernible in the events of the past which sprang ultimately from the mind of man, a pattern, consequently, which is recoverable by the application of the historical method (a process invented by the mind of man) and which can be represented by the art of historical writing.

"Historical writing," says C. H. Dodd, "is not merely a record of occurrences as such. It is, at least implicitly, a record of the interest and meaning they bore for those who took part in them, or were affected by them. . . ." And he concludes: "Thus the events which make up history are relative to the human mind which is active in those events."[33] Later, Dodd defines history "as consisting of events which are of the nature of occurrences plus meaning."[34]

If we accept Dodd's definition, it becomes clear that the task of selecting and interpreting the facts to be chronicled is an essential part of the historian's function. While the exercise of these two will vary according as he writes cultural, political, or economic history, the historian must choose and he must interpret. Assuming, for instance, it were possible to film a battle in its entirety, such a newsreel record would not be history, but only a source for history.

Selection and interpretation, of course, presuppose some criterion of judgment. The very choice, of course, will be governed by the type of history to be written. The political historian will find much of his data in government archives; the cultural historian discovers valuable

material in folklore, local customs, family traditions, even legends.
It is the fashion, at least in clerical circles, to smile superiorly at the
stories occasionally found in the lives of the saints commemorated in
the Roman breviary: e.g., the heroic fasts of the infant St. Nicholas,
or the marvelous prayer feats of St. Patrick. While indeed in the
future revision of the Divine Office we can expect that many of these
legends will be excised, it should be remembered that these stories
constitute (and this not despite, but because of, their incredible
character) the essential proof of the people's belief in the holiness of
these saints. Thus, in this respect, the stories do represent historical
reality. *Vox populi, vox Dei,* in the age before official canonization,
was the principle which justified the cultus paid to the saints. These
legendary tales are the popular expression of a solid faith in the
heroic sanctity of these ancient Christian heroes.

The historian's work will ultimately be judged by the correctness
of his interpretation of the evidence he has unearthed. In some instances he will be led to highlight an event which in itself, or at the
time of its occurrence, may have been almost insignificant. Thus the
historian of the Counter Reformation will direct attention to the
battle of Pampeluna, a tiny incident in a series of border skirmishes,
because an impoverished Basque nobleman, Inigo de Loyola, there
received the wound which led to his "conversion" and eventually to
the founding of the Society of Jesus.

But before he selects and interprets the events about which he intends to write, the historian must satisfy himself as to their situation
in space and time. "When" and "where" are two of the historian's
most elementary queries. Chronology and geography have been
called "the eyes of history." "If the modern historian cannot tell you
when and where something happened, he will not call it a historical
event, although he does not thereby deny that it happened."[35]

It is of considerable significance for any understanding of what is
meant by the historical nature of the Gospels to be aware that the
evangelists show a strongly marked tendency to dissociate most of
the episodes of Jesus' public life which they record from both time
and place. While some explanation of this phenomenon will appear
later in this essay, it must be noted here as one indication of the distance which separates the Gospels from modern historical writing.

The evangelists' lack of interest in the specific geographical or chronological settings of many of their narratives unquestionably sets a
limitation upon our attempts to prove these events "historical" in the
modern sense.

We might note, as one consequence of this fact, that the historicity
of the Gospels is not as simple as some apologetics manuals would
lead us to think. Their authors' purpose was quite different from that
of the modern historian. Their primary aim was to testify to the divine-human fact of God's intervention in human history which
brought man salvation in Jesus Christ. In order to express this fundamental fact, the evangelists have chosen narratives of varying type,
from parables to eyewitness accounts. Attention to this point will reveal the supreme importance of studying the many subsidiary literary
forms found in the Gospels. If an apologetic is to be valid, it must
face the fact that the Magi story, for example, is not "historical" in
the sense in which the narrative of the Crucifixion may be said to be
"historical." Jesus' earthly life, to be sure, is located in Palestine; his
birth occurred "*in diebus regis Herodis,*" his death "*sub Pontio
Pilato.*" The dates of both events, however, are known only approximately. As for the period of his public ministry, the impression given
by the first three Gospels is that it lasted about six months.

What, then, is the biblical conception of history, and how do our
Gospels differ from "history" in the modern acceptation of the word?
The biblical notion of history rests upon the belief that God has, in
the past, revealed himself in a special way within the cadre of human
affairs. "This is in fact the assertion," says C. H. Dodd, "which Christianity makes. It takes the series of events recorded or reflected in
the Bible, from the call of Abraham to the emergence of the Church,
and declares that in this series the ultimate reality of all history,
which is the purpose of God, is finally revealed, because the series is
itself controlled by the supreme event of all—the life, death and
resurrection of Jesus Christ."[36]

Through specific events, personalities, and human utterances, God
has intervened in the world of man. From this point of view, it is
clear that the intelligibility to be seen in the biblical narratives is essentially that of a divine, not a human, pattern. It is this viewpoint
which distinguishes all biblical history from the profane, or so-called

scientific, history, and indeed constitutes its superiority vis-à-vis "history" as we understand it today. It is best described as "a Mystery," in the Pauline and Johannine sense, namely, as God's revelation, in time, to men of his eternal plan for the world's salvation.

This Mystery was disclosed to mankind in two stages: one incomplete and rudimentary to God's chosen people in the Old Testament; the second, complete and definitive, through his only Son, Jesus Christ, to the Church of the New Testament. This genre of history, which we call salvation history or *Heilsgeschichte,* is the story of God's self-revelation to us; and its purpose is obviously very different from that modern scientific history which is written without reference to the divine point of view.

Here, in fact, we have touched upon one of the profound differences between the *Weltanschauung* of modern man, the product of a distinctively Greek culture, and the ancient Semitic mentality. Where we moderns habitually discuss the meaning of happenings in terms of secondary or finite causality, the Semitic genius interested itself principally in God, first cause of all things. The attitude may, now and then, strike us today as somewhat naïve. How many Christians, for instance, after smiling indulgently at the explanation, offered by Ps 28, of the thunderstorm as the "voice of Yahweh," turn to the newspaper or television broadcast for an analysis of the weather? They find, we must admit it frankly, that the meteorologists' pronunciamentos, couched in mythological terms of "high- and low-pressure areas," are eminently more satisfying than the insight of the Psalmist. Yet if, as the Christian surely believes, God causes the weather as he causes everything else, which explanation touches the reality more profoundly? At any rate, the example provides a useful illustration of the radical difference between the two viewpoints of which we are speaking.

Before we proceed further, one may well ask upon what grounds the validity of this suprahuman interpretation rests, if, as we have asserted, salvation history is simply God's revelation of himself. Obviously, it cannot be proven (or disproven) *solely* by the use of modern historical method. For while it is quite possible to demonstrate scientifically the "historical" (in our modern sense) character of the Gospel, still the fact that God has spoken to many by means of books written by human beings is an object of faith. Faith's guarantee that these writers have infallibly expressed the revelation of Jesus Christ as incarnate Son and universal redeemer is founded upon the supernatural fact of scriptural inspiration. Thus for an adequate comprehension of the evangelists' testimony we must realize that it possesses not merely the authority of reliable eyewitnesses, but also the authority of God himself.

The evangelists do indeed propose, in the written accounts of Jesus' life upon earth, to give their reader a narrative that is based upon ocular testimony. It is of paramount importance, however, to appreciate the fact that they aim principally at writing salvation history, which entails testimony to something that lies beyond the competence of any eyewitness. They offer, that is, an insight into the meaning of the Mystery of Jesus Christ. They disclose to the reader (in whom they presuppose Christian faith) something which cannot be seen with the eye or perceived by the ear, namely, the *propter nos et propter nostram salutem* (for us and for our salvation). A careful reading of 1 Jn 1:1–2 will substantiate this statement.

And this, we should not forget, is these sacred authors' primary intention. They claim to be not only eyewitnesses, but witness of the Good News of salvation, since their message, like the rest of the Bible, is addressed not simply to man's mind for his information, but to the whole man for his redemption.

We see this twofold nature of the apostolic testimony to Jesus Christ already consciously present in Peter's sermon to Cornelius and his household at Palestinian Caesarea (Acts 10:34–43). The apostolic preachers are, in the first place, "witnesses of all he (Jesus) did in the country of the Jews and Jerusalem" (v.38), or "witnesses appointed beforehand by God, who ate and drank with him after his resurrection from death" (v.41). But they have the office of witnessing in a deeper, more important sense, because they have received a mandate from the risen Lord "to preach to the People and to bear witness that he is the judge of living and dead, constituted by God" (v.42).

This same twofold purpose is manifest also in our written Gospels. Mark, whose account reflects, perhaps more strikingly than any other

Gospel, the influence of an observant eyewitness, has entitled his book "The Good News of Jesus Christ, Son of God" (Mk 1:1). A study of this Gospel reveals that its author, while providing us with some of the most vivid and detailed scenes of Jesus' public life, was innocent of anything like literary art or a creative imagination. This strange combination of two seemingly contradictory qualities happily vouches for the authenticity of the early testimony of Papias, namely, that while Mark was not a disciple of Jesus himself, he "wrote down accurately all that he remembered" of Peter's preaching. Thus the liveliness of the Markan narratives, so rich in minute detail, goes back to Peter's all-seeing eye.

Mark's intention, expressed in the title of his book, of providing us with a profounder realization of Christ's divinity, with a grasp, that is, of a supernatural truth which does not fall under the observation of the senses, implies something more than ocular testimony. Even Luke, whose prologue reveals a spirit not unacquainted with "historical method," manifests to his aristocratic convert, Theophilus, his aim of writing salvation-history. True, he has "investigated it all carefully from the beginning"; he has "decided to write a connected account of it." But both the thorough examination of his sources and the ordering of his narrative have been carved out "in order that you may more clearly grasp the authentic character of the oral instructions you have received" (Lk 1:4). The term we have translated "the authentic character" (*asphaleia*) meant "security" in the contemporary commercial and military usage. Since he is writing for a man who is already a believer in Christianity, Luke aims at more than establishing the historical character of the events and sayings he records. He means to interpret their Christological significance, as indeed the whole of his two-volume work reveals.

The author of the fourth Gospel declares, as he reaches the conclusion of his book, that "these things have been written in order that you may persevere in your belief that Jesus is the Messias, the Son of God, and that persevering in this belief you may possess life in his Name" (Jn 20:31). John's use of the present subjunctive with the Greek verb usually translated "that you may believe" is to be given its full value: it denotes not the beginning but the continuance of an action. These words are an appendage to the scene which John describes between the doubter Thomas and the risen Christ, a scene which brings out clearly the relative importance of eyewitness experience and the intelligibility apprehended by Christian faith. It is obvious, from Christ's insistence that Thomas touch him and so have the reality of his Lord's risen body impinge upon his senses, that there can be no doubt of the necessity and the value of eye-witness testimony. But Jesus points out to his disciple that belief implies much more than mere seeing with bodily eyes. "Is it because you have seen me that you have believed?" Faith, these words teach us, belongs to a higher order, providing the superior perceptiveness expressed in Thomas' "My Lord and my God." It is for this reason that Jesus pronounced a new beatitude upon all future generations of Christians. "Happy those who, though they did not see, yet become believers" (Jn 20:28–29). In the eyes of the evangelist, we of a later age are at no disadvantage in comparison with the disciples who saw and heard Jesus. We possess the *unum necessarium,* that perception of the salvific character of Jesus' earthly life through Christian faith which, if it reposes of necessity upon the apostles' eyewitness testimony, grasps, quite as accurately as they, the supernatural meaning of that life, which is beyond the reach of mere historical investigation.

How do the evangelists convey this "fourth-dimensional" quality of the salvation history they write? We can only find the answer to this question (1) by appreciating the very personal manner in which each of these sacred writers has represented to himself the Good News of salvation in Jesus Christ, (2) by investigating how he employs the various kinds of materials that have gone into the making of his book, and finally (3) by determining the manifold literary types[37] through which he has expressed what he wishes to tell us.

Before we attempt to illustrate our answers to these three aspects of the problem by means of concrete examples, however, several observations of a general character are in order. First, it must be evident that to treat these questions thoroughly demands exact and detailed literary and historical analysis, which would be out of place here. Secondly, we must not allow ourselves to forget that there is no rule-of-thumb solution to the question of the historicity of the Gospels:

each narrative must be examined for itself and for the problems it presents. Thirdly, if we are to avoid the fundamentalist mentality, we must be on our guard against the superficial conclusion that, because one may be led to admit that certain details in an evangelist's narrative (or even its general framework) are due to the literary form used or to his specific purpose, the whole story has been invented. Such a "black-or-white" attitude is simply the result of the failure, on the part of a modern, Occidental mind, to comprehend the Semitic viewpoint evinced by the inspired author. Finally, it will not infrequently happen that, after the most patient and painstaking literary analysis, we cannot decide with any certainty "what did actually happen," and we must content ourselves with such imprecision. The phrase "what did actually happen" implies, of course, the modern point of view. For the early Christians and the biblical writers, "what did actually happen" was what was recorded upon the sacred page. The term *dabar* in Hebrew means both "word" and "event." It is of course quite true that we can, by an investigation of the original historical context (*Sitz im Leben*) in which a scriptural passage was originally employed, satisfy the curiosity of the modern mind. Still, it must not be overlooked that, however useful such investigation may be, it is the meaning intended by the sacred author which holds the primacy.

In this connection, it may be useful to recall the remarks of J. Cambier in an essay to which we have already referred:[38] "It is important not to forget that the literary analysis of a narrative gives no warrant for affirming or denying its historical value. This depends upon other factors: most basically, so far as our Gospels are concerned, upon the quality of the witnesses and the nature of the tradition reporting Christ's sayings and his deeds. The problem of the historicity of our Gospels is much more intimately bound up with that of tradition than with the study of literary forms."

"THE DISTINCTIVE GENIUS" OF OUR FOUR EVANGELISTS

The ancient titles which tradition has given the Gospels show that from a very early period the Christian Church was conscious that,

while there is only one Gospel (*to euangēlion*), each of the four
evangelists has presented that one Gospel according to his own
personal understanding of it (*kata Matthaion,* etc.) by means of
those aspects of the person and mission of Jesus which struck him
particularly. In fact, we may say that our four evangelists present
us with four different Christologies, provided, as Oscar Cullmann
has recently reminded us, that we do not forget that this Christology
is inseparable from the Christian *Heilsgeschichte.* Doctor Cullmann
rightly insists that "the question of Jesus in primitive Christianity
was answered, not on the basis of a ready-made myth, but of a series
of real facts, which occurred during the first century of our era,
facts which went unnoticed by the 'history-makers' of the time . . .
but which, for all that, are no less historical: the life, mission, and
death of Jesus of Nazareth; the experience of his presence and his
continued activity after his death within the community of his
disciples."[39]

Such a Christological interpretation of the history of Jesus is
seen already operative in the Markan Gospel, in many respects the
least artistically presented of the four, adhering as it does so closely
to the scheme provided by Peter for the apostolic preaching. Mark's
principal theme is that the incarnate Son of God, Jesus Christ, has,
in his public life, his death and resurrection, realized the prophetic
fulfilment of his vocation as the Servant of God. It is in terms of the
Deutero-Isaian suffering and glorified *'Ebed Yahweh* (Servant of
Yahweh) that Mark has couched the Gospel message. At Jesus'
first appearance in his book, on the occasion of his baptism by John,
the heavenly voice proclaims him the Son of God, who is also the
Suffering Servant. "You are my beloved Son. In you I take delight"
(Mk 1:11). The words contain an allusion to the first Servant
Song (Is 42:1). Rightly called the Gospel of the Passion, Mark's
book announces Jesus' death as early as the third chapter (Mk 3:6);
and the Passion account occupies a proportionally large place in
this shortest of the Gospels. Jesus' statement of the purpose of his
life's work, which is taken as typical of Mark, is expressed in terms
of the Servant theme: "Why, even the Son of Man has come to act
as a servant, not to be served, and to lay down his life as a ransom

for all the rest of men" (Mk 10:45; cf. Is 53:5–8). Another echo of this same motif is perceptible in the Transfiguration episode, which forms the literary center of Mark's Gospel: "This is my beloved Son. Pay heed to him" (Mk 9:7).[40] Moreover, the threefold prophecy by Jesus of his future passion is expressed in terms of the Servant's mission (Mk 8:31; 9:31 = Is 53:10–11; Mk 10:33 = Is 50:6).

Since it is as the *incarnate* Son that Jesus acts as the Servant, in the eyes of Mark, his narrative underscores the reality of Jesus' human nature to the point where the reader is almost disconcerted. Indeed, it would seem that the author of Greek-Matthew, who would appear to have re-edited many of Mark's narratives (compare Mk 4:38 with Mt 8:25; Mk 6:5–6 with Mt 13:58; Mk 5:30–31 omitted in Mt 9:22), was also disconcerted by such candid realism. Jesus can become impatient, angry, sharp in his rebukes, sensitive to his hearers' reactions, surprised at the turn of events, in Mark's Gospel. Yet Mark presents undeniable evidence of Jesus' divinity, while stating implicitly that the reality of Jesus' adoption of the Servant's role hid this profound truth during his public life from all, even his chosen followers, until, at his death, even a pagan centurion could be moved to confess, "This man was really God's Son!" (Mk 15:39).[41] Mark provides his Christian reader with incontrovertible evidence that Jesus is the Son of God: by his power to forgive sins (Mk 2:1–11), his assertion of authority over the sabbath (Mk 2:28), his control of even inanimate nature (Mk 4:35–41). Thus the second Gospel provides an unmistakable picture of the Son of God incarnate, who "despoiled himself by taking on the Servant's character," and "carried self-abasement, through obedience, right up to death" (Phil 2: 7–8).

Matthew, in contrast with Mark, presents a conception of Jesus and his redemptive work which is intimately bound up with the mystery of the Church which he came to found. For it is in the Church, the divine or "heavenly Kingdom," that Matthew discovers the realization in this world of God's dominion or sovereignty over all creation. Matthew's characteristic title for Jesus is Emmanuel, a name foretold by Isaiah in his prediction of Jesus' virginal conception (Is 7:14), as Matthew informs us, and explained at the outset of this Gospel as meaning "with us is God" (Mt 1:24). As he brings his story to a close, Matthew refers once again to this image of Jesus Christ, when he records the promise of the glorified Christ at his departure from this world: "And remember, *I am with you* all the time until the end of the world" (Mt 28:20). Thus we have an example of the Semitic *inclusio,* which enunciates the theme which dominates the whole book.

Matthew's version of Jesus' public life is so constructed as to bring home to us the truth that, in his Galilean ministry—particularly in his preaching (Matthew's chief interest is in the logia of Jesus, while the event is of importance mainly for the doctrinal message it contains)—Jesus has begun to found that Church through which he will remain with us until the end of time. Behind the immediate reality of five long instructions, into which Matthew has grouped Jesus' sayings, we are given a glimpse of the future Church. The Sermon on the Mount (Mt 5–7) is an expression of the Church's spirit and function as the perfect fulfilment of Old Testament religion. The missionary discourse (Mt 10), particularly its second half, is a prediction of the evangelizing activities of the Church in the apostolic age (cf. Mt 10:17–42). The wider perspective of this second part of the discourse can be seen in the heightened opposition to the Christian gospel (16–17) both in Palestine itself (17) and in the Diaspora (18). The disciples are now endowed with the Pentecostal Spirit (20). The divine visitation of "Son of Man" in the destruction of the Temple in the year A.D. 70 is mentioned (23), and the apostolic kerygma is pictured as already being preached universally (27), since the apostles have now, in the primitive Christian Church, been entrusted with the office of prophets (41).

The instruction in parables (Mt 13) discloses the mystery which is involved in the supernatural character of the Church. Matthew's appended explanations of the Sower (Mt 13:19–23) and of the Cockle (Mt 13:36–43) reflect the experiences of the apostolic Church. The point of the Sower centers upon the harvest, a symbol of the eschatological judgment: the future judgment will reveal what is decided in the present (represented by the varying fortune of the seed). In the explanation of this parable, however, the original point is overshadowed by a psychological allegorization, which dwells upon the reception of the *logos* (the apostolic kerygma) by various classes of men. One type of hearer is characterized as *proskairos* (inconstant) (21), a term otherwise found only in the Pauline writings. Such a "lack of perseverance" or inconstancy can be judged only in relation to an organized community, a conception implied also in the reference to persecution (*thlipsis, diōgmos*) directed against it. Another type of listener is led to abandon the Christian faith by what is called the *merimna tou aiōnos* or the *apatē tou ploutou* (22). The classic example of this category may be seen in the story of Ananias and Sapphira (Acts 5:1–11). Accordingly, it appears to be not implausible that we are dealing here with applications of the Lord's teaching made by the apostolic Church as a result of her experiences in the early years after Jesus' death.

Matthew is the only evangelist who records the explanation of the Cockle. Here again, while the point of the parable, the eschatological judgment, indicated by the command, which contradicts normal Palestinian agricultural practice, to collect the cockle *first* (30), has been preserved in the explanation, still it appears that we are dealing with an allegorical application to the Church of the apostolic age. Jesus' habitual custom of addressing his message only to his fellow Jews during his lifetime has here been abandoned for the universal Gentile mission (38: *ho de agros estin ho kosmos*). Moreover, the good seed is construed as symbolizing the members of the Christian Church (38b: *hoi huioi tēs basileias*), here distinguished (43) from heaven (*basileia tou patros autōn*), a distinction reminiscent of the Pauline epistles.

The importance of recognizing that these explanations (which, in Matthew's Gospel, appear upon the lips of Jesus) are *in their present form* the creation of the apostolic Church, must not be lost sight of. They provide a most valuable piece of evidence that the primitive Christian community was already doing what the Church has, in every age, claimed the right to do, namely, render explicit the doctrinal implications of her Master's teaching.

The community discourse (Mt 18) prescribes the mutual rela-

tions of the Church's members, which are all governed by brotherly
love. The prophetic description of the fall of Jerusalem and the ruin
of the Temple (Mt 24–25) gives a preview of the ultimate liberation
of the Church from the Judaism in which she was born. This essential
autonomy of Christianity vis-à-vis the Mosaic code and cult, which
includes the Church's *visible* character, is depicted as a necessary
consequence of Jesus' exaltation through his Passion and Resurrection. A. Feuillet[42] has convincingly demonstrated that this discourse applies directly and *in toto* to the events of the year A.D. 70,
and hence only in a typical sense to the end of the world.

For Luke, Jesus is primarily the Savior. He, alone of the Synoptic
evangelists, gives Jesus the title *sōtēr* (savior) (Lk 2:11; cf. also
1:69.71.77; 19:9; 2:30; 3:6). The gospel is the message of mercy
and salvation which provides the God-given answer to the religious
aspirations of that Hellenistic world for which Luke writes. Jerusalem, the principal scene of man's salvation, is the focal point of the
third Gospel, which describes all the events of Jesus' life as orientated
toward the holy city. The Infancy Gospel and its narrative revolves
about Jerusalem and its Temple; and almost ten chapters of the
book are devoted to Jesus' last journey to the scene of his Passion
and Resurrection (Lk 9:51; 19:27). Once the disciples arrive there,
Luke insinuates, they "tarry in the city" (Lk 24:49) until the coming of the Holy Spirit.

John's Gospel is markedly different in spirit and style, as in the
episodes narrated, from the first three. John is absorbed in the contemplation of God's Son, the divine Word, or perfect expression of
the Father. The Logos becomes "flesh" in order to "interpret" to us
the God "no man has ever seen" (Jn 1:18). It is above all the
sacramental quality of Jesus' actions during his public life which
has impressed John. Christ speaks to man of the Father, not only
by what he says, but even more forcibly by the symbolic character
of his actions. His miracles are "signs" (*sēmeia*), which have a
supernatural significance for the eyes and ears of faith. They are
so many symbols of the Christian sacraments. Baptism, for example,
is symbolized by the cure of the blind man (Jn 9:1–41), who
washes in a pool bearing Christ's name, "the One sent" (Jn 9:7).

The author employs popular etymology for the place name Siloë (which actually means a conduit), in order to indicate that the pool, in which the man is cured of blindness (symbol of a lack of Christian faith), is a type of the baptismal font. The miracle of the multiplication of loaves (Jn 6:1–13) is narrated in such a way as to reveal its Eucharistic significance, as I have pointed out elsewhere.[43] In brief, John's message, directed as we have seen to those Christians who have believed without having seen Jesus upon earth, is that the glorified Christ, who lives on in the Church and in her sacraments, is the same Jesus of Nazareth, whose "signs" reveal to men the character of his unseen Father.

THE EVANGELISTS' USE OF THEIR SOURCES

An examination of the manner in which the evangelists have employed the data about Jesus furnished them by tradition will reveal their utter fidelity to the reality of the sacred history. At the same time, it will be seen that they employ considerable freedom in their expression of the meaning of *Heilsgeschichte*. Thus, while Matthew and Luke present Jesus' temptations in the desert as a rejection of the false messianic ideals, current in contemporary Judaism, Mark, who devotes but a single verse to the episode, portrays Jesus in this episode as the New Adam in the New Paradise. The Lukan account of Jesus' visit to Nazareth, which appears to be a synthesis of three visits, or of three distinct scenes, forms the solemn introduction to Jesus' public life in the third Gospel. Matthew in fact mentions two visits: one at the beginning of the public ministry (4:12–13), another later (13:54–58). In addition, Luke has, in his well-developed travel story of the last journey to Jerusalem (Lk 9:51–19:27), assembled together the bulk of those materials which his own independent research has unearthed.

Matthew has his own characteristic method of dealing with narratives. Since he is primarily interested in highlighting their religious meaning, he habitually compresses these episodes by eliminating such details as he considers insignificant. Matthew appears also to have abbreviated his descriptions of events, in order to leave room for the inclusion of the many logia of Jesus, with which he is principally concerned. At times, this Matthean brevity can lead to obscurity: to understand Mt 9:2b ("Jesus seeing their faith") one must read Mk 2:4; similarly, the incomprehensible "I repeat" of Mt 19:24 is clarified by Mk 10:23–24. Matthew will suppress secondary characters in an episode, when he considers the mention of them to be unnecessary. Thus, the centurion seeking a cure for his sick "boy" comes in person to make his request (Mt 8:5–13), which, according to Luke's version, was actually made through two groups of intermediaries (Mk 7:1–10). This same technique may be seen to operate in Matthew's story of the raising of Jairus' daughter (cf. Mt 9:18–24 with Mk 5:21–43). By having Jairus announce to Jesus that his daughter "has just died," Matthew can tell his story without introducing the messengers that appear in Mark, where they bring to Jairus (who had told Jesus his daughter "was dying") the news of the little girl's death. Matthew described the fig tree which Jesus cursed as withering up "instantaneously" (Mt 21:19), while the Markan version of this parabolic event is notably lengthier (Mk 11:12–14.20–25).

Occasionally, we see an evangelist create a new literary unit out of materials garnered from different traditions. In the first chapter of the fourth Gospel, for example, the author presents a series of testimonies given by Jesus' disciples, in which we can discern a Christological rather than a simple historical purpose. John wishes to provide, at the outset of his Gospel, a fairly complete record of the disciples' conception of their Master and his work; and he does this by means of seven titles given to Jesus (the Prophet, the Lamb of God, the Son of God, rabbi, the Anointed, King of Israel, Son of Man). A comparative study of the other Gospels will reveal that these titles were given at various times throughout the early or the risen life of Christ and that the realization of their significance was the result of a long evolution. At the same time, an examination of this chapter shows that John has recorded much valuable historical data, namely, that Peter, Andrew, John, Nathanael, and Philip, even Jesus himself, had originally been for some time followers of John the Baptist, or that the change of Simon's name to Peter occurred at quite an early stage of Jesus' public ministry (as Mk 3:10 and

Lk 6:14 also attest), and hence not as late as the event at Caesarea Philippi, where Mt 16:18 places it.

THE EVANGELISTS' USE OF
LITERARY FORMS

Each of the four Gospels, if they be considered as a whole, belongs to a special type of literature which took shape from the oral form of the apostolic preaching. The kerygma was a proclamation to non-believers of Jesus' work of universal redemption through his Passion and Resurrection, to which certain episodes and sayings from his public life were added. On the other hand, the written Gospel, as we have stated earlier, was intended for readers already possessed of the Christian faith, to provide them with a more profound understanding of the mysteries of the faith. Thus it may be classified as a particular genre of that religious history of which the encyclical *Divino afflante Spiritu* speaks. Like the preaching, however, it attempts to express that reality which surpasses the limits of our time-space world and its experiences. Indeed, it would be no exaggeration to say that the external historical events which the written Gospel records are subordinate to the infinitely more important, less easily perceptible fact that God has, in Jesus Christ, personally entered our human history. It should never be overlooked that the historical happenings which form the warp and woof of our Gospels are not introduced solely (or even primarily) for the sake of the "history" (in our modern sense) which they contain, but for their Christological signification. To assess fully the evangelical *genus litterarium* (literary genre), we must attend above all to the dialogue between the inspired author and his Christian reader, to that witnessing to Christ which, as Paul characterizes it, is "from faith to faith" (Rom 1:17). It is this which makes the Gospel "God's power unto salvation for every believer" (Rom 1:16). It is only when this fact is borne in mind that the historical character of the Gospels can be rightly evaluated.

Incorporated under this specific literary type, the Gospel form, which we have called salvation history, we can discern many other

literary forms whose study can aid us in grasping the meaning of
the Gospels' historical character. At this point it may not be in-
opportune to recall Pius XII's insistence upon the very wide variety
of historical literary forms found in the Bible, all of them perfectly
consonant with the divine dignity and veracity. To decide how God
should (or should not) have transmitted his revelation to us, without first putting ourselves to school to his inspired writers, is scarcely
a reverent (or intelligent) approach to the scriptural Word. No
sincere Christian should feel called upon to apologize for the divine
choice of certain media of God's self-revelation.

Let me put this another way. The problem posed by the presence
of certain literary forms in the Gospels is in no sense to be regarded
as one of reconciling the "history" with the Christology. Once we
grant the supreme truth of the Incarnation of the Son with all the
consequences for human history which that fact involves, then the
Christology *is* admittedly the history. Oscar Cullmann has remarked:
"The life of Jesus constitutes the point of departure for all christological thought in a twofold manner: in Jesus' own consciousness of
himself and in the concrete realization, which his person and his
work awakened in his disciples and in the people."[44]

Here we must also mention a question frequently put to the
Catholic critic, when he is discussing the literary form of certain
Gospel narratives, "Where do you stop?" If we accept that incarnational view of Sacred Scripture which has been proposed by *Divino
afflante Spiritu* ("just as the substantial Word of God became like to
men in all things, 'without sin,' so the words of God, expressed in
human language, became in all things like to human speech, except
error"),[45] then the answer to the question is clear enough. Just as
the Word became incarnate to reveal to men some understanding
of the unseen God, so the scriptural Word contained in the Bible
was intended, in the divine plan, to be understood by man's intelligence aided by faith. Accordingly, we "stop" when we have been
satisfied that we understand the words of the inspired writer, since
then we know we have grasped the divine message contained in a
particular biblical passage. In addition, we might draw attention
here once again to the false implication contained in such a question,

namely, that the attempt to understand the Bible by the use of literary criticism calls in question or destroys the historical character of the events recorded in the Bible.

Among the subordinate literary forms in the Gospel narratives, we might enumerate the genealogy, the eyewitness account, popular traditions, family reminiscences, externalized representatives of interior experiences, and finally, midrash. The biblical genealogy, it is to be noted, is an art form, and hence it is not to be confused with those family trees found appended to modern histories or biographies, which profess to trace all the ancestors of a given individual back through many generations. The biblical genealogy has some doctrinal significance: in the Old Testament and in the New, it is frequently put at the service of the messianic idea. Matthew's genealogy testifies that Jesus is an Abrahamid and also of the royal Davidic dynasty. Luke's purpose in employing an ascending genealogy underscores the universality of the Christian religion, by tracing Jesus' lineage back to Adam, "who was of God." This last phrase, whose signification is so clearly different from the other in the series, attests the divine filiation of Jesus.

It is perhaps Mark's Gospel which contains the greatest number of eyewitness accounts, since that evangelist is the faithful recorder of what Peter's observant eye had noted. Striking examples of the genre are to be found in Mk 1:23–27; 2:1–12; 3:9–11, etc.

The popular tradition is that type of story told, especially in the ancient Near East, among the people. By the nature of things, there are many more examples of this form to be found in the Old than in the New Testament. However, the two accounts of Judas' death (Mt 27:3–10; Acts 1:18–19), to which we have already referred, provide an instance of it. Possibly, the same genre is to be seen in the account of the strange happenings in Jerusalem after the death of Jesus (Mt 27:51–53). For those who boggle at the suggestion that God has condescended to use "the story" as vehicle of his revelation, we recommend John L. McKenzie's masterly discussion in *The Two-Edged Sword*.[46]

Certain elements in Matthew's and Luke's Infancy Gospels belong to the class designated as family reminiscences, as does also perhaps the strange story preserved in Mk 3:21–22.

There are certain scenes in the Gospels which may be best described as externalized descriptions of an inner experience. The account of Jesus' triple temptation (Mt 4:1–11; Lk 4:1–3, the latter is more subtly narrated), or of Joseph's dream (Mt 1:20–21) belongs in this category. Related to this genre are the sacred writers' attempts to describe some supernatural phenomenon which defies human expression. In Acts' description of Pentecost, there is the "sound *like that of* a violent wind blowing," or the "tongues *as if* of fire" (Acts 2:2–3). In the Lukan Passion, we find the statement, "his sweat became *as it were* clots of blood . . ." (Lk 22:44b).

The midrash is a literary form much cultivated in biblical literature, as well as in noninspired Jewish writings. Its distinctive character consists in supplementing with scriptural passages the description of some event about which usually little detailed information is available. The principle operative in this form of literature, particularly in biblical accounts, appears to be the continuity and consistency of God's actions throughout the course of sacred history. It is important to remember that at the base of any midrashic account there is always an historical nucleus, even though the nature and extent of the original happening may be difficult to determine. René Laurentin, in his interesting book, *Structure et Théologie de Luc I–II*,[47] discusses several instances of this type in the Lukan Infancy narrative.

With regard to the sayings and sermons of Jesus, there are undoubtedly certain logia which retain the very form and idiom of their author. These can often be determined quite accurately by a comparison of the varying forms in which a logion is represented in the evangelical tradition. The simplest and most obvious example, perhaps, is Mt 5:40 which contains the *ipsissima verba* of Jesus (cf. Lk 6:29b).

There are, however, discourses which the sacred writer himself has constructed from Jesus' utterances and sermons; and these can even be expressed (as frequently in the fourth Gospel) in the author's own style and terminology. There are parables which, in the course of oral tradition, have undergone a certain historicization. The Wedding Feast in Mt 22:1–14 exemplifies this. The detail in v. 7 is probably a reference to the destruction of Jerusalem under Titus in A.D. 70, which has borrowed from the actual occurrence. The Matthean epilogue concerning the guest without a wedding garment (vv. 11 ff.), intended as a warning to the Gentile Christians, probably reflects the changed complexion of the Church by the year 80, when the Greek edition of the first Gospel was written. Again, there are parables which appear, in the form in which we possess them, to have been allegorized. While it is a delicate question to determine how much or how little allegory was present in Jesus' own version of certain parables, it is not implausible that three Matthean parables (the Steward, Mt 24:45–51, the Virgins, Mt 52:1–13, and the Talents, Mt 25:14–30) reflect the ecclesiastical organization of the apostolic Church of the author's day, and represent respectively the hierarchical authorities, groups of consecrated women, and the body of the faithful.

At times, it is possible to discern liturgical texts which enshrine the pronouncement of Jesus dealing with the ritual or sacramental life of his future Church. An instance of this literary type may be seen in Mt 28:18–19 and Jn 9:35–38; Acts 8:34 ff. appear to reflect the prebaptismal instructions given in the early Church, as we have pointed out in an article, "Liturgical Influences on the Foundation of the Four Gospels."[48]

While this list of literary genres found in the Gospels is by no means exhaustive, it exemplifies sufficiently the great variety of types of literature which they contain. It should also serve to demonstrate the truth of the statement by Pius XII already referred to, that, prescinding from divine inspiration, the pre-eminence of the Israelites in historical writing lies in the *religious* character of the history they wrote. Indeed, it is this quality which so sharply distinguishes the literature of Israel from that of her neighbors and explains the remarkable way in which the sacred writers, at least in the Old Testament, were able to take over literary forms and even myths from their pagan contemporaries and transform them into suitable media for the expression of divine revelation. With regard to the evangelists, it is clear that while they were concerned with the historical and employed eyewitness accounts where these were available, they were always engaged upon their predominating purpose, the recording of the Good News of Jesus Christ, which is the supreme example of salvation history.

CONCLUSION

In closing this essay, I should like to refer to an episode in the fourth Gospel which, I believe, illustrates in a very striking way the conception of salvation history which we have been discussing in these pages. I have in mind the scene in which a baffled Sanhedrin is resolving to put Jesus effectively out of the way. "If we permit him to go on this way, everybody will find faith in him. Besides, the Romans will intervene and do away with both the Temple and the Nation" (Jn 11:48). To them in their quandary, Caiaphas, "as high priest of that year" (of the accomplishment of man's redemption), addresses an inspired pronouncement: "You have completely mis-understood the case. You do not realize that it is better that one man die for the People, and that the whole Nation should not perish" (Jn 11:50). This remark is designated as "prophecy" by the sacred author. The term is not used in the sense of a mere predic-tion of Jesus' approaching death, which the supreme council of Judaism was at that very moment discussing. Rather, it is meant in the sense of an utterance which voices the divine verdict about the saving nature of that death. In John's view, Caiaphas here has be-come God's official spokesman. Accordingly, the high priest gives expression (whether unwittingly or not, John does not tell us) to the *propter nos et propter nostram salutem,* (for us and for our salvation), which is the principal preoccupation of the evangelist himself.

John's reflections upon the true significance of Caiaphas' words are germane to our study, since they imply not only his own awareness as an inspired writer of the nature of salvation history, but also a con-viction that, to deliver such a statement, a special divine charism was at work. John immediately adds: "He did not say this on his own. But, as high priest of that year, he prophesied that Jesus was destined to die for the Nation—indeed, not only for the Nation, but that he might reunite God's dispersed children" (Jn 11:51–52).

NOTES

This article is a slightly revised version of "The Conception of Our Gospels as Salvation-History," which appeared in *Theological Studies,* Vol. 20 (1959), pp. 561–589. It is reprinted here with permission of the editor, to whom we are indebted as we are to Fr. Stanley for his revisions.

1. Among recent studies on these subjects the following are noteworthy: P. Synaeve, P. Benoit, *La prophétie* (*Somme théologique,* ed. Revue des Jeunes; Paris, 1947); P. Benoit, "L'Inspiration," in Robert-Tricot, *Initiation Biblique* (3rd ed., Paris, 1954), pp. 6–45; P. Benoit, "Note complémentaire sur l'inspiration," *Revue Biblique,* Vol. 63 (1956), pp. 416–422; Karl Rahner, "Über die Schriftinspiration," *Zeitschrift für katholische Theologie,* Vol. 78 (1956), pp. 137–168; J. Coppens, "L'Inspiration et l'inerrance biblique," *Ephemerides theologicae Lovanienses,* Vol. 33 (1957), pp. 36–57; Johannes Schildenberger, *Vom Geheimnis des Gotteswortes: Einführung in das Verständnis der heiligen Schrift* (Heidelberg, 1950); R. A. F. MacKenzie, "Some Problems in the Field of Inspiration," *Catholic Biblical Quarterly,* Vol. 20 (1958), pp. 1–8.

I have attempted to review and evaluate the more significant contributions in a recent paper, "The Concept of Biblical Inspiration," *Catholic Theological Society of America: Proceedings of the Thirteenth Annual Convention (1958)* (New York, 1959), pp. 65–89. Other studies which treat biblical questions are: Charles Hauret, *Origines de l'univers et de l'homme d'après la Bible,* 2nd ed. (Paris: J. Gabalda, 1950); R. A. F. MacKenzie, "Before Abraham was . . . ," *Catholic Biblical Quarterly,* Vol. 15 (1953), pp. 131–140; Bruce Vawter, *A Path Through Genesis* (New York: Sheed and Ward, 1956); John L. McKenzie, *The Two-Edged Sword* (Milwaukee: Bruce, 1956); B. Rigaux, "L'historicité de Jésus devant l'exégèse récente," *Revue Biblique,* Vol. 65 (1958), pp. 481–522; Frederick L. Moriarty, *Introducing the Old Testament* (Milwaukee: Bruce, 1960).

2. John L. McKenzie, "Problems of Hermeneutics in Roman Catholic Exegesis," *Journal of Biblical Literature,* Vol. 77 (1958), pp. 197–204.

3. London, 1938: cf. his chapter, "The Historical Tradition in the New Testament," pp. 41–74.

4. *Scripture,* Vol. 8 (1956), pp. 2–12.

5. *La formation des évangiles* (Bruges: Desclée de Brouwer, 1957), p. 196.

6. *Biblica,* Vol. 39 (1958), p. 502.

7. *Theological Studies,* Vol. 14 (1953), p. 465.

8. McKenzie, "Problems of Hermeneutics . . . ," *op. cit.,* p. 200.

9. *The Two-Edged Sword,* p. 105.

10. *Acta Apostolicae Sedis,* Vol. 33 (1941), pp. 465–72.

11. "Problems of Hermeneutics . . . ," p. 198.

12. *Acta Apostolicae Sedis,* Vol. 35 (1943), p. 314. Hereafter, citations from

the encyclical *Divino afflante Spiritu* will be taken from the translation of
Canon G. D. Smith, published by the Catholic Truth Society, London, 1944.

13. *Acta Apostolicae Sedis,* Vol. 35 (1943), p. 319.

14. *Ibid.,* p. 314.

15. *Acta Apostolicae Sedis,* Vol. 42 (1950), p. 569.

16. *Ibid.,* p. 570.

17. G. Lambert, "L'encyclique 'Humani Generis' et l'écriture sainte,"
Nouvelle Revue Théologique, Vol. 73 (1951), p. 226.

18. *Acta Apostolicae Sedis,* Vol. 35 (1943), p. 314.

19. *Ibid.*

20. London: Dacre Press, 1953.

21. *Bible et Vie Chrétienne,* Vol. 18 (1957), pp. 7–26.

22. *Acta Apostolicae Sedis,* Vol. 35 (1943), p. 315.

23. *Ibid.*

24. *Ibid.*

25. *Ibid.,* p. 316.

26. "Problems of Hermeneutics ... ," p. 198.

27. Cf. "De glossolalia Pentecostes eiusque significatione," *Verbum Domini,*
Vol. 24 (1944), pp. 65–75.

28. *Acta Apostolicae Sedis,* Vol. 35 (1943), p. 319.

29. One recent and striking instance is the interpretation of Mt 1:18–22 by
Xavier Léon-Dufour, "L'Annonce à Joseph," *Mélanges bibliques rédigés en
l'honneur de André Robert* (Paris: Bloud & Gay, 1957), pp. 390–397; or the
brilliantly simple solution of the Matthean divorce logia by Alberto Vaccari,
"La clausola sul divorzio in Matteo 5, 32:19, 9," *Revista Biblica,* Vol. 3
(1955), pp. 97–119.

30. *Acta Apostolicae Sedis,* Vol. 35 (1943), p. 319.

31. *The Idea of History in the Ancient Near East* (New Haven-London,
1955), p. 172.

32. *The Two-Edged Sword,* p. 60.

33. *History and the Gospel,* pp. 26–27.

34. *Ibid.,* p. 36.

35. *The Two-Edged Sword,* p. 62.

36. *History and the Gospel,* p. 30.

37. To those who still need convincing that certain literary forms are
actually to be found in the Bible, we recommend Jean Levie, *La Bible:
parole humaine et message de Dieu* (Paris-Louvain: Desclée de Brouwer,
1958).

38. "Historicité des évangiles ... ," p. 211.

39. Oscar Cullmann, *Die Christologie des Neuen Testaments* (Tübingen:
J. C. B. Mohr, 1957), pp. 326–327.

40. Cf. the plan of this Gospel proposed by Willibald Michaux, "Cahier de
Bible: l'évangile selon Marc," *Bible et Vie Chrétienne,* Vol. 1 (1953), pp.
78–97.

41. On the meaning of this confession, cf. D. M. Stanley, "Balaam's Ass, or a Problem of New Testament Hermeneutics," *Catholic Biblical Quarterly*, Vol. 20 (1958), pp. 55–56.
42. "La synthèse eschatologique de Saint Matthieu (XXIV–XXV)," *Revue Biblique*, Vol. 56 (1949), pp. 340–364; Vol. 57 (1950), pp. 62–91, 180–211.
43. "The Bread of Life," *Worship*, Vol. 32 (1957–58), pp. 477–488.
44. Cullmann, *op. cit.*, p. 328.
45. *Acta Apostolicae Sedis*, Vol. 35 (1943), p. 316.
46. Cf. the chapter, "The Hebrew Story," pp. 60 ff.
47. Paris, 1957.
48. *Catholic Biblical Quarterly*, Vol. 21 (1959), pp. 24–38.

SELECTED READINGS

1. *La Bible de Jerusalem.* Paris: Éditions du Cerf, 1955. A one-volume edition in which the introductions and notes of the original fascicles are condensed. Many scholars consider this the best modern Catholic Bible translation.
2. *The Catholic Biblical Quarterly.* Organ of the Catholic Biblical Association of America, Cardinal Station, Washington 17, D.C.
3. Charlier, Célestin, O.S.B., *The Christian Approach to the Bible.* Westminster, Md.: Newman, 1957. 298 pp. An introduction for the nonspecialist reader.
4. Congar, Yves M. J., O.P., *Le Mystère du Temple.* Paris: Éditions du Cerf, 1958. 345 pp. A biblical study of the presence of God from Genesis to the Apocalypse.
5. Durrwell, F. X., C.S.S.R., *The Resurrection. A Biblical Study.* New York: Sheed and Ward, 1960. 371 pp. Combines complete respect for the individual genius of each sacred writer with contemplation of the Christian mystery as a whole.
6. McKenzie, John L., S.J., *The Two-Edged Sword. An Interpretation of the Old Testament.* Milwaukee: Bruce, 1955. 317 pp. Deals boldly and colorfully with the problems involved in understanding the Old Testament.
7. *New Testament Reading Guide.* Collegeville, Minn.: Liturgical Press, 1960. Fourteen pamphlets averaging a little under a hundred pages each. Introduction, text, and commentary.
8. *Pamphlet Bible Series.* New York: Paulist Press, 1960. This series began with the Old Testament and a new pamphlet will appear monthly until the whole Bible is completed. Introductory commentary and text.
9. *Pius XII, Biblical Studies,* trans. by Canon G. D. Smith of encyclical letter *Divino afflante Spiritu.* London: Catholic Truth Society, 1943. The Magna Charta of modern biblical studies.

10. Robert, A., and Feuillet, A., eds., *Introduction à la Bible*. Tome I. *Introduction générale, Ancien Testament*. 1959². 880 pp. Tome II. *Nouveau Testament*. 1959. 939 pp. Tournai: Desclée. Twenty-two leading French-speaking Catholic biblical scholars.

11. Robert A.; and Tricot, A., eds., *Guide to the Bible*, Vol. I (1960²). 812 pp. Vol. II (1955), 622 pp. Tournai: Desclée. A collection of studies by French scholars to help the reader understand the Bible.

12. Vawter, Bruce, *A Path Through Genesis*. New York: Sheed and Ward, 1956. 308 pp. A running commentary on Genesis which gives the results of modern scholarship in readable style.

13. Wheaton, Anthony, ed., *Son and Savior. The Divinity of Jesus in the Scriptures*. London: Geoffrey Chapman, 1960. 151 pp. Five studies by French Catholic biblical scholars.

14. Wikenhauser, Alfred, *New Testament Introduction*. New York: Herder and Herder, 1958. 580 pp. Translation of a standard German introduction; treats of the canon, the text, and each of the books of the New Testament.

PART THREE

The Church

INTRODUCTION:

THE PROTESTANT VIEW OF
THE CHURCH

THE discussion between Roman Catholicism and Reformation as regards the understanding of the Church has definitely entered a new stage. Since the time of the sixteenth century the usual accusation from the Roman Catholic side leveled against the Reformation has been that its ecclesiology is markedly spiritualistic. According to this Roman Catholic interpretation, the Reformation not only distinguished between the invisible, one, holy, Catholic Church of the creed and the visible Church of history and daily experience, but it actually went so far as to divorce them.

And, on the other hand, the traditional description which one most frequently met in circles of the Reformation was that in Roman Catholic ecclesiology the Church and her Lord Jesus Christ are so identified that the Church comes to be seen as the extension of the existence of the Son of God and thus as the continuation of the Incarnation.

Properly understood, this description of the Church as the extension of the Incarnation could well be acceptable to many Protestants; but the uneasiness over the phrase remains, as it has led to what is widely held among Protestants to be a Roman Catholic understanding of the Church as a self-sufficient divine entity. This makes the Roman Catholic ecclesiology pronouncedly institutionalistic: the Church becomes a self-contained structure whose only task in history is to actualize its built-in potentialities. Such a doctrine of the Church sharply divorces (not merely distinguishes between) the holiness of the teaching Church with its sacramental

149

priesthood and doctrinal infallibility, on the one hand, and the peccability of the listening Church, on the other hand.

Three new developments should be noted here which have necessarily affected the traditional presentation of the Protestant view of the Church.

(1) A searching self-analysis on the part of Protestants due to the charge of spiritualism has resulted in a more precise definition of the terms "invisible" and "visible" as applied to the Church. There can be little discussion regarding their validity to designate respectively the Church triumphant and the Church militant. But the rediscovery of the teaching of the Reformers led to a never-forgotten but renewed emphasis on the fact that the invisible Church of the elect of God is only to be found *in* the institutional visibility of the Church of time and space.

(2) The deep awareness of the essential unity of the Church in Christ, her only Head, appeared in and was stimulated by the establishment of the World Council of Churches in 1948. The disunity of the Church which had nourished an idealism of pluriformity and had enhanced too easy a distinction between the Church visible and invisible was unmasked as flagrant disobedience to the one Lord of the Church. This acknowledgment underlies the statement made by the Central Committee of the World Council at its 1950 meeting in Toronto: "The member Churches of the Council believe that conversation, cooperation and common witness of the Churches must be based on the common recognition that Christ is the divine Head of the Body." Growth toward corporate unity is not an apocalyptical dream: the acknowledgment of *essential* unity necessarily leads toward *existential* unity.

(3) In a self-contained organism there is no place for obedience to the Lord who stands above the Body of His faithful; in a self-contained organism there is only the causal sequence of development according to inherent divine laws and embryonic structures. In the tradition of the Reformation, however, a twofold obedience is stressed. The Church is in the first place understood not as the kingdom of God itself but as a function of the kingdom of God, as the realm whereby God continues to call on the world. This means that the Church has to understand itself as subordinated to the

kingdom and as standing in a *relation of obedience* to the God of creation. In the second place, the Church is placed in a *relation of service* to the world. The real purpose of God is not to save his *Church* but his *world;* the Church as God's instrument in reclaiming his creation in revolt has time and again to ask itself whether it has fallen for the temptation to make itself the *purpose* instead of the *means* of God's plans for the world.

The following article, written by a theologian who has left a unique mark on Reformation thought today, is a succinct and representative treatment of this theme of obedience and allegiance to the kingdom of God and the world of God. Professor Barth himself suggested this article for the present collection and stated that he still holds the position expressed in it is representative of his ecclesiology if the article is read in conjunction with *Church Dogmatics,* paragraphs 62, 67, and 72.

Karl Barth's first work, *The Epistle to the Romans* (1918), marked the beginning of a career which has taken him from a pastorate in Switzerland to professorships at the Universities of Göttingen, Münster, and Bonn. When he was driven out of Germany by the Nazis he returned to his native Switzerland and is today a professor at the University of Basel. Although he is the author of a number of important works, his multivolume *Church Dogmatics* is a landmark in contemporary Reformation thought.

6

THE CONCEPT OF THE CHURCH

KARL BARTH

WE must be quite clear in our minds and not deceive ourselves for a moment: our meeting here today signifies a very daring undertaking. I have shouldered only half of the responsibility by accepting this most kindly proffered invitation; and I admit I am glad of that.

Is it at all possible for Catholics and Protestants to enter into a theological conversation which concerns itself seriously with a *substantial* question, which concerns itself with a concept of Christian *dogmatics* and not merely with an historical or practical subject; which deals, moreover, with that concept which, as everyone with experience knows, tends to make its appearance as the boundary and limit whenever a halfway thorough attempt is made to further mutual understanding; a concept which is the boundary where *Sic et Non* (Yes and No) clash without any mitigation, where all mutual understanding comes to an end and where all understanding which has been apparently accomplished, again becomes questionable—the concept of the *Church?*

I would answer: *if* one should dare to enter into such a conversation (and Münster[1] suggests itself as the place where this venture, for once, might be essayed) and if it is to be meaningful, then it should concern itself with a serious question, i.e., with a question of dogmatics and precisely with this question which, if all signs do not mislead, is the very touchstone of spiritual division. This should be done even though at the very most the result of this conversation can be no other than that we come to agree why and in what respect as matters stand now we cannot come to an agreement. That is why what we undertake today is a daring venture, since even at best its

153

results can be no more than the one I have described. Yet I, for my part, would certainly count even this result as a gain.

In the sixteenth and seventeenth centuries Catholics and Protestants still looked each other in the eye, wrathfully to be sure, but they faced each other; and then they engaged in conversation, harshly and angrily, but they truly engaged in *conversation*. But we today, tired of the long quarrel, possibly also tired of Christian seriousness in these matters, rather look past each other and speak without making contact with one another on almost all points. Thus we oppose each other in an unfruitful manner (more precisely, we stand disengaged side by side) that is not worthy of the high mystery which, in any event, is at stake on both sides. I have accepted the invitation to come here to this meeting because I conceive of our being together as an attempt to take each other seriously.

Among those who are *ultimately* not one, who are not one in *Christ*—and indeed, here we are *not* one—taking each other seriously cannot mean: to meet urbanely, in a friendly fashion, to listen to each other quietly and attentively and to extend recognition to each other's position in various nonessential matters. Nor can it mean to grant each other a certain *bona fides* in the great and decisive main issue while at the same time we hold each other to be in error. Certainly we have the will to do all this. Nevertheless, taking each other seriously means: mutually to bear the whole burden of our opposition, both as a burden and as the burden of our being opposed to each other. (So often we dispense ourselves even from thinking of the fact that this burden is present.) It means to *see* the other over there, who also calls himself a Christian, but really to see him in his whole, horrifyingly different faith, in his uncanny turning away from that which for us is the most central and unshakeable Christian truth; while we at the same time make clear to ourselves that he, on his part, is just as horrified about us. It means: again to listen willingly to the great and painful enigma of the Church's division, the split which exists on a level where no separation should exist, where division is a *contradictio in adjecto,* so that we may leave here as better, more convinced, but probably also more thoughtful Catholics or Protestants yearning more than ever before for the peace in Christ that now is not given to us. Considering that we might in this sense

succeed in taking each other seriously, I can assume the responsibility for speaking here.

Perhaps nowhere is the cleavage of Western Christendom more
glaringly apparent than in the disagreement about this very concept of the Church. Neither side can seriously deny that it is truly
the *same object* on whose proper conception no agreement can be
reached. Nor can either side deny that this disagreement entails very
grave consequences. This is what makes the breach so serious. Matters do not stand thus that Catholics and Protestants mean totally
different realities when they speak of the Church. Of course, in part,
we do *also* see different realities. But the dissension engendered by
this difference becomes necessary and important only because each
side sees first and foremost the *same* reality so *very differently*. Perhaps we should even say that this dissension becomes necessary and
important because, in accordance with God's inscrutable council, the
same reality *looks at* each side in a wholly different manner. So great
is the difference that we cannot come to an understanding of the
Church's proper concept, that we are not one in Christ but divided,
that we cannot think of the Church without thinking of her disastrous
cleavage. Because we look at things so differently (*aliter*) we really
see partially different objects (*alia*). To the primary dissension concerning the *quale* (of what nature) is added, therefore, the dissension,
secondary in principle, concerning the *quantum* (in what measure):
e.g., about the ranking of the functions of the Church, whether she
is a sacramental or a preaching Church; about the relationship of
those invested with ecclesiastical powers to the remainder of the
membership; about the extent of ecclesiastical authority; about the
particular predicates belonging to the magisterial and jurisdictional
powers which the Bishop of Rome holds in respect to the entire
Church; and about other, similar questions. All these are burning
and decisive questions. But they are burning and decisive because
ultimately we contend about *something quite different*. To make clear
to you in what this altogether different reality consists I should like
to underscore emphatically that, in speaking of the Church, we see
as regards the substance the same reality—though we are not in
agreement. If we do not take this into account, then each side makes

the discussion much too easy for itself. Then we tend, by neglecting to listen to the most important things which our opponent *also* knows and *also* says, to picture him as if he worshipped before some strange idol. If we listened more attentively, we would have to say to ourselves that he adores the same God, but in such an incompatible and different manner that adoration in common does not occur. We must take into account that—despite all kindly and enlightened toleration —both sides deny the presence of the true Church on the other side. Hence there remain in force the bitter words: he is of a different faith. Permit me now, through a discussion of the most important determinations of the concept of the Church, to explain this statement (which in no way is ironically intended) that Catholics and Protestants see the same reality when they speak of the Church.

"*I believe in one holy, catholic, and apostolic church.*"[2] Thus the words of the common creed and confession. Let us inquire briefly into the meaning of these words.

1. "The word *ecclesia* (church) means 'a calling forth.' "[3] The Church is the calling together of God's people; of the people of the faith who have been created on the basis of the covenant through Christ between God and men and who have been awakened by the Holy Ghost. If on the Protestant side it is held that Catholicism understands by *evocatio* only the calling together as such, in other words the Church understood as an institute of salvation which functions through "magic," that is as erroneous as holding on the Catholic side that Protestantism does not understand the Church as a divine foundation but only as a corporation of the pious or of people who intend to be pious. Listen to these two definitions of the Church: a) What do you believe of the holy universal Christian Church? That from the beginning of the world to its end from the whole human race the Son of God collects, protects, and maintains for Him through His spirit and word in the oneness of the true faith a community of the elect for life eternal of which I am and remain forever, a living member; b) The Church is a *gathering together of believers, "that is, of those who have been called by faith to the light of truth and the knowledge of God, so that putting aside the darkness of ignorance and error, they may worship the true and living God in piety and holiness and serve him with their whole heart.*"[4] Who

would not admit that the first formula shows more the foundation character of the Church, while the second shows more the communal character of the Church? There Christ is the subject; here the *fideles* (believers) are the subject. But the first formula is taken from the Heidelberg Catechism, while the second is found in the *Roman Catechism*.[5] I mention this merely to point out that Protestantism also knows of the objective aspect in its conception of the Church and Catholicism too knows the subjective aspect in its conception. There is, therefore, little meaning in attacking each other on this point.

2. The Church is *one*. This is as certain as that there is only one God. She is the body of Christ on earth which can only be one. It is absurd to speak of several opposing churches. If such a situation actually exists, then one Church is the true Church and the others are false churches, nonchurches. In that case all we can do is recall the divine foundation of *the* Church and fall back on the fact that the members of the other church are in error *sine fraude* and belong ultimately to the one true Church—in somewhat the same way as Pope Pius IX asserted in dealing with Emperor Wilhelm I.

We must distinguish between the *ecclesia triumphans* (church triumphant) in heaven and the *ecclesia militans* (church militant) on earth, between the Church of the old covenant and the Church of the new covenant, between the visible and the invisible Church. But in none of these distinctions can the unity of the Church become doubtful. Protestantism emphasizes this distinction, as is well known. But it should not be overlooked on the opposing side that also according to Protestant doctrine the visible Church and the invisible Church are one and the same; that they are not two species of one genus, but two predicates of the same subject. The *coetus electorum* (group of the elect), the invisible Church made up of those who are not only called but chosen, is not a *civitas platonica* (Platonic commonwealth) somewhere above the visible Church but identical with the latter in its ambiguous state. Catholic dogmatics which emphasizes the visibility of the Church nevertheless recognizes that there obtains in reference to the Church something akin to the relationship of body and soul, where the latter can be perceived only in the spirit and "only to a degree."[6] The *Roman Catechism*[7] expressly teaches that in the Church the good and the wicked coexist without external mark of distinction, as the pure and the impure animals coexisted in Noah's Ark. Apparently here too there is provided a visually imperceptible delimitation of the Church within the Church; in which case—as we know—conditions might be such that even a pope may find himself standing on the left side.

Also as regards the unity of the Church, it must be noted that in respect to viewing the Church as a necessary instrument of salvation no substantial controversy seems to exist. Protestant dogmatics too professes belief in the famous words of the Fathers to which Catholic dogmatics habitually refers on this point. Some examples are: *"Where the Church is, there also is the Spirit of God, and where the Spirit of God is there is the Church."*[8] *"Outside the Church there is no salvation."*[9] *"I would not believe the Gospel unless the authority of the Catholic Church impelled me."*[10] According to Luther, the Church is ". . . the mother that begets and bears every Christian through the Word of God. The Holy Spirit reveals and preaches that Word, and by it he illumines and kindles hearts so that they grasp and accept it, cling to it, and persevere in it."[11] And Calvin holds that *discessio ab ecclesia* (to leave the Church) is no more, no less than *Dei et Christi abnegatio* (denial of God and Christ).[12]

3. The Church is *holy;* she is set apart from every other institution and community as the place and the instrument of divine revelation and atonement. In what respect is she *sancta* (holy)? Listen again to two definitions: a) She is holy *"among so many sinners . . . because she is joined to Christ the Lord as a body to its head;"*[13] b) *"because all of those whom God chose, he justifies and reforms in holiness and innocence of life so that his glory may shine for them."*[14] Who would not believe that in this instance the first objectively determining formula is Protestant, probably Calvinist, and that the second formula which emphatically underscores the sanctification of the members is Catholic. But in fact the first formula is found in the *Roman Catechism,*[15] while the second has Calvin as its author.[16] No doubt the Catholic can subscribe joyfully to the second formulation and the Protestant, with equal joy, can subscribe to the first.

In this context belongs the proposition, also held in common, that the Church in its entirety cannot err *in fundamenta fidei* (in basic matters of faith), that God's people as such cannot miss its goal, whatever might be said about individuals and particulars; in short, the proposition which enunciates the essential infallibility and perennial existence of the Church. There seems, moreover, to be a prevailing agreement that the Holiness of God must be clearly distinguished from the holiness of the Church. Hence not only Calvin[17] but also the *Roman Catechism*[18] emphasizes that in the creed we read *credo ecclesiam* (I believe the Church) and not *in ecclesiam* (in the Church) as we do in regard to the three Divine persons: "*so that also by this different way of speaking, God, the Creator of all things, may be distinguished from created things, and so that we may attribute to the divine Goodness all those wonderful favors which are bestowed on the Church.*"[19]

4. It also seems impossible that there should be basic disagreement concerning the predicate *catholicam* (catholic, universal) either when we understand thereby the absolute priority of the ecclesiastical community to the communities of race, of language, of culture, of state, of class; or when it is emphasized that the body united to its head is prior to its members. We also appear agreed that this predicate must be understood to express a spiritual quality and not a mechanical quantity. In other words, the divinely given title of the Church cannot be proven numerically, but only through the objective superiority of the truth.[20] Catholicity means virtual universality and not numerical majority. From the Catholic side this fact receives remarkable and valuable illumination from the fact that since the pope is not bound to the majority he can assent to the opinion of the *pars minor et sanior* (smaller and more sensible group)[21] when issuing the necessary certification of a conciliar decision.

5. Again both sides appear to have perceived and recognized in principle the mark of the *apostolicity* of the origin of the doctrine and of the succession of the Church. The Catholic must be aware that in addition to God's authority Protestantism knows also very well the authority of the Church, insofar as the latter is grounded and must continually return to its ground in the testimony of the apostles, which is normative both for the understanding and the preaching of divine revelation. The Protestant on the other side who at first glance, and quite understandably, thinks he perceives only a god-

like authority of the Church as such, must make it clear to himself that, according to Catholic doctrine, we are confronted here with the delegated relative power which Christ handed over to the apostles, or, more precisely, to *the* apostle Peter. Objectively considered, this position is identical with that which Protestantism understands as the authority of the written and of the preached word of the Bible. There is, therefore, no need to contend about the existence of an apostolic authority in the Church which, by the way, is documented in Matthew 16. In principle, therefore, no one need become upset by the well-known use of the *Tu es Petrus* (Thou art Peter) in the Basilica of St. Peter in Rome.

6. I mention as the last point: both sides appear to be in agreement that close attention must be paid to the word *credo,* with which the section of the creed we are discussing begins. This attention is necessary for comprehending that the Church, although visible in her existence and thus rationally intelligible, must be believed through the mystery on which her existence is based and through which she is maintained. She must be believed with all her characteristics by virtue of which she is not just *any* church but the Church of God. We appear also agreed that the word *credo* is requisite to understanding that, as the Church of God, she is visible and becomes visible only through grace. Once more I read, not in a Protestant work bearing witness to the Reformers' point of view, but in the *Roman Catechism*:[22]

Therefore, since this article [of the Creed] surpasses the capacity and power of our intelligence as fully as the other articles, we are altogether justified in acknowledging that it is not by human reason that we know the origin, the functions and the dignity of the Church, but we see all these things by the eyes of faith. . . . For it was not men who were the founders of this Church, but the immortal God himself. . . . And the power she received is not human but granted by God's gift. That is why, just as this cannot be accomplished by natural human powers, so also it is *by faith alone that we understand* that the keys of heaven are in the Church, and that the power of forgiving sin, of excommunicating, and of consecrating the true body of Christ have been committed to her.[23]

In view of this rather broad basis of apparent agreement, to which more could easily be added, one may marvel momentarily how it was possible, and is possible, that the Reformers of the sixteenth century, in the emphatic language of that time, unanimously rejected the Roman Church as the church of the anti-Christ; how it was, and is, possible that the Roman Church, regenerated at Trent, offered on her part nought but a monotonous anathema to the Church of the Reformation and that today, all on either side who are serious-minded, though with a heavy heart and in the more muted expressions of our day, must nevertheless ratify this attitude of their respective ancestors with an impartial Amen. But why? Indeed why? Because—and this must be said to all those good and well-meaning persons who might wish to step into the middle and exhort us to recognize this quite respectable common minimum and to get along with each other—because everything that we have mentioned, everything without exception, and much else besides which could be brought up is understood so differently by both sides; because the reality of the Church which undeniably is perceived in common is visible in so different a manner and viewed in so different a manner, that we disagree as to what she is. This entails immediately that we disagree on our attitude toward her and our position in her. Therefore, even with the best of wills on both sides, we cannot recognize ourselves as one flock under one shepherd, but we must leave it in the hand of God, whether and in what respect we might be such.

Where do our ways part? This is what we must discuss now. Our differences could be developed in detail, starting with any of the points mentioned earlier. The last-quoted sentences from the *Roman Catechism* offer the best means of transition. It is said there that in respect to the divine reality of the Church "it is *by Faith alone that we understand*" (*Fide solum intelligimus*). We can safely maintain that if we interpreted these words in the same sense, then there would be no division in the Church; then we would not need to prefix "Catholic" or "Protestant"[24] to the name of "Christian." Were we agreed on this point, we could then discuss all other things—and I do mean *all* other things—papacy and sacrament, dogma and ritual. If a Protestant conceives these three words in a Catholic sense, which in this case would be according to the sense of the

text, then he is at bottom a Catholic, even though he happens
to be a professor of Protestant theology. And if a Catholic understands these three words in a Protestant sense, then he has turned
Protestant in his heart no matter what the outward appearances. A
genuine Catholic and a genuine Protestant, however, cannot come to
agree on the meaning of these words. This is the final reason why they
cannot discuss other disputed points. They can only discuss why it
is impossible to discuss them.

I shall now try to develop briefly how we Protestants understand
those three words *fide solum intelligimus,* or rather how we would
understand the Church in the light of these three words if we knew
not where and by whom they were written.

We Protestants understand by *faith* man's acceptance and grasp
of God's grace, which itself is the effect of grace. Here grace is grace
and God's ineffable *favor* precisely to the extent that it is, and *remains, God's* grace both in respect to that which has been accepted
and also in respect to the acts of acceptance and comprehension;
where the reality of the Logos and the Spirit of God acquire power
over man so that he perceives grace sensibly (through Word and sacrament), knows it rationally and experiences it within his heart. But
in all this, and this is the decisive point, man never acquires the least
power of disposition over grace, as he has power of disposition over
other realities which he perceives, knows, and experiences. Man does
not receive this power of disposing over grace, because in grace man
has to do with the holy *God* who, even when he is graciously inclined
toward us, dwells in a light where none can come; because man is a
sinner whose community with God is not possible for a single moment or in any way except through God's action. Man's community
with God is without reciprocity and man is never in a position to lay
his hand upon God as God lays His hand upon *him*. In other words,
man's condition is such that at every moment, in every respect, he is
held by God and by God alone, and in no way at all by himself. Although his faith is a perceiving, a recognizing and an experiencing,
man cannot keep himself in community with God either by means of
his perception, or by means of his cognition, or by means of his experience. For God is God, but man is a creature and a sinful creature at that. How should he be able to maintain himself in com-

munity with God through his acts of perception, cognition, and experience? For man to be supported by his own self would be the
equivalent of sin without grace, of death without hope. That *God*
keeps him, that therein consists his redemption and salvation, that he
is maintained by God Himself, by God alone, this is what faith believes.

But this precisely is also the meaning of *credo ecclesiam* (I believe
the Church). The Church is the place and the means of God's grace.
It is there, in and through the Church, that the act of faith takes
place. For there speaks, and there is heard, the reality of the Logos
become flesh and of the holy Spirit of God. The Church, however,
shares, as place and means of grace, the characteristic that she has
power over us, while the reverse is not the case. We do not have the
Church as we have other things, but we have her as we have God—
that is, if, and insofar as, He has us. There is, of course, this decisive
difference that we deal here with a visible historical quantity which
becomes tangible in men and human thoughts, in human institutions
and enterprises, and which as such, as the earthly body of the
heavenly Lord, is the place and means of grace. How else could she
be the *place* and the *means,* the *accessible* place and the *usable*
means of grace? But this does not alter the fact that we have her only
as we have God; thus, that in her and through her the consoling message God has consigned to us, comes to us in a manner which on our
part does not give rise to a claim on God and on those matters reserved to Him and to Him alone. When anyone else addresses us, a
corresponding claim on our part may arise, a claim now to assert
effectively as our own what has been addressed to us. But when God
addresses us, *no* such claim arises. To have the Church, the *evocatio,*
the assignment of divine grace cannot mean that we are furnished a
claim; that in that visible historical and human place and means of
grace, there is given to us the instrument by which we could have the
power of disposing over grace and even could *secure* ourselves in respect to grace. If there were in the Church some other security than
that founded in God Himself, how could grace still be grace? Therefore, however dear grace be to us, we should not wish to have the
Church in any other way than as we have God, i.e., as beggers who
live from hand to mouth and not as rich, secure, and powerful peo-

ple. The Church is placed between Jesus Christ and the pardoned sinner. Jesus Christ and the pardoned sinner have in common that in both takes place God's entrance into time, into the twilight, into the relativity and ambiguity of history and of human life, into that hiddenness where he can be recognized only through the presence of his will and of the act of his love, and where there cannot be any direct and self-evident recognition of him.

This is the manner in which the Church too is divinely founded; *thus* is she the community of saints. It is an essential characteristic of grace to be objectively real in the Logos become flesh. Christ took His Cross upon Himself and was obedient unto death (and for this, for this God has raised Him up) and therewith the Church too is shown her position and character. It is an essential characteristic of grace to be subjectively real in pardoned sinners. The pardoned sinner cannot live anywhere else but under the judgment and the promise of God before whom he is dust, and Who alone can set matters right with him; and therewith the Church is told where she belongs and how she should stand before God. The Church who is placed between Jesus Christ and the pardoned sinner cannot stand under any other law than these two. The Church is the place and the means of grace in the *hiddenness* of God, in the lowliness of things human, or she is in no way the place and means of grace. Because of the fact of this hiddenness we must have her as we have God and in no other way. We do perceive her, we recognize her, we experience her. Yet we do not have her through our perception, through our recognition, through our experience. No, we have her because God has *us* in our perception, recognition, and experience of the Church, because he deals with us as the Lord, has elected *us* in this manner which is suited to us, and not because we have, and even in the most subtle way, elected Him. If we wanted to invert the relationship, what else would we retain of the Church than the lowliness of everything human which, at best, might be idealized and decked out but would not thereby vanish; the poor servant maid who, even most beautifully draped, would no longer be the handmaid of Christ, but just an ordinary maid like any other? Now for us to have in her the one handmaid and bride of Christ depends on our not making her into a grand lady and thus—for we ourselves are the Church—making ourselves into

lords. And note well, this means making ourselves lords in our relation to God. It is not permissible to invert this relation because we
want to have a Church without lowliness, with her lowliness covered
by a royal robe. Her glory can consist only in that she hears, in her
honestly admitted poverty, the word of the eternally rich God and
that she makes it heard. Her glory does not consist in acquiring control over His word as one acquires control over the things of this
earth. Nor does it consist in possessing His word as material or intellectual goods are customarily possessed. Nor can she count on it, as
if she owned anything which had not been given to her. Her glory
cannot, and may not, shine forth anywhere else than where the glory
of the Lord and where the glory of the pardoned sinner shines forth.
But the place where that occurs on earth is the *Cross*. Whatever
shines forth in some other place is some other glory, namely, the
glory of this world which passes away; the Church should not put
herself on this level.

This is the way in which the Church is the *one* Church. Yes, the
one Church beside whom there is no other. Her oneness, however, is
not at her disposal, but she herself is at the disposal of the one God,
and that in two ways. She is the one Church insofar as God has set
her apart and keeps her separate from every false church, but not so
as she herself is able to set herself apart in an inevitable, but also very
relative, manner from other structures which also call themselves
churches. She is the one Church insofar as it pleases God to make
visible in her and through her what He as the Lord of the Church
can make visible, but not insofar as she herself renders her invisible
reality visible. She is the one Church, not to the extent that she might
be able to prove through words and deeds that she is necessary for
salvation, but to the extent that in her and through her God Himself
gives the proof of spirit and power which honors not her but Him.

This is the way in which she is the *holy* Church. Her holiness is not
at her own disposal, but she herself is at the disposal of the holy God.
Her holiness does not consist in her constituting herself as a second
Christian world in opposition to the world. Indeed, she must constitute herself in the world, but in doing *that* she is not yet anything more
than the world. She is more than the world because she *has been* constituted, and *continuously* is constituted in the world, not by Canon

Law but by God's law. The act of her institution is never something past and gone, precisely because she is instituted by God. She is holy to the degree that she obeys, not to the degree that she commands. Her freedom from error does not arise because infallibility and perfection are attributes of the precepts she necessarily gives and which necessarily are conditioned by the human factor; but she is free of error to the degree that she bears witness and confirms through her precepts that she has heard the infallible word of God, to the degree that she, as Calvin has it, "*puts aside her own wisdom and allows herself to be taught by the Holy Spirit through the Word of God.*"[25] Insofar as she does not do this she is not a church at all. But to the extent that she does this she will always seek infallibility in what has been *said to her.* That which she can say herself and ought to say herself does not come from heaven, in contrast to what has been said to her, but is spoken on earth; it is not *the* dogma but *a* dogma; it has not divine authority but the specific ecclesiastical authority, which *by its own nature* is weighty and demands respect. This ecclesiastical authority is truly genuine authority because it is ready at every moment to submit to the higher authority which is really set over her. The Church is under obligation to will her *purity;* first and foremost the purity of her teaching. She must fight for this and, if it become necessary, suffer for it. But she cannot will to be holy. She can only *believe,* under the judgment and promise of God, that she is holy.

This is the way in which she is the *catholic* Church. Again it must be said: her catholicity is not at her disposal, but she herself is at the disposal of the eternal, omnipresent God. She will, therefore, not boast about her centuries and millennia—the idolatrous church of ancient Egypt for instance could have done so with much greater justification. Nor will she insist on the territorial extent she might perhaps have in common with the Roman or the British Empire. What would that have to do with her real catholicity, which is a spiritual and qualitative thing? Where two or three among you are gathered together in *my* name, there I am in their midst. I! This establishes, maintains, and preserves the catholicity of the Church. Without this she *is* not a church at all. But this also is the content of a promise which can only *become* true, for which one can only pray, which no one on earth can *make* true, whatever the means and guar-

antees used. Once more faith is demanded. The great truth of the
catholicity of the Church also requires faith.

This is the way in which the Church is also *apostolic*. She has that
quality by *serving* the Logos and the Spirit of God in accordance with
the testimony and the model of the apostles. For this were the
apostles chosen; for this Peter was chosen among the apostles; and
for this were all his genuine successors chosen. How else could the
Church prove and enact the apostolicity of the origin of her doctrine
and of her succession, if not through the *ministerium verbi divini*
(ministry of the Word of God) in which these men are our models
and predecessors? Assuredly, she exercises by this *ministerium* a
power, the *potestas ecclesiastica* (churchly power), the power to bind
and to loose, beside which all other powers are stunted and meager.
But if she, as apostolic Church, exercises such power, then it is a
power which she, by virtue of the apostolicity of her origin, of her
doctrine and of her succession, knows is not in *her* hand. On the contrary, while she binds and looses on earth she knows that this power
is wholly in the hand of Him who alone can forgive sin and who alone
can make man accountable for sin.

This is the meaning of *credo unam sanctam catholicam et apostolicam ecclesiam*. I believe the Church as the place where God is
honored and where, therefore, divine honors are rejected. For these
reasons and in this manner I believe the Church as a means of grace. I
believe the Church as the divine foundation by virtue of which there
shall not be a palace but rather a hovel of God among men until the
end of the world. I believe the Church as the community of saints;
that is, of sinners set apart and called by God, who, even as a *community* of saints, even as preachers and hearers of the divine word,
even as God's people—and particularly as that—wish to live by
God's mercy (and do not consider this too little!) until the beginning
of the realm of glory. There everything that passes away, even the
transitory character of this community, the earthly body of the
heavenly Lord, will put on permanence, where, also in this respect,
what has been sown in weakness shall rise up in strength.

This is the way in which *we* understand the *fide solum intelligimus*
as it refers to the Church. I do not wish to develop that all this is, and
in what way it is, a sharp antithesis to Roman Catholic doctrine. You

will have perceived, without effort, the boundary and limit of which I
spoke in the beginning and you will have heard the protest of Protestantism. The authors of the *Roman Catechism* presumably understood these three words somewhat differently. How? It may be left
to our discussion to bring that into the light of day.

Translated by U. Allers

NOTES

A translation of "Der Begriff der Kirche," which appeared in *Zwischen
den Zeiten,* Vol. 5 (1927), pp. 365–378. A lecture given to the University
Group of the [Catholic] Center Party in Münster i. W., July 11, 1927. It is
reprinted and translated here with the gracious permission of Professor
Barth and of the Christian Kaiser Verlag, Munich.

1. The treaties of Münster and Osnabrück in 1648, commonly known as the
Peace of Westphalia, marked the end of the religious wars in Germany and
Holland. [Ed. note.]
2. "Credo unam sanctam catholicam et apostolicam ecclesiam."
3. *Catechismus Romanus,* Part I, Chapter 10, Number 2. ["Significat ecclesia evocationem."]
4. "Congregatio fidelium qui scilicet ad lucem veritatis et Dei notitiam per
fidem vocat sunt, ut, rejectis ignorantiae et errorum tenebris, Deum verum
et vivum pie et sancte colant illique ex toto corde inserviant."
5. *Ibid.* [*Catechismus Romanus.*]
6. Bernhard Bartmann, *Lehrbuch der Dogmatik,* Vol. II, pp. 189 f.
7. *Catechismus Romanus,* Part I, Chapter 10, Nos. 6 and 7.
8. "Ubi ecclesia ibi et spiritus Dei et ubi spiritus Dei illic ecclesia."
9. "Extra ecclesiam nulla salus."
10. "Ego evangelio non crederem nisi ecclesiae catholicae commoveret auc-
toritas."
11. *The Large Catechism* (1529), Part II, Article 3. English translation
cited from *The Book of Concord,* trans. and ed. by Theodore G. Tappert
(Philadelphia; Muhlenberg Press, 1959), p. 416.
12. *Institutio Christianae Religionis* (1959), Book IV, Chapter 1, Number
10. [English trans., *Institutes of the Christian Religion* (Philadelphia: Westminster Press, 1936), Vol. II, pp. 282–283.]
13. "Inter tot peccatores . . . quod, veluti corpus cum capite, Christo Domino
conjungitur."

14. "Quia quoscunque elegit Deus eos justificat reformatque in sanctitatem ac vitae innocentiam quo in illis reluceat sua gloria."
15. *Catechismus Romanus,* Part I, Chapter 10, Number 12.
16. *Catechismus Genevensis,* ed. by K. Müller, p. 125.
17. *Institutio Christianae Religionis,* Book IV, Chapter 1, Number 2. [English trans., *Institutes, op. cit.,* Vol. II, pp. 270 ff.]
18. *Catechismus Romanus,* Part I, Chapter 10, Number 19.
19. "Ut hac etiam diversa loquendi ratione, Deus omnium effector a creatis rebus distinguatur, praeclaraque illa omnia, quae in ecclesiam collata sunt, beneficia divinae bonitati accepta referamus."
20. Bernhard Bartmann, *Lehrbuch der Dogmatik,* Vol. II, p. 199.
21. *Ibid.,* p. 161.
22. *Catechismus Romanus,* Part I, Chapter 10, Nos. 17 and 18.
23. "Cum igitur hic articulus, non minus quam ceteri, intelligentiae nostrae facultatem et vires superet, jure optimo confitemur, nos ecclesiae ortum, munera et dignitatem non humana ratione cognoscere sed fidei oculis intueri. . . . Neque enim homines huius ecclesiae auctores fuerunt sed Deus ipse immortalis, . . . Nec potestas quam accepit, humana est, sed divino munere tributa. Quare, quemadmodum naturae viribus comparari non potest, ita etiam fide solum intelligimus in ecclesia claves caelorum esse eique potestatem peccata remittendi, excommunicandi, verumque Christi corpus consecrandi traditam." *Ibid.*
24. The word Barth uses is "Evangelical," which is used in Germany much as the word "Protestant" is used in this country. [Ed. note.]
25. *Institutio Christianae Religionis,* Part IV, Chapter 8, Number 13. "Abdicato omni sua sapientia a spiritu sancto doceri se per verbum Dei patitur." [English trans., *Institutes., op. cit.,* Vol. II, pp. 429 ff.]

SELECTED READINGS

1. Barth, Karl, *Church Dogmatics,* Vol. II, Pt. 2, trans. by G. W. Bromiley, *et al.* Edinburgh: T. and T. Clark, 1957, "The Election of the Community," pp. 195–308; "The Real Church," *Scottish Journal of Theology,* Vol. 3 (December 1950), pp. 337–351. The Dogmatics selection is an original discussion of Israel and the Church in the context of the doctrine of election; the article is a lecture given on Barth's trip to Hungary in the spring of 1948.
2. Barth, Karl, and Hamel, Johannes, *How to Serve God in a Marxist Land.* New York: Association Press, New York, 1959. Contains the full text of Barth's controversial letter to a pastor in East Germany, and the response and article by the East Zone Pastor Hamel.
3. Bonhoeffer, Dietrich, *Sanctorum Communio.* Munich: Chr. Kaiser Verlag, 1954. *Ethics,* ed. by Eberhard Bethge, trans. by Neville Horton Smith. New

York: Macmillan Co., 1955, pp. 297–325. The first selection is a study of the Church in its theological and sociological dimensions; the second is a reflection on the relation of the Church and the State during Bonhoeffer's final internment before his execution by the Nazis.

4. Dillistone, F. W., *The Structure of the Divine Society*. Philadelphia: Westminster Press, 1951.

5. Hromadka, Joseph Lukl, "Church of the Reformation Faces Today's Challenges," *Theology Today*, Vol. 6 (January 1950), pp. 446–464. Interesting mainly because written by a representative of those theologians who have tried to express their political loyalty to a Communist regime and yet not to sacrifice the Church's specific witness.

6. Jenkins, D. T., "Christology, the Holy Spirit and the Ecumenical Movement," in *Essays in Christology for Karl Barth*, ed. by T. H. L. Parker (London: Lutterworth Press, 1956), pp. 229–241.

7. Mehl, Roger, *Du catholicisme romain: approche et interpretation* (Cahiers Théoligiques No. 40). Neuchâtel: Delachaux & Nistlé, 1957.

8. Newbigen, Lesslie, *The Household of God*. New York: Friendship Press, 1954. A bishop of the Church of South India brings the theological, exegetical, missionary experience of the Church of South India (a union of Anglicans, Presbyterians, Congregationalists, Methodists) to bear on the question of the nature of the Church itself.

9. Niebuhr, H. Richard, *The Purpose of the Church and Its Ministry*. New York: Harper and Bros., 1956. Study on the aims of theological education, with the collaboration of D. D. Williams and J. M. Gustafson.

10. Nygren, Anders, *Christ and His Church*, trans. by Alan Carlsten. Philadelphia: Westminster Press, 1956. An attempt to bring ecclesiology into line with, and have it delineated by, Christology as the latter stands in present investigation.

11. Robinson, J. A. T., *The Body: A Study in Pauline Theology*, Studies in Biblical Theology, No. 5. Naperville, Ill.: Alec R. Allenson, (copyright, S.C.M. Press). An Anglican scholar figures that the concept of body forms the keystone of Paul's theology and has profound relevance for the modern problem of mass man.

12. Tomkins, Oliver S., *The Wholeness of the Church*. London: S.C.M. Press, 1949.

13. Torrance, Thomas F., *The Royal Priesthood, Scottish Journal of Theology* Occasional Papers No. 3. Edinburgh: Oliver and Boyd Ltd., 1955. Written for the discussions initiated by World Conference on Faith and Order, held at Lund in 1952, this paper attempts to apply the concept of the corporate episcopacy to the Church of England and Church of Scotland talks on reunion.

14. *The Universal Church in God's Design*, Vol. I of the World Council of Churches' Amsterdam Assembly Series on Man's Disorder and God's Design. New York: Harper and Bros., 1948. Articles on this topic by G. Aulen, K.

Barth, P. Craig, P. D. Devanandan, H. R. Niebuhr, E. Schlink, K. E. Skysgaard, and others.

15. Visser 't Hooft, W. A., *The Renewal of the Church*. London: S. C. M. Press, 1955. The General Secretary of the World Council of Churches examines the ecumenical movement in its historical context as one of the great new facts of our times.

INTRODUCTION:

THE ROMAN CATHOLIC VIEW OF THE CHURCH

OVER thirty years ago Otto Dibelius predicted that this would be the century of the Church, and history has surely proved him right both about the life of the Church and about the reflection on that life which we call ecclesiology.

The simplest way to characterize this renewed vitality as it shows itself in Catholic ecclesiology is to say that it has been moving beyond the limited boundaries of post-Tridentine theology of the Church, following the lead already set in the last century by pioneers like Möhler and Newman.

Theologians had put together the treatise on the Church, Congar observes, as the Jews built the Temple after the Exile—sword in hand. But now they have put aside the sword and the result has been a whole new set of emphases. There has been more stress on the interior aspects of the Church, more stress on the role of the laity, and a deeper ecumenical concern. There has been a move away from *ad hoc* defensive argumentation and a return to primary theological sources: the Scriptures and the Fathers of the Church.

Even before the sixteenth century, the tendencies of the "spirituals" had led Catholic theologians to put heavy emphasis on the exterior aspects of the Church, and the stand taken by the Reformers and later by the Jansenists intensified and prolonged this emphasis. But recent Catholic work tries to restore the proper balance by renewed emphasis on the interior life of the Church.

The attitude of an earlier generation of Catholics toward the role of the layman in the Church is illustrated by a story Cardinal Gasquet told quite a number of years ago. A priest had been asked what was the position of the layman in the Catholic Church. "The layman has two positions," answered the priest. "He kneels before the altar, and that is one. And he sits below the pulpit; that is the other." The Cardinal added that there was a third the priest had forgotten. The layman also puts his hand into his pocketbook. Now none of these positions is ever likely to become outmoded, but laymen are now becoming steadily more active in the Church, in liturgical participation, in apostolic movements, in the work of education, in the Catholic press. Furthermore, this increased activity of the layman in the Church has stimulated theological reflection on the role of the layman in the Church and this reflection has had a healthy effect on the theologian's total view of the Church.

Another trend in Catholic ecclesiology is its growing ecumenical concern. Catholic theologians seriously study the work of their Protestant colleagues. They show a growing sympathy for the work of the World Council of Churches, and the establishment of the Secretariat for Promoting Christian Unity has provided a permanent channel of communication which augurs well for the future. Furthermore, there is solid ground for hope that the developments which are taking place in Catholic ecclesiology will make it more suited to dialogue with other Christian theologians.

Nothing fosters this hope more than the new way in which Catholic ecclesiologists study the Scriptures and the Fathers of the Church, not as arsenals for proofs, but as sources for understanding the mystery of the Church. Undoubtedly much remains to be done, but such studies seem eminently well-suited to the methodology which the study of the Church demands.

The Church is a living organism of great complexity; perhaps no object of theological reflection has more numerous and varied aspects. She is both visible and invisible. She unites present reality and eschatological hope. She is both human and divine, active and contemplative, collective and individual. She is eminently personal, yet transcends individual persons. She is united in love yet ruled by laws. Nevertheless, all of these aspects make up one living organism.

No theologian has yet worked out a methodology adequate to this complex reality, but surely biblical and patristic studies of the kind which are appearing foster the kind of method which is needed: a method in which the concrete, existential, historical reality of the Church in all its dynamic vitality will not be allowed to escape.

The following article by Father Weigel was originally given as the first of the three 1960 Taylor lectures at the Yale University Divinity School. He is the first Catholic priest to fill an endowed lectureship there.

The article is of special interest because it comes from the best-known Catholic ecclesiologist in this country. Since 1948 Father Weigel has been Professor of Ecclesiology at Woodstock College in Maryland, the oldest Jesuit theological seminary in the United States. Before coming to Woodstock he had spent eleven years in Chile, where he was dean of the Faculty of Theology of the Catholic University of Chile at Santiago. Father Weigel has said that his three principal concerns are ecumenism, the need of serious scholarship in American Catholic colleges and universities, and Latin America. He lectures widely and writes many articles on these themes. He is the author, among other books, of *A Catholic Primer on the Ecumenical Movement* and *Faith and Understanding in America.*

7

CATHOLIC ECCLESIOLOGY IN OUR TIME

GUSTAVE WEIGEL, S.J.

IN this treatment of Catholic ecclesiology it will become evident to all that certain concerns and positions in Catholic theology can also be found in its Protestant counterpart. This is not strange. At a given moment, there is a prevailing wind which affects all the people in a given area. Under the pressure of this wind, all will react to it. Different people will react differently, but all the reactions will be functions of the same force working on all.

Because ecclesiology is my own specialization, I might by prejudice think that it is the most vital branch of Catholic theology. I do think so, but I do not think that it is mere prejudice which has led me to this position. At any rate, ecclesiological meditation is conspicuous in our time and we must deal with it.

The Church has been with us since the days of the apostles. Much is said of her in the New Testament, and yet nowhere in Scripture is she defined. Nor did the Councils of the Church nor yet any pope supply us with such a definition.

Many of the Fathers of the Church speak of the Church in connection with some other theme. Clement of Rome, Ignatius of Antioch, Polycarp, Irenaeus of Lyons, John Chrysostom, Leo the Great, and John of Damascus supply us with many ecclesiological insights, though they did not do so systematically nor by way of a formal treatise. Augustine must be mentioned in particular because he has so much to tell us about the idea of the Church in spite of the fact that he never prepared a systematic ecclesiology. There were indeed formal treatises on the Church in the early Fathers. Cyprian, Optatus,

177

and Pacian wrote such ecclesiological tractates, but they did not try
to give an ecclesiological synthesis. In a word, the Fathers give us
much material for ecclesiological investigation, but they do not give
us a formal ecclesiology.

In the early stages of the Middle Ages theoretical ecclesiology was
not done. Instead, there was much canon law being written. Here
is another instance where data, but only data, are given to the
ecclesiologist. Even in the thirteenth century, the bloom time of the
Middle Ages, the great masters who gave us the classical divisions of
theology did not include a treatise on the Church. St. Thomas in his
Summa theologica deals with the Church briefly in terms of the Mystical Body of Christ as an appendage to his Christology. Many ecclesiological ideas are present in his treatment of the sacraments, but
there is no ecclesiological treatise as such. The same may be said for
the other great Scholastics of the thirteenth century. The reasons for
these oversights are not evident to us, but certainly Peter Lombard's
Book of the Sentences in the twelfth century was used as a basic
guide by all, and the Lombard does not propose a formal ecclesiology.

The fourteenth century was a period of strife between the princes
and the popes. In this period Juan de Torquemada, O.P., wrote his
Summa de ecclesia. This sounds like a systematic ecclesiology, but it
really was not. He was defending the primatial rights of the pope over
Christendom. There was much ecclesiological writing in this century, but it was primarily pointed to the place of the bishop of Rome
in the unwritten constitution of the *res publica christiana*.

It was in the sixteenth century that ecclesiology as a formal theological treatise was born. It was a consequent of the Protestant Reform. But the tractates on the Church all suffer from one common
defect. Catholics and Protestants were engaged in bitter polemics. It
was the time of controversial theology, in many ways fruitful but
essentially quarrelsome. By the time of the nineteenth century
Protestantism was not too concerned with the notion of the Church,
and ecclesiological work was not too prominent. In Catholic circles
ecclesiology had become a fixed part of the total theological *cursus,*
but it was considered as an essay in apologetics. The quarrel with
the Protestants was still manifest, but new adversaries had arisen.
Rationalism plagued the eighteenth century and liberal historicism

haunted the nineteenth. The work of the Catholic ecclesiologists slowly came to a point which manifested itself in the ecclesiological doctrine of the First Vatican Council. But nowhere was there a consideration of the total reality of the Church. Phases of its nature and being were examined, but a total picture was not essayed.

It was after the first World War that ecclesiology became more holistic and more vital. On the Catholic side the man who brought this out into the open was Professor Karl Adam of Tübingen. His *Wesen des Katholizismus* (1924), badly turned as *The Spirit of Catholicism* in its English translation, was a point of departure for modern Catholic ecclesiology. This book was a reaction to the Protestant Friederich Heiler's analysis of Catholic theory.

Adam used the Pauline symbol of the Church as the body of Christ as the guiding thread of his systematic outline. This was an innovation in Catholic academic ecclesiology. All through the nineteenth century the key concept was the Church as the kingdom of God. Nor was this idea used according to its scriptural meaning but rather after the fashion of Bellarmine's thought in the sixteenth century. Kingdom in Bellarmine's treatise was employed as a sovereign society as manifested in the Kingdom of France or the Republic of Venice.

It is interesting to see the reaction of the Catholic theological brotherhood to the work of Adam. At first it was well received, but not as a theology. It was considered as an essay in homiletic piety. Adam had not used the severe logical schematization then in use in the schools. In consequence, anything not so structured was not considered theology. For the same reason Cardinal Newman's work was not taken too seriously in theological circles.

However, in the twenties Adam's work inspired many to see in it a strict theology and they used it as such. The result was opposition from the theologians because it was an unintentional criticism of their work. They resented the introduction of the concept of the Mystical Body as the matrix for the ecclesiological treatise. They considered it quite in place in the pulpit or in spiritual reading, but it should not intrude into the theological enterprise. But much work was being done along the lines suggested by Karl Adam, and the result was a war between those who used the kingdom of God concept as central and those who replaced it with the notion of the *sōma tou Christou.* In 1943, during the second World War, Pius XII published his encyclical *Mystici corporis,* which was the outline of an ecclesiology based on the symbol of the body of Christ. After that moment there could be no opposition to the newer essays in ecclesiology.

Yet it would have been too hard for the older theologians to reconstruct their treatises completely. Some continued their old efforts and added a supplement on the Church as the Mystical Body. This, however, was hardly an organic vision. Outlines for the newer ecclesiology were being offered in Europe by many theologians, but even to this moment there is no set ecclesiology in Catholic circles. To use the words of Koster, a Dutch Dominican theologian, ecclesiology is in the making.

But there are certain common trends which can be detected in the many ecclesiological essays appearing in the journals. Little theological centers will still be following the manuals which were distinctive of the theology of the first years of this century. But the livelier centers have dropped that approach and are working in a newer style.

Concerning this newer style one can say something. The interest now is biblical and patristic. Ecclesiology itself is not polemical. There is a general recognition that the Church is a mystery. We can profitably explain these three outlooks.

With the revival of a biblical concern on the part of the theologians, the Scriptures, especially the New Testament, were carefully scrutinized by the divines. The use of Scripture is nothing new in Catholic theology. In fact, St. Thomas equated sacred doctrine with the science of Scripture. Yet by the end of the nineteenth century so many Catholic theologians were using a method which was quasi-fundamentalist, though it could never be pure fundamentalism. Texts were taken in isolation, and they were used as rigorous philological proofs for theological theses. Key words in the Bible were indeed used, but a meaning was given to them without a thorough investigation of these ideas in their biblical milieu. Meanings were stuck on the words in the light of postscriptural developments and concerns. I remember my own student days in ecclesiology when the Kingdom concept was dominant in the development of the ecclesiological treatise. Yet the notion of Kingdom was not explained in the biblical setting. Kingdom was understood as the sovereignty in a people with the functions explained by Montesquieu in the eighteenth century. Under such circumstances the biblical notion was not even touched. Rather, in its place another idea was introduced under the guise of being biblical, though it was not.

Today this tactic would be quite impossible. The Catholic scriptural scholars would not tolerate it. Moreover, the legalistic accent so strong in the earlier treatises is unpleasant to the modern ecclesiologists, and they are anxious to be ontological rather than juridical. They also want to be vital rather than schematic. Thirdly, they are searching for the supernatural factors in the constitution of the Church.

In all these concerns the current biblical scholars and the patristic investigators have been of great aid and serve as a stimulus. The return to Scripture has led to the abandonment of the text-proof. In its place there is the total scriptural burden which must be considered. Fundamentalist literalism has been transcended, but the biblical affirmation has been kept.

However, the Catholic notion of the inseparable union of Scripture and Tradition functions today as much as in the days of St. Vincent of Lérins. In recent times there has been much clarification of the meaning of Tradition. It would be well for non-Catholic theologians to understand this development. In Protestant theology there is also a renewed awareness of the role of Tradition in the faith of the Christian, and the work of Albert Cook Outler here in America is quite indicative of this trend. However, by and large, Protestants understand by tradition the faith of the historical church in the light of historical science. This is not true in Catholic theology. For the Catholics Tradition is not a mere appeal to history; it is a strictly theological conception.

As the Catholics see it, Tradition is the teaching of the Church. The same Church always teaches the same doctrine through the power of the indwelling Spirit within the Church. The magisterium under that power formulates the doctrine adequately for the moment of its teaching. Such formulation is dogma, which is the normative expression of the truth of revelation. Truth does not evolve, be-

cause there is only one truth which the Church communicates and
that is the total revelation of Christ. The Church grows in awareness
of the revealed truth and in that sense there is an evolution, and that
evolution will become externally manifest by the progress of dogmatic affirmation. The point to be stressed is that the new dogma
does not deny the old one, but rather absorbs it into a fuller constella-
tion of meaning wherein the older dogma is completely and without
inner change related to the new.

This process takes place in history, but it is not an historical process. It is strictly ecclesiological. The Catholic theologian goes to older
dogmas convinced that he already has the truth in them because of
his adhesion to the teaching Church of his own time. In principle he
can see no contradiction in what is taught now and what was taught
in ages past. Nor does he try to resurrect ancient positions in the hy-
pothesis that they have been lost later.

It is here that Catholic theology can be a scandal to non-Catholics.
The Catholic does not approach teachings of the Council of Chalcedon with the uncommittedness of the non-Catholic. The latter with
a bag of historiographic tools meets Chalcedon with no obsessive
concern for what the later Church taught. He tries in freedom to
formulate Chalcedonian thought as he sees it in its historical isolation. His findings can well go counter to the doctrine of the living
Church. His conclusion will be either that the living Church ought to
go back to the doctrine of Chalcedon or that Chalcedon cannot be
normative for the Church of our day. Neither of these two conclusions can be accepted by the Catholic theologian. He insists that the
actual Church is teaching Chalcedon and that Chalcedon will always
be normative for Christian doctrine. The result will be reconciliation of positions which seem to the non-Catholic dishonest subter-
fuges.

This scandal is needless if the non-Catholic understands the
methodology of Catholic theology. This form of divinity begins with
the principle that revelation can be adequately achieved only by following the teaching of the Church to which he here and now belongs.
This is definitive, normative, peremptory. Here is his commitment of
faith. He cannot as a Catholic theologize in any other way because
theology is the intelligent formulation of faith. It does not create a

faith; it is itself a product of a faith which is already there. If the theologian questions his faith, he has already lost it. He is on the road of making a faith rather than attempting to understand the faith he has.

For the Catholic, the Protestant readiness to question any dogma with the inner freedom to reject it, seems something less than faithfulness. As the Catholic sees it, the construction of a faith is not the task of theology. Its proper function is to understand the faith which is there. The Catholic cannot quarrel with it without abandoning it. When this happens, he is not the follower of Christ but turns out to be a new prophet. Concerning his prophetic claims no judgment need here be made. Suffice it to say that he is not a Christian, one who clings to the faith once and for all delivered to the saints. The Catholic has made his decision to cling to that faith and no other.

The trend to reconstructionism which is highly visible in Protestant theology deeply puzzles the Catholic. The freedom presupposed in the reconstructionist enterprise is undoubtedly alluring, but the Catholic simply cannot understand how such freedom can be tolerated by the commitment of faith.

This brings up the current Catholic ecclesiologist's conception of the Church. This is a matter of greatest importance to Catholicism itself. The Catholic proposes an equation wherein the equal signs are not indications of equality but of equivalence. God, Christ, and Church, these three terms are ultimates. Usually Protestants find this doctrine to some degree scandalous and we had better explain the terms and their relations.

God is the transcendent ultimate, the ground of being, and man's *telos*. Union with God is the destiny for which man is created. This destiny is now physically impossible because of man's congenital alienation from God through what in theology is called Original Sin. Yet God in gracious condescension deigned to overcome for man his radical estrangement, and revealed Himself and His saving plans progressively until the definitive revelation and salvation was achieved in the Incarnation of God in Christ Jesus. This was the high moment of history, ushering in the final stage of human existence in preparation for the posthistorical eschatological era.

The historic Jesus of Nazareth was truly God and truly man. In

Him the ideal of man's union with God was absolutely perfect in its achievement. It could not be verified exactly in any other man because other men have human personalities while Christ's personality is formally divine. Yet a pattern had been set ontologically. If the concrete human nature of Christ could be shared with other men, then all things would be given to mankind. In Christ a concrete historical humanity was eternally united to divinity. Sharing, then, in Christ's humanity, any man would be bound internally and objectively with God. If man shared the human nature of Christ, he would be living in Christ. His would be the position of a coheir of all the promises.

The Incarnation must therefore be considered not merely as one historical event but as a total re-creation of the human situation. This re-creation was simultaneously the creation of the Church. There are some forty symbols used for the Church in the New Testament. All give us insight into her being and none must be overlooked. But of them all, the richest and most revealing is Paul's daring symbol of the Church as the body of Christ.

In this symbol the Church is an organism as much as an organization. There is one life, and that is the life of Christ transfused in all the members by the Spirit of Christ, the Holy Ghost. The Church is thus more than a means of salvation; it is salvation already achieved as far as the present human condition allows. When the Christian shares death with Christ, his salvation through resurrection will be complete.

The Church is then Christ prolonged in history until He comes again in judgment and power. Christ is here and now in the Church. Moreover, we must avoid the notion that this is purely figurative language. Figures of speech are only external analogies, but the analogy of the Church with the living body of Christ is intrinsic and ontological. It is, of course, an analogy beyond a doubt, but it is an analogy which uncloses reality as it truly is. In Catholic circles the *sōma tou Christou* is usually translated as the Mystical Body of Christ. The word *mystical* fulfills three functions: (1) it distinguishes the present earthly body of Christ from the body that walked the roads and streets of Palestine; (2) it distinguishes the Church from the Eucharistic presence of Christ; (3) it indicates that the Church is the body of Christ by analogy rather than material reality.

Now the point to be stressed is that intrinsic analogy objectively describes reality in terms of proportional equivalence. It does not ascribe a term in univocal identity. There is here no instance of literalism, but on the other hand there is more than a transfer of language.

The consequences of this understanding of the Church as the body of Christ are many. All of the Christ-functions are performed by the Church in analogous language with Him. He was the revealing prophet, king, priest, redeemer, sanctifier, judge, and healer. Within the limits of analogy the Church must have the same attributes. The definitive revelation came from Christ, and so it must now come from the Church. Sanctification came from Christ and Him alone, and so it must now come from His Mystical Body. The way of true life and conduct was shown by Christ, and so now it must come from the Church as Christ prolonged. The heavy emphasis which Catholics place on the Church is logically inevitable in the light of the symbol of the Church as Christ's living body.

The second feature which is corollary to this ecclesiology is that the action of the Church is as symbolic as its being. The Church symbolically is Christ and her actions will be symbolic by the same reason. The sacraments are therefore the most proper action of the Church. In symbol she, the great symbol, manifests herself and does her work.

The third feature which derives from the conception of the Church as the symbolic presence of Christ is an apologetic one. The Church is made up of sinners, and yet the Christ is no sinner. The Church as an historical thing shows all the limitations of finite, defective humanity, and yet the Christ is above such shortcomings. But all the miseries of the Church are only facets of her physical being. The judge's robes may be tattered and soiled; they may fit the judge badly indeed; they may show signs of anachronism; but all these things belong to the robe as cloth. In their symbolic value and action the robes are as powerful as if they were beautifully made, beautifully fitted, and beautifully appropriate. The Church as a sheerly empirical thing will be no different from any other empirical reality.

However, this is only the lesser part of her being. We must move from her historical appearance to her symbolic meaning. This ascent is, needless to say, an ascent of faith. From that vantage point, what is seen is the Christ, that same Christ who in His own journey to death was a scandal to the faithful of His time: poor, tired, depressed, and persecuted. To see in Him the incarnation of God, the anointed of the Most High, required a revelation from the Father, and only in such revelation could He be seen for what He truly was.

The vision of the Church as seen in modern Catholic ecclesiology is a very moving thing. It humbles and exalts the believer; it consoles and stimulates him; it puts his feet on earth and his head in heaven.

For a Christian of the Reform tradition this vision will have difficulties.

First of all, he will think of many passages in Protestant theology and worship which are echoes of the Catholic paean. But in the Protestant expression it is the invisible Church which is praised. For the visible Church the Reform tradition has many harsh words. For the Church invisible the Protestant has as high a regard as the Catholic. He just cannot see how this admiration can be caused by the Church before our eyes. It is here that the symbol of the Mystical Body is so helpful. Although the distinction between the visible and invisible Church can be understood in a good sense, yet radically it is a poor distinction. There are not two Churches but only one. That the Church has two facets which are distinct is true; but the facets, though distinct, are not separated. If the Church of Christ is the body of Christ, then she is by essence visible. Nothing could be less invisible than a body. That in this body an invisible activity is going on can be admitted without losing the value of the body symbol. Man is like that. We see his bodily actions, but not therefore do we see his true life, which is a life of thought, insight, choice, and deliberation. There is, therefore, within the Church which is most visible an invisible vitality which somehow manifests itself even in that which is visible.

Perhaps the Christian of the Reform tradition is afraid of deriving too much from the body symbol. He may see in such derivation an affirmation of hierarchy in the Church. This he feels is too much. Yet this difficulty is nonexistent for the Catholic who does believe that the Church is hierarchically structured. For him, therefore, the body symbol is most comforting. If the Church is a body, then it is not like an undifferentiated blob of protoplasm. It will be an organism made up of different organs, differentiated from each other by structure and function. The very nature of a body demands a hierarchy of parts in order to insure unity and vital efficacy. One is the life, but many are the members; nor is the eye the ear, nor the hand the foot. It spells out unity of life identical with multiplicity of distinct functions for which there are distinctly structured parts.

We all know that symbols must not be taken as allegories where every element in the proposed image has univocal verification in the reality of the thing allegorized. Symbols are greater than allegories, and they reveal great lines of reality without seeking a one-to-one relationship between the factors of the symbol and the thing symbolized. Yet the notion of an hierarchically structured, visible Church fits uncommonly well with the symbol of the body of Christ. The detailed structure of the hierarchical parts is not given by the symbol itself. Such information must be sought for elsewhere.

In spite of all that can be said for the Catholic approach to the symbol of Mystical Body as a deep description of the Church, I think that Protestants will be uneasy with the Catholic effort. Paul Tillich seems to go to the root of the matter. He believes Catholics put the historical Church in the place of God, and for him this is heteronomy, or, in a more usual term, idolatry. From what has been said so far, we can see grounds of Tillich's fear. In this question it seems to me that Tillich is speaking for all Protestants, although his total theology may not be acceptable to all who follow the Reform pattern of faith.

That the modern Catholic conception puts the Church in place of God is partially true and partially false. If we understand heteronomy in Tillich's terms as the substitution of something finite and historical in the place of the transcendental God, then Catholic ecclesiologists are not heteronomists. They loudly confess that the Church is a finite and historical reality and as such cannot be God. On the other hand, they make much of the doctrine of the Incarnation. This for them is the great act of Christian faith. In this faith God did identify Himself with something historical and finite: the human Christ. If this is not accepted, then Incarnation is not taken seriously. On the rock of Incarnation all theologies must be tested. Gnosticism, Arianism, and Nestorianism denied the Incarnation in one form or other, and the Church could not in loyalty tolerate their rejections.

That God is nothing finite and imperfect is a good Christian theological position. What is more, it is necessary for any Christian belief. But this does not deny that God can take into His own mysterious and infinite being something historical and finite. If it were to deny that, then the Incarnation is denied. If this is denied, then we are sinners indeed and in penance we must return to Israel according to the flesh. Israel refused the doctrine of the Incarnation as a contradiction of the infinity and perfectness of God. On this refusal it continues to exist.

Granted the transcendence of God, we must yet admit that the divine *shekinah,* a material presence of God, is possible. The ancient rabbis saw that, even though they refused to see the *doxa* of God in Jesus the Christ. *Shekinah, doxa,* the glory, are all words which tell us that God in love transcends even His transcendence. The human figure of Jesus of Nazareth was the divine *shekinah* just as was the cloud on Sinai. The Christ *shekinah* was prolonged and extended in time and space in the form of the Church. The cloud on Sinai foreshadowed the Christ to come, and the Church prolongs the historical Christ until the end of time.

Is God His *shekinah?* One must answer both Yes and No. It is God's real presence in time and space. It is not God's pure essence, but it is God coming to material man in love and condescension. In the *shekinah* God is there, and only where He is, can He be met. Only in the encounter with Him in His *shekinah* can man be saved. We have here another formula for the great ecclesiological axiom: *extra ecclesiam nulla salus* (outside the Church there is no salvation).

We have here the strong realism of Catholic theology. This is its peculiar characteristic. Its approach to revelation is ontological, not with an ontology of gnostic mysticism but with the ontology of intelligence enlightened by faith.

A Protestant may well say that this is evident enough, but is it biblical? That question is an ambiguous one. What is the meaning of the Bible in the question? Does it mean a book, self-sufficient and self-standing, which can be understood by the exclusive use of the scientific method of philology? If that is the meaning, then the answer can only be that current Catholic ecclesiology can be constructed out of the biblical data, but it is not the only construction possible. If by biblical we mean the burden of the Bible as it shows up interpreted in the unbroken preaching of the Church, then it alone is biblical. This second answer, which is the Catholic answer, supposes that the Bible and the Church are inseparably joined. The Bible is the Church's book. It is not over her or separated from her being. It can only be read profitably when read from her holding hands. To grab the book from her hands and study it in isolation is to lose the Bible. In such a human action it transforms itself from a word of God into a word of man. It no longer is salvific.

It is at this point where Catholic and Protestant ecclesiologies will divide. The Catholic's stand is simply that the Bible is in the Church and the Church is in the Bible. It is hard to formulate the Protestant stand. Certainly not all Protestants would say that the philological method is the exclusive way to understand the Scriptures. Some do say it. Yet all gives the theologian and the believer a right to judge the Church in the light of their grasp of the biblical message, whether that be achieved in the light of philology, in the warmth of piety, or in the light of existence.

Here begin the divisions. The Catholic simply rejects the thought that a believing Christian can judge the Church, and by the Church he means the one Church, both visible and invisible. The Catholic with the Protestant believes that the prophetic protest of the Spirit must be addressed to the members of the Church, so that they live up to the great ecclesiastical calling. Such protest is not against the Church but against the sinners in the Church. As the believer protests against the sinner, he must remember that he himself is under judgment; and the Church, the Christ *shekinah* in the world, the locus of God in history, will do the judging.

The Catholic paradoxically believes that the Church, being Christ prolonged, is all-holy and yet made up of sinners who must be built up to the stature of the full Christ. For him the faithful are the saints, not because of their own sinlessness, but because they live, act, think, and pray in Christ who certainly is sinless because He is truly the Son of God.

NOTES

This essay is also published in Father Weigel's book, *Catholic Theology in Dialogue* (New York: Harper & Bros., 1961; copyright by Gustave Weigel, S.J.). We are grateful to Father Weigel and to Harper & Bros. for kind permission to print it here.

SELECTED READINGS

1. Adam, Karl, *One and Holy*. New York: Sheed and Ward, 1951. 131 pp. How the situation has changed since Luther.

2. Cerfaux, Lucien, *The Church in the Theology of St. Paul*. New York: Herder and Herder, 1959. 417 pp. An essay in Pauline theology, aiming at the underlying synthesis of the epistles.

3. Congar, Yves M. J., O.P., *Lay People in the Church. A Study for a Theology of the Laity*. Westminster, Md.: Newman. 1956. 447 pp. The most complete study of this question by a Catholic scholar.

4. Jàki, Stanislas, O.S.B., *Les tendances nouvelles de l'ecclésiologie*, Rome: Herder, 1957. 274 pp. The most complete account of recent trends.

5. Leeming, Bernard, S.J., *The Churches and the Church. A Study of Ecumenism*. Westminster, Md.: Newman, 1960. 340 pp. A clear and sympathetic study by an English theologian with experience in the ecumenical movement.

6. De Lubac, Henri, S.J., *Catholicism. A Study of Dogma in Relation to the Corporate Destiny of Mankind*. New York: Sheed and Ward, 1958. 283 pp. Emphasizes the essentially social character of the Church.

7. Mersch, Emile, S.J., *The Whole Christ. The Historical Development of the Doctrine of the Mystical Body in Scripture and Tradition*. Milwaukee: Bruce, 1938. 623 pp. In three parts: the Scriptures, the Greek Fathers, the Western tradition.

8. Pius XII, *The Mystical Body*, translation of encyclical letter *Mystici Corporis* by Canon G. D. Smith. London: Catholic Truth Society, 1943. The most important recent ecclesiastical document on the Church.

9. Rahner, Karl, S.J., *Free Speech in the Church*. New York: Sheed and

Ward, 1959. 50 pp. Explains why free speech within the Church is the right of both layman and cleric, and necessary for the health of the Church.

10. Vögtle, Anton, "Jesus und die Kirche," in M. Roesle, O.S.B., and Oscar Cullmann, eds. *Begegnung der Christen* (Stuttgart: Evangelisches Verlagswerk, and Frankfurt am Main: Verlag Josef Knecht, 1960), pp. 54–81. An exegetical study for the specialist.

11. Vollert, Cyril, S.J., "Bibliography on Mary in the Church," *Theology Digest*, Vol. 4 (1956), pp. 34–36. An annotated bibliography of forty-nine titles.

12. Winter, Michael M., *St. Peter and the Popes*. Baltimore: Helicon Press, 1960. 236 pp. An historical study of the first five centuries.

PART FOUR

The Sacraments

INTRODUCTION:

THE PROTESTANT VIEW OF
THE SACRAMENTS

In Article 31 of the Anglican *Articles of Religion,* the point of departure for sacramental thought in the Reformation tradition is succinctly formulated: "The Offering of Christ once made is that perfect redemption, propitiation, and satisfaction, for the sins of the whole world, both original and actual; and there is none other satisfaction for sin, but that alone." With minor variations, this articulation of the completeness and comprehensiveness of God's identification with his suffering creation and his victory over the demonic powers of this age in and through his Son, Jesus Christ, reappears in all Reformation confessions. This formulation is basic for the understanding of the Reformation doctrines of the sacraments and justification to which this and the last section are dedicated.

With respect to the sacraments, four areas of discussion can be designated as most prominent, existing long before but especially since the time of the Reformation: (1) the number of the sacraments instituted by Christ; (2) the relation of the preaching of the Word to the administration of the sacraments; (3) the *ex opere operato* character of the sacraments of the New Covenant; (4) the doctrine of transubstantiation, an interpretation of the effect of the consecration defined in terms of medieval Aristotelian philosophy.

While Protestant theologians widely acknowledge a number of sacramental acts such as confirmation and absolution, ordination and marriage, these are to be distinguished from the sacraments proper, Baptism and the Lord's Supper, which according to apostolic witness were instituted by Christ.

Since reasons for disagreement with the Roman Catholic accept-

195

ance of seven sacraments lie in the different view on the relation of
Scripture and Tradition, we can refer here to the first section which
deals with this issue.

The following selections have been chosen as samples of contemporary Protestant treatment of the three other indicated issues.

The second of the two contributions by Max Thurian, a leading
theologian of the Protestant *Communauté de Taizé* in France, deals
with the problem of the mode of the real presence of Christ. More
than ever before, this question is acknowledged as the most decisive
one. We have not included this as a separate point in our enumeration
of principal issues because it is necessarily *implied* in the discussion
of the relation of Word and sacrament, *ex opere operato* and transubstantiation. Modern discussions, however, have increasingly
turned to this aspect, stimulated by a deep longing for intercommunion and by the variety of solutions within the Reformation tradition
itself. The 1956 consensus on the Lord's Supper between Reformed
and Lutheran synods in Holland and the searching discussions,
especially in Germany and Scandinavia, on precisely this point are
indicative of this development.

Differentiation between a confessional statement and a theological
formulation may well lead to a wide interconfessional agreement on
the real presence of Christ as in some way connected with the sacramental signs. On the theologian then rests the task of clarifying and
interpreting this statement in a form understandable and helpful for
his age and time.

8

TOWARD A RENEWAL OF THE DOCTRINE OF TRANSUBSTANTIATION

MAX THURIAN

THEOLOGY AND PHILOSOPHY

In the Catholic theology of the Eucharist, the dogma of transubstantiation is not an essential one. The central element of the Catholic belief in the Eucharist, as of ours, is certitude about the real presence. The dogma of transubstantiation has a protective and defensive purpose. It was explicitly formulated in the Middle Ages, and its sole purpose was to express the mystery of the real presence in an understandable way to the men of this period.

This effort to embody Christian truth in the thought of a period is a constant phenomenon in Catholic theology. This effort must be praised and imitated, for it allows contact with the world. Protestants are handicapped in such attempts by a certain kind of pietism. This spirit of adaptation is above all a profoundly apostolic one: "To the Jews I became as a Jew, in order to win the Jews; to those under the law I became as one under the law ... I have become all things to all men, that I might by all means save some" (1 Cor 9:20, 22).

It is this kind of apostolic zeal in the realm of human thought that drives all the great doctors of the Church to become all things to the men of their time, to their philosophy, to their science, to their art ... St. Augustine, St. Thomas Aquinas, Calvin .... However, the effort is full of risks, for in attempting to embody the gospel in the thought of a period, one runs the danger of seeing it assimilated, dissipated, deprived of its savor and of its revolutionary force. The truth of the gospel must not be compromised and confused with human philosophy. It must certainly take modern philosophy into account, make use of it, become embodied in it, accomplishing its work of resurrection and revolution. Christian truth, like Christ himself, must "become flesh," but with the purpose of resurrecting and sanctifying this flesh. The embodiment of Christian truth in "philosophical flesh" must never compromise the liberty of this truth. "Though I am free from all men, I have made myself a slave to all, that I might win the more" (1 Cor 9:19).

We must have great admiration for St. Thomas, who in a masterful way embodied the gospel in the philosophical thought of his age. Thanks to him and to other doctors, Christian thought was in a position to attempt a synthesis, a harmonization, and a unification, in a way rarely known before this great scholastic period. However, St. Thomas did not escape the danger of compromise. Embodiment sometimes became assimilation or confusion; and he deprived certain truths of their proper evangelical savor, substituting insipid Aristotelianism. In his desire to be "to all men," he no longer remained "all things." We find in him an excessive natural optimism, which prevents him from seeing the sinful character of all human philosophies and the danger that always threatens Christian truth when it undertakes this necessary embodiment in the philosophy of an age. And this attitude is characteristic of the theologians before and after him who developed the dogma of transubstantiation.

THE REAL PRESENCE AND TRANSUBSTANTIATION

The aim of these theologians was to provide the dogma of the real presence of Christ in the Lord's Supper with a philosophical framework which would give it a point of contact with contemporary thought, a protection from this same human and sinful thought, and a defense against all heresy. Here again, there is nothing objectionable. All the truths of the gospel have a theological aspect, which simply states the mystery, and a philosophical aspect, which explains this same mystery to the human thought of a given period. Each revealed truth must be theologically expressed with a biblical basis which guarantees that it is true; and it must have a philosophical explanation which clearly presents the mystery to the mind without exhausting it. Theological and philosophical systems are all subject to change. Only the Word of God, contained in the canonical Scriptures, is immutable. However, the theological expression of truth, by reason of its contact with Scripture and its absolute nature, is much more immutable than any philosophical explanation, whether it be Thomistic or Calvinistic. Above all, the theological expression of truth belongs to the whole Church, which alone is authorized to make changes in it, whereas a philosophical explanation can be proper to a particular school.

It is surprising that for centuries Catholic theology has continued to explain the dogma of the real presence by transubstantiation, while human thought has moved forward so that this explanation has become quite out of date and unreal. Perhaps the theological truth which it defends is so fundamental for faith and piety that one dares not touch it for fear that the whole structure will crumble. And yet it seems that this dogma constitutes an obstacle and a real difficulty for the faith and piety of many. The ordinary members of the Church have perhaps not gone beyond the primitive concept of transubstantiation, but those who have been influenced by modern philosophy and recent scientific discoveries are no longer satisfied. They give the word a content which no longer corresponds to the word itself and especially to its historical context. They remain profoundly Catholic, for they know that the essential thing is the affirmation of the real presence, but they find another philosophical explanation for this dogma. It seems that one can discern an effort on the part of the teaching Church to make this task easier for them. Indeed, it is an urgent matter that this dogma of the real presence be thought out again in modern concepts. Not only will this result in an increase of spirituality for Catholic faith and piety, but it will be one step more toward the unity of the Church.

The formation of the dogma of transubstantiation is explained by the realist and substantialist bent of medieval thinking. For the men of that period, each being was composed of an inner reality, substance, and of certain appearances and accidents. Since after the consecration of the host and of the wine, no change in the appearances is visible, it is certain that to the words "This *is* my body" there corresponds a modification of the substance of "this" (the bread) into the substance of the "body" of Jesus Christ. In the place of that which is the subtle and unobservable inner reality in the host and the wine, there comes the substance of the body and blood of Jesus Christ, dead on the Cross. There is no question here of the material body of the historical Christ multiplying itself in the Eucharists, nor of his glorified body which is in God. We must not conceive of transubstantiation according to the flesh or in an angelic sense. The new substance of the host and of the wine, after transubstantiation, is the sacramental body of Jesus Christ. Besides the historical body and the glorified body there is the sacramental or Eucharistic body which reproduces, under the appearances of the bread and wine, the substance of the body and blood of the crucified Christ. As St. Thomas writes, in transubstantiation the body of Christ is not in the sacrament "in the way a body is in a place, by the juxtaposition of its dimensions to those of a place, but in a special manner which is proper to this sacrament."[1] This special manner is the manner of substance. Each time that transubstantiation occurs, "Christ's eucharistic body is produced in the manner in which his divine hands produced bread when he multiplied the loaves,"[2] and he replaces the inner nature of the bread and wine in the way one substance can be substituted for another. One could say, according to this theology, that the person of Christ has the unique power of being presented to us with an appearance which is foreign to itself. Not only was the substance of the body of Christ presented to his contemporaries under the veils of human flesh—which is common to all men here below, not only is it presented to the angels, and will be to us, in a glorified state, but now it is presented to us under the appearances, the accidents, the species of bread and wine.

For a good, brief understanding of this idea, we must reread this text of St. Thomas, which is all-important for our purposes: "Christ does not have the same mode of being (*esse*) in himself (in history and in heaven) and in this sacrament (the Eucharist), for when we say of Christ that he is (*esse*) in this sacrament, we signify *a certain relation which unites him to this sacrament.*"[3]

This is the method which the scholastic theologians and St. Thomas judged suitable as a means of making the real presence understandable during a period of realist and substantialist philosophy, strongly influenced by the thought of Aristotle.

NOTES

A translation, done under the direction of the editors, of "Vers un renouvellement du dogme de la transubstantiation," which appears as Appendix 2 of *Joi du Ciel sur la Terre*, pp. 179–184, published by Éditions Delachaux & Niestlé, Neuchâtel et Paris, 1946. We would like to thank Delachaux & Niestlé for permission to undertake this translation.

1. *Summa Theologica*, IIIa Pars, q. 75, a. 1.
2. Anscar Vonier, O.S.B., *A Key to the Doctrine of the Eucharist* (London: Burns Oates and Washbourne, 1925), p. 190.
3. *Summa Theologica*, IIIa Pars, q. 76, a. 6.

9

THE REAL PRESENCE

MAX THURIAN

OUR purpose so far has been to study the sacrificial character of the Eucharist in the light of the biblical notion of memorial, and not the problem of the real presence of Christ in this sacrament. As is well known, much has been written on this subject during the history of the Church. Works on the real presence are not lacking, and we would like to call attention at this point to the remarkable treatise of Professor F. J. Leenhardt, *Ceci est mon corps, explication de ces paroles de Jésus-Christ,* the best recent work on this question and the most ecumenical.[1] We can agree with the author on all points in his study of the real presence.[2] We do not intend to repeat what has already been said excellently by others about the real presence of Christ in the Eucharist. Our intention is simply to draw the conclusions from our research on the memorial of the Lord and on the Eucharistic sacrifice by showing that our study leads us quite naturally to affirm the real presence of Christ in the mystery of the Eucharist. If the Church accomplishes in the Lord's Supper the unique memorial of the Lord which we have described, then Christ is truly present therein. The memorial of the Lord, the sacrament of the sacrifice of the Cross and of Christ's heavenly intercession, has no meaning unless the Lord himself is sacramentally present in the Eucharist. Otherwise the memorial is nothing but a game of symbols, impressive perhaps, but without ontological significance. It is because of the real presence of Christ in the Eucharistic sacrament that it can be a true memorial of the Lord, a true Eucharistic sacrifice in the biblical sense. Nothing we have said can have any actuality and meaning unless Christ himself, really and personally present, is acting in the Eucharist as priest, as offering, as food. This real and personal presence of Christ in the bread and wine, his body and blood, is a mystery that will always remain beyond the Church's power to understand or explain. She can only present it as an undeniable fact and defend the belief in the real presence by protecting it from every explanation that would minimize or exaggerate the reality, from all disembodied spiritualism, and from any semblance of magic or materialism. In a striking passage, St. Irenaeus of Lyons expressed the mystery of the real presence in this way: "As the bread from the earth, receiving the invocation of God, is no longer common bread, but a Eucharist composed of two things, terrestrial and celestial; so also our bodies, which partake of the Eucharist, are no longer corruptible, since they have the hope of the eternal resurrection . . . ."[3] And elsewhere: "When therefore the cup which is mingled with water and the bread which is made, receive the Eucharist of the body and blood of Christ, and bring food and sustenance to our flesh, how can they affirm that flesh is incapable of receiving the gift of God which is eternal life, that flesh which has been nourished by the body and blood of the Lord, and is one of his members . . . that flesh which is nourished by the cup which is his blood, and receives increase from the bread which is his body. Just as the cutting from the vine, planted in the ground, has borne fruit in its season, or as the grain of wheat, falling into the earth and corrupting, has sprung with manifold increase by the power of the Spirit of God, and receiving the Word of God, then becomes the Eucharist, which is the body and blood of Christ; so also our bodies, being nourished by it and put into the ground where they undergo corruption, shall rise again at their appointed time."[4]

Would to God that we had remained with these simple affirmations of the real presence, safeguarding all of its mystery without encumbering ourselves with pseudo explanations of that which can only be stated and believed. But we must not be too severe with the theology that down through the centuries has desired to preserve belief in the real presence against dangerous deviations.

It is in this context that the doctrine of transubstantiation was intended to be a safeguard for the truth of the real presence.[5] It was not intended to be a rational explanation of the mystery but a categorical affirmation of the reality of the presence of Christ. Unfortunately, the vocabulary of transubstantiation, worked out to present and to safeguard the real presence, not to explain it and make it understood, was to become obscured in theology and was no longer truly understood during the sixteenth century either by many Catholic theologians who retained it or by the Protestants who rejected it.

The Council of Trent, in its thirteenth session, October 11, 1551, was to affirm first of all the real presence in the first chapter and the first canon; it then took up the doctrine of transubstantiation in the fourth chapter and the second canon. The Council speaks of the real presence as a "conversion" (*conversio*) of the bread and wine into the body and blood of Christ, "which conversion is called (*appellata*) fittingly and properly transubstantiation by the Holy Catholic Church."[6] The Council considers "that the Catholic Church calls this conversion most appropriately (*aptissime*) transubstantiation."[7] Thus, transubstantiation is first of all an appellation, a name, which designates the reality of the presence of Christ, who is "truly, really and substantially" present in the Eucharist.[8]

Luther was to affirm just as forcibly that the bread and wine are the body and blood of Christ, but rejected transubstantiation which he understood to be an explanation: "The Sacrament of the altar is the true body and true blood of our Lord Jesus Christ, instituted by Christ himself under the bread and the wine so that we Christians may eat and drink."[9] In the *Smalkald Articles,* Luther wrote in 1537: "We do not concern ourselves with the sophistic subtlety of transubstantiation. . . . For that which agrees best with Scripture is that the bread is there and remains, as St. Paul himself calls it: 'the bread which we break,' and 'let him eat of the bread' (1 Cor 10:16; 11:28)."[10] Luther's biblical preoccupation is to affirm at the same time both the real presence of the body and blood of Christ, in and under the bread and wine, and to maintain the natural and chemical permanence of the bread and wine. Luther wished to keep the mystery intact in the very vocabulary of the New Testament: "This is my *body* . . . . The *bread* which we break . . . ."

THE CALVINIST DOCTRINE OF THE
REAL PRESENCE

Calvin affirms the real presence just as vigorously: "We must confess therefore that if the representation which God effects for us in the Supper is true, the interior substance of the Sacrament is joined together with the visible signs; and as the bread is put into our hands, so also is the body of Christ communicated to us that we may become partakers of it."[11] Substance for Calvin does not mean a sort of invisible material substratum, nor the natural body of flesh, the matter of Christ's physical body. For him the term "substance" signifies the profound reality of a being or of a thing.[12] Calvin's doctrine on the Eucharist is a doctrine of the efficacious sign. We must examine the terms of this doctrine carefully to grasp its full meaning as well as the difficulties involved. It must be stated first of all that Calvin wishes to preserve an ecumenical position between Zwingli and Luther. The text that follows will shed light on the idea of sign as applied to the Lord's Supper, and we will see that his foremost concern is to preserve in the Eucharist its twofold terrestrial and celestial aspect, according to the terms used by St. Irenaeus:

Our Lord, wishing his Spirit to appear at the baptism of Christ, represented him in the figure of a dove. In narrating this incident, St. John the Baptist says that he saw the Holy Spirit descending. If we investigate more closely, we will discover that he saw only the dove and that he saw that the Holy Spirit in its essence is invisible. However, knowing that this vision was not an empty figure, but a sure sign of the presence of the Holy Spirit, John does not hesitate to say that he has seen Him, because he has represented himself to him according to his capacity. So it is with the communication we have with the body and blood of the Lord Jesus. It is a spiritual mystery which is not visible to the eyes nor comprehensible to the human mind. It is therefore represented to us by means of visible signs, as is required by our frailty. However, it is not an empty representation but one united with its truth and substance. Rightly then is the bread called body, since not only does it represent it to us but also presents it to us.[13]

Not only does the sign represent communion with the body and blood of Christ and not only does this representation, willed by God and backed by his promises, confirm the Christian in his faith, but by reason of the profound meaning which "sign" has for Calvin, it also "presents" the reality which it signifies.

Before continuing, we should clarify a few ideas in order to keep from thinking that the power and efficacy of the sacrament are due to the fact that it belongs to the category of signs or symbols. If it is true to say with St. Thomas that "sacraments are classified as signs,"[14] it is still necessary to determine what singles it out from other revealed or natural signs or symbols in order to avoid falling into the error of natural theology, which attempts to understand the supernatural through natural realities, the higher by means of the lower, following the way of analogy.

Although the symbol, or the sign, leads the mind in a mysterious fashion to the truth which it signifies, the relation which it establishes between the object signified and the person thinking remains a subjective one, both on the intellectual and the psychological level. The symbol is a powerful instrument of understanding and perception. The sacrament, insofar as it is a sign or symbol, is all of this, but it is even more than this, by the will of him who instituted it. Not only does it lead the mind, in an infallible and mysterious way, to the truth which it signifies, but it also guarantees the presence and efficacy of the reality which it symbolizes. The sacrament of the Supper, as revealed sign, gives our faith a clear grasp of the body and blood of Christ as food; as sacrament or efficacious sign, it truly gives what it symbolizes; that is, it communicates the body and blood of Jesus Christ as spiritual food.

This understanding of sign, which is that of the Fathers of the Church, brings Calvin to the idea of real presence. The Supper is a sign that guarantees. Now because it is a sign and because it is a guarantee, that which is signified and guaranteed must be really present, otherwise the sign is meaningless and the guarantee empty.

The Supper is an efficacious sign because its substance is Jesus Christ himself. "The matter and substance of the Sacrament is the Lord Jesus; the graces and blessings we receive through him are the efficacy."[15] Calvin, and after him, all of Reformed theology, make a very strong affirmation of the real presence. "Christ with all his riches is presented to us (at the Supper) no less than if he were placed before our eyes and were touched by our hands."[16] The *Petit traité de la sainte cène* gives this summary of Reformed teaching: "All of us therefore profess with one voice that by receiving the Sacrament with faith, according to the ordinance of the Lord, we truly become partakers of the very substance of the body and blood of Jesus Christ."[17]

If Calvin had stopped with a simple statement of the real presence, agreement with the Lutherans might have been a possibility. But he was troubled by Zwingli's rationalistic questions. And he was not satisfied with Luther's mystical vagueness: of him he wrote that "he added comparisons which were somewhat harsh and crude . . . for it is difficult to give an understanding of so lofty a thing without making use of some less apt ideas."[18]

This led to his teaching on the role of the Holy Spirit in the Supper.[19]

His thought can be summed up as follows: Christ with his glorified body rose to heaven on the day of the Ascension and from there he will come to judge the living and the dead at the end of time. It would be a misunderstanding of the nature of a human body, even a glorified one, or it would make of this body a "phantasm," as did the Gnostics and the Docetists, and thus undervalue the Incarnation, if one thought that this body could be joined locally to the Eucharistic appearances. This "joining together" therefore of the body and blood of Christ with the sacramental signs takes place through the Holy Spirit; in the sacrament the Holy Spirit is as "channel or conduit by which all that Christ is or possesses comes down to us."[20] And Calvin compared Christ to the sun, and the Spirit to the rays which bear its warmth to the earth.

Calvin and Reformed theology have never felt very comfortable with this explanation of the mystery. Calvin himself will betray some hesitancy in the *Petit traité de la sainte cène,* in which he states at first: "It is not *only* that we are *participants of his Spirit,* but we must *also partake of his humanity,* in which he gave full obedience to God his Father to satisfy our debt."[21]

Further on, as a refutation of the idea of local presence we find a contrary declaration:

To maintain this [local presence] one must admit either that the body of Christ is without measure or that it can be in different places; and in so saying one finally comes to the point where it is in no way different from a phantasm. Therefore the attempt to establish such a presence, by which the body of Christ would be enclosed within the sign or would be joined to it locally, is not only folly, it is also a damnable error, opposed to the glory of Christ, and destructive of what we must hold concerning his human nature. For Scripture everywhere teaches us that just as the Lord Jesus assumed our humanity on earth, so he raised it to heaven, freeing it from its mortal condition but without changing its nature in the process. Thus we have two things to consider when we speak of this humanity: we must not detract from the integrity of its nature and we must not take away anything from its glorious condition. To do this satisfactorily, we must *always raise our thoughts on high* in search of our Redeemer. For if we wished to bring him down among the corruptible elements of this world, besides doing away with what Scripture shows us about his human nature, we would be destroying the glory of his Ascension.[22]

Finally, in the summary which he gives at the end of the treatise:

How this comes about [our participation in the substance of Christ] some can better deduce and more clearly explain than others. This being so, we must, on the one hand, exclude all phantasies of the flesh, raise our hearts on high to heaven, not thinking that the Lord Jesus lowered himself to the point of being enclosed within a few corruptible elements. On the other hand, lest we lessen the efficacy of the holy mystery, we must think that it happens through the secret and miraculous power of God, and that the *Spirit of God is the bond of this participation,* by reason of which it is called spiritual.[23]

Whenever the matter of spiritual participation in the body and blood of Christ is discussed in Reformed theology, it must not be understood in terms of a certain form of liberal spiritualism which looks on communion as a comprehension of the symbol by the mind of man. It should mean rather that the body and blood of Christ are really communicated with the signs by the "channel" of the Holy Spirit.

In his exposition of the real presence, Calvin seems to have too material a concept of the body of Christ.[24] Calvin is very emphatic in affirming the humanity of Jesus Christ. But he does not distinguish clearly enough between the Christ who lived and suffered from the Annunciation to Calvary and the risen and glorious Christ of Easter to the Ascension, and in eternity. He identifies too closely the state of the crucified with that of the risen Christ. Perhaps for Calvin the two natures of Christ, the human and the divine, are too autonomous, and he does not realize to what extent they are united, according to the words of St. John's prologue: "The Word became flesh" (Jn 1:14). So it happens that the Christ who lived and suffered from Christmas to the Cross is for him too suffused with the effects of his divinity—divinity almost juxtaposed to his humanity. In Calvin's Christology there seems to be, as it were, something intermittent about the divine and the human. While holding fast to the humanity of Jesus Christ—the human and direct qualities of his preaching prove this by the way it presents Christ as true man like us—Calvin is not always free of a kind of Docetism, however contradictory this may seem. This explains, for example, his refusal to allow Christ to be represented by images and his rejection of the crucifix. The divinity of Jesus Christ is so resplendent that it would be blasphemous either to wish to portray it, or by prescinding from it, to present only his humanity. In the first case, one would fall under the condemnation of the second commandment of the Decalogue; in the other, one would undermine the mystery of the Incarnation and of the union of the two distinct natures. There is no doubt that Calvin believes in the reality of the Incarnation, but he fails to grasp its full meaning; he does not see clearly enough that the Incarnation is an emptying of self (Phil 2:7). It often seems that for him Christ came *with flesh* and not that he truly *became flesh*. In general, the distinction between the two natures is too pronounced in Calvinistic theology: this distinction often becomes a juxtaposition.

This explains why Jesus is both human and resplendent with divinity, even during his Passion and on the Cross, and why, in turn, strict Calvinistic theology cannot allow any representation of the Son of Man, not even the crucifix. It also explains how it is that Christ, risen and seated at the right hand of the Father, is both glorified in nature and also limited by his human nature.

By making at times too sharp a distinction between the two natures in Jesus Christ, Calvinistic theology runs the danger of not fully grasping the difference that exists between Christ before the Cross and Christ after the Resurrection. This point is important with reference to the Reformed doctrine on the sacrament, for it gives rise to one of its greatest problems. New Testament Christology, especially that of St. John, will help us to understand this difficulty and to find a solution by correcting the overly narrow view Calvin took of the body of Christ in his efforts to counterbalance the dogmatic excesses of Luther.

"This is the changeless truth about bodies: they are contained in place and they are defined by their dimensions,"[25] wrote Calvin in 1536. The question arises whether this narrow definition of body is applicable to the idea of "glorified body" developed by St. Paul in 1 Cor 15, and to St. John's concept of Jesus Christ's body after the Resurrection.

For it is remarkable that St. John, the witness of the Incarnation and the one who makes of this dogma the center of the Christian faith, is at pains to call attention to the mysterious character of the body of Jesus Christ after the Resurrection. John wrote his Gospel in the light of this line from his preface: "The Word became flesh" (Jn 1:14). In his first Epistle he states that "every spirit which confesses that Jesus Christ has come in the flesh is of God" (1 Jn 4:2). Jesus Christ, true Son of God, true God, therefore became man; he became flesh, *"He emptied himself,* taking the form of a servant, and becoming like men" (Phil 2:7). "He had neither beauty nor brilliance to draw our attention to him, and nothing in his appearance which could make us love him" (Is 53:2). There was no "physical" natural resplendence in the person of Christ. He was truly like us, and it took all the power of the Holy Spirit to stir up the disciples' faith to the point where they recognized God in this humble itinerant preacher. Do not object that he performed miracles and that these miracles revealed his divinity and surround him with a sort of aura. No, miracles are for men of faith; they are acts of divine condescension by which God accommodates himself to human frailty and strengthens man's ever-wavering faith. Miracles were all the more necessary during Jesus' earthly life in proportion as his presence as a man was more of a "scandal" to the faith. For how could one believe that this poor man was God himself? A miracle then means nothing to someone who does not have faith through the Holy Spirit. "If they do not hear Moses and the prophets, neither will they be convinced even if someone should rise from the dead" (Lk 16:31). Indeed, miracles can always be explained physically or psychologically. This was well demonstrated by Renan. Miracles are miraculous only through faith.

Jesus Christ has therefore truly "emptied himself" in his humanity, from the crib to the Cross. He is like any other man and we must think of him and picture him as we do any other man. The mystery of the two natures can be known only through faith.

After his Resurrection, the humanity of Jesus Christ is covered over by his divinity, as his humanity previously covered over his divinity. He had performed miracles of power to strengthen his disciples' faith in his divinity; now it is miracles of lowliness that he performs to prove to them that he, a man, is always close to them, with them until the end of the world. Earlier, the miracles had been calming the tempest and walking on the waters; now the miracle is that he eats with his friends, as a man, and that he allows himself to be touched by Thomas (Lk 24:41–42; Jn 20:27).

The mystery of his glorified body is strongly emphasized in the accounts of his apparitions, especially in John and Luke. He tells Mary Magdalene not to touch him, as if it were not normal that he, having been glorified, should be visibly present to his disciples when his actual state would demand that he be present in heaven with the Father. It is to justify the faith of those who followed him that he chooses to show himself during the forty days (Jn 20:17). Elsewhere he calls on his astonished and doubting disciples to touch him, a miracle granted because of the weakness of their faith (Lk 24:39). He enters the house where the disciples are present, "the doors being shut." John insists on this fact (20:19, 26) and points out in this way the new and glorious character of his person. However, with his apostles he eats a piece of broiled fish, thereby manifesting the humanity of his person.

All these indications therefore point to the newness of nature in the person of the risen Christ. If he remains human, if he remains the Word Incarnate, Jesus Christ now has a new body, assumed in the glory of his divinity. This body can no longer correspond to the restrictive definitions of human, natural bodies; it can no longer be limited by a place and the dimensions of place, as Calvin put it. This body is a part of the mystery, and the presence of the body of Jesus Christ at the Supper must be understood in terms of the mystery of the Lord's apparitions to his disciples that took place from Easter to the Ascension.

In keeping with his restricted concept of Christ's body, Calvin quite anthropomorphically localizes this body in heaven and he bids us to "raise our hearts on high to heaven," to find our Lord who cannot be "brought so low that he is confined beneath a few corruptible elements."

This is an obvious reaction against the curious Lutheran concept of the ubiquity of Christ's body. The Lutherans claimed that by reason of its assumption into the divinity, the glorified body of the Lord could enjoy from the advantages of divinity, for example, the possibility of being everywhere at once, i.e., ubiquity. This was an awkward attempt to explain the mysterious characteristics of Christ's risen and glorified body and his real presence in the Lord's Supper.

If Calvin's idea of Christ's body seems to us at times to be deficient, especially in his theology of the sacrament and of the real presence, there is also another difficulty: his theology of the Holy Spirit. Calvin and all orthodox Reformed theologians are Trinitarians, and they believe in the divine personality of the Spirit. But in point of fact, when he applies this dogma to his sacramental ideas, Calvin diminishes the personal character of the Holy Spirit. In his role at the Lord's Supper, the Holy Spirit becomes the Spirit of Jesus Christ, "channel or conduit by which all that Christ is or possesses comes down to us." Further on, Christ is compared to the sun, and the Spirit to the rays which communicate its substance to the earth; it is again a question of the "glow and irradiation" of the Spirit of Jesus Christ. All these expressions bespeak a certain indetermination in Calvinistic pneumatology. The Spirit is not so much the third Person of the Trinity as he is an instrument of the Person of the Son, the Spirit of the Son. A personal concept of the Holy Spirit has shaded over into an instrumental concept. The Spirit becomes, in Eucharistic theology, "the bond which links together" the person of Christ, localized "in heaven," and the faith of the communicant, through the intermediation of the appearances. The Holy Spirit is no more than a unifying power bridging the distance between Christ and the believer.

Once we understand the difficulty Calvin experienced with Luther's doctrine, and if we remember that his chief concern was to safeguard the full humanity of the glorified Christ (which is referred to in the words "sitting at the right hand of God"), the fact remains that the Reformer was a firm believer in the real presence of the body and blood of Christ.[26] In a letter of December 27, 1562, to Bullinger, he writes:

Although the flesh of Christ is in heaven, we are nevertheless truly nourished by it on earth because Christ, by the unbounded and all-pervading power of his Spirit, has so made himself ours that he dwells in us without change of place. . . . I see no absurdity in saying that we truly and in all reality receive the flesh and blood of Christ, and that he is thus substantially our food so long as it is admitted that Christ comes down to us not only by means of external symbols but also by the secret workings of his Spirit, so that we through faith may rise up to him.[27]

Whatever dogmatic and exegetical difficulties may be involved in Calvin's Eucharistic doctrine, one must acknowledge that his piety would be satisfied only by very positive statements about the real presence, in spite of the fact that his doctrinal pronouncements prevented his teaching from being perfectly clear.[28]

Finally, Calvin wishes to preserve a great respect for the mystery of the Eucharist and the real presence. He says:

As for me, I am lost in astonishment at the profundity of this mystery, which surpasses our understanding; I am not ashamed to stand in wonder and profess my ignorance, as St. Paul does. For is it not better to act in this way than by my earthly understanding to diminish what St. Paul calls a great mystery? And reason itself teaches us to act in this way. For everything which is supernatural surely surpasses our power of understanding. Therefore let us strive harder to feel Christ living in us than to make the means by which he communicates with us in this Sacrament completely understandable.[29]

Peter Martyr Vernigli, the companion of Theodore Beza, declared at the Colloquy of Poissy in 1561:

. . . the substance of his flesh and of his blood is truly promised and offered and given to us. . . . The Holy Spirit, by his secret and ineffable activity, effects in us here on earth this communication and participation of the body which dwells in heaven and not elsewhere, adapting in a divine fashion his loftiness both to our capacity and to different places according to their distance; as if by his power he visibly joined heaven with earth to establish his royal throne in the midst of the Supper and to give himself more intimately as food for our souls.[30]

The Reformed Church will always maintain its belief in the real presence, leaving the manner of this presence a mystery. Thus, in 1931, the Synod of the Reformed Churches of France made this statement: "As to the manner in which the Lord is present in the Sacrament, the faithful may differ in their opinions, but not as to the fact of the real presence itself. It is a real presence according to the Spirit, inseparable from the elements of the Supper in the very act of celebration."

The Orthodox, more than the Christians of the West, had this respect for the mystery of the real presence, without showing too much desire to specify the manner of Christ's presence. Before the sixteenth century, most Orthodox theologians prudently did not go beyond simple faith in the real presence, beyond the idea of a change of bread and wine into the body and blood of Christ; they did not inquire philosophically into the nature of this change. Some, having read St. Thomas, introduced the idea of transubstantiation, but without any explanations, or else only explaining the comparisons used in presenting it. After the sixteenth century, one can distinguish three tendencies: 1) one which holds the idea of transubstantiation, 2) one which accepts the dogma of the Council of Trent but without transubstantiation, 3) one which does no more than affirm the truth of the real presence, while rejecting even the idea that accidents remain.

It should be noted carefully that all these tendencies, whether they be of the West or of the East, are closely linked with different Christological positions and with different doctrines on the relation between the two natures. Those who tend to separate the humanity and the divinity in Christ (a Nestorian attitude) will also tend to separate the bread from the body and the wine from the blood of Christ, and they will have difficulty in expressing the relation existing between the Eucharistic appearances and the person of Christ. In the fourteenth century, Timothy II, the Nestorian patriarch, would express these thoughts: "This bread and this wine which, of their nature, are neither body nor blood, by the grace of the Holy Spirit which is poured out on them, are called the body and blood of Christ. . . . Since we say that the bread and wine are body and blood by grace, we cannot conclude that of their nature they are God."[31] Those who tend to confuse the humanity and the divinity of Christ (a Monophysitic attitude)[32] will tend also to confuse the bread and the body, the wine and the blood of Christ, and will refuse to maintain even the Catholic distinction between the substance which changes and the accidents which remain. Here, as in Christology, the mystery of the dogma of Chalcedon ought to be respected. If the substance of the Eucharist, its inner reality, is the body and blood of Christ, its chemical nature remains bread and wine, without our being able to define the manner of their relation, a relation which is such that we must say, with Scripture, that the Eucharist *is* the body and blood of Christ.

THESES ON THE REAL PRESENCE

1. The body and blood of Christ, his whole humanity and divinity, are truly, and in all reality, and substantially present in the Eucharist.

This real presence of Christ's body and blood is the presence here and now of the crucified and glorified Christ, under concrete signs. Bodily presence always means that a person is concretely present and can communicate concretely with others. Because of the real presence of the body and blood, the Church is certain that Christ is there in her midst concretely, and she receives him under a concrete form. Substantial presence of Christ does not signify material presence in the natural sense, but the presence of the inner reality of the body and blood of the crucified and glorified Christ.

2. The glorified Christ, in his humanity and in his divinity, sits at the right hand of the Father; how it is possible that he be also bodily present in the Eucharist is a mystery, the work of the Holy Spirit, which the Church cannot resolve.

The real presence of Christ must not be understood as a localization limited to the appearances of the bread and wine; Christ cannot be enclosed within these limits of creation. But the bread and wine in the Eucharist become a privileged site where it is possible to encounter and to receive concretely Christ himself in his humanity and his divinity. It is the glorified Christ who, by his power to submit all things to himself, acts through the Holy Spirit and by his Word upon the bread and wine to make of them a place where Christ encounters him and receives him bodily, and an instrument through which the Church can contact him in the fullness of his humanity and divinity.

3. Christ therefore, through the Holy Spirit and by his Word, masters with full dominion the elements of the bread and wine; he draws them to himself and assumes them into the fullness of his humanity and his divinity, in such a way that they truly, in all reality and substantially, become his body and blood, according to the Gospel.

The glorified Christ assumes the form of bread and wine to manifest his bodily presence in the Church. The bread and wine of the Eucharist are no longer ordinary bread and wine. No doubt the chemical constituents remain those of bread and wine, but behind these chemical constituents, we must recognize by faith the new and real substantial nature of this bread and wine: the body and blood of Christ. The Church does not stop at the fact that this is real bread and real wine, in the chemical sense; but she believes that this bread and this wine are changed, not chemically, but in this sense, that the glorified Christ assumes them to make of them a concrete symbol of his presence in our midst (his Eucharistic form), his body and blood. They constitute a place where he can be found locally, contemplated with the senses, communicated in concrete fashion.

4. It is the Holy Spirit, asked from the Father, and the Word of Christ, spoken by the Church during the memorial that is accomplished in the great Eucharistic prayer, which make of the bread and wine the body and blood of Christ.

It is not necessary to determine the one moment at which the mystery actually takes place. For it is by reason of the entire Eucharistic action and in particular by the whole of the great Eucharistic prayer (from the *Sursum corda* to the *Amen*) that the bread and wine are made into the Eucharist by the Holy Spirit and the Word of Christ, in the memorial presented to the Father. In the unfolding of the liturgy we should not look for a privileged moment at which the consecration takes place nor should we create opposition between the words of Christ and the invocation of the Holy Spirit. The normal liturgical order would call for the Holy Spirit to be invoked before Christ's words of institution. This would show that the Holy Spirit vivifies the words and gives them efficacy and that as a result the bread and wine become the body and blood of Christ. A second epiklesis or invocation of the Holy Spirit is not out of place after the words of consecration and the Anamnesis, but this time with the purpose of preparing the faithful for the reception of the body and blood of Christ. These two invocations of the Holy Spirit are given in these places in the ancient Alexandrine liturgy said to be of St. Mark.

5. The form of bread and wine is the sign that Christ is our food; it is through this sign of bread and wine that the real presence of the body and blood of Christ comes to us. This real bodily presence must be contemplated and received within the liturgical action in which Christ acts with us and for us, in which he gives himself to us in communion.

The Eucharist is not a sacred object but an action and a communion; the signs of the bread and wine become the Eucharist for the sacrifice of thanksgiving and intercession which takes place in the communion. The sick who cannot leave home are joined to the Eucharistic action if they so desire: communion is brought to them at home, as an extension of the celebration.

6. The body and blood of Christ, objectively present in the Eucharist for communion, really affect all those by whom they are received: those with a right intention, for their sanctification; and for their condemnation, those who refuse to acknowledge the body of Christ out of incredulity, or the body of the Church out of selfishness.

St. Paul expresses the objective nature of Christ's Eucharistic presence by pointing out the disastrous consequences of communion which is selfish or without faith, without discerning the body of Christ or the body of the Church by faith and charity (1 Cor 11:27–34). In the event of an unworthy communion, he who does not have faith and charity encounters Christ, who is really present, but without receiving the fruits of this encounter; rather, he is condemned for his lack of faith and charity.

7. After the Eucharistic celebration, completed by the communion of all the faithful, even of the sick in their homes, the real relationship between Christ and the Eucharistic elements which remain is a mystery which we must respect.

The purpose of the Eucharist being communion ("Take, eat. . . . Drink of it all of you . . ."), we will not allow ourselves to define what kind of relation exists between Christ and the Eucharistic elements which remain after communion has taken place. It is not our task to take a stand either for or against the permanence of the real presence. Here we must respect the mystery. In this attitude of respect, it is proper that the remaining Eucharistic elements be consumed after the celebration.[33] Negligence in this area compromises belief in the real presence, while a reasonable respect is a sign that one truly believes in the presence of Christ's body and blood and that at least the material basis of this presence merits our respect. If one believes in the efficacy of the Word of Christ, he must also believe that this Word would not leave unaffected the creatures it touches.

8. Communion in the body and blood of Christ is at the same time communion of each person with the ecclesial body; united in the same offering by the Church in Christ, the faithful are inseparably joined together by communion in the body of Christ.

If the Church makes the Eucharist, the Eucharist makes the Church. The Eucharist unites and welds together the members of Christ's body. United in the Eucharistic and also in the ecclesiastical body of Christ, the baptized are all formed into a unity, and cannot but seek to deepen and extend their unity and to bring it to total perfection. As the sacrament of unity, the Eucharist is the sacrament of charity, which it preserves and deepens. Therefore in the search for Church unity, intercommunion in the same Eucharist cannot be considered as an end but as a means of acknowledging and of living the fact that it is Christ who effects the unity of the ecclesiastical body through communion in his Eucharistic body. And in the life of a local community, the Eucharist is the place par excellence where the Church is built up, is formed, and grows in charity. The Church, by frequently celebrating the Eucharist, increases her charity and unity and makes effective in the world her words and her life.

Translated under the direction of the editors

NOTES

A translation of "La Présence réelle," which appeared as a part of *L'Eucharistie* by Max Thurian, pp. 255–273, Éditions Delachaux & Niestlé, Neuchâtel et Paris, 1959. An English edition will be published under the title *The Eucharistic Memorial*, Part II: *The New Testament* by the Lutterworth Press, London. We are indebted to Delachaux & Niestlé for permission to translate this contribution.

1. Cahiers Théologiques, No. 37, (Neuchâtel-Paris, Delachaux-Niestlé: 1955).
2. But the chapter on "The Lord's Supper as Sacrifice" calls for some reservations. It will be quite clear where we differ from F. J. Leenhardt on this point.
3. *Adversus Haereses*, IV, 18, 5.
4. *Ibid.*, V, 2, 3.
5. For the Catholic doctrine of transubstantiation, see the excellent article "Eucharistie" of J. de Baciocchi in the encyclopedia *Catholicisme*; the article is also very enlightening on the Catholic doctrine of the Eucharistic sacrifice.
6. Chapter IV, Denzinger, *Enchiridion Symbolorum*, 877.
7. Canon II, *ibid.*, 884; see also the *Professio fidei Tridentina, ibid.*, 997.
8. *Ibid.*, 874.
9. *The Small Catechism*, VI; *The Large Catechism* has: ". . . in and under the bread and wine. . . ."
10. Part III, Art. VI.
11. *Petit traité de la sainte cène*, p. 112.
12. Cf. the analysis of the idea of substance in Calvin by H. Gollwitzer, *Coena Domini* (Munich, 1937), p. 120 ff.
13. *Petit traité de la sainte cène*, p. 111.
14. "Sacramentum ponitur in genere signi." *Summa Theologiae*, IIIa Pars, q. 60, a. 1.
15. *Petit traité de la sainte cène*, pp. 108–9.
16. *Instruction* of 1537, article "De la Cène du Seigneur."
17. P. 141.
18. *Petit traité de la sainte cène*, p. 138.
19. He certainly found this idea in a sermon which Erasmus attributed to St. John Chrysostom in the edition of his works published at Basel in 1530.
20. *Institution chrétienne*, 1541, Ed. Belles Lettres, t. IV, p. 24.

21. P. 110.

22. Pp. 129–30.

23. P. 141.

24. *Institution chrétienne*, t. IV, pp. 29–31.

25. "Haec est perpetua corporis veritas, ut loco contineatur, ut suis dimensionibus constet."

26. F. Wendel, *Calvin, sources et évolution de sa pensée religieuse* (Paris: Presses universitaires de France, 1950), has some very enlightening pages on the doctrine of the Lord's Supper, pp. 251–71; see also A. Graf, "La doctrine calvinienne de la cène," *Revue de théologie et de philosophie*, Vol. 83 (avril-juin 1932), pp. 135–50; W. Niesel, *Calvins Lehre vom Abendmahl*, 2nd ed., (Munich: Ch. Kaiser Verlag, 1935); H. Gollwitzer, *Coena Domini* (Munich, 1937); E. Bizer, *Studien zur Geschichte des Abendmahlstreites im 16. Jahrhundert* (Gütersloh, 1940); J. Cadier, *La doctrine calviniste de la cène* (Montpellier, 1951).

27. There is a similar passage in his Commentary on 1 Cor 11:24 (Calvin, *Commentaires sur le Nouveau Testament*, t. III [Toulouse, 1864], p. 355): "I conclude that the body of Christ is in all reality (as is commonly said) given to us at the Supper; that is, that it may truly be salutary food for our souls. I speak in ordinary language, but I mean that our souls are nourished by the substance of his body that we may in all reality become one with him; or what amounts to the same thing, that life-giving strength, derived from the flesh of Christ, be poured forth in us through the Spirit though the flesh of Christ remain distant from us and though it be not mingled with us."

28. Wendel, *op. cit.*, p. 271.

29. Commentary on Eph 5:32, *op. cit.*, p. 666; Calvin here applies "the great mystery" to the Lord's Supper, and criticizes those who wish to understand the how of the real presence in order to believe in it.

30. Quoted by J. Cadier, *op. cit.*, p. 113.

31. *De sacramentis*, in G. S. Assémani, ed., *Bibliotheca orientalis* (Rome, 1719 ff.), Vol. III, pp. 294–95; Nestorius, *Livre d'Héraclide*, ed. Nan, p. 52; W. de Vries, *Sakramenten Theologie bei den Nestorianern*, Orientalia Christiana analecta (Rome, 1947), Vol. 133, pp. 214–20. Nestorians always find it difficult to abstract the ideas of substance or nature from their concrete manifestations; cf. I. H. Dalmais in a review of the book by W. de Vries, *Maison-Dieu*, Vol. 19, pp. 127–30. Modern Nestorians now hold the Orthodox position. See *Dictionnaire Théologique Catholique*, "Tables Générales," art. "Eucharistie," col. 1322 ff.

32. W. de Vries, *Sakramenten Theologie bei den syrischen Monophysiten*, Orientalia Christiana analecta (Rome, 1940), Vol. 125. I. H. Dalmais, "Note sur la théologie des Mystères dans les Églises Syriennes (occidentales et orientales)," *Maison-Dieu*, Vol. 19, pp. 60–61: "One discovers . . . the old Semitic concept of holiness as of a quasi-physical fluid which is communicated by contact."

33. To avoid having too great a quantity of wine left over, one consecrates only the wine which is contained in the cups necessary for communion: if more wine is needed during communion, more is to be added to the cups, while they still contain enough "Eucharistic" wine. This will safeguard the full truth of the Eucharistic prayer.

This practice is founded in tradition. When the faithful were very numerous, it was not possible to consecrate on the altar all the wine necessary. The celebrant would consecrate only his own cup, and before communion the deacon consecrated the cups for the faithful by putting into them a small amount of the wine consecrated by the celebrant or a particle of the consecrated bread. The prayer of the Roman Mass now in use, *Haec commixtio et consecratio* [This commingling and consecration], was understood in those days in a more literal sense. Moreover, after the Council of Trent the word *Haec* [This] replaced an earlier *Fiat* [Let it take place]; the meaning of the prayer had been: "May the commingling and the consecration of the body and blood of our Lord Jesus Christ take place. . . ." The three signs of the Cross made with the particle over the chalice still recall today this earlier consecration; even today the priest drops this particle into the wine, an action that no longer has the meaning of a consecration. This very complex rite also has other origins, but it was important to call attention to the primitive significance of a consecration by commingling a particle of the consecrated bread (or of a little consecrated wine) with the wine destined for the communion of the faithful. De Jonge, "L'arrière-plan dogmatique de la commixtion," cited by T. Mertens, "L'histoire de la communion au service de sa pastorale," *Paroisse et Liturgie* (1958), No. 5, p. 352.

10

REFORMATION, PREACHING, AND EX OPERE OPERATO

HEIKO A. OBERMAN

IT has been repeatedly suggested that *the* discovery of the Reformation was the re-enthronement of the sermon tradition of Augustine and Chrysostom. However, if we were to point to the main characteristic that the Middle Ages and the Reformation had in common it would be, without doubt, the emphasis on preaching,[1] its frequency and popularity. From Bernard through Savonarola and Knox princes and citizens were confronted from the pulpit with the Scriptures as the standard for living. The later Middle Ages especially show such a colorful, even confusing, spectacle of conventicle and itinerant preaching[2] that this phenomenon can only be compared with the activities of the Radical Reformers. The idea that there was a disappearance of preaching with the sole emphasis on the Eucharist along with the "Chained Bible" should be removed to the realm of fable.

New indeed is the understanding of the function of the sermon and its relation to the sacraments. Due to the various emphases of the Reformers and to the overarching Catholicity of the Reformation we cannot epitomize this understanding in one single sentence. As far as I can see, at least three aspects should be mentioned here: (1) the sermon as apocalyptic event, (2) the sermon as corporate act of worship, and (3) the relation of the written and the spoken Word of God.

The Heidelberg Catechism answers the question, "How is the Kingdom of Heaven opened and shut?" by pointing to the preaching of the gospel, proceeding to explain it with the following words:

In this way, when according to the command of Christ it [the gospel] is proclaimed and openly testified to believers, one and all, (that) as often as they receive the promise of the Gospel with true faith, all their sins are truly forgiven by God for the sake of Christ's merits; and on the contrary to all unbelievers and hypocrites, (that) the wrath of God and eternal condemnation lie on them so long as they are not converted. It is according to this testimony of the Gospel that God will pass judgment both in this life and in the life to come.[3]

Three things should be noted here. First, the sermon has absorbed the medieval sacrament of Penance. In the medieval and Roman Catholic tradition, however frequently the preaching of the Word may occur, it never has any other function than to dispose the fallen Christian for the infusion of grace in the sacrament of Penance or —in a more theoretical case—to dispose the heathen for Baptism. As the leading Jesuit theologian at the Council of Trent, Jacob Lainez, put it, ". . . the Scriptures have been made for the special purpose of producing good inclinations by way of threats and promises."[4] The function of the sermon is to provide proper doctrinal information especially as regards the First and Second Advents of Jesus Christ. The more mystical tradition would stress the psychological effects: the condescension of God in the First Advent should produce love, his return in the Second Advent to judge the quick and the dead, fear.[5] Preaching is here essentially teaching, communication of revealed truths, exhortation through *didache*.

The sermon, then, has the propaedeutic task of convincing the listener of his sin and of showing him the way to holiness; the sermon helps the sinner to climb the steps that lead to the entrance of the cathedral. But just as Dante has to change guides when he enters heaven, so the sermon has to stop at the gates of the sanctuary and refer the sinner to the baptismal font, the penitential, and the altar. Only in the sacraments is communication between God and man established. To be sure, what takes place is not the encounter with the living person of Jesus Christ but with the fruits of his works: ". . . all true justice either begins or being begun is increased or being lost is repaired by the Sacraments."[6]

For the Reformers the sermon had certainly also a didactic and paraenetical function—but only because and insofar as the kerygma forced for itself a way to the heart and mind of the congregation: not a *preparation* for the encounter with the sphere of the holy but the *decisive* encounter with the Holy One himself. The sermon does not inspire good inclinations, but moves the doors of heaven(and hell. It is *the apocalyptic event*—apocalyptic in the pure sense: that which reveals—with its double connotation; it reveals God and devil alike. It does not call man *out* of his sinful situation to the unassailable safety of the sacred but reaches man *in* his worldly situation: Jesus Christ becomes present under the veil of the preached Word, *outside* the cathedral, on the steps. But however drastically— and dramatically—"contemporaneous" preachers like Luther and Calvin may have been preaching with direct relevance to social or political situations, they never presumed that the gospel simply answers the questions the members of the congregation bring with them. Luther said that the most dangerous task in the world is that of preaching the Word: Where Christ appears the devils start to speak.[7] The other aspect of the sermon as apocalyptic event is therefore that man's real existence is revealed in confrontation with Jesus Christ and so even his religious and pious questions are unmasked as expressions of self-love. The pietistic-revivalistic tradition has rightly stressed this point: Where the Word is preached and man encounters Christ, he is forced to answer Yes or No.

This leads us to two further comments on the sermon as apocalyptic event. The doors of heaven and hell are put in motion by the preached Word. The problem of predestination arose out of the homiletic surprise that some understood and others did not. From there it was transferred, both in the Augustinian and Thomistic tradition, to the realm of philosophical prolegomena or theological speculations on the properties of God. The Reformation has reassigned this doctrine its primary, systematic place in homiletics. In the sermon Christ and the devil are revealed, Creator and creature, love and wrath, essence and existence, Yes and No.

The sermon does not have to try desperately to be actual because it has the highest possible actuality; it reveals and responds—in this order!—to the creation which "waits with eager longing for the revealing of the sons of God."[8] This means finally that the Last Judgment is not the feared tribunal, chaired by an unknown, unpredictable God at the end of time.[9] The sermon is also apocalyptic in the sense that, far from merely referring to the final evaluation of our records, it reveals to us *now* in time and space the final will of God for the individual Christian. It is God's last word, to which no syllable will be added.

For this reason the Reformation could preach the *certitudo salutis* (certainty of salvation), because he who will judge us is the same who fulfilled the law. In the words of Calvin: "When a Christian looks into himself, he finds cause to be afraid or even to despair . . . [but] he will win a sure hope of eternal perseverance when he considers that he belongs to Him who cannot fall or fail."[10] Insofar as the term "certainty of salvation" carries none of the restrictive connotations of the traditional three *sola*'s [*sola scriptura, sola gratia, sola fides*], it is to be preferred as the more revealing single-term description of the kernel of Reformation theology.

The sermon as *corporate act of worship* is the second aspect to which we turn to describe the rediscovery of the meaning of preaching in the Reformation. The great English liturgist Dom Gregory Dix stated in his influential *The Shape of the Liturgy*[11] that the Eucharist in the late Middle Ages became for the first time something said rather than something done.[12] He argues that the Reformation did not change this. The Reformed liturgy was still essentially something said rather than something done. It remains individualistic rather than corporate.[13]

I should like to make a few comments on these statements of Dix which—I believe—bear directly on our topic.

In a more liturgical-formal sense the Reformed form of worship seems only a variation on the late medieval liturgy.

It is indeed more typical of the Radical Reformers, with their Donatist inclinations, to reverse the stream of history and return to the pre-Constantinian *form* of Christian life than of the major Reformers to do so.

All three Reformers, Luther, Zwingli and Calvin, believe that the outward forms of worship are nonessential and variable human traditions insofar as they are not "instituted by God's Word and done in faith."[14] Any reform in nonessentials would only confuse and thus mislead the simple folk. The so-called "liturgical conservatism" of the magisterial Reformers, where present, stems from this pastoral concern.[15]

The observation that Reformation worship is verbalistic and individualistic instead of corporate, however, seems to me to be indefensible on several counts.

In the first place, the rejection of Latin as the liturgical language and the introduction of liturgies in the vernacular not only broke down the wall separating the altar from the nave of the church but enabled the congregation to participate again in the service; prayers and responses were no longer the sole prerogative of clergy or choir.

Secondly, the Reformation sanctioned a development which originated in the later Middle Ages—n.b. Surgant's *Manuale Curatorum*, 1502—by introducing some rubrics which formerly had a solely private function. The reading and singing of the Decalogue stems from the instruction of converts before Baptism; the confession of sins is first the private preparation of the priest before the beginning of the service; the declaration of grace is the transformation of the private absolution by the priest in the sacrament of Penance. All these *private* devotions were made *corporate* by the Reformers to structure the worship of the Church.

Nevertheless, more important and constitutive for these other developments is the fact that the administration of the Word itself is understood as a corporate action. This is true for the visible Word, the sacraments. Baptism becomes the visible sign of God's gracious operation in which not only the godparents, but the whole *con*-gregation is involved. And in the Eucharist the emphasis shifts from the consecration of the elements and the sacrifice of the priest on *behalf* of the congregation to the communion *by* the congregation.

It may surprise us that Huldreich Zwingli—for a long time more highly rated as soldier and politician than as theologian—formulated this operation of the Holy Spirit so succinctly that there is reason to say that he taught a doctrine of transubstantiation—not the medieval doctrine of transubstantiation of the elements, but the apostolic doctrine, mentioned in the *Didache* (*The Teaching of the Twelve Apostles*)—according to which the dispersed congregation is assembled and changed into the body of Christ.[16]

Here, then, we may conclude that the Reformation, far from being the illegitimate child of individualism is, on the contrary—in one of its many aspects—the answer to the challenge of late medieval individualism. This, now, is equally true for the preaching of the Word.

If asked to state in just one phrase the most fundamental rediscovery of the Reformation, one should not simply answer: the authority of the Scriptures, or the sole efficacy of grace. The debates prior to the fourth session of the Council of Trent show with how much hesitancy the dogma of equal reverence for Scripture and Tradition was received; and throughout the Middle Ages, in Augustinian and Dominican circles, the sole efficacy of grace was clearly stated.

It seems to me that one of the most important aspects of Reformation thought is best described as the rediscovery of the Holy Spirit, as the *Christus pro nobis*. To be sure, medieval theology had a powerful doctrine of the Holy Spirit. But this was localized in the sacramental infusion of created grace and in special individual charisms. The Reformation returned to an understanding of the Holy Spirit as the dynamic presence of God in His creation. The prime function, now, of the Holy Spirit is to gather his Church; and, though this may happen at any place and any moment, the preaching of the gospel is the specially God-chosen way. In his second exposition of *Galatians* Luther remarks: "As God at first gives faith through the Word, so He hereafter also exercises, increases, confirms and perfects it through the Word. Therefore the worship of God at its best and the finest keeping of the Sabbath consists in exercising oneself in piety and in dealing with the Word and hearing it."[17]

The double operation of the Holy Spirit in opening the Bible through the preacher and opening the hearts of the listeners constitutes the sermon as corporate action which links speaking and listening. Just as the Holy Spirit is not effective in the sacraments when faith is absent, so no preaching of the gospel is possible without the whole congregation being involved, positively or negatively, accepting the Word or rejecting it.

But the recovery of the vision of the dynamic operation of the Holy Spirit has yet another consequence. In contrast with the medieval and Roman Catholic tradition the Reformation understands the church service not as the time and place of refuge from a devil-ridden world which is only the passing scenery for the *viator,* the traveler to the Holy City. That the wall between secular and sacred, between natural and supernatural, is broken down means in this context that the congregation does not flee the world for the sanctuary, nor for that matter does it bring the world into the church, but the service takes place in the world; the world as God's creation with its needs and promises is not lost from sight for one moment.

Dr. Pelikan's widely hailed *The Riddle of Roman Catholicism*[18] in trying to be as sympathetic as possible toward Roman Catholicism has not been fortunate in presenting the genius of the Reformation. Mariology is one of the points where he expresses a deep concern and hesitancy. He hastens to add, however, that "the mother of God is also a bridge to the entire world of nature,"[19] and "only in our own day has Protestant thought begun to realize the riches it has lost by excluding the world of nature so radically from its purview and it remains to be seen whether its reconsideration of this area will approach the profundity evident in Roman Catholic Mariology."[20] Dr. Pelikan seems to me to ignore here the basic thrust of the Reformation: the linking of body and soul, society and Church, creation and re-creation.

The Reformation service is essentially a "trilogue" between God, His creature, and His creation. In this sense the program of the Reformation is *radical secularization,* secular meant in the same sense in which we may speak of God as having secularized His transcendent Holiness by becoming time and space in Jesus Christ. For this reason worship could never mean a total absorption in the worship of heavenly angels and archangels: with the world all around it was not difficult to be mindful of the difference between the Church Triumphant and the Church Militant. As Luther's distinction between Gospel and Law and, therefore, between kingdom and world, is so often misrepresented, we quote him once again: "To be sure, it is true that the foremost and highest worship of God is preaching and hearing God's Word, administering the Sacraments, etc., performing the works of the First Table of the Ten Commandments. Nevertheless, also *the performance of all work of the Second Table* of the Ten Commandments, such as honoring father and mother, living a patient, chaste and decent life, is worshiping God. For he who leads such a life is serving and honoring the same God."[21] And again: "Where the true obedience of faith toward God is to be found, there *everything* one's calling requires to be done is a holy and God-pleasing act of worship."[22]

Zwingli became a Reformer not primarily because of the anguish of his own soul, but because he was driven by a deep concern for the social and political conditions in Switzerland. The Church of Zürich offers one of the purest examples of the earthy and concrete relevance of the preaching of the Word in the Reformation.

Turning to Calvin, we find this expressed in an even clearer way in the structure of his Genevan catechism. The administration of Word and sacraments, i.e., let us say, the "Sunday operation" of the Holy Spirit, is only one of the four parts to honor God. The other three parts, true faith and knowledge, obedience to the law, and prayer, form the worship of the Church as much as the part mentioned last: the Sunday service. Though it is definitely wrong to say that according to the Reformation "real worship starts outside the church" the church service has no meaning as a dialogue between God and the soul, as religious education or edification: faith *and* knowledge, task (*Amt*) *and* prayer are as many aspects of the dynamic operation of the Holy Spirit which is not limited to the souls of more or less pious men but directed to all the works of God's hand. In short, not *dialogue,* but *trilogue* characterizes the Reformation conception of worship.

At this point, then, before dealing with the last part, we may conclude that in contrast with the medieval and Roman Catholic preaching of the Word, the Reformation sermon is not legalistic but redemptive, not only directed to individual souls but especially to the corporate existence of the congregation, not elevating but mobilizing, not a refuge but a starting point, and, finally, not holy and vertical but secular and horizontal: time, space, and dust.

There are few Latin words left in the vocabulary of the Protestant layman. But with little doubt one may say that one of these is a short, almost magical phrase which tends to evoke a world of emotion: *ex opere operato.* From the time of the *Apology of the*

Augsburg Confession[23] it is used in the official Protestant confessions, and even before 1547 when Trent[24] gave it official sanction it had become a Protestant battle cry.

In this last section we should like to show that the Reformation had its own *ex opere operato* doctrine, in connection not with the sacraments, the visible Word, but with the audible Word, the sermon. If this were the case, it would affect deeply our understanding of Reformation theology, on the one hand, and on the other, it would contrast the sixteenth-century concept of preaching not only with its medieval predecessor but also with its twentieth-century counterpart.

The term *ex opere operato* has a triple, and not always sufficiently differentiated, meaning. Each meaning stands in contradistinction to the phrase *ex opere operantis* and stresses, therefore, the independence of the results of a certain operation from the acting subject. Applied to the sacraments, this means, in the first place, that the validity of the administration of a sacrament is independent from the dignity and standing of the administering clergyman. Taken in this sense, the doctrine of *ex opere operato* is not typically Roman Catholic or medieval. Since the fourth century the Church has rejected the claim of the Donatists that at least the clergy should be holy men. The Reformation, on the whole very sensitive to the sovereignty of God, agreed that human weakness and sin in the ministrant could not form an obstacle to God's operation. None of the Reformers puts this in more precise words than Luther: "Although a rascal, a godless and unbelieving person takes or gives the Sacrament, he takes or gives the true Sacrament . . . just as truly as he who administers and receives it most worthily. For the Sacrament is not based on the holiness of man but on the Word of God."[25] Although Calvin does not hold the real presence of Christ apart from the participation by faith, he, too, can say that "the power of the mystery remains intact no matter how much wicked men try their utmost to nullify it."[26]

We may, therefore, conclude that according to the Reformation the sacraments are administered *ex opere operato* in the indicated first sense. At the same time Luther's *Babylonian Captivity of the Church*[27] makes it perfectly clear that he agrees with the other Reformers in rejecting the doctrine of *ex opere operato* in a second sense, that accepted by the Council of Trent, implying a ritual which is supposed to impart grace simply by virtue of its having been properly performed, without reference to any faith or lack of faith on the part of the person for whom it is performed.[28]

Before we return to the preaching of the Word we must recall the above indicated important difference between Luther and Calvin as regards the Lord's Supper. While both rejected the automatic *saving* efficacy of the participation in this sacrament, Calvin felt that Luther conceded too much to Roman Catholic doctrine by accepting the *ex opere operato* availability of Jesus Christ in the Eucharist. In this Lutheran conception of the Lord's Supper we meet therefore with a third meaning of the term *ex opere operato*.

When we keep in mind this excursus on the Eucharist in the Reformation we are in a better position to answer the question, How far did the Reformers teach a doctrine of *ex opere operato* with respect to the preaching of the Word? There can be no doubt about their subscribing to the *ex opere operato* in the first, anti-Donatist sense, identical with that which we noted in connection with the administration of the sacraments.[29] *Ex opere operato* in its second sense is unanimously rejected by the Reformers as only the *faithful* receive the Word of God unto salvation.

It should not surprise us that Luther also teaches an *ex opere operato* doctrine in the third sense as the certain presence of the Word of God in the mouth of the preacher: "Yes, I hear the sermon; but who is speaking? The minister? No, indeed! You do not hear the minister. True, the voice is his; but my God is speaking the Word which he preaches or speaks."[30]

Heinrich Bullinger, the author in 1562 of a personal confession, later officially accepted as the *Confessio Helvetica Posterior,* was instrumental in unifying the Zwingli-Calvin tradition[31] with that of Luther. Due to this confession the *ex opere operato presence* of God's Word in the preached Word has become *common doctrine for the whole Reformation.* Bullinger formulated this in the following words: "When this Word of God is proclaimed in the church by preachers who are officially called, we believe that they proclaim and the faithful receive, the very Word of God and that no different Word of

God is to be imagined or expected from heaven; we believe also that in the present day we should concentrate on the very Word that is preached and not on the minister that is preaching, for though he be wicked and sinful, the Word of God remains nonetheless true and good."[32] Central in this quotation is the equation of the preached word with the Word of God. The title of this part of the confession is given succinctly: *Praedicatio verbi Dei est verbum Dei* (the preaching of the Word of God is *the* Word of God).

In a few points we can now evaluate the significance and relevance of this Reformation insight:

1. This doctrine finds its close parallel in the Lutheran *ex opere operato* doctrine of the Eucharist. The Word of God is not only automatically present if preached by properly ordained ministers, but it is *ipso facto* effective. The Word of God does not return empty; it may be rejected or accepted in faith. At the same time we may conclude that, in contrast to the Tridentine position, faith is necessary to effect salvation.[33]

2. The Word of God must be *preached* to become fully effective. The seventeenth-century identification of the biblical canon with the Word of God has led to many tragic developments. More than that black sheep, the doctrine of verbal inspiration, this identification is mainly responsible for a static conception of revelation which laid itself wide-open to the uprooting consequences of biblical criticism.

It also led to a misunderstanding of the meaning of individual reading of the Bible. If the perspicuity of the Bible for the most simple believer is overemphasized, the task of the sermon cannot be much more than a scholarly aid to clear up some difficult points. The doctrine of the perspicuity of the Bible, however, functions properly only when correlated with the preaching of the Word. Even the most simple believer is in a position to safeguard the proper administration of the Word and to distinguish between the Word of God and the word of man. This is the point where the Reformation doctrine of the priesthood of all believers should be stressed against the neo-Protestant conception of a priesthood of all Old Testament and New Testament professors.

3. At this point one may well wonder why it is necessary for the faithful to distinguish between these two, if indeed the Word of

God is present *ex opere operato.* Here we must stress the fact that
the content of the sermon is not secondary or even irrelevant, but
that the Word of *God* must be preached, that is, the Word of God
as contained in the Scriptures. Not only faith on the part of the
congregation but obedience on the part of the preacher is a condition for the *ex opere operato* saving presence of the Word of God
in the sermon. One can point here to the medieval and Roman
Catholic requirement of the "proper intention" in the administrant
to perform the rite in accordance with the teaching of the Church.

Father George Tavard in his book *Holy Writ or Holy Church*
pays no attention to this Reformation understanding of preaching
as the living authority and actualization of the Scriptures. If this
had been true, he would not have been in a position to state that the
Reformers ignored and denied what he called "the coinherence of
Church and Scripture."[34] The preaching of the Word in the Reformation is the living *magisterium* and bridge between Church and
Scripture.

4. It is not possible in the context of this short article to deal
at length with the history and present state of biblical hermeneutics.
But it is clear that the rediscovery of the Reformation adage *praedicatio verbi Dei est verbum Dei* is *the* precondition for dealing with
this most urgent of modern theological tasks, and only this principle
can help today's preacher properly to understand his own task.

It seems to me that Dr. Krister Stendahl has done just this by
advocating what he terms the "bilingual approach." In an article on
"The New Testament and the Preaching of the Church" he says:
"There is no short cut by which the original meaning of a text and
its implication for our present situation could be grasped in one
existential glimpse. The preacher needs a command of biblical
thought . . . which allows him to move within the first century categories with idiomatic ease . . . . He also needs the same competence
in the 'language' of his own time and setting. Only with such
bilingual competence will he be able to communicate the message
of his text. Only then will his preaching become 'biblical' in a true
sense and the text be allowed to cut into men's lives."[35]

Preaching cannot be just reading of the biblical record. This
would fence in the Scriptures and transform the kerygma for the

world into a secret language for the chosen few. The right wing—the fundamentalist wing of the Reformation—found this a temptation. But as great a temptation for what one may call, in a broad sense, liberal Protestantism, is the other extreme: the frantic search for a "vital message for our time." Here the Scriptures function merely as a point of departure for dealing with problems of contemporary life. Bullinger had this approach in mind when he said that we believe that the preaching of the Word of God is the Word of God and that we therefore should not compose a new message.

In summary, we may say that the Reformation rejected the authority of the suprascriptural *magisterium* but not to replace it with the static authority of the paper pope, the Bible, nor with the time-bound authority of individual ministers who manage to reach the ranks of theological, psychological, or social specialists. The Reformation heard the divine charge to preach in the words of Luke 10:16. "He who hears you hears Me, and he who rejects you rejects Me. . . ." In the sermon the Word of God meets the faithful with authority. There the apocalyptic event takes place wherein the real dimensions of the created world are revealed. There, finally, the congregation is transformed into the body of Christ situated not in the sanctuary but in a secular world, sinful, to be sure, yet endowed with the first fruits of the Spirit.

NOTES

This article is a revised version of "Preaching and the Word in the Reformation," which appeared in *Theology Today*, Vol. 18 (1961), pp. 16–29. We are indebted to the editor for his kind permission to publish it.

1. R. Cruel, *Geschichte der deutschen Predigt im Mittelalter* (Detmold, 1879), pp. 370 ff.; G. R. Owst, *Preaching in Medieval England* (Cambridge, 1926), *passim;* D. Roth, *Mittelalterliche Predigttheorie* (Basel, 1956).
2. See the interesting analyses of Calvin in his reply to the letter of Cardinal Sadolet, *Corpus Reformatorum* [hereafter abbreviated *CR*] (Brunsvigae: apud C. A. Schwetschke et Filium, 1891), Vol. 33, p. 396; e.g., "Only a few expressions were thrown in from the Word of God." This judgment is not applicable in general, but is correct as far as the "popular" late medieval sermon is concerned.

3. Question and Answer 83 and 84. Quoted from Thomas Torrance, ed., *The School of Faith* (New York: Harper and Bros., 1959), p. 87.

4. ". . . ad impellendum affectum in bonum, ut minae, promissa etc. Ad hoc enim scripturae factae sunt." Disputationes morales. VII Documenta ad bene interpretandas scripturas, in Diego Lainez, *Disputationes Tridentinae*, Hartmannus Grisar, S. J., ed. (Cincinnati: Fr. Pustet, 1886), Tomus II, p. 502.

5. *Sermones Dominicales Gabrielis Biel*, Hagenau 1510, Dominica I Adventus domini. Sermo I. Cf. Trent, Sessio VI. cap. 6. *Denz.* 798. It is noteworthy that we find the same with Erasmus, *Opera Omnia*, ed. Clericus, V Lugduni Batavorum 1704, 1319 E.

6. Trent, Sessio VII, Proemium: ". . . visum est, de sanctissimis Ecclesiae sacramentis agere per quae omnis vera iustitia vel incipit, vel coepta agetur, vel amissa reparatur." *Denz.* 843a. Though I do not claim that the Eucharistic presence of the *Christus passus* would be denied, it is nevertheless characteristic for fourteenth- and fifteenth-century academic theology to limit itself to issues concerning transubstantiation in contradistinction to those concerning offer, *recordatio,* and *praesentia realis.* The presence of the *Christus glorificatus* was treated in connection with the Second Advent.

7. Martin Luther, *Werke, Kritische Gesamtansgabe* [hereafter abbreviated *WA*] (Weimar: Hermann Böhlan, 1883 ff.), Vol. 25, p. 253. Cf. Zwingli on preaching: "Non possunt tacere daemones praesenti Christo." *CR*, Vol. 94, p. 485. Among contemporary theologians Karl Barth has again pointed most clearly to this dual aspect of preaching. Cf. his 1922 paper on "Not und Verheiszung der christliche Verkündigung," in *Das Wort Gottes und die Theologie,* 2nd ed. (Munich, 1925), pp. 99 ff.

8. Rom 8:19.

9. Luther on John 6:37. Jan. 1931. *WA*, Vol. 33, p. 83 f.

10. *CR*, Vol. 49, p. 313; cf. Luther, *Operationes in Psalmos*, Ps. 4:9; *WA*, Vol. 5, p. 124 f.

11. London: Dacre Press, 1945.

12. *Ibid.*, p. 16.

13. *Ibid.*, p. 10.

14. *Apology of the Augsburg Confession,* Art. XXVII, in Theodore G. Tappert, ed., *The Book of Concord* (Philadelphia: Muhlenberg Press, 1959), p. 281.

15. Calvin, *Institutes,* IV, Vol. 43; Luther, *WA,* Vol. 25, p. 128; Zwingli, *CR,* Vol. I, p. 536. Within the limits of this principle the Reformed tradition especially has originally been most active in liturgical reform (Zürich, Strasbourg, Geneva!). Cf. especially the relevant passage in a letter (April 23, 1561) written by Calvin to John Knox in Scotland. *CR,* Vol. 47, ep. 3377.

16. Cf. Zwingli's *Aktion oder Bruch des Nachtmals* (Zürich, 1525). Text in R. Christoffel, *Huldreich Zwingli* (Elberfeld, 1857), p. 412. It seems to me that this is not an isolated element in the theology of Zwingli; it should be seen against the background of his peculiar interpretation of the *imago Dei:*

mankind *in its totality* carries the image of God. Gottfried W. Locher noted this latter point in *CR,* Vol. 87, p. 168. Cf. his careful *Die Theologie Huldrych Zwinglis im Lichte seiner Christologie* (Zürich: Zwingli-Verlag, 1952), Vol. 1, p. 107.

17. *WA,* Vol. 40, Pt. I, p. 130. One can clarify the relation of the administration of the Word to that of the sacraments according to the Reformation by comparing it to the medieval conception of the relation of Baptism and Eucharist. In the former, the "redeeming" grace is given; in the latter, an *augmentum gratiae.* This shows at the same time that stress on the preaching of the Word does not for that reason diminish the significance of the sacraments. Cf. Luther, *WA,* Vol. I, p. 1168; *WA,* Vol. 47, p. 33. Calvin very clear in *Inst.* IV 14.9; Zwingli (*Huldreich Zwingli's Werke* [hereafter abbreviated *SS*], ed. by Melchior Schuler and Joh. Schulthess [Zürich: F. Schulthess, 1828 ff.] Vol. IV, p. 11).

18. New York: Abingdon Press, 1959.

19. *Ibid.,* p. 134.

20. *Ibid.,* p. 139.

21. *WA,* Vol. 45, p. 682.

22. *WA,* Vol. 43, p. 20.

23. 1531; cf. Art. IV on Justification.

24. In the canons added to the seventh session: *Denz.* 851.

25. *WA,* Vol. 6, p. 6770.

26. *Institutes,* IV, p. 17–33; cf. Craig's Catechism, 1581; 8. The sacraments in general: "*Q:* Do all men receive the favor of God by means of them? *A:* No; only the faithful receive it. *Q:* How then are they true seals to all men? *A:* They offer Christ truly to all men."

27. In *Luther's Works,* ed. by Abdel Ross Wentz (Philadelphia, 1959), Vol. 36, Word and Sacrament, pp. 55 f.

28. *Ibid.,* p. 37.

29. In *The Babylonian Captivity of the Church* this *ex opere operato* validity of the sacraments is even *founded* on that of preaching the gospel: "For it is true beyond a question that the testament or sacrament is given and received through the ministration of wicked priests no less completely than through the ministration of the most saintly. For who has any doubt that the Gospel is preached by the ungodly? Now the mass is part of the Gospel. . . ." *Loc. cit.*

30. *WA,* Vol. 47, p. 229.

31. Thirteen years earlier Bullinger and Calvin had reached agreement on the understanding of the Lord's Supper in what is known as the *Consensus Tigurinus* and thus preserved the unity of the Reformed tradition.

32. Proinde cum hodie hoc Dei verbum per praedicatores legitime vocatos annunciatur in Ecclesia, credimus ipsum Dei verbum annunciari et a fidelibus recipi, neque aliud Dei verbum vel fingendum vel coelitus esse exspectandum: atque in praesenti spectandum esse ipsum verbum, quod annunciatur non annunciantem ministrum, qui etsi sit malus et peccator, verum tamen et

bonum manet nihilominus verbum Dei. *Confessio Helvetica Posterior,* Vol.
I, p. 4, in Philip Schaff, *The Creeds of Christendom* (New York: Harper
and Bros., 1882), Vol. III, pp. 237 f.
33. Dogmatically, this conception reflects the widely debated question of the
interdependence of the universality and the particularity of God's loving
will for His world, *Ex opere operato* (again!) God's love in Jesus Christ is
present and *ipso facto* effective for mankind. For the *salutary* effect on the
rational part of the creation the response in faith is necessary, and here the
concept of predestination stands guard over the sovereignty of God in the
confession of justification without works.
34. *Holy Writ or Holy Church: The Crisis of the Protestant Reformation*
(New York: Harper and Bros., 1959), p. 245 and *passim.*
35. *Lutheran World,* Vol. VI (1959), No. 1, p. 32. This approach has already been stressed by J. S. Semmler, *Vorbereitung zur theologischen
Hermeneutik* 1760 (!); quoted by G. Ebeling, *RGG* 3rd ed. s.v. "Hermeneutik," Vol. III, col. 254.

SELECTED READINGS

1. Baillie, Donald M., *The Theology of the Sacraments.* New York: Charles
Scribner's Sons, 1957. Includes discussion of the real presence, the Eucharistic
offering, sacrament, and sacred history.
2. Baillie, D. M., and Marsh, John, eds., *Intercommunion.* New York: Harper
and Bros., 1952.
3. Barth, Karl, *The Teaching of the Church Regarding Baptism,* trans. by
Ernest A. Payne. London: S. C. M. Press Ltd., 1954. Out of Barth's thorough
re-examination of the nature of the Church and the Christian life has come,
among other things, this work which Oscar Cullmann called "the most
serious challenge to infant Baptism which has ever been offered."
4. Cullmann, Oscar, *Baptism in the New Testament,* trans by J. K. S. Reid.
London: S. C. M. Press Ltd., 1956. In this study Cullmann, in part writing
to confront Barth's view of Baptism, argues that a study of the New Testament shows that, whereas proof of infant Baptism is at best indirectly
demonstrable from observations, "infant Baptism is in every detail congruous
with the *doctrine* of Baptism" in several important ways.
5. Dillistone, F. W., "Atonement and the Sacraments," *Church Quarterly
Review,* Vol. 159 (April–June 1958), pp. 193–203.
6. Forsythe, P. T., *The Church and the Sacraments.* London: Independent
Press Ltd., 1947. First printed in 1917. Lectures by a man whose theology
has a newly found relevance.
7. Fuchs, Ernst, *Das Urchristliche Sakramentsverständnis.* Bad Connstatt;
R. Müllerschon Verlag, 1958.

8. Gilmore, A., ed., *Christian Baptism*. London: Lutterworth Press, 1959. A re-examination of this doctrine from biblical, historical, and theological points of view by a group of Baptist churchmen.

9. Hodgson, Leonard, *Church and Sacraments in Divided Christendom*. London: S. P. C. K., 1959.

10. Leenhardt, Franz J., *Ceci est mon corps*. Cahiers Théologiques, No. 37. Neuchâtel: Delachaux and Niestlé, 1955; *Le baptême chrétien, son origine, sa signification*. Cahiers Théologiques de l'actualité protestante, No. 4. Neuchâtel: Delachaux and Niestlé, 1946.

11. Pittenger, Norman W., *The Christian Sacrifice*. New York: Oxford University Press, 1951. A study of the offering of the Eucharistic memorial as the central and characteristic action of the body of Christ.

12. Reid, J. K. S., "A Christological View of the Sacraments," *Essays in Christology for Karl Barth*, ed. by T. H. L. Parker. London: Lutterworth Press, 1956, pp.

13. Church of Scotland's Special Commission on Baptism, *The Biblical Doctrine of Baptism*. Edinburgh: Saint Andrew Press, 1958.

14. Thurian, Max, *The Eucharistic Memorial: Part I, The Old Testament*, trans. by J. C. Davies. Ecumenical Studies in Worship, No. 7. Richmond, Va.: John Knox Press, 1960. The second part of Thurian's *L'Eucharistie: Mémorial du Seigneur, Sacrifice d'action de grâce et d'intercession* (Neuchâtel and Paris: Delachaux and Niestlé, 1959) will be published in this same series soon.

15. Tillich, Paul, *The Protestant Era*, trans. and with a concluding essay by James Luther Adams. Chicago: University of Chicago Press, 1948, pp. 94–112. An important statement of Tillich's manner of reinterpreting sacramental language and usage in light of the new understanding of the intrinsic powers of nature for which he argues.

INTRODUCTION:

THE ROMAN CATHOLIC VIEW OF
THE SACRAMENTS

How does man reach God? How does he make contact with Him? That is the basic question which all religions try to answer. Since the Christian believes that it is through the historical person of Jesus Christ and through his saving death and Resurrection that man reaches God, he has a concrete link to God which no other religion provides. But he also has a special problem: How does a man who lives in the twentieth century (or the fourth or the sixteenth) bridge the time gap between his present life and the saving events of the life of Jesus Christ?

A religion which is not centered on a contingent, historical event has no need of such a bridge; it claims to relate man directly to the timeless God. But the Christian must make contact with Jesus Christ and his saving deeds which were performed in the first century. That is why the Christian religion has sacraments.

During the first four centuries the Church did not theologize about the sacraments. It was enough that the life of the Church was lived through the sacraments and that Christians were aware of the objective presence of the saving acts of Christ in the sacramental mysteries of the Church. St. Augustine was the first to attempt a theological definition of a sacrament and the emphasis which he placed on the sign character of the sacraments dominated theological thought until the scholastic movement of the twelfth century, which reached its climax in St. Thomas Aquinas, emphasized that the sacraments *cause* what they signify. In the centuries which followed, rational analysis of the *modes* of causality of the sacraments became an absorbing concern of sacramental theology, and this, together with the failure to

emphasize that it is *Christ* who acts in the sacraments, had several
unfortunate consequences.

This proliferation of theories about modes of causality of the
sacraments in producing grace was accompanied by a failure to
stress that a sacrament is a personal act of Christ wrought on me.
This tended to obscure the importance of the personal response of
faith to the personal action of Christ in the sacraments.

In our own time several factors have conspired to restore the
more integral and balanced view of the sacraments which the following article of Father Schillebeeckx represents.

The return to the sources, to the Bible, the Fathers, and the
liturgy, which is at present revitalizing Catholic theology, has not
failed to have a healthy effect on sacramental theology and practice;
and the general intellectual climate of our time, which finds little
relish in the purely rational, analytic, impersonal approach, has also
provided a favorable atmosphere for a return to the kind of emphasis,
integral, concrete and personal, which had been neglected.

The liturgical movement, by its stress on active participation in
the sacramental life of the Church, has provided a powerful cor-
rective for the tendency to think of the sacraments as automatic
mechanisms, demanding only passivity from him who receives them.

And recent theologians have insisted more strongly that it is the
subjective dispositions of the one who receives the sacraments which
are the measure of their fruitfulness.

The sacraments, then, are enduring and efficacious bonds uniting
us to the unique act of God's love in Christ Jesus. It is true that both
Protestant and Catholic agree that the sacraments are where the
Christian meets Christ. But there is a significant difference in the
way the Catholic conceives this meeting. He believes that just as
God has not merely shown special favor to the man Jesus, but has
truly entered into him and permanently dwells in him, and just
as Christ has not only shown loving concern for his Church but
truly dwells in it, so also in the sacraments, there is more than a
symbolic attestation of the gracious love of God for us, giving a
certainty of forgiveness and assuring man that he is a son of God.
In the sacraments, above all in the Eucharist, Christ is objectively

present; he meets us personally and concretely, and works a real ontic inner transformation of our very being.

The following article is by one of the most highly respected living Catholic theologians of the sacraments. In it Father Schillebeeckx, a Dutch Dominican, brings forth new things and old. All the new developments in the theology of the sacraments find an echo here, especially the emphasis on the concrete and personal character of our meeting with Christ.

Father E. Schillebeeckx, O.P. was born at Antwerp, Belgium, in 1914 and entered the Dominican Order in 1935. He received his doctorate in theology in 1951 at "le Saulchoir," Etiolles, France. From 1943 until 1957 he was Professor of Dogmatic Theology at the Dominican House of Studies at Louvain. From 1956 until 1957 he was professor at the Higher Institute for Religious Sciences of the Catholic University of Louvain. Since January 1958 he has been Professor of Dogmatic Theology, History of Theology, and of Christian Anthropology at the Catholic University of Nijmegen, Holland. Since 1958 he has also been Chief Editor of the periodical *Tijdschrift voor geestelijk Leven* (Louvain-Nijmegen) and, since 1960, coeditor of the newly founded theological journal, *Tijdschrift voor Theologie* (Nijmegen). He is the author of a number of books, the most prominent, perhaps, being his *Christus, sacrament van de Godsontmoeting* (1959), which has already been translated into German and French and will be published in an English translation by Sheed and Ward.

11

THE SACRAMENTS: AN ENCOUNTER WITH GOD

E. SCHILLEBEECKX, O.P.

THE SACRAMENTAL PRINCIPLE OF REVELATION

IT may be true that Rudolf Bultmann's attempt to demythologize the Christian kerygma, that is, to abandon its objective character and interpret it existentially, is unacceptable. It is true, nonetheless, that traditional theology has not alway brought out clearly enough the distinction between the mere physical presence (*Vorhandensein*) of the things of nature and the unique character of conscious human reality (*Dasein*) and human existence (*Existenz*). The personal call which the living God addresses to man in his human situation often seems endangered by a reduction of religious life to the impersonal level. And it was precisely in the theology of the sacraments that this kind of approach resulted in treating sacramental life too exclusively as an impersonal cause-effect relationship. This led to the idea that our reception of grace in the sacraments is mainly a passive affair.

Our aim in this present work is to throw some light on the essential sacramental character of the Church from the standpoint of *intersubjectivity* or *existential personal encounter*.[1] Religion, after all, is a dialogue between God and man. By his created powers man can reach God only through the medium of his creation as its First Cause. At the utmost, all man can do is arouse only a powerless longing for the person of the living God (in reality, the three Persons) and for the immediacy of an I-Thou relationship with him. But by reason of the gratuitous, saving initiative of the living God, the religious man finds himself in direct converse with his God. In this divine encounter or personal fellowship with God—called saving grace—consists *salvation.* This encounter is, from God's side, *revelation;* from man's side, his *religious response.*

Revelation and religion—or, in other words, the mutual encounter of man, created and situated in history, with the uncreated God—of their very nature create history and hence, in the widest sense of the word, are truly sacramental. We call sacramental every supernatural saving reality which presents itself in our lives historically. God directs what he plans for man through history, and he does it in such a way that his interventions can be recognized by men as divine. God's giving grace to man makes history by revealing itself, and it reveals itself by becoming history.

Precisely because the supernatural saving reality, veiled in historical events, and surrounded by the darkness of mystery, is present to us only in earthly form (*sacramentum*), it demands the revealing word (*verbum*) as the interior aspect of its earthly appearance. Only in and through the prophetic word is the divine dimension of saving history brought to light. "Word" and "sacrament" are therefore the fundamental constituents for revelation in the Old Testament as well as in the New and, after this revelation has been brought to an end, for the life of the Church which grows out of it.

CHRISTIANITY AS PERSONAL COMMUNION
OF MAN WITH THE LIVING GOD IN
CHRIST

Intersubjectivity or the dialogue structure of revelation (as "Word and sacrament") appears already in the Old Testament. Yahweh is the God of the Covenant. He personally intervenes in favor of the one determined people he himself has freely chosen out of the community of nations—Israel. He intervenes *personally,* not just as the Creator who by his power guides the historical course of all nations in creative transcendence, but as one who takes part in the vicissitudes of history and who stands on the side of Israel. The core of Israel's history, as it was interpreted through the prophetic word, is set forth over and over again in the Old Testament as: "I will be *your* God, you *my* people" (Lv 26:11–12; Jer 7:23; 11:4; 24:7; 31:33; Ez 11:20; 14:11; 37:27; Os 1:9; etc.).

The burden of all God's revelation in the Old Testament is exactly the course of history which results from the alternation between God's constant fidelity and the ever-recurring infidelity of his people. This revelation, then, is accomplished in a dialectical situation: Out of the dialogue struggle between God and his people, in fidelity and infidelity, the concrete content of revelation takes shape. In one way, of course, this arises from a decision of the living God which is completely and sovereignly free. But looked at from the viewpoint of history, this revelation remains the result of a dialogue of acts: between the invitation and proposal of love by God and the personal, loving response or refusal of love by God's people.

Through all the vicissitudes of this history God desires to lead his people in spite of everything to a final and definitive fidelity. This intention of God appears to be a failure—at least for the majority: The Jews reject their Messiah. The revelation which leads up to Christ then, evolves in history as a dialogue in which God wrestles with human freedom in his desire to save mankind. It is an existential, two-way struggle between God who calls and man who resists—until this God who invites to a faithful love, himself personally responds as true man to this courtship, with a return of love whose fidelity knows no bounds—which does not shrink even from the death of the Cross.

In the man Jesus is realized the fidelity of the covenant in a twofold way. At last the dialogue which was ever breaking down finds a full and perfect human resonance. In a single person both elements are fulfilled: the invitation, and the reply of perfect fidelity, and in such a way that both the invitation and the response constitute the completed revelation of God.

The man Jesus is not only the one sent by the Holy Trinity, he is also the one called to be the representative of all humanity. He is not only the visible embodiment of God's wooing of man, but also the representation and highest fulfillment of the human response of love to God's courtship. Jesus, the free man, who in his humanity reveals to us the divine invitation of love, is at the same time, as man, the person who in the name of all of us and as our representative accepts this invitation. As head of redeemed humanity, he is in a sense the

whole of mankind. That is why it is possible for his sacrifice to be at
the same time our redemption. Only by uniting ourselves to the man
Jesus does our own personal fidelity to the covenant become possible.
Our personal communion with God can only take place, explicitly or
implicitly, by an interpersonal relationship with the man Jesus.

SACRAMENTAL ENCOUNTER WITH GOD
THROUGH ENCOUNTER WITH
THE MAN JESUS

The encounter of man with the invisible God through the medium
of the visible embodiment of the love of that same God in a man we
call a *sacramental encounter with God*. To be personally addressed
by the man Jesus is for the believer personal encounter with God; for
God himself, the eternal Logos, is *personally* this man. Whoever
touches with faith the hem of Christ's garment is immediately healed.
That is why the human interchange, the interpersonal relationship
between Jesus and the men he encounters, is the sacrament of their
encounter with God. It means grace and redemption for all who in
living faith actually come face to face with the man Jesus.

Social intercourse between men, however, occurs through and in
bodily forms. Spiritual influence on a fellow man requires bodily
means of communication; it remains a human activity which must
find its bodily expression. Jesus was a real man. He was the Son of
God appearing in a truly human form, an incarnated human spirit.
His contacts with other men required, as do every man's, bodily
means of communication. Nevertheless, the encounter of Christ with
his fellow men and his properly human activity remain a personal
deed of the Son of God, although in human form. It is consequently
a divine encounter with men in a truly human form. And as the activity of the Son of God, this encounter of Christ as man with men
possesses divine saving power; it is the friendship of God himself for
man, translated and transformed into the form of human encounter.
Although this is true of every truly human activity of Christ, it is
especially true of those human actions of Christ which are exclusively
actions of God, although accomplished in a human manner, that is,

his miracles and, more especially, redemption itself which finds its consummation in the sacrifice of the Cross.

But since the translation of God's encounter with man into an encounter between men includes bodily elements making it visible, this human encounter of Christ with his fellow men possesses not only *divine* saving power in a very general way (since it is a personal action of the Son of God) but divine saving power which is specifically *sacramental;* for the human actions of Jesus in their visibility and corporality are the human outward manifestation of the divine bestowal of grace. They are "signs and causes" of grace, and this in such fashion that the same reality which is externally visible (the sign) is the inner saving power itself in visible form: the concrete embodiment of the offering of grace.

That the human actions of Jesus have sacramental saving efficacy in themselves means, finally, that our "body-spirit" encounter with the man Jesus is the sacrament of our encounter with God. And because redemption through the man Jesus is achieved "once and for all," and in such a way that every communication of grace remains essentially bound up with this man, therefore, every bestowal of grace or encounter with God will come about in an encounter with this man Jesus. The intersubjective relationship of the believer with Christ, the primordial sacrament (*Ursakrament*), remains the basic event of the Christian religion as personal communion with the three divine persons.

SACRAMENTAL ENCOUNTER WITH CHRIST
AS THE FULL DEVELOPMENT OF RELIGIOUS
ENCOUNTER WITH GOD

In the appearance of the man Christ, the anonymity of the living God is removed. The man Jesus shows us the true face of the living God in such a way that the universal religious themes come to the fore only in Christ. For in fact God reveals himself not only interiorly through his mysterious appeal to our souls (the impulse of the Holy Spirit drawing us to belief); he has, as we have said, concretized his inner invitation to personal communion with him in saving history and (fully at last) in the human appearance of Christ in this world. God desired not only to be God for us, he wanted to be God for us in a *human* way. For the first time we can fully grasp what sanctifying grace means; how it reveals, on the one hand, God's boundless desire for a personal communion with us, for the man Jesus who longs to befriend us is precisely revelation of God. On the other hand, it also reveals how profoundly meant our human response to that divine love ought to be, for the man Jesus whose devoted, childlike intimacy with his Father remaining faithful even unto death is also a vicarious realization of our devotion, the highest realization of religious intimacy with the living God which man has ever undertaken.

The bodily manifestation of divine life through Christ's human soul, the Incarnation, also plays a decisive role in solving the mystery of God's anonymity in the world. That its sacramental character makes Christianity the perfect form of religious life can be elucidated from insights into the true nature of man.

The human body is not only the appearance and countenance of the human person who reveals himself, it is also that in which and by which the soul develops into a full-fledged person. To join both ideas together: in and through the body the soul externalizes its process of becoming a person. By going out into the world, the human person gains self-consciousness. It is only in incarnation, becoming-flesh, that personal activity is completed. Thus, embodiment serves as the sign, although a sign that also veils, of the most intimate personal activity.

The point here is that dynamic personality constitutes itself in and through an activity which externalizes itself also in bodily form. In the body the soul presents itself to another. "What we in encounter call body is that through which we situate ourselves, express ourselves, and make ourselves known; in short, the form of man's being-in-the-world. The person we encounter *has* this form, but he also *is* this form."[2] It is through the body and in the body that human encounter takes place. In virtue of this, human relationships of a spiritual nature, no matter how independent they are in themselves of bodily encounter, nevertheless do attain their high points in such an encounter because in it the spiritual interrelationship is made fully present.

Of course, we should by no means overlook the unique characteristic of the man Christ. He is truly God-man, divine in a human way and human in a divine way. Nonetheless, he is truly man. What we have said about the human dimension pertains also to Christ in his personal relations with his fellow men. For the apostles, the moments of their companionship with Christ in both soul *and* body were the decisive high points of their experience of Christ. The Last Supper is a typical example, or Jesus' glance to Peter after his denial, which was enough to move him to tears.

In such bodily-spiritual encounters Christ himself makes the gift of his presence an intensely vivid reality, while in those also bodily encounters the disciples experience their spiritual bond with Christ more deeply than ever. On both sides the bodily personal encounter is the point at which spiritual encounter culminates. And since the spiritual intervention of the man Jesus, the redeeming God, is an intervention in grace, this means that the sacramentalizing or the embodying of this gracious intervention is the culmination of Christ's will to bestow grace and bring salvation. Conversely, whoever in faith encounters the man Jesus and is offered his mercy in a visible and tangible form can achieve through this a fully developed religious attitude.

In the encounter with Christ the anonymity of man's experience of God is removed. In religions outside of Christianity man cannot normally reach to an experience of God except in a vague and often nameless way. It is only in the sacramental encounter with Christ that this experience of God can develop into a mature and fully personal religious worship. The full unfolding of religious life has, therefore, a sacramental basis: the primordial sacrament (*Ursakrament*), Christ Jesus.

Against this one could object: Christ himself has said that "the Spirit gives life and the flesh profits nothing" (Jn 6:63); or, better: "It is good for you that I go. . . . If I do not go, the Consoler will not come to you" (Jn 16:7). The corporal absence of Christ seems to be the very thing which ushers in the perfection of religious life.

It is true, of course, that Christ had to go where we cannot yet follow him. He rose and vanished out of our visible world of empirical experience. But it is not his invisibility as such that "is good for us," but his *glorification* out of death. For us, this necessarily involves his withdrawal because we have not yet been glorified ourselves. But this means precisely that the definitive, eternal, and unsurpassable fulfillment both of the Incarnation and of our religious life takes place there where we ourselves enjoy the privilege of being together with Christ in transfigured *bodily* form, after his return. From this very fact it is clear that our earthly Christian life and (since this life, as we will see, demands sacraments) our sacramental life must fundamentally be an eschatological advance toward the Parousia. What at first seemed an objection, in reality confirms our position; precisely since the fullness of religious worship can only be realized in the sacramental, bodily-spiritual encounter with Christ, therefore Christianity, as the life which elapses between Pasch and Parousia, is fundamentally eschatological. In the last analysis the saying of Tertullian proves true: *"Caro salutis est cardo,"* (It is on the flesh that salvation hinges).[3]

THE SACRAMENTS OF THE CHURCH AS HUMAN ENCOUNTER WITH THE GLORIFIED KYRIOS (LORD)

Another objection may perhaps be raised: Must we who have never encountered Christ in the flesh and who have not yet been taken up in glory—must we manage to get along meanwhile without bodily encounter with Christ? Must our Christ encounter occur in a purely mystical fashion, in the purely spiritual contact of faith, as our Protestant brothers in the faith suppose? The first answer that suggests itself is: in a certain sense, yes; just as those of the Old Covenant and also the other non-Jewish and non-Christian religions had to and still have to get along without any bodily encounter with Christ, although all of these were and are already indebted to Christ for everything. This makes Catholic life fundamentally a life of *waiting:* "waiting for the blessed hope" (Ti 2:13). Our eschatological eagerness is a vigil, an advance toward a meeting, an encounter not yet complete. Christianity is the religion of *Maranatha:* "Come, Lord Jesus!" (Ap 22:20); "Thy Kingdom come!" (Mt 6:10; Lk 11:2).

But this is only one aspect. This active expectation of the perfect encounter is not sustained merely through an encounter with Christ which is only spiritual, or achieved through a mystical act of faith; but it is sustained just as much through an encounter with the living *Kyrios* (Lord) which, though unique, is nevertheless real and quasi-bodily—this encounter takes place in the sacraments of the Church and through them. And this quasi-bodily or strictly sacramental encounter with Christ is for that very reason a pledge and anticipation of the eschatological and perfect encounter with Christ.

From behind the cloud of his glorification, behind which he withdraws from our still earthly eyes, the Lord in his visible Church reaches for earthly, unglorified elements which for that very reason are visible to us, elements as unpretentious as the child in the crib: a little bread and wine, oil and water, a warm, fatherly hand upon the forehead, in order to make his heavenly, saving act effectively present to us here and now. The Church's sacraments are, therefore, our quasi-bodily encounters with the transfigured man Jesus, a veiled contact with the Lord but, nonetheless, one which is concretely human in the full sense because both body and soul are involved. Therefore, based on the historical redemptive event of Christ who is himself the *Eschaton,* the sacramental encounter is a celebration in mystery of the Parousia.

From this we see the "why" of the Church's sacraments. The man Jesus, the visible, fully human image of the redeeming God is, as we have said, the "once-for-all" sacramental sign in which the mystery of the divine redeeming love is visibly represented to us and through which the redeeming God introduces us into existential, personal communion with himself. Since the Ascension has withdrawn the man Jesus from the visible horizon of our lives, our encounter with the living Lord Christ, our perennial mediator, would take place purely mystically by faith if there were no sacraments. Irremediably one of the human dimensions of the Incarnation would in fact be lost for all of us who have never encountered Christ in his earthly life. But God has remained true to his pedagogy. With sympathetic consideration for the characteristic situation of the human person who, because of his bodily nature, lives in a world of men and things, and reaches spiritual maturity in them and through them, God ever offers us the kingdom of Heaven in earthly garb. Thus it was in the days of the covenant; thus it was at the *ephapax* (once and for all) (Heb 9:12) of the human appearance of the redeeming God; and this is what the divine pedagogy requires now in the sacramental Church which is the earthly, visible instrument of salvation employed by the living, invisible *Kyrios*.

The divine plan of salvation is essentially a sacramental economy of salvation. It is true that the spiritual Christ can meet us and influence our lives outside the sacramental visibility of the Church. Nonetheless, *by reason of his glorified body,* he can only make himself *fully present for us and to us* (and thus exploit his grace-giving approach to the full) by using earthly, untransfigured elements as visible symbols, prolonging and manifesting his invisible, heavenly, saving act. The concrete presence of this heavenly saving activity of Christ demands that the *Kyrios* embody his invisible, saving efficacy in this earthly world by employing unglorified corporality which becomes an interior element of his heavenly, symbolic action. The sacramentalism of the Church bridges the disproportion between our untransfigured world and the Christ: the world, that is, which at one point, at its center, is already glorified.

In the context of the historical milieu in which we live, the sacraments are a visible expression of the celestial, present, saving action of Christ, the *Eschaton*. In the sacraments we encounter Christ, though he be bodily absent, in a tangible, bodily way. The Eucharist is for us the crowning point of this actual encounter with Christ.

Thus we see immediately that the so-called *sacramenta separata* (separated sacraments) are not things, but rather personal encounters with the glorified man Jesus and in him with the living God. We now wish to investigate, first, the objective structure of these sacraments, and then reflect on the religious spirit in which we personally should celebrate them.

The Sacraments of the Church

THEIR OBJECTIVE FORM AS MYSTERIES

The man Jesus himself is the primordial sacrament (*Ursakrament*). The redemption wrought through him is "once for all" and conclusive. The sacraments of the Church have no new and additional meaning; they merely bring us in their own way into living contact with the "perennial Christ," who through the power of the Holy Spirit remains the permanent mediator between the Father and men. The sacraments of the Church, consequently, rest on an essentially Christological foundation: "For there is no other Sacrament of God but Christ."[4]

If the sacraments of the Church are only the points of contact on earth with Christ the primordial sacrament (*Ursakrament*), that means that they *sacramentalize* the redeeming work of Christ for us and in us here and now: "What was visible in Christ passed over into the sacraments of the Church."[5] The significance of the Christological dimension of the sacraments can be made clear only after we have explained their ecclesiological basis.

a. The Ecclesiological Dimension of the Sacraments

We have already said that in God's economy of salvation the man Jesus represents the whole human race. In the sense of being its origin, he himself, as head of the human race he has redeemed, is personally the Church. In the fullest sense of the word this means that in the sacrifice of the Cross of Jesus, the whole human race became "Church." "Christ died so that by His death might arise the Church."[6] Christ's sacrifice on the Cross has meaning as a real fact only if it is at the same time the sign of the sacrifice of all mankind; and it has this value as a representative sign effectively only to the extent that it is at the same time a real fact. In this respect the Church exists only in germ, that is, in the representative humanity of Jesus, sacrificed, yet glorified.

The earthly Church is the sign, present within the world, of this victorious and definitive redemption which introduces the *Eschaton*. When we spoke of the sacraments as that which makes present in the world in earthly garb the saving action of Christ in glory, we meant, first of all, the sacramental *Church* herself. She is the visible, historical representation in the world of the definitive redemption. Christianity is essentially a belief in earthly realities as the appearance in mystery of the supernatural realities of the redemption.

Accordingly, the Church as the institution of salvation is essentially sacrament and Word. Both form the specific area of endeavor for the hierarchical ministry. The norm for ministry, sacrament, and Word is, on the one hand, the *ephapax* (once-and-for-all character) of the historical appearance of Christ and of the apostolic, primitive tradition, and on the other hand the earthly form of the saving action of the glorified *Kyrios* through his Spirit. The whole visible Church is ruled by the glorified *Kyrios* who, through the mediation both of his Holy Spirit and of the apostolic ministry of his earthly Church, brings to completion in this world the building up of the people of God. Christ *sends* the Holy Spirit (Jn 14:16, 26; 15:26) and he also *sends* his apostles (Jn 13:16, 20; 17:18).[7] Both of these sendings are organically connected with one another. Pentecost, the day on which the Church with her sacramental and kerygmatic activity stepped forth into the full light of day, is the mystery event of the manifestation of both these missions precisely in their conjointly acting unity, a unity which is vitalized from a single source of life, the *Kyrios* himself. What the visible Church does in the order of historical, external visibility, the Spirit sent by Christ does interiorly both in her authorized ministers and in the souls of the faithful. That is why the Church as the representation of the mystery of Christ can herself be called a primordial sacrament (*Ursakrament*) insofar as she is (1) *sacramentum humanitatis Christi* (sacrament of the humanity of Christ) or the sacramental Christ, and (2) the subject in which the seven sacraments, the specific ministerial actions of the sacramental Church, are found.

This means that the seven sacraments, even before they are this or that particular sacrament, are first of all and primarily the visible official action of the Church or, better, the action of Christ in heaven sacramentalized in the visible action of the Church. They are the activity of the *Church* from a sevenfold perspective. This is the reason why the power of orders and the power of jurisdiction are interwoven in every sacrament and why the validity of an action of the power of orders can be limited, altered, or nullified by the power of jurisdiction. The validity or authentic sacramentality of the seven sacraments, therefore, fundamentally depends on whether or not the sacrament in question is truly an action of the Church of Christ. The so-called "matter" and "form" point out two complementary ways of giving concrete form to the ecclesial character of this celebration in mystery, which being "sacrament" includes "sacramental Word" as an inner constituent because the supernatural dimension of the earthly event is only made fully present to us in the Word.

The primary aspect, which reveals itself in a variety of shadings, in the reception of each of the seven sacraments, is the setting up of living contact with the visible Church in the actions as Christ's representative which are characteristic of her as the Church. It is precisely this visible contact with the Church through the reception of her sacraments in faith that *is* the encounter with Christ.

This already implies that the *main* lines of this economy of the seven sacraments were established by Christ when he founded the Church. The fullness of the gift of redemption is bound up, through Christ's founding of the Church, with the great external sign: the Church as the historical reality which renders the achieved redemption present. Thus, Christ's founding of his Church as primordial sacrament (*Ursakrament*) is basically also the institution of the seven sacraments. What the sacraments do is nothing more than make concretely present here and now what the Church herself is in her essence. True enough, Christ himself also said, implicitly or explicitly, that the sevenfold treasure of the grace of redemption should be shared in through the visible activity of the Church. But apart from the fact that for a few sacraments he himself also determined the outer form of the visible action (e.g., washing with *water,* the sacrifice of *bread* and *wine*), he gave full scope to the Church to determine for herself the external symbolic form of her visible action which would be the outward sign of the sevenfold sacramental grace. But the fundamental and decisive factor, the joining of the sevenfold grace to a visible action of the Church—*that* comes directly from Christ. The *substantia sacramenti* (essential element of a sacrament)—that element in the external sign which cannot be changed by the Church[8] and hence was determined by Christ himself—signifies, simply, the sacramental meaning as expressed in external form, that is, the sacramentalizing of a sevenfold grace. (With regard to certain sacraments this can also involve the concrete determination of the external symbolic form.)

The fact that the sacramental meaning is expressed in an *action* of the Church implies, as we have said, that it has as an intimate constituent element the sacramental Word. It is this alone that makes fully present to us in a visible action the supernatural saving presence. Both together—the liturgical action joined to the sacramental Word of the Church, made one in the liturgy—are the elements which go to make up the external symbolic action of the Church and turn it into a sacrament where we meet Christ. The sacraments are, therefore, the specifically churchly actions which make visible on earth the fulfilled messianic activity of her high priest in heaven.

That there are *seven* sacraments derives, in the last analysis, exclusively from the saving will of Christ. But this number seven should be explained not so much anthropologically, through an analogy with human life on a biological level, as ecclesiologically, i.e., from the essence of the Church as the kingdom of God existing on earth in historical form. For the sevenfold sacramental grace is the grace of redemption which comes to us in visible form, in the seven dimensions presented us by the Church. The fundamental reality which takes on a special shading in each of the seven sacraments is the personal contact with the inner dynamism of the holy Church, which contact itself is the effective sign of our personal encounter with the glorified man Jesus and in him with the living God. The special symbolism of each sacrament's liturgical action, taken as a whole in which the Word elucidates the symbol, highlights that special aspect under which the one redeeming action of Christ reaches us in the Church through the various sacraments.

On this account it is the progressive realization of the kingdom of God in each individual person and in the human race as a whole which demands a sevenfold, sacramental saving activity of the Church.[9]

b. The Christological Content of the Sacraments of the Church

The necessity of the sacraments is based upon the fact that grace continues to be mediated through the man Jesus. Since Christ's Ascension, this further continuation demands, as we have seen, the introduction of the sacramental Church with her sacramental activity (*sacramenta separata*) in which this mediation of grace visibly enters into our earthly world. Therefore, even after the Ascension, the conferring of grace continues to be on the basis of intersubjectivity between us men and the man Jesus, which is the sacrament of our personal fellowship with God. Since the Ascension, the perfect form of this intersubjectivity with the man Jesus takes place only within the sacred domain of the Church of Christ. This proposes for us the problem of "presence in mystery" (*Mysteriengegenwart*). Without allowing ourselves to become involved in the numerous and various opinions concerning this theory which have grown out of the discussion of the work of Dom Odo Casel, nor in the problem of what exactly Casel meant to affirm, we present a solution which immediately suggests itself from the standpoint of a sound Christology.

To put it in terms of time: When God became man, the eternal Redeemer entered into time. Now time is irreversible. What has happened historically can, in no way, be made actual again, not even by God. As an historical incident it is irrevocably past. Since, therefore, Christ was *really* man, the sacrifice of the Cross as an historical event is also a reality that is past; and it cannot actually be made to be present again even "in mystery." Of course, it is true that an historical action of a human person, being a personal action, in a certain respect surpasses time because it is a *spiritual* act and it had a part in fashioning the person into what he now is. But this does not alter the fact that the historical element of that act as a human act belongs irrevocably to the past and as such it can no longer be made actually present, not even in a mysterious way. The past of the human acts of Jesus inescapably shares in this irreversibility of the time event, otherwise we fall into a kind of Docetism.

On the other hand, the historical human acts of Christ, who is personally God, are the *personal* acts of the second divine Person, even though performed through his humanity. Therefore, Jesus' sacrifice on the Cross, as a personal action of God, is an eternally present actuality which is imperishable. The sacrifice of the Cross, not in its historical form as human act, but as *this* kind of human act which proceeds from the *Son of God* who *personalizes* the *human* act of Jesus—this sacrifice of the Cross, in its inner nature a truly divine act of sacrifice (although performed in the humanity and therefore in time) is—as is everything which is divine—eternal, and not past. Redemption, therefore, if considered *exclusively* as an action of God (only God can redeem us), is, although achieved in this humanity, an eternally present divine act. The death on the Cross, then, itself possesses a "mystery" content which transcends time.

Since Jesus did not cease to be man after the Resurrection but remains man, we must also speak of the *permanence* or perennial character of the *Kyrios*: "Christ yesterday, today, and forever!" (Heb 13:8). To be sure, the eternally present redemptive act has in itself a "changing" human mode of expression—a "movement" which we, of course, cannot measure by earthly time because it is the human act of a man who has risen and shares in the vision of God. There is a difference between the mode of expression in the historical sacrifice on the Cross and in the Christ in glory. The historical human mode of appearance of the inner act of sacrifice of the Son of God is forever past; but it remains in its mystery content as an action of God. It possesses an eternal contemporaneity in the now living Christ, in whom it becomes humanly incarnate in a new "heavenly" manner. Rooted in an act of God, the death on the Cross has, therefore, an eternally permanent content, a content which had us in view in the sacrificial death and which still presents itself to us now.

The man Jesus is in a glorified state and is for that reason (to us) invisible. We, on the other hand, find ourselves in an untransfigured earthly condition. Consequently, the eternally-present redemptive act of the sacrifice of the Cross indeed can have a direct influence on us, but it can no longer be made present to us "in Christ's own body." The eternally-present divine redemption consummated in human nature can be rendered present now, as has been shown, only through sacramental, earthly symbols, especially those of the Eucharist. From this it automatically follows that there is inescapably a "presence in mystery" in the seven sacraments—and in a very special way for the Eucharist.

The whole redeeming mystery of Christ, not in some way or other in its historical content, but as the act of God, becomes actively present in the sacrament, so that in these sacraments we are immediately encompassed by the redemptive efficacy of the "redeeming Incarnation." It thus becomes clear that the core of the sacramental efficacy is the eternally-present act of redemption of the Son of God; and that this is *identical* with both the mystery content of the saving action of the historical sacrifice of the Cross and with the mystery content of the saving activity of the living, glorified *Kyrios* and, finally, with the mystery of the saving power of the sacramental Church; although in all of this the *human* form given to the divine redeeming act of the man Jesus is different in each case. From this viewpoint the *ephapax* and the sufficiency of the historical event of redemption is shown to be in no way threatened or cancelled out by the sacraments of the Church; and it becomes clear that to support this we do not have to call on the questionable theory which says that a past, temporal event can be made somehow actual again in our own time *in mysterio* or in some "mystical" way.

Yet for all this the sacraments are truly also a celebration in mystery of the past *acta et passa Christi* (actions and sufferings of Christ) and always contain a reference to the historical coming of Christ. For on the Cross—and *only* there—at that historical moment, God offered for us his human life. Therefore, the eternally-present redemptive act of God retains a reference to the past sacrifice on the Cross. The eternally-present redemptive act of the Son of God made man is actively made present in the sacraments precisely as referring to the historical sacrifice of the Cross. That is why St. Thomas says with all Tradition that the sacraments draw their saving power from the death of Christ. We must maintain at the same time, however, that it is the glorified Christ now living who gives to the sacraments their saving efficacy. "It is Christ himself, who, through his Church baptizes, teaches, rules, absolves, makes sacrifice."[10]

The sacraments as a medium between Christ and us should be situated, then, not so much between the historically past sacrifice of the Cross and our present situation in the twentieth century, as between the now living, glorified Christ, the *Eschaton,* and our own human world which is not yet transfigured and which strains toward the *Eschaton.* In other words, we should conceive of the sacraments as a "medium" in a real encounter *between living men*: between the man Jesus and us men and, therefore, *as this very encounter itself.* For although personal encounter through the medium of the body in a certain respect is indirect, it is, nevertheless, also *immediate* since in the body subjectivity immediately and directly expresses itself.

It is only this encounter with Christ in and through the actual presence in the sacraments of the eternally-present redemptive act of the living Christ (and of the redeeming Christ himself in the Eucharist) which explains the historical perspective in the sacraments insofar as they are: (1) an *Anamnesis* (commemoration) or celebration in mystery of the past sacrifice of the Cross (*signum rememorativum*), because precisely at the sacrifice of the Cross the eternally-present redemptive act of the Son of God amounted to really giving up his life; (2) *actual bestowal of grace* (*signum demonstrativum*), because the receiving subject is here and now really drawn into the eternally-present redemptive act; (3) an *anticipation,* in germ, of the eschatological Parousia (*signum prognosticum*),[11] because they are the sacramental act of rendering the *Eschaton* itself present (in the Eucharist) or at least of making present the eternally-actual redemptive act of the Son of God in his efficacy as the glorified *Kyrios* (in the other six sacraments); they allow our own time to be grasped in a visible way by the *Eschaton* itself. The sacramental encounter of man with Christ in the Church is, therefore, on the basis of the historically-past redeeming event, the beginning or the *arrha* (pledge) here and now of eschatological salvation; and the supporting substratum of all this is the permanence of the redeeming man Jesus, who is God and who, through his sacraments, receives us into his redeeming mercy.

SACRAMENTAL MYSTERY OF WORSHIP
AND SACRAMENTAL SANCTIFICATION

In the concrete, the man Jesus is not only the person who offers us in his humanity the grace of God; he is also the person who in his humanity as our representative and in our name in obedient religious love accepts the offer of grace. Tradition expresses this by saying: "The man Jesus *gives* us the grace that as man he *merited* for us on the Cross. In the saving acts of Christ we find, therefore, a double aspect: worship for God and sanctification for man. These are two aspects of the same *mysteria carnis Christi* (mysteries of Christ's flesh). This idea must now be further developed.

Even to the very core of what is most human in him, Jesus is the Son of God the Father. In grace, therefore, he enjoys the perfection of the intimacy with the three-in-one God. He is the consummate actualization of the communion of love of man with God. He is "grace become man": As God-man, he is essentially dialogue between the holy man Jesus and the Father in the unity of the Holy Spirit. As God, Christ is the second Person, the Son of God, in all things like to the Father. "Living through the Father" (Jn 6:57), receiving all things from him, the Son is nevertheless true God and, in this sense, not "dependent" on the Father. There is question here of an intimacy by which (without prejudice to full equality) the Father is the source without origin. We find ourselves, then, before the incomprehensible mystery of a divine and, therefore, "independent" person Who, nevertheless, "derives" from the Father and possesses all things from him (derivation of origin without proper dependence) *a Patre* and *ad Patrem* (from the father and to the Father).

Now the *human existence* of Jesus is the revelation of this divine inner-trinitarian life relationship: its translation into human forms of appearance. What is translated onto a human level in the man Jesus is primarily this divine intimacy of love of the Son for His Father. In the humanity of the Son the divine intimacy of love be-

tween Son and Father is brought to the *created* level, and thus in
the man Jesus a real dependence toward the Father now comes into
existence *in* this loving intimacy of the Son become man. "The
Father is greater than I" (Jn 14:28). In and through this condition
the Son reveals to us his divine loving intimacy with the Father—
to the "principle without origin." The "being-from-the-Father" of the
Son is made known to us by the man Jesus in His *obedient* or *dependent* love for the Father. The man Jesus is essentially *obedient* love
and adoration of the Father as the human translation of his divine
relationship of origin. Thus considered, the whole earthly life of
Jesus is spent before the Father in "living out" this childhood which
he acquired by becoming man. In obedient love for his Father, he
has accepted his whole human existence (*Dasein*) which, through
the intrigues of his fellow men, ended in his being murdered, as the
religious expression of his ever-unshaken devotion to his Father.
Through this supreme religious worship of Christ we have been redeemed.

But Christ reveals to us through and in his humanity not only
his divine relationship to his Father but also his relationship to the
Holy Spirit. The Son of God is also a *coprinciple of the Holy Spirit*:
"who proceeds from the Father through the Son." The mission of
the Holy Spirit *to us* is also the externalizing of this inner trinitarian
structure. The "from the Father through the Son" as expressed in
the Incarnation signifies that the Holy Spirit is given to us from
the Father in and through the perfection of the Son's religiously
obedient love (the human level of divine filiation as *a Patre* and *ad
Patrem*). That is why John twice mentions that Christ could send
us the Holy Spirit only after his Resurrection from the dead (Jn
16:7; 7:37–39; cf. also Acts 2:33). Theology says the same when
it tells us that Jesus through his human life has *merited* for us the
Holy Spirit. Only with the final closing, the crowning of his earthly
obedient life, is the "incarnation" concluded; only then is the *a
Patre* and *ad Patrem* character of the Son fully translated on the
human level. "Into thy hands I commend my spirit" is the consummate incarnational translation of the "*ad Patrem*" which is the Son.
The Father's responding acceptance of His Son—on the level of
the Incarnation—is the Resurrection and Ascension which con-

cludes the cycle of loving intimacy between the Father and the Son become man. Only now can the Son—who on the trinitarian level in his *"ad Patrem"* is the coprinciple of the Holy Spirit—only now can he on the level of the Incarnation send the Holy Spirit to us, too. Thus, through the worship mystery of his life which culminated in death, the man Jesus "merited" for us *"the spirit* of sonship" (Rom 8:15); and thus he effectively bestows on us, as *Kyrios,* his own Spirit.

In this primordial sacrament (*Ursakrament*) which is Christ himself, who is personally God, we see that the redemptive act is a *mystery of worship* which is *liturgical* because it was done in our name (*leiton* or *laiton ergon* [work of the people]), and at the same time is the gift of redemption or *sanctification.* Both are achieved by God in human nature.

We find these two aspects again in the sacraments of the Church as celebrations in mystery of the Redemption; in them the Church celebrates the "mysteries of Christ's flesh," a liturgical mystery of worship in which Christ in and through the Church remains the actual high priest. In and through his Church, Christ sacramentalizes his intercession for us in heaven. It is the way he as Lord manifests his eternally-present divine redeeming act, so that every sacrament that is performed for one of the faithful is a *sacramental prayer for grace* for this believer: the prayer of Christ himself to which the Church joins her prayer here and now (*sacramenta fidei Ecclesiae*— sacraments of the faith of the Church). On the other hand, the sacraments are also the sacramentalizing of Christ's *effective sanctification* from heaven in and through his Holy Spirit. In virtue of the eternally-present redeeming act of the *Kyrios,* both efficacious and an act of worship, the sacraments *bestow* the grace which they *ask* of God by this act of worship.

Thus the sacraments of the Church give grace because the Church herself is visibly and perceptibly full of grace. She is, after all, the historical, tangible presence of the redeeming grace of the Cross here and now in the world. In her sacramental activity the Church is not only the effective instrument of salvation employed by the living *Kyrios* by which he establishes on earth among men a community in faith and love (i.e., the Church as a community in grace) and interiorly intensifies and deepens the life of her members, but this visible sacramental expression also makes visible the inner community of faith and grace of *the ever-holy Church* itself. The Church is community of worship and community of sanctification in such a way that in the very act of giving expression to her holiness in sacramental worship she is seen to be *carrying on the work itself of sanctification.* The grace which operates in the sacraments is Christ's fullness of grace shared in his living Church. The sacraments, therefore, are not only the saving sign of the sanctifying worship of Christ, but no less the worship of the Church herself, the expression of the Church's life of grace as community with Christ. The *pleroma Christi* (fullness of Christ) operates in each sacrament. In and through the performance of a sacrament, Christ and his whole Church surround with prayer the man who receives the sacrament. "The *faith* of the Church contributes to the efficacy of baptism,"[12] a faith which is always vivified by charity.[13] In every sacrament the believer enters more deeply into the living bond which the community of the Church has with the "mysteries of Christ's flesh." The mystery of worship, precisely because of its sacramentality, is not only the worship of Christ himself in and through his Church, but by the very fact a *liturgical* mystery of worship of the Church: the liturgical expression of the inner worship of God by the Church's community of the faithful in union with Christ. All this belongs to the constitution of a *sacrament* considered *valid* by the Church and which, consequently, if the receiving subject sets up no obstacle— i.e., if the recipient also joins himself in a religious spirit with faith to this mystery of worship—through the very fact of the liturgical celebration (*ex opere operato*), efficaciously bestows the grace prayed for in this act of liturgical worship.

From this we can see the meaning of the traditional formula *Sacramenta causant quod figurant* (the sacraments cause the grace to which they give visible expression). As distinguished from the holy humanity of Jesus, which is hypostatically united to the Son of God, the sacraments are *sacramenta separata,* i.e., earthly manifestations in symbolic signs of the invisible, saving act of the man Jesus in heaven. They are truly, therefore, the personal acts of the God-man in and through the minister of the Church. They are, in visible sacramental form (*signum*), the redeeming will of Christ himself with respect to the man who receives them. The eternally-present redemptive act as designed for us personally is sacrament-alized by the glorified Christ in and through his Church. Essentially, therefore, this visible proof of Christ's redemptive love is meant for the believer to whom it is directed: the receiver of the sacrament. That it be directed to this definite man belongs to the essence of a sacramental proof of Christ's love.

Because they are the visible appearance on earth of this celestial saving act, the sacraments have, as a natural consequence, the same divine saving efficacy. The earthly symbolism of the Church visibly represents the heavenly salvific activity. If we consider the sacra-ments "from below," we can say that they are symbolic acts of worship of the Church in which Christ accomplishes a deeper mys-tery. Seen thus, the symbolic acts of the Church are *charged* with divine saving efficacy. But if we look at the sacraments "from above," from the standpoint of the saving act in heaven which is sacra-mentalized in the Church, as the personal human act of Christ through the official mediation of the Church, then the sacraments are the visibility in the Church, or the historical "incarnation," of the sanctifying will of Christ; they are this saving will itself in visible and tangible form. And thus because of their sacramental visibility, they are the effective bestowal itself of grace made manifest in a visible and therefore meaningful way. Just as the body is the soul itself made visible (but in such a way that the proper activity of the body can in no way be made equivalent to the spiritual activity of the soul), so also at Baptism, for example, the corporal washing of the Church is the divine grace of reconciliation made visible on earth. As the action of Christ manifest in symbol, the washing is more than what it is on the merely physical level; insofar as it is symbolic activity, it is a bearer of salvation because it is a *sign*. It is only when we consider the physical aspect just in itself and then afterward proceed to give it a higher significance that we unneces-sarily complicate the relation between "sign" and "saving causality." Because we are dealing with *sacramenta separata,* we can rightly call this symbolic causality an instrumental saving causality.

We should not forget, however, that this saving efficacy can be viewed in a twofold respect: as mystery of worship and as sancti-fication. In every sacrament, but especially in the Eucharist, both aspects operate *ex opere operato;* that means that in its sacramental manifestation the power of the redemptive grace of Christ operates *of itself,* both as prayerful *worship* and as efficacious *sanctification.* As sacramental mystery of worship, every sacrament, since it is supported by Christ and the whole community of the faithful in the Church, wins *ex opere operato* the sacramental grace for the one who is to receive it. This grace is then bestowed *ex opere operato* through the same sacrament as long as the man puts no obstacle in the way (i.e., if the adult recipient joins himself actively and reli-giously to the request included in this act of worship—a point which we will deal with in a moment). Precisely because of the efficacy of this act of worship or the sacramental value of the sacrament as prayer, as the sacramentalizing of the prayer of Christ in and through his Church, a valid sacrament that was received unfruitfully can *subsequently* "revivify." Even when a sacrament is perhaps un-fruitful at the moment of reception, still, in a certain respect, no sacrament is *completely* unfruitful because of its value as a sacra-mental prayer of Christ and his entire Church.

THE SACRAMENT AS RELIGIOUS
EXPERIENCE

The inner religious condition of the receiving subject is not merely a disposition which precedes or parallels the sacrament; it enters into the very essence of the fruitful sacrament. Of course, the reli-gious experience contributes in no respect to the *validity* of the sacra-ment. Christ's demonstration of love has absolute priority over every human response and does not depend on it; rather, this response is supported by Christ's love. However, it remains true that only when some inchoate religious ardor is present in the believer who is to receive the sacrament will his sharing in the mystery of worship of the Church be a worthy sacramental expression of his inner spirit. Then this worthily received sacrament will become not only the worshipping petition of Christ and his Church but also that of the receiver: the sacramental expression of his religious desire for grace and his will to encounter Christ. If such a religious desire for encounter does not exist, the valid sacrament (i.e., Christ's will for encounter in and through his Church) cannot develop into a real mutual encounter. As a personal encounter with the glorified *Kyrios*, the sacrament which is completely genuine, therefore, necessarily implies the religious ardor of the receiving subject.

The personal religious dispositions of the receiver (which differ depending on whether we are dealing with a sacrament of the living or of the dead) will, therefore, be sacramentalized *in* the worshipping activity of the Church, which, then—solely by virtue of the redemption of Christ—bestows sacramental grace *ex opere operato*, that is, brings about the actual encounter with Christ. From this we see that the sacraments do not work automatically, but rather that, as a result of faith and a deep religious longing, they lay hold of the sanctifying power of Christ which is at work in the sacramental Church. But this grasping of salvation in faith is actually the person's *being grasped* by the redeeming Christ. ("The passion of Christ obtains its effect in those to whom it is applied through *faith and charity* and through the *sacraments of faith*."[14])

The sacraments are, therefore, no easier path to holiness, as though they could dispense us from a part of that religious striving which is demanded in order to attain the grace of reconciliation or interior intimacy with God outside the sacraments. As we have seen, the significance of sacraments as incarnations of the religious disposition is rather that they bring about *moments of supreme ardor* in the everyday Christian life. In contrast to the extrasacramental communion with God, the sacramental life of grace and love is the full and mature stature of the Christian life. As modern anthropology points out, there are in human life, besides the *decisive* or *momentous* actions in which the person achieves more intensive self-expression, also *everyday* actions in which personal freedom expresses itself in a lesser or more moderate degree. So also there are decisive Christian acts and also everyday acts of grace. Because of their sacramental incarnation, the sacramental acts of worship are intended to be decisive and momentous actions of the Christian life. They demand, therefore, more intensive deliberation and reflection; otherwise they become flat and are reduced to a soulless formalism. On the part of Christ too, the sacraments, as earthly embodiment of his heavenly saving act, are the tangible and complete intervention of his gracious will. Therefore, what is normally experienced as something *ordinary* outside of the sacraments should grow in and through the sacraments toward a special crowning experience, toward full and complete maturity.

Thus, the seven sacraments indicate the high points of our Christian existence (*Dasein*). They give sharp and clear dimensions to everyday Christian life, which at regular intervals raise up the level of everyday spiritual life to new heights. In them the ordinary day-to-day pattern must once again be left behind and surpassed if it is not to fade into that colorless anonymity which, once sacramental practice is abandoned, leads in time to the surrender of Christianity itself and, finally, of all religious spirit.

The sacraments are God's own saving act as it manifests itself in the sacred realm of the Church, as it concretely addresses man and takes hold of him as perceptibly and visibly as a mother embraces her child. Although the child already realizes that his mother loves him, still this felt embrace gives the experience of love in its fulness. "Now we truly know." On our way to Emmaus which leads to the *Eschaton,* the sacrament is the veiled encounter in which our heart, listening with eager and ardent faith, burns within us. "Were not our hearts burning within us while he spoke to us on the road?" (Lk 24:32). Precisely because of their sacramental character, i.e., because the sacraments are an authentic, visible proof of Christ's desire to give grace to the one who receives them, they give us a tranquil, moral certitude of the reality of this gift of grace—a certitude which is lacking in grace bestowed outside the sacraments. This very fact makes us experience the divine graciousness of redemption even more intensely than the bestowal of grace outside the sacraments.

ANALYTICAL DEFINITION OF THE SACRAMENTS OF THE CHURCH

On account of the different levels and the numerous factors which we discovered in the sacramental order of the Church, it is impossible to put together into a single sentence all the elements which go to make up a sacrament. The definition which has become classical, *signum efficax gratiae* (an efficacious sign of grace), is only a schematic cross-section of the abundant riches contained in the notion of sacrament. In concluding, we can now attempt to give a descriptive definition which progressively indicates the different essential elements of a sacrament.

A sacrament of the Church is (1) a personal saving act of the glorified Christ, an act of worship as well as sanctification—(2) in and through his Church which, in virtue of the authority and the sacramental character given to her by Christ, *sacramentalizes* this invisible act of the glorified Christ in a sanctifying mystery of worship of the Church. In this way, the once-for-all, eternally-actual redeeming act of the God-man is given a public, historically situated visibility on earth which renders it present among us and for us, and which is at the same time the manifestation of the Church's holy participation in it. The Church does this through the medium of her authorized minister who, therefore, must have the intention of "doing what the Church does." This intention is necessary to authentically sacramentalize the celestial saving act of Christ. What is essential to this early sacramentalizing is the ritual action of the Church in liturgical unity with the sacramental word of the Church. The symbolic signs and actions are borrowed from ordinary human life and, for the most part, they are things which already had a sacred meaning for religious man (ritual washing, anointing, imposition of hands, sacred meal, etc.). But through the word, this basic symbolism is caught up in the higher vision of the Church and thus elevated to the specific sacramental symbolism of the Church. In this ordinary *matter* supplied by man, which of itself is lifeless and impotent, Christ accomplishes in his Church, by the power of his salvific *word,* a deeper, divine mystery of salvation.

(3) This sanctifying act of worship of the glorified high priest in heaven, sacramentalized in and through the Church, is *directed essentially* to that particular man in whom the sacrament is performed (consideration being made for the unique character of the Eucharist as sacrifice of the Church and for the entire Church). This is so completely true that this personal involvement is part of the very essence of the sacrament; for this reason, the intention of the

person to receive a sacrament also contributes toward determining the validity or authentic sacramentalizing (i.e., the making visible in an earthly way in the ministry of the Church) of Christ's will to sanctify this person. These first three elements are what constitute a *valid* sacrament.

(4) However, this sanctifying sacramental mystery of worship of Christ in and through his Church can only develop *ex opere operato* all the rich fecundity for which it was established when the subject for whom the sacrament is intended also actively enters with a religious spirit into this mystery of worship with faith and an earnest longing for grace. Thus it will also become the sacramental expression of his personal desire to encounter Christ in faith.

This vital religious participation by the (adult) recipient in the sacramental mystery of worship—a participation which is itself already the fruit of grace—now grows, through the saving efficacy of the sacramental celebration, toward a more interior, personal communion with Christ, toward a deeper bond with the Church's community of grace, and, therefore, to an increased intimacy of grace with the living God: with the Father, the Son, and the Holy Spirit.

From all of this it becomes quite clear that the sacraments are neither "things" nor "automatons" but rather, by virtue of genuine incarnation, a mutual personal involvement on the part of Christ and his Church (through the medium of her authorized minister) and also on the part of the believer who receives him, and who in his longing for grace lays hold of the living power of Christ which alone sanctifies and which is actively present in the Church. He does this through his reception in faith or, more correctly, through the *active part* he also plays *in the celebration* of the sacrament. The one same objective reality appearing in veiled sacral symbolic actions, namely, the sanctifying sacramental mystery of worship, thus becomes the expression of both the condescending *agape* (charity) of God and of the longing of the man of faith who strives to reach above and beyond himself. In the liturgical, sacramental mystery of worship the theophany of the redeeming God is accomplished and man succeeds in returning home to the Father in Christ through the Spirit of sanctification. "You have showed yourself to me face to face, O Christ; it is you that I find in your sacraments."[15]

Translated by Rev. John L. Boyle, S.J.

NOTES

This article is a translation of "Sakramente als Organe der Gottbegegnung," which appeared in J. Feiner, J. Trütsch, and F. Böckle, eds., *Fragen der Theologie heute* (Einsiedeln: Benziger Verlag, 1957), pp. 379–401. It has been translated and reprinted here by kind permission of the author and of Benziger Verlag.

1. This article gives the main themes of our book *Christus, sacrament van de Godsontmoeting* [Christ, sacrament of encounter with God], German and French translations of which have recently appeared. An English version, to be published by Sheed and Ward, is in preparation.
2. F. J. J. Buytendijk, "Zur Phänomenologie der Begegnung" in *Eranos-Jahrbuch*, Vol. 19 (1950), p. 468. See also G. Gusdorf, *La découverte de soi* (Paris: Presses universitaires de France, 1948); L. Binswanger, *Grundformen und Erkenntnis menschlichen Daseins* (Zürich: M. Niehans, 1952); K. Rahner "Persönliche und sakramentale Frömmigkeit," *Schriften zur Theologie*, II (Einsiedeln, 1955), pp. 115–142.
3. Tertullian, *De carnis resurrectione*, 8; Migne, *Patrologia Latina (MPL)* 2, 806.
4. "Non est enim aliud Dei Sacramentum nisi Christus." Augustine, *Ep.* 187, 34; *MPL* 38, 845.
5. "Quod conspicuum erat in Christo, transivit in Ecclesiae sacramenta." Leo the Great, *Sermo* 74, 2; *MPL* 54, 398.
6. "Moritur Christus ut fiat Ecclesia . . . mortuo Christo." Augustine, *In Evangelium Joannis*, tr. 9, n. 10; *MPL* 35, 1463.
7. On this point see Y. Congar, *Esquisses du Mystère de l'Église* (Paris, 1953²), pp. 129–179. (English trans.: *The Mystery of the Church* [Baltimore: Helicon Press, 1960].)
8. Pius XII, "Constitutio Apostolica 'Sacramentum Ordinis,'" *Acta Apostolicae Sedis*, Vol. 40 (1948).
9. We cannot analyze further here the ecclesiological foundation of each sacrament in particular. On this point see K. Rahner, "Kirche und Sakramente," *Geist und Leben*, Vol. 28 (1955), pp. 434–453.
10. Pius XII, Encyclical *Mystici Corporis*, Acta Apostolicae Sedis, Vol. 35 (1943), p. 218.

11. Cf. *Summa Theologica*, III, q. 60, a. 3.

12. "Operatur ad efficaciam baptismi *fides* Ecclesiae," *Summa Theologica*, III, q. 39, a. 5. Emphasis added.

13. "Fides Ecclesiae est (. . .) fides formata [caritate]," *Summa Theologica*, II–II, q. 1, a. 9, ad 3m.

14. "Passio Christi sortitur effectum suum in illis quibus applicatur *per fidem et caritatem* et per *fidei sacramenta,*" *Summa Theologica*, III, q. 49, a. 3, ad lm. Emphasis added.

15. "Facie ad faciem te mihi, Christe, demonstrasti, in tuis te invenio sacramentis." Ambrose, *Apologia prophetae David*, XII, 58; *MPL* 14, 875.

SELECTED READINGS

1. Aquinas, St. Thomas, *Summa Theologica*, Vol. III, pp. 60–69. This "Treatise on the Sacraments" is found in English in *The Summa Theologica*. New York: Benziger, Vol. 17, 1914 (468 pp.) and Vol. 18, 1917 (pp. 1–97). The classic scholastic treatise on the sacraments.

2. Diekmann, Godfrey L., O. S. B., "Two Approaches to Understanding the Sacraments," *Proceedings of the 18th North American Liturgical Week* (1957), pp. 12–27. Approach through cause and approach through sign.

3. Henry, A. M., O.P., ed., *Christ in His Sacraments*. Vol. 6 of Theology Library. Chicago: Fides, 1958. 466 pp. The best treatment in English both of sacraments in general and individual sacraments. Extensive annotated bibliographies.

4. Howell, Clifford, S.J., *Of Sacraments and Sacrifice*. Collegeville, Minn.: Liturgical Press, 1954. 183 pp. The inner meaning of the liturgy.

5. Leeming, Bernard, S.J., *Principles of Sacramental Theology*. Westminster, Md.: Newman, 1956. 690 pp. Most comprehensive recent treatment in English of sacraments in general. Does not deal with individual sacraments.

6. O'Callaghan, Denis, "The Theory of the '*Mysteriengegenwart*' of Dom Odo Casel, a Controversial Subject in Modern Theology," *Irish Ecclesiastical Record*, Vol. 90 (1958), pp. 246–262. Father O'Callaghan wrote his doctoral dissertation on Casel.

7. Palmer, Paul F., S.J., *Sacraments and Worship: Liturgy and Doctrinal Development of Baptism, Confirmation and the Eucharist*. Westminster, Md.: Newman, 1955. 227 pp. A collection of source materials.

8. Pius XII, *Christian Worship*, translation by Canon G. D. Smith of encyclical letter *Mediator Dei*. London: Catholic Truth Society, 1947. 84 pp. The most important recent ecclesiastical document on the nature of the liturgy.

9. Rahner, Karl, S.J., "Personal and Sacramental Sanctity," *Theology Digest*, Vol. 3 (1955), pp. 93–98. These two aspects do not exclude one another, but form a unified way of sanctity in faith and sacrament.

10. Roguet, A. M., O.P., *Christ Acts Through the Sacraments*. Collegeville, Minn.: Liturgical Press, 1954. 162 pp. One of the best short introductions.

11. Semmelroth, Otto, S.J., *Die Kirche als Ursakrament*. Frankfurt: Knecht, 1953. 244 pp. The Church herself is the primal sacrament.

12. Vagaggini, Cyprian, *Theological Dimensions of the Liturgy*, Vol. I. Collegeville, Minn.: Liturgical Press, 1959. 242 pp. The nature of the liturgy and its place in the plan of salvation. So far only Volume I has been translated from the Italian original.

13. Van Roo, William, S.J., *De Sacramentis in Genere*. Rome: Pontifical Gregorian University, 1957. 368 pp. Noteworthy for its analysis of the causality of the sacraments.

14. *Worship*, a monthly which concerns itself principally with the liturgical life of the Church. Published by the Benedictines of St. John's Abbey, Collegeville, Minn.

INTRODUCTION:

THE PROTESTANT VIEW OF JUSTIFICATION

BECAUSE of the great amount of attention given in our times to the doctrine of the Church and the sacraments on the one hand and the concept of Tradition and its hermeneutical aspects on the other, it may seem that the proper understanding of justification is no longer held to be the *articulus stantis et cadentis ecclesiae,* the heart of the Christian faith.

Nevertheless, the doctrine of justification is so much the thermometer of the understanding of God, man, and his mediator that there is hardly a theological statement which does not imply, presuppose, and betray a particular interpretation of God's redemption of man in space and time.

The selections and introductions of this volume have necessarily been mainly concerned with Reformation *thought.* It is worthwhile at least to indicate here that the centrality of the doctrine of justification by faith through grace is even more explicit in Reformation life, and a fundamental factor in the Protestant *experience* of the Christian faith.

It has been said that the basic difference between the Protestant and the Roman Catholic doctrines of justification is that according to the Reformation, God justifies the sinner on the level of man while according to Roman Catholic belief God justifies the sinner on the level of God. By justification of the sinner on God's level is meant the view that God's justice would be compromised if he should finally accept a man who had not, through the help of grace, become sanctified enough to be worthy of that divine acceptance. By justification of the sinner on the sinner's level is meant that view that God's justice is shown precisely in his gracious condescension to accept and so to justify man *as he is,* i.e., man who is unacceptable without his being covered by Christ's righteousness. This formulation, which brings out that God in both traditions is seen as the author of justification, has the advantage that it does away with the popular distortion that Roman Catholicism in contrast with the Reformation sees man as self-sufficient to earn his own salvation. At the same time, it articulates the basic insight of the Reformation that God's justification of the sinner is *unconditional,* that it is the acceptance of the sinner, i.e., that the transformation of the sinner to a child of God does not presuppose a set degree of wholesomeness or sanctity. In the Reformation tradition, predestination is subordinated to this understanding insofar as it protects and preserves the unconditional character of justification.

From the very first decades of the Reformation, Protestants have tried to make clear that justification thus understood does not exclude but includes the performance of "good works." The contrast of justification by *faith* or justification by *faith and works* can be misleading when it is not clearly seen that the acceptance of the sinner is a real transformation in the sense that the new relationship to God through faith in Jesus Christ carries with it the willingness and joy to execute the will of God.

Even in our times it is not redundant to make this same point again. One should add, however, that these "good works" do not form the missing link in the lifeline between God and man—this is firmly and completely established in Jesus Christ—but function in the realm of man and fellow man and are therefore not *heaven,* but *world,* directed, and in this instrumental way glorify God.

In contemporary Protestant discussion, the primary points at stake within the described context concern the formulation of the realistic character of this transformation, the question whether the traditional distinction between grace as act or grace as gift is adequate, and the question as to how the salvation of man is related to the restoration of the created cosmos as such.

To mention only the latter issue in particular, the theological discussion today seems to indicate that behind the Protestant-Roman Catholic disagreement on the point of the doctrine of justification lies a basic difference as regards the created order. In Protestantism, time and space—"our world" and "my body"—do not constitute obstacles for communion with God, but form the God-given realm *within* which alone one can regain the original dignity of man. Therefore, one can say that in Jesus Christ God has reclaimed not souls, but his creation. The individual participation in this act, justification, does therefore not mean a progressive liberation from the chains of time and space in a return to God and *union* with God. It means the discontinuation of the struggle for equality with God and the obedient acceptance of the set realm for *communion* with God, which is the created order itself. The hope of the Christian is, therefore, not merely concerned with his own salvation; it is at the same time a looking forward to the liberation of this cosmos from the fetters of sin.

The following article is representative of the contemporary Protestant interest in illuminating the Christian faith from its own central point: the Person and work of Jesus Christ in whom creation, redemption, and liberation have been and are being brought about.

Thomas F. Torrance was born in 1913. He was educated at the University of Edinburgh and received his D. Theol. at the University of Basel. He is a minister of the Church of Scotland, and at present he is Professor of Christian Dogmatics in the University of Edinburgh and Editor of the *Scottish Journal of Theology*. Professor Torrance is the author of numerous books and articles including *Conflict and Agreement in the Church*.

12

JUSTIFICATION: ITS RADICAL NATURE AND PLACE IN REFORMED DOCTRINE AND LIFE

T. F. TORRANCE

THE TEACHING OF JOHN KNOX

IN his debate with the Jesuit James Tyrie, John Knox claimed that the controversy of the Reformers with the Roman Church was the same as that of St. Paul with the Judaizers of Galatia, in which the Gospel of Grace was at stake, "for it concerneth the chief head of justification," as Knox expressed it.[1] On the other hand, when we examine the writings of Knox we do not find that "justification," as a term at any rate, plays a prominent part, while the expression "justification by faith" is hardly ever found—for when he did speak of justification he preferred to be more concrete and to use an expression like "justification through the blood of Christ."

This calls for two observations. (1) The whole question of the Reformation is at stake in the doctrine of justification. (2) Justification is not a principle in itself: it directs us at once to Jesus Christ and His mighty acts.

When we turn to the *Scots Confession* of 1560 and ask what place justification occupies in it, we find ample confirmation for the two observations we have just made. There are, in fact, three important facts about justification in the Confession that we must note.

(1) There is no separate article on justification. It has no place of its own; rather does justification belong to the inner texture of the Gospel and becomes evident as its cutting edge. That is to say, justification makes decisively clear the very essence of the Gospel of salvation by Grace.

(2) What is absolutely central is Jesus Christ. Man's salvation is exclusively the work of God in Christ, God in union with Man, and

therefore Man in union with God. It is an outstanding characteristic of all the documents of the Scottish Reformation that a place of centrality is given to the union of God and Man in Christ, and therefore of our "blessed conjunction" or "society" or "fraternity" with Christ. That union with Christ lies at the heart of our righteousness in Him, for it is through that union that we actually participate in His holy life. Knox laid immense stress upon the saving humanity of Christ, that is, upon His positive obedience and filial life in our flesh. Consider, for example, this sentence that comes from the *Form of Confession* in the *Book of Common Order:* "We mast alwais have our refuge to the free justice which procedeth of the obedience which Jesus Christe hath prayed for us."[2] What Knox refers to there is the fact that the prayer of Jesus was part of His atoning obedience and oblation to God—it was the worship of God the Father with His Life. In that Life of the worshipping and obedient Son we are made to share and are well-pleasing to the Father as through that participation we are clothed with the Name and Holy Life of Christ. In His unity with man the Son of God lived out a perfect Life on earth in obedience, love and worship, and as such died and rose again. Therefore it is in and through our union with Him, that all that is His becomes ours. It is only as such, that is in the Name of Christ, that we appear before God, and as such that He regards us—in Christ.

(3) The accent lies very strongly here on the positive side of salvation. Thus justification is expressly linked with the resurrection of Christ,[3] to which a whole chapter is given in the *Confession* of 1560, while a further chapter is devoted to the Ascension of Christ.[4] Now that is one of the great characteristics of Knoxian theology—Resurrection and Ascension are part of the Atonement—indeed, "the Resurrection" is often called "the chief article of our faith." What is the significance of this emphasis? In the Resurrection and Ascension we have the affirmation of man by God, and his exaltation to be a partaker of a new humanity, a new righteousness, and a new freedom as a child of God, as a brother of Christ, as a joint heir with Him, as one who together with Him has the same Father. Justification is not only the forgiveness of sins, but the bestowal of a positive righteousness that derives from beyond us, and which we have through union with Christ. Justification is not the beginning of a new self-righteous-

ness, but the perpetual end of it, for it is a perpetual living in Christ, from a center and source beyond us. To be justified is to be lifted up above and beyond ourselves to live out of the risen and ascended Christ, and not out of ourselves.

Justification is interwoven with Incarnation—the union of God and Man in Christ, and with the fulfilment of that union in Reconciliation and Mediation between God and man which was wrought out in the Life, Death, Resurrection and Ascension of Christ—although the final execution of it so far as we are concerned awaits the coming again of Jesus Christ. Justification is rooted in the Incarnation and therefore it reaches out to the final Advent of Jesus as the Incarnate Son—it is both christological and eschatological. In none of the Reformers was the stress upon incarnational union so strong as in Knox; and in none of them was the place given to the *Parousia* so powerful; while it is Knox's highly distinctive doctrine of the Ascension that links those two together, or rather reveals the relation of the Incarnation to the *Parousia*. It is in the Ascension that we have *the fruit* of the Incarnation (including the Death and Resurrection) of Christ, and it is in the *Parousia* that we have the full *fruit* of the Ascension.

Now the reality of all this is what Knox called *Veritie,* that is, the truth and reality of our justification and renewal in Jesus Christ. But the *Veritie* is in Christ and *is* Christ, and it is in us through the operation of the Spirit, and through faith. The *Veritie* of God is in us only as by faith we seek it, not in ourselves, but in Christ alone, for it is through the Spirit that we partake of the blessed conjunction between Christ and ourselves and are presented before the Father in the Body of the Son as those who share in His Life and Righteousness, and are one with Him.

If it is through the Spirit that this Verity is in us, it is through the two Sacraments as instruments of the Holy Spirit's operation that we are *exercised,* as Knox expressed it, in that Verity or blessed conjunction, unity, society, or fraternity with Christ. In Baptism we are ingrafted into Christ to be made partakers of His justice by which our sins are covered and remitted, and in the Supper we are continually nourished through that union with Christ.[5] Both Sacraments tell us that we live not out of ourselves, but we find our life and righteous-

ness outside of ourselves, in Christ alone, through union and communion with Him. Therefore, we are required, as Knox and his colleagues put it in the *Confession,* "to spoil ourselves of all honour of
our own creation and redemption and also of our regeneration and
sanctification."[6] That is the radical nature, and the cutting edge of
Justification.

To bring out the full significance of that a more systematic exposition is necessary.

THE NATURE OF JUSTIFICATION

The Greek word *dikaioun,* like the Scots word *to justify,* may mean
to condemn as well as to vindicate. The basic meaning, which we find
in biblical Greek, is *to put in the right, to put in the truth.* Thus, if a
man is guilty he is put in the right by being condemned, for that is the
truth of the matter; if he is innocent he is put in the right by being declared guiltless and set free. Justification always involves a fulfilling
of the righteousness, or the enacting of the truth.

The Gospel teaches "the justification of the ungodly," and the
astounding thing about it is that that means such a putting of the ungodly man in the right that through fulfilment of his condemnation he
is justified, justified in both senses: judged and acquitted, condemned
and vindicated, exposed as guilty and made righteous—but that is
truth, *alētheia,* concrete reality, only in Jesus Christ.

Let us consider what that means, by thinking of it in terms of *objective justification* and *subjective justification.*

A. *Objective justification* takes place in Christ, before the Father.
The *Scots Confession* expounds it in this way. There was "enmity
betwixt the justice of God and our sins,"[7] and therefore the Son of
God descended to take to Himself a body of our body, flesh of our
flesh, and bone of our bones, and so to become *Mediator* between
God and man. Three conceptions are involved here which we may
allow three words of the *Confession* in its Latin edition to express.
(a) *Frater.* The Son of the Father has made Himself our Brother, for
through His incarnational union with us, He has established our
union with Him. By making Himself our Brother, He has made us

brothers of His and therefore sons of the Father. Through this incarnational fraternity, that which was lost in Adam is restored.[8] (b) *Mediator* or *Interpres*. Through His Sonship, that is, through His obedient Life in filial relation toward the Father, and through His brotherhood with us in our estrangement, Christ is the active Agent who reveals God to us and reconciles us to God—and that He does through the whole of His Life lived out in our flesh and bone in which He brought us back to union with God. The positive emphasis here is upon the obedience of the Beloved Son.[9] (c) *Pacificator*. As our Mediator or Redeemer it behoved Jesus Christ to be very God and very Man "because He was to underlie the punishment due for our transgressions, and to present Himself in the presence of His Father's Judgment, as in our persone, to suffer for our transgression and inobedience, by death to overcome him that was the author of death."[10]

All this could only be done in the hypostatic union, "the wondrous conjunction betwixt Godhead and Manhood,"[11] and out of it issues our justification in resurrection.[12]

This is the doctrine which Reformed theology has called the *Active* and *Passive Obedience* of Christ, and His incarnational *Assumption* and *Sanctification* of our human nature.

(1) *By active obedience* of Christ is meant the positive fulfilment in the whole Life of Jesus of His Sonship. From the very beginning to the very end He maintained a perfect filial relation to the Father in which He yielded to Him a life of utter love and faithfulness, or praise and thanksgiving and confidence and trust, and in which He perfectly fulfilled God's Holy Will and received and laid hold of the Love of the Father. This active obedience was therefore His own loving self-offering to the Father in our name and on our behalf and also His own faithful appropriation of the Father's Word and Will in our name and our behalf.

(2) *By passive obedience* is meant the submission of Jesus Christ to the judgment of the Father upon our sin which He assumed in our humanity when He was "made under the Law" in order to bear it in our name and on our behalf. This is the passion He endured in the expiation of our sins, but it is also His willing acceptance of the divine verdict upon our humanity. The passive obedience is mani-

fested above all in the obedience of Jesus unto the death of the Cross, but that was a passion that began with His very birth, for His whole life, as Calvin says, was in a real sense a bearing of the Cross, but it was in the Cross itself that it had its *telos* or consummation.

This distinction between the active and passive obedience of Christ has been emphasized in Reformed theology not in order to divide or separate them but in order to insist that the whole course of Christ's active obedience is absolutely integral to His work of reconciliation, and that atonement cannot be limited to His passive obedience, that is, to His passive submission to the penalty for our sin inflicted upon Christ in His death. As Calvin put it, immediately He put on the person of the servant He began to pay the price of liberation for our salvation.[18] How could it be otherwise when in the Incarnation there took place a union of God the Judge and the man judged in one Person, so that all through His life, but especially in His death, Jesus bore in Himself the infliction and judgment of God upon our sinful humanity, and wrought out in His life and His death expiation and amendment for our sin?

The active and passive obedience of Christ thus do not differ in regard to time, for both extend to the very beginning of the Incarnation, to the birth of Jesus, and both reach out to its fulfilment in His death and resurrection. Nor do they differ in regard to their Subject, for they are both manifestations of the one obedience of the Son of God in our humanity. They are set in mutual unity in the whole life of Christ. Since this is so we must speak of the active obedience as *actio passiva* and the passive obedience as *passio activa*. This mutuality of Christ's active and passive obedience is important, for it means that in our justification we have imputed to us not only the passive righteousness of Christ in which He satisfied for our sins in suffering the judgment of God in His death on the Cross, but the active righteousness of Christ in which He positively fulfilled the Father's holy Will in an obedient Life. In other words, justification means not simply the nonimputation of our sins through the pardon of Christ, but positive sharing in His divine-human righteousness. We are saved, therefore, not only by the death of Christ which He suffered for our sakes, but by His Life which He lived in our flesh for our sakes and which God raised from the dead that we may share in it through the power of the Spirit. It is in that light, of His atoning and justifying Life, that we are to understand the Incarnation of the Son in the whole course of His obedience from His Birth to His Resurrection.

(3) By the *sanctification of our human nature* we refer to what was wrought by the Son, not only in His active and passive obedience, but through the *union* He established in His birth, life, death, and resurrection between our fallen human nature and His divine nature. In this union He both assumed our fallen human nature, taking it from the Virgin Mary, and sanctified it in the very act of assumption, and all through the holy Life He lived in it from the beginning to the end. Thus our redemption begins from His very Birth, so that we must regard the Incarnation, even in its narrower sense, as redeeming event, reaching out to its full *telos* in the death and resurrection. In His holy assumption of our unholy humanity, His purity wipes away our impurity, His holiness covers our corruption, His nature heals our nature.[14]

If we are to think of the active and passive obedience of Christ as dealing with our actual sin and its penalty, we are to think of the incarnational union of the Holy Son with our unholy nature as dealing with our original sin, or as sanctifying our human nature, through bringing it into a healing and sanctifying union with His own holy nature. That applies, as Calvin insisted in a famous section of his *Institutes,* to the whole life of Jesus, His conception, birth, childhood, youth, manhood, for by living His holy Life through the whole course of our life He has sanctified our conception, birth, childhood, youth, manhood, and death, in Himself.[15]

This is supremely important, for it is only through this union of the human nature with His divine nature that Jesus Christ gives us not only the negative righteousness of the remission of sins but makes us share in the positive righteousness of His obedient and loving Life lived in perfect filial relation to the Father from the cradle to the grave. If we neglect this essential element in the obedience of the Son, then not only do the active and the passive obedience of Christ fall apart in our understanding and doctrine, but we are unable to apprehend justification as anything more than a merely forensic non-imputation of sin. Moreover, if we neglect this essential element, we

are unable to see the Humanity of Jesus Christ in its saving significance, that is, to give the whole life of the historical Jesus its rightful place in the doctrine of the atonement. It is necessary for us, then,
to give the fullest consideration to the place of the union of human
and divine natures in the being and Life of the incarnate Son, for it is
that saving and sanctifying union in which we are given to share that
belongs to the very substance of our faith and life in Christ. In other
words, what we are concerned with is the *filial relation* which the Son
of God lived out in our humanity in perfect holiness and love, achiev-
ing that in Himself in assuming our human nature into oneness with
Himself, and on that ground giving us to share in it, providing us with
a fulness in His own obedient Sonship from which we may all receive.

B. *Subjective Justification.* It is illuminating to recognize that subjective Justification, as well as objective Justification, has already
taken place in Jesus Christ. Not only was the great divine act of
righteousness fulfilled in the flesh of Jesus, in His Life and Death, but
throughout His Life and Death Jesus stood in our place as our Sub-
stitute and Representative who appropriated the divine Act of saving Righteousness for us. He responded to it, yielded to it, accepted
it and actively made it His own, for what He was and did in His human nature was not for His own sake but for our sakes. That is true
of all that He did. He was the Word of God brought to bear upon
man, but He was also man hearing that Word, answering it, trusting
it, living by it—by faith. He was the great Believer—vicariously believing in our place and in our name.[16] He was not only the Will of
God enacted in our flesh, but He was the will of man united to that
divine Will. In becoming one with us He laid hold upon our wayward
human will, made it His very own, and bent it back into obedience
to, and in oneness with, the holy Will of God. Likewise in Justification, Jesus Christ was not only the embodiment of God's justifying
act but the embodiment of our human appropriation of it. In that
unity of the divine and the human, Justification was fulfilled in
Christ from both sides, from the side of the justifying God and from
the side of justified man—"He was justified in the Spirit," as St. Paul
put it.[17] Justification as objective act of the redeeming God and Justi-

fication as subjective actualization of it in our estranged human existence have once and for all taken place—in Jesus.

The New Testament employs other language to speak of this—*hagiazein* (to sanctify), and *teleioun* (to consecrate), especially in their application to Christ. Thus in the Fourth Gospel, in His great high-priestly prayer, Jesus spoke of sanctifying Himself that we also may be sanctified in Him, and prayed that we may be consecrated in one with Him as He and the Father are one. Similarly the Epistle to the Hebrews spoke of Christ as our High Priest who has consecrated Himself for our sakes, and pointed out that He who sanctifies and those who are sanctified are all one. Once and for all we have been sanctified and consecrated in Christ's vicarious work.

That aspect of justification tended to drop out of sight when Protestant scholastic theology began to operate with an *ordo salutis* in which it assigned justification and sanctification to successive and different stages in a process of salvation. In the New Testament itself, however, sanctification or consecration in Christ (for the two words express the same thing) is spoken of in the perfect tense. Christ has already consecrated or sanctified Himself for our sakes, so that we are already consecrated or sanctified in Him—therefore sanctification or consecration is imputed to us by His free Grace just like justification. But it would be a mistake to think of these as two different things, for in the Johannine literature and in the Epistle to the Hebrews the words "sanctification" and "consecration" correspond closely to the Pauline "justification"—they have their special nuance, without doubt, for they are more closely associated than "justification" with the priestly work of Christ, but it is the same reality, the same verity, to use Knox's terms, which they describe.

This teaching is found deeply embedded in the theology of John Calvin and it is an immense pity that later "Calvinism" overlaid and obscured it, although it is once more being brought to light and appropriated in our Reformed doctrine.[18] Our concern here is with *subjective justification,* that aspect of it in which the mighty act of God's righteousness and holiness is appropriated and translated into human life—and that is precisely what Calvin spoke of as the consecrated and sanctified flesh or Life of Jesus in which we are given to share. Let us take as a text for our discussion his answer in the *Geneva*

Catechism to question 342: "Since the whole affiance of our salvation rests in the obedience which He has rendered to God, His Father, in order that it may be imputed to us as if it were ours, we must possess Him: for His blessings are not ours unless He gives Himself to us first." The same essential point is made by Knox in the *Book of Common Order* in which he says that justification, regeneration, sanctification flow out of *adoption*.

We may single out of this two points immediately relevant for our concern at the moment. (1) It is only through union with Christ that we partake of the blessings of Christ, that is through union with Him in His holy and obedient life. Through being united to Him we share in His judgment and His exaltation, in His passive and active obedience, in His Death and also in His Resurrection and Ascension —but first of all it is necessary that we be united to Him, that is, have part in the union which He wrought out between us in His Incarnation and the whole course of His Life. Unfortunately this was reversed in the later teaching of the Church of Scotland, as found in the Westminster Standards—for they put justification first, and then spoke of union with Christ and sanctification as following upon the judicial act that took place in justification by faith.[19]

(2) But there is a second point we have to note in Calvin's statement, the meaning of "affiance." As Calvin used it, this term had a covenanted significance, for it referred to the "fiance" or trust which we have within the covenant mercies of God. A great deal of harm has been occasioned through a sharp distinction between *fides quae creditur* and *fides qua creditur,* or between *credere* and *confidere,* belief and trust. Once this distinction is drawn, faith is separated off from its objective ground and is understood as "trust," *fiducia*—then justification by faith means justification through our trust in God. Now of course there is a truth here which must not be neglected. The Latin term for trust, *fiducia,* which Calvin often translated *fiance,* was a legal term taken from conveyancing, and referred to the conveying of a property from one person to another without any documented receipt; it is an act of trust that relies solely upon the word of another without any tangible pledge of his deed. As Calvin used the word *affiance,* however, the trust or faith of the believer was regarded as grounded and pledged in the faithfulness

of Christ, not only in His spoken promises but in His flesh. He has already received from God all His blessings and has sealed that reception of it for us in His own life and death. Faith is thus a polar concept that reposes upon and derives from the prior faithfulness of God which has been translated permanently into our actual human existence in Jesus Christ. We do not rely, then, upon our act of faith, but upon the faith of Christ which undergirds and upholds our faith. But His faith is not in word only; it has been translated into His life and saving action and set forth in the Covenant of His Body and Blood. The text which we have taken from Calvin comes from his account of the Lord's Supper, for it is in our participation in the Supper and our union with Christ which it gives us that we discern what *affiance,* faith depending upon the faithfulness of Christ, really means.

We may summarize this by saying that Jesus Christ was not only the fulfilment and embodiment of God's righteous and holy Act or *dikaioma,* but also the embodiment of our act of faith and trust and obedience toward God. He stood in our place, taking our cause upon Him, also as Believer, as the Obedient One who was Himself justified before God as His beloved Son in whom He was well pleased. He offered to God a perfect confidence and trust, a perfect faith and response which we are unable to offer, and He appropriated all God's blessings which we are unable to appropriate. Through union with Him we share in His faith, in His obedience, in His trust and His appropriation of the Father's blessing; we share in His justification before God. Therefore when we are justified by faith, this does not mean that it is *our* faith that justifies us, far from it—it is the faith of Christ alone that justifies us, but we in faith flee from our own acts even of repentance, confession, trust and response, and take refuge in the obedience and faithfulness of Christ—"Lord I believe, help thou mine unbelief." That is what is meant to be justified by faith.

We may express it in still another way. Justification has been fulfilled subjectively as well as objectively in Jesus Christ, but that objective and subjective justification is objective to us. It is freely imputed to us by Grace objectively and we through the Spirit share in it subjectively as we are united to Christ. His subjective justification becomes ours, and it is subjective in us as well as in Him, but only subjective in us because it has been made subjectively real in our own human nature, in our own human flesh in Jesus, our Brother, and our Mediator.

When we look at it like this, we understand why John Knox hesitated to use the expression "justification by faith" and preferred instead concrete expressions which made it clear that we are justified only in Christ, by what He has done alone, and not by any act of ours, even if that act be an act of believing. We believe in Christ in such a way that we flee from ourselves and take refuge in Him alone—and therefore we can hardly speak about "justifying faith" without transferring the emphasis away from Christ and His faithful act to ourselves and our act of trust or believing. At this point Calvin and Knox stood in contrast to Luther, who approached the whole question from a point that tended to be anthropocentric: "How can I get a gracious God?" Luther made it indubitably clear that justification does not derive from the act of the self, but from a righteousness outside of us in Christ, from an *aliena justitia,* as he called it. But his basic question demanded an answer to the self, and inevitably gave the whole question of assurance undue prominence. With Calvin and Knox it was different—assurance had little place, because it was not needed. The very act of faith was pivoted upon Christ and His faith, not upon my faith or my need for this or that answer, and hence the assurance was unshakable, because it was grounded in the solid faithfulness of Christ. It was only later in Scottish theology when the anthropocentric questions emerged, questions of conscience and soul-searching, when the eyes of the believer were turned inward upon his own heart rather than outward upon his Lord and Savior, that the demand for assurance became clamant. Whenever there is talk of "justifying faith" then uncertainty creeps in, for all our acts, even of repentance and faith, are unworthy before God. If it is upon our repentance and our faith that we have ultimately to rely, who can be saved, not to speak of being sure of his salvation? It is against this false notion of justification and this false notion of faith that Fraser of Brea directed his profound writings, for what disturbed him more than anything else was the new legalism and the new self-righteousness that had crept into the Reformed faith under cover of "justifying faith."[20] If we are to use the expression "justification by faith alone," and there is no reason why we should not, then let it be crystal clear that "by faith alone" is meant "by the Grace of Christ alone," that faith is but an empty vessel to be filled by the Covenant Mercies and faithfulness of God in Christ.

THE RADICAL CONSEQUENCES OF JUSTIFICATION

Justification means Justification by Christ alone—that is the reference of the expressions *sola fide, sola gratia, sola scriptura,* used in Reformed theology. Justification means that we look exclusively to Christ, and therefore that we look away from ourselves altogether in order to live out of Him alone. That radical nature of justification is expressed and its radical consequences drawn by the *Scots Confession* in the words we cited earlier: "we willingly spoil ourselves of all honor and glory of our own salvation and redemption, as we also do of our regeneration and sanctification."

This is something that very badly needs to be reiterated today within the Churches of the Reformation. Justification by Christ alone means the rejection of *all* forms of self-justification and all forms of justification by anything or out of any source other than Jesus Christ. Let us consider what this means in several areas of doctrine and life.

(*a*) At the Reformation Justification by the Grace of Christ alone was seen to set aside all *natural goodness,* and all works— righteousness; but this applies to all goodness, Christian goodness as well, that is, to "sanctification" as it came to be called. This is powerfully driven home by the *Scots Confession* in several articles, such as the twelfth and the fifteenth. All that we do is unworthy, so that we must fall down before you and unfeignedly confess that we are unprofitable servants—and it is precisely Justification by the free Grace of Christ alone that shows us that all that we are and have done even as believers is called in question. Justification by Grace alone remains the sole ground of the Christian life; we never advance beyond it, as if justification were only the beginning of a new self-righteousness, the beginning of a life of sanctification which is what we do in response to justification. Of course we are summoned to live out day by day what we already are in Christ through His self-consecration or sanctification, but sanctification is not what we do in addition to what God has done in justification. And yet that is the tendency of the *Westminster Catechisms,* where we have a return to the Roman notion of infused sanctification that has to be worked out through strict obedience to legal precepts—hence the exposition of the Ten Commandments takes up the greater part of the Catechisms. But the *Scots Confession* laid the axe to the root of any such movement when it insisted that we have to spoil ourselves even of our own regeneration and sanctification as well as justification. What is "axed" so radically was the notion of "corredemption" which in our day has again become so rampant, not only in the Roman Church, but in Liberal and Evangelical Protestantism, e.g., the emphasis upon existential decision as the means whereby we "make real" for ourselves the *kerygma* of the New Testament, which means that in the last resort our salvation depends upon our own personal or existential decision. That is the exact antithesis of the Reformed doctrine of election, which rests salvation upon the prior and objective decision of God in Christ. It is Justification by Grace alone that guards the Gospel from corruption by "Evangelicals," "Liberals," and Romans alike.

(*b*) Justification by the Grace of Christ alone calls in question not only all natural goodness but all *natural knowledge.* Natural knowledge is as much the work of the flesh as natural goodness; it is a work of the natural man. It is at this point that Karl Barth has made such an immense contribution to the Reformation. We cannot separate knowing and being for they belong to the same man, and it is the whole man, with his knowing and his acting, with the whole of his being, who is called in question by Justification. Justification puts us in the right and truth of God and therefore tells us that we are in untruth. Now, let it be clear that Justification by Grace alone does not mean that there is no natural goodness in man, but that man with his natural goodness is called in question. Jesus Christ died for the whole man (with his good and his evil) not for part of him, the evil part, but for the whole man. He died for all men, the

good and the bad, and all alike come under the total judgment of
His Death and Resurrection; all alike have to be born again in Him,
and made new creatures. That is the radical nature of the Gospel,
which becomes so clear to us when we communicate at the Holy
Table in the Body and Blood of our Lord, for there we feel ashamed
for our *whole being,* for our good as well as for our evil. But the
same applies to our natural knowledge. Justification by the Grace of
Christ alone, does not mean that there is no natural knowledge—what
natural man is there who does not know something of God even
if he holds it down in unrighteousness or turns the truth into a lie?[21]
But it does mean that the whole of that natural knowledge is called in
question by Christ, who when He comes to us says: "If any man
will come after me, let him deny himself, take up his cross and follow
me." The whole man with his natural knowledge is there questioned
down to the root of his being, for man is summoned to look away
from all that he is and knows or thinks he knows to Christ who is
the Way, the Truth, and the Life; no one goes to the Father but by
Him. The theology of Barth can be described, then, as the application
of Justification of the whole realm of man's life, to the realm of
his knowing as well as the realm of his doing. In that, he has sought
to follow through the radical consequences of the Reformation
from which our forefathers resiled when they took refuge again, like
the Romans, in the works of the natural man, for justification.

But if we are to take the *Scots Confession* seriously, then we have
to apply this not only to natural knowledge but to *all* Christian
knowledge; we have to learn to spoil ourselves of our own vaunted
knowledge, we have to let our own theology be called into radical
question, by Christ. If we translate the word "justification" by the
word "verification," we can see the startling relevance of this to
modern theological and philosophical discussions. Justification by
Grace alone tells us that verification of our faith or knowledge on
any other ground, or out of any other source, than Jesus Christ, is to
be set aside. Justification has an *epistemological* as well as an ethical
reference—epistemologically it insists that the only legitimate demonstration of Christian truth is that which is in accordance with its
nature, which is Grace, and that to seek justification of it on any other
ground is not only fundamentally false in itself but to falsify the

Gospel at its very basis. But apart from the contemporary debate on "verification," Justification means that at every point in our theological inquiry we have to let our knowledge, our theology, our formulations, our statements, be called into question by the very Christ toward which they point, for He alone is the Truth. Justification means that our theological statements are of such a kind that they do not claim to have truth in themselves, for by their very nature they point away from themselves to Christ as the one Truth of God. Therefore whenever we claim that our theological statements or our formulations have their truth in themselves we are turning back into the way of self-justification. Out of sheer respect for the majesty of the Truth as it is revealed in the Holy Scriptures, we have to do our utmost to speak correctly and exactly about it—that is the meaning of orthodoxy and the way of humility—but when we have done all this, we have still to confess that we are unfaithful servants, that all our efforts fall far short of the truth. Far from seeking justification on the ground of our "orthodoxy," we can only serve the Truth faithfully if we point away from ourselves and our statements to Christ Himself, and direct all eyes to Him alone. He who boasts of orthodoxy thus sins against Justification by Christ alone, for he justifies himself by appeal to his own beliefs or his own formulations of belief and thereby does despite to the Truth and Grace of Christ. Once a Church begins to boast of its "orthodoxy" it begins to fall from Grace.

(c) Justification by the Grace of Christ alone calls in question all *tradition*. The radical consequence of Justification was keenly felt in this direction at the Reformation. Concentration upon the Word of God, the self-utterance of the Truth, and the acknowledgment of its primacy, cut the strings of prejudice and prejudgment and made clear the path of faith and obedience. Justification here meant that faith is determined by the objective Word of God as its ultimate authority, and so it was freed from the shackles of every lesser authority, for devotion to the Truth of the Word (the whole Truth and nothing but the Truth) inculcated a readiness to rethink all preconceptions and to put all traditional ideas to the test face to face with the Word. In other words, sheer attachment to the Word of God as the real object of knowledge meant detachment from all other sources and norms of knowledge, and the demand that all traditional ideas and notions had to be tested at the bar of the Word. That did not mean that tradition was to be despised, but that it was to be subjected to the criticism of the Word and the Spirit, and corrected through conformity to Jesus Christ. The Reformation stood, therefore, for the supremacy of the Word over all tradition, and for theological activity as the repentant rethinking of all tradition face to face with the Revelation of God in Jesus Christ.

But that applies no less to the Reformed and Evangelical tradition; to our Presbyterian tradition as well as to the Roman tradition. When we examine our own position today, it is astonishing to find how close we have come to the Roman view even in the Church of Scotland. How frequently, for example, we find that appeal is made to "Christian instinct" or to "the mind of the Church" over against the plain utterances of Holy Scripture, and often just at those places where the Word of God offends our will, opposes our habits, or cuts against the grain of our desire! And how massive is the effect of our several traditions upon the interpretations of the Bible! How easy it is to allow the Presbyterian tradition to determine our reading of the New Testament, especially when it is a question of justifying our tradition before the critique of others! There can be no doubt that every one of the great Churches of the Reformation—the Lutheran, the Angelican, and the Reformed—has developed its own masterful tradition, and that that tradition today exercises massive influence not only over its way of interpreting the Bible and formulating its doctrine but over the whole shape and direction of its life. Those who shut their eyes to this fact are precisely those who are most enslaved to the dominant power of tradition just because it has become an unconscious canon and norm of their thinking. It is high time we asked again whether the Word of God really does have free course amongst us and whether it is not after all bound and fettered by the traditions of men. The tragedy, apparently, is that the very structures of our Churches represent the fossilization of traditions that have grown up by practice and procedure, have become so hardened in self-justification that even the Word of God can hardly crack them open. There is scarcely a Church that claims to be *ecclesia reformata* that can truthfully claim to be *semper reformanda.*

(*d*) Justification by Christ alone calls in question all *systems* and *orders,* and calls them in question because Jesus Christ alone is central and supreme in the one Church of God. In any true theological system, Justification is by reference to Christ alone, for conformity to Christ as the Truth of God for us is the one ultimate principle of unity. Likewise Justification in ecclesiastical order or polity ought to be through appeal to Christ alone. Our quarrel with the Church of Rome in doctrinal matters concerns the centrality of Jesus Christ, the primacy and supremacy of Christology which is so obscured and compromised by Roman doctrines of merit and tradition, and above all by Mariology. In our debate with the Church of England over questions of order, we are also concerned with the centrality of Christ, and the primacy of Christology—and therefore the doctrine of the Church as the Body of *Christ* is in the forefront. It is Justification by Christ alone that makes it so, for He alone is the ground and Head of the Church, and in Him alone is the Church's unity constituted and its order maintained. But for that very reason Justification by Christ alone disallows any appeal from one Church to another for recognition of its orders, as it also rebukes the self-justification of a Church in calling in question the orders of another Church. Justification by Christ alone means that we renounce the way of the flesh in seeking honor from men, or justification from one another; and therefore Justification by Christ alone means that in any movement for reconciliation between Churches, the question of the recognition of orders cannot have priority without radical betrayal of the Reformation, nay, without radical betrayal of Christ for He is thereby ousted from His place of centrality.

It becomes more and more clear that in the ecumenical movement it is the doctrine of Justification by Christ alone that is at stake, and that it can just as easily be sinned against by those who shout loudest that they are upholding the Reformation tradition as by those who make no such boast. He is truest to the Reformation tradition who is always ready to subject it to the ruthless questioning of the Word of God.

(*e*) Nowhere does Justification by Christ alone have more radical consequences than in regard to the pastoral ministry. Justification by Christ is grounded upon His mighty Act in which He took our place, substituting Himself for us under the divine judgment, and substituting Himself for us in the obedient response He rendered to God in worship and thanksgiving and praise. In Himself He has opened up a way to the Father, so that we may approach God solely through Him and on the ground of what He has done and is—therefore we pray in His Name, and whatever we do, we do in His Name before God. Thus the whole of our worship and ministry reposes upon the substitutionary work of Christ. Now the radical nature of that is apparent from the fact that through substituting Himself in our place there takes place a displacement of our humanity by the humanity of Christ—that is why Jesus insists that we can only follow Him by denying ourselves, by letting Him displace us from a place of centrality, and by letting Him take our place.

At the Reformation this doctrine had immediate effect in the overthrow of Roman sacerdotalism—Jesus Christ is our sole Priest. He is the one and only Man who can mediate between us and God, so that we approach God solely through the mediation of the Humanity of Jesus, through His incarnate Priesthood. When the Humanity of Christ is depreciated or whenever it is obscured by the sheer majesty of His Deity, then the need for some other human mediation creeps in—hence in the Dark and Middle Ages arose the need for a human priesthood to mediate between sinful humanity and the exalted Christ, the majestic Judge and King. There was of course no denial of the Deity of Christ by the Reformers—on the contrary, they restored the purity of faith in Christ as God through overthrowing the accretions that compromised it; but they also restored the place occupied in the New Testament and the Early Church by the Humanity of Christ, as He who took our human nature in order to be our Priest, as He who takes our side and is our Advocate before the judgment of God, and who once and for all has wrought out atonement for us in His sacrifice on the Cross, and therefore as He who eternally stands in for us as our heavenly Mediator and High Priest.

The Church on earth lives and acts only as it is directed by its heavenly Lord, and only in such a way that His Ministry is reflected in the midst of its ministry and worship. Therefore from first to last the worship and ministry of the Church on earth must be governed by the fact that Christ substitutes Himself in our place, and that our humanity with its own acts of worship, is displaced by His, so that we appear before God not in our own name, not in our own significance, not in virtue of our own acts of confession, contrition, worship, and thanksgiving, but solely in the name of Christ and solely in virtue of what He has done in our name and on our behalf, and in our stead. Justification by Christ alone means that from first to last in the worship of God and in the ministry of the Gospel Christ Himself is central, and that we draw near in worship and service only through letting Him take our place. He only is Priest. He only represents humanity. He only has an offering with which to appear before God and with which God is well pleased. He only presents our prayers before God, and He only is our praise and thanksgiving and worship as we appear before the face of the Father. Nothing in our hands we bring—simply to His Cross we cling.

But what has happened in Protestant worship and ministry? Is it not too often the case that the whole life and worship of the congregation revolves round the personality of the minister? He is the one who is in the center; he offers the prayers of the congregation; he it is who mediates "truth" through his personality, and he it is who mediates beween the people and God through conducting the worship entirely on his own. Nowhere is this more apparent than in the case of the popular minister where everything centers on him, and the whole life of the congregation is built round him. What is that but *Protestant sacerdotalism,* sacerdotalism which involves the displacement of the Humanity of Christ by the humanity of the minister, and the obscuring of the Person of Christ by the personality of the minister? How extraordinary that Protestantism should thus develop a new sacerdotalism, to be sure a psychological rather than a sacramental sacerdotalism, but a sacerdotalism nonetheless, in which it is the personality of the minister which both mediates the Word of God to man and mediates the worship of man to God! Protestant Churches are full of these "psychological priests" and more and more they evolve a psychological cult and develop a form of psychological counselling which displaces the truly pastoral ministry of Christ. How frequently, for example, the minister's prayers are so crammed with his own personality (with all its boring idiosyncrasies!) that the worshipper cannot get past him in order to worship God in the name of Christ —but is forced to worship God in the name of the minister! How frequently the sermon is not an exposition of the Word of God but an exposition of the minister's own views on this or that subject! And how frequently the whole life of the congregation is so built up on the personality of the minister that when he goes the congregation all but collapses or dwindles away!

There can be no doubt that the whole concept of the ministry and of worship in our Reformed Churches needs to be brought back to the criticism of the Word of God in order that we may learn again the meaning of Justification by Christ alone in the midst of the Church's life and work. Jesus Christ must be given His rightful place by being set right in the center, as Head and Lord of the Church, as its sole Prophet and Priest and King, and that means in the midst of our preaching, in the basic notion of the ministerial office, in the fundamental mode of worship, and in the whole life of the congregation as the Body of *Christ alone*.

NOTES

Reprinted from the *Scottish Journal of Theology*, September 1960. This article was the Presidential address delivered to the Scottish Church Theology Society, January 18, 1960, and is reprinted here with the kind permission of Professor Torrance.

1. *The Works of John Knox*, ed. by Laing, Vol. VI, p. 499.
2. *Ibid.*, p. 364.
3. Rom 4:35—a favorite verse with Knox, as with Calvin.
4. *Scots Confession*, Articles X and XI.
5. *Scots Confession*, 1560, Art. XXI.
6. Art. XII
7. *Scots Confession*, Art. VIII.
8. *Ibid.*
9. Arts. VII and VIII.

10. Arts. VIII and X.
11. Art. X.
12. Art. IX.
13. *Institutes*, 2.16.5.
14. See Robert Bruce, *Sermons Preached in the Kirk of Edinburgh* (ed. by Cunningham), pp. 268 f.
15. *Institutes*, 2.16.19.
16. This is the significance of the expression "the merits of Christ" employed in our Reformed Confessions and Catechisms. See T. F. Torrance, *The School of Faith* (London: James Clarke, 1959), pp. lxxxiii f.
17. 1 Tm 3:16.
18. Cf. R. S. Wallace, *Calvin's Doctrine of the Christian Life* (Edinburgh, 1959) in which Dr. Wallace shows that for Calvin Christ's self-consecration on our behalf governs the whole of the Christian life.
19. Torrance, *op. cit.*, pp. cvi f .
20. James Fraser of Brea, *A Treatise on Justifying Faith*, and *Meditations on Several Subjects in Divinity, Particularly Trusting upon God*. etc.
21. Rom 1:18, 25.

SELECTED READINGS

1. Barth, Karl, *Church Dogmatics*, Vol. IV, Pt. 1, trans. by G. W. Bromiley. Edinburgh: T. and T. Clark, 1956, pp. 614–642. These pages comprise one paragraph (61) of Barth's treatment of the doctrine of reconciliation, and include one subparagraph on a re-examination of the doctrine of justification by faith alone and its inevitable consequences for sanctification.
2. Bonhoeffer, Dietrich, *Ethics*, ed. by Eberhard Bethge, trans. by N. H. Smith. New York: Macmillan Co., 1955, pp. 3–230. This volume is a result of the editing and compilation of sections which have survived of the *Ethics* Bonhoeffer himself was never to complete; any study of contemporary Protestant thought on justification cannot ignore this theologian.
3. Bring, Ragnar, "Preaching the Law," *Scottish Journal of Theology*, Vol. 13 (March 1960), pp. 1–32.
4. Bultmann, Rudolf, "Grace and Freedom," in *Essays, Philosophical and Theological*. London: S.C.M. Press Ltd., 1955, pp. 168–181, and "Christ and the End of the Law," *Essays* etc., pp. 36–66. Two excellent expressions of the justification of man as viewed from within existentialist categories.
5. Cox, David, *Jung and St. Paul*. London: Longmans, Green, 1959. "A study of the doctrine of justification by faith and its relation to individuation."
6. Cully, K. B., "Grace and Justification Today: An Interpretation of the Theme of Romans," *Interpretation*, Vol. 11 (October 1957), pp. 421–428.
7. Dillistone, F. W., Lampe, G. W. H., *et al.*, *The Doctrine of Justification*

by Faith. London: A. R. Mowbray and Co. Ltd., 1954. This book had its origin in papers read at an informal conference in 1953 by representatives of two quite different groups within the Church of England.

8. Flew, R. Newton, *The Idea of Perfection in Christian Theology.* London: Oxford University Press, 1934. An important biblical, historical, and critical treatment of a controversial term.

9. Lehmann, Paul Louis, *Forgiveness: Decisive Issue in Protestant Thought.* New York: Harper and Bros., 1940. This work seeks to point in the direction Protestantism must move on the central issue of forgiveness in view of "the gradual disintegration of liberalism and the still uncertain ascendancy of the dialectical movement."

10. Maury, Pierre, *Predestination and Other Papers,* trans. by Edwin Hudson. Richmond: John Knox Press, 1960. Karl Barth's foreword indicates the importance of Pierre Maury's thought.

11. Miller, Alexander, *The Renewal of Man: A Twentieth Century Essay on Justification by Faith.* New York: Doubleday and Co., Inc., 1955. One of the "Christian Faith Series," edited by Reinhold Niebuhr. This study sets the problem of justification in the social and political context of modern man's life.

12. Neill, Stephen, *Christian Holiness.* London: Lutterworth Press, 1960.

13. Niebuhr, Reinhold, *The Nature and Destiny of Man,* Vol. II. New York: Charles Scribner's Sons, 1955. Chap. 4, "Wisdom, Grace and Power (The Fulfillment of History)," pp. 98–126, and Chap. 9, "The Kingdom of God and the Struggle for Justice," pp. 244–286. Justification in the traditional sense is here understood and treated as a part of God's purpose of social, economic, and political justice in history.

14. Tillich, Paul, "Estrangement and Reconciliation in Modern Thought," *Review of Religion,* Vol. 9 (November 1944), pp. 5–19; *Systematic Theology,* Vol. II. Chicago: University of Chicago Press, 1957, pp. 165–180.

15. Watson, P. S., "Luther and Sanctification," *Concordia,* Vol. 30 (April 1959), pp. 243–259.

INTRODUCTION:

THE ROMAN CATHOLIC VIEW OF JUSTIFICATION

IN 1957 Hans Küng, a young Swiss Catholic theologian, published a book called *Rechtfertigung* (Justification), with the subtitle *The Teaching of Karl Barth and a Catholic Reflection*. The first part of the book explained Barth's teaching on justification and the second part explained the Catholic teaching, particularly as it was proposed by the Council of Trent. In this second part, Küng insisted that there is no real opposition between Trent and Barth. He maintained that Catholic doctrine takes seriously both the omnipotence of God and man's righteousness and that the only difference between Barth and Trent is one of emphasis. Barth begins from above and stresses the divine, uncreated aspects of justification, while Trent begins from below, from the created, human aspect. Nevertheless, for Trent, as for Barth, it is always God, in Jesus Christ, who reconciles man with himself in an absolutely gratuitous act. Trent teaches that no human, created reality is the cause or condition or disposition for that justification. At the same time, unless the internal consent or conversion of the individual occurs, justification does not take place. Küng pointed out that Trent was speaking polemically and defensively, emphasizing the truths which the Reformers denied, and consequently did not say all that could be said about justification. Küng's book went on to fill out these omissions by bringing together what many other Catholic authors, both ancient and modern, had said about justification. He concluded that the Catholic doctrine in its fullness not only does not contradict the Scriptures but contains in an eminent way all that was nearest to the hearts of the Reformers.

This was remarkable enough, but the cordial letter from Barth which was published at the beginning of the book was even more remarkable. In this letter Barth praised the complete and accurate account Küng had given of his teaching on justification, and assured the reader that Küng had faithfully reproduced both what he said and what he meant. Barth went on to say that if the second part of Küng's book really described the Roman Catholic teaching on justification, he had to admit that his (Barth's) teaching on justification agreed with it. However, he said that he would suspend judgment until he had the chance to see the reception given Küng's book by his Catholic colleagues. He wanted to see whether they would agree that Küng's description of the Catholic teaching on justification was accurate.

Naturally, the book evoked much comment. A roundup in the Spring 1959 issue of *New Testament Abstracts* lists thirty-one reviews. The interesting thing about these reviews is that, although the reactions are understandably varied, no Catholic reviewer suggests that Küng has not accurately presented the Catholic teaching on justification. Juan Alfaro, in an extended review article written in the *Gregorianum* in 1958, which takes into consideration nineteen reviews of the book which had already appeared, concluded that Küng has discovered the profound intention of Barth's thinking on justification which coincides fundamentally with Catholic theology.

In the light of all this, the following article by Küng takes on a special interest. In it he examines in more detail the relation between justification and sanctification, a problem which his book had been able to deal with only briefly. By making it exclusively a study of justification and sanctification in the New Testament he goes behind the different emphases given to these words in Catholic and Protestant language and provides a concrete illustration of the conviction he expressed in his book: the most fruitful way for Catholic and Protestant theologians to meet is through joint study of the inspired Word of God.

Hans Küng was born in 1928. He studied at the Gregorianum in Rome and at the Sorbonne and the Institut Catholique in Paris. At the age of thirty-two he was appointed Professor of Fundamental Theology at the University of Tübingen. His most recent book, published in 1960, is *Konzil und Wiedervereinigung,* an English translation of which will be published by Sheed and Ward in the Spring of 1962.

13

JUSTIFICATION AND SANCTIFICATION ACCORDING TO THE NEW TESTAMENT

HANS KÜNG

JUST as there are saints who only seem to be saints and just men who are not really just, so also there is a process of justification which really is not justification, and a process of sanctification which is sanctification in appearance only. Justification and sanctification of sinful man are found in every religion. In some of them it is accomplished through nature magic, in some through pantheistic absorption in the divine, in others through a piety which expresses itself in ritual worship or through a morality which emphasizes active fulfilment of duty. However, what we are speaking of here is not just *any* justification at all or *any* sanctification, and certainly least of all man's autonomous self-justification and self-sanctification, but rather *God's* sanctification and justification of sinful man. In other words, we are speaking of justification and sanctification as they are understood in the Scriptures, which, for the Christian, are binding. It is the Scriptures, God's gracious liberating gift to men, which are the norm not only for what a Christian does, but also for what he says. It is not only "ideas" that Holy Scripture communicates to us, but words freighted with "ideas." An uncommitted "philosophy of religion" may allow itself the liberty of by-passing the biblical words in its search of "ideas"; not so Christian theology, which does not aim at self-interpretation, but at making clear the meaning of the Word of God.

Christian theology will not shun the hard work involved in probing the meaning of the terminology of the Bible, of the words it uses, and the way it uses them. There are a number of different ways of explaining the justification-sanctification relationship. If we want an explanation which comes from the Word of God, we must let ourselves be taught by the terminology of the Bible. Categories which come from outside the Bible need not be eliminated, but the biblical categories must be the standard against which they are checked. Now in the light of Scripture, what is the relationship between justification and sanctification? They must be seen in the unity which underlies their differences.[1]

The New Testament word for justification is the noun *dikaiōsis* with the verb *dikaioun* (to justify), both (together with *dikaiosunē* [righteousness]) derived from *dikaios* (just, righteous), which in its turn goes back to the root word *dikē* (punishment). The New Testament term for sanctification is the noun *hagiasmos* with the verb *hagiazein* (to sanctify), which stems from *hagios* (holy), as do also *hagiotēs* (holiness) and *hagiosunē* (holiness). If we compare both word groups, we quickly notice that justification and sanctification cannot be separated. It is the same God who is both the Just One (Jn 17:25; 2 Tm 4:8; Ap 16:5) *and* the Holy One (Jn 17:11; 1 Jn 2:20), who justifies (Rom 3:26, 30; 4:5; 8:30, 33; Gal 3:8) *and* sanctifies (Jn 17:17; 1 Thes 5:23). It is the same Jesus Christ who is the Holy One *and* the Just One (Acts 3:14), the Just One Acts 7:25; 22:14; 1 Jn 2:1; 3:7) *and* the Holy One of God (Mk 1:24; Lk 4:34; Jn 6:69), who was justified in the Spirit (1 Tm 3:16) *and* sanctified by the Father (Jn 10:36), in whose name we are justified (1 Cor 6:11; Gal 2:17) *and* sanctified (1 Cor 6:11; 1:2). It is the same Spirit, the Spirit of holiness (Rom 1:4; 2 Thes 2:13), in whom we are justified *and* sanctified (1 Cor 6:11; cf. Rom 15:16). It is the same redemption in which Christ became our righteousness *and* sanctification (1 Cor 1:30); we were justified (Rom 5:9) *and* sanctified (Heb 10:29; 13:12) in the same blood. By being cleansed in the same baptism, we have been justified *and* sanctified (1 Cor 6:11; Eph 5:26). It is the same Christians who are just (Mt 13:43; Rom 2:13; 5:19; 1 Pt 4:18 and *passim*) *and* holy (Acts 9:13, 32; Rom 8:27; 12:13; 15:25 and *passim*), who are the justified (Rom 3:24) *and* the sanctified (Heb 10:14; Acts

20:32; 26:18), and who nevertheless actively await justification
(Gal 5:5) *and* sanctification (Rom 6:22; 1 Thes 4:3).

Whoever would tear justification and sanctification one from the
other does not let the Scriptures teach him, but rather makes up his
own teaching. The same theocentricity prevails in both justification
and sanctification. It is the just and holy Father *alone* who justifies
and sanctifies: "It is God who justifies" (Rom 8:33). "May the
God of peace himself sanctify you through and through" (1 Thes
5:23). And the same Christocentricity likewise prevails in both:
Only in Jesus Christ who is *the* Just One and *the* Holy One does the
justification and sanctification of sinful men take place directly and
primordially. "Jesus Christ, who was our righteousness and sanctification" (1 Cor 1:30). As in justification, so also in sanctification
it is *man* who is being genuinely affected by the justifying and sanctifying action of God. Man receives through the Holy Spirit a real
share in the justification and sanctification of Christ and is changed
in his very being. "Now you *have* been sanctified, now you *have* been
justified through the name of the Lord Jesus Christ and through the
Spirit of our God" (1 Cor 6:11).

In both justification *and* sanctification the movement proceeds
from above downwards, from the Father who is the *solus sanctus*
(the only Holy One) and *solus justus* (the only Just One), through
his crucified and risen Son Jesus Christ, who is one with him in the
Holy Spirit, to the man who is to be justified and sanctified. Not
only justification but sanctification as well are rooted in God's
eternal decree: "From the beginning God has chosen you for salvation in sanctification through the Spirit" (2 Thes 2:13). "Thus has
he truly chosen us in him (Christ) from the foundation of the
world, so that we might be holy and blameless before him" (Eph
1:4). Sanctification is not simply—as has often been asserted—the
human counter-movement from below, the responsive action of men
in sanctification answering to the divine action of justification. No,
the origin and beginning of justification and sanctification are from
above, in the action of God. The center and the basis of justification *and* sanctification are in Jesus Christ. The power and the seal
of justification *and* sanctification is the Holy Spirit of Jesus Christ,
and of the Father, through whom justification *and* sanctification

develop and reach their goal in individual men. Man *receives* justification *and* sanctification. Whereas a *justification* from below, coming
from men, appears at least as a possibility in the purview of the New
Testament, a *sanctification* which would take its beginning from
below appears to be ruled out from the start. That sanctification can
take place only from above downwards is, for the New Testament,
an evident presupposition which does not even need to be argumen-
tatively established. All sanctification in the New Testament proceeds
from God. That the Temple (Mt 23:17), the altar (Mt 23:19),
and the sacrifice (Heb 9:13) are able to sanctify, are able to
possess sanctifying power, all this presupposes the holiness of God.
Just as the kingdom of God comes (in men) through God himself,
just as the will of God is done (in men) through God himself, so
also the name of God is sanctified (in men) through God himself
(Mt 6:9; Lk 11:2). It is not merely a benediction but a genuine
request to our Father: May he himself reveal his holiness. God
himself—in cautious passive paraphrase—is the logical subject of
sanctification (cf. Ez 36:23; 20:41; 28:22; 38:16; Is 5:16). And
the divinity of Jesus Christ becomes manifest in the fact that he—
sanctified by the Father (Jn 10:36)—sanctifies himself (Jn 17:19),
and then also his disciples (Jn 17:19) and the Church (Eph 5:26;
Heb 2:11; 10:10, 14; 13:12). It is not without cause that the concept of sanctification in St. Paul is employed mainly in the passive
sense: the sanctified in Jesus Christ (1 Cor 1:2), in the Holy Spirit
(Rom 15:16), those *called* by God to be saints (1 Cor 1:2; Rom
1:7). Christians can and ought to sanctify Christ in their hearts (1
Pt 3:15), *because* they themselves are saints through God (1 Pt
1:15 f.). So, in contradistinction to other religions, it is God's sanctifying will and Word which stand altogether in the foreground. *He*
sanctifies his people and sanctifies individuals; *he* brings his claim
upon the whole of life. In view of this work of God, only this can
be said about the work of man: "As he who has called you is holy,
you also ought to be holy in all your dealings, for it is written: 'Be
holy, *for I* am holy' " (1 Pt 1:15 f.; cf. Lv 11:44). The phrase
"sanctification of man" is speaking more of the production of this
sanctification by God in man than of man's possession of this sanctification. The Father sanctifies the Son (Jn 10:36) and the Son

sanctifies himself (Jn 17:19) so that men may be sanctified (Jn 17:19) in him who is the "holy one of God" in the absolute sense, that is, in him who as the sanctifier produces those who are sanctified (Heb 2:11).

Justification and sanctification belong together, form a unity in the single event of salvation in Jesus Christ. This does not mean that justification and sanctification may be confused. A theological reduction of these two concepts to one would not correspond to exegetical findings; it would pass over the contrasts which are fruitful precisely for theological reflection, and it would lead eventually to a very dangerous distortion of the Christian message.

1. *Justification has a legal character.* The root word for *dikaioun* (to justify) and *dikaiōsis* (justification) is *dikē* (punishment), which occurs only three times in the New Testament and is always understood as criminal justice and punishment (Acts 28:4; 2 Thes 1:9; Jude 7). Whatever its etymology may be, it is a basic concept of the *legal* sphere. This holds good especially for the Greek of the classical and Hellenist periods. The enormous theological significance of the idea of justice in the Old Testament is well known. Consider in the present context the importance of the legal trial as the typical image of God's dealings with the just and unjust men.

But even the verb form *dikaioun* (to justify) is no less obviously legal in character. In this all lines which lead to the New Testament word agree: the Old Testament *ṣdq* means a "court pronouncement of justification" (which is of the highest importance precisely for Pauline terminology because of its general dependence on Old Testament terminology). In classical Greek also, in Hellenism, and in the Septuagint (which Paul cites), *dikaioun* (to justify) is a legal concept. Especially significant, finally, is the legal aspect of justification in the synagogue teaching, with which Paul had to carry on controversy. In all his other attacks, this aspect is never placed in question. For his own terminology he has drawn extensively upon the juridical language of the Pharisees.

And thus in New Testament usage as well the legal keynote of *dikaioun* (to justify) is unmistakable. Though not everywhere emphasized, nevertheless, it is operative throughout. And even if it is not apodictically provable in every text, its presence can still be easily detected. It is certainly clear in the Synoptics: Mt 11:19 (cf. Rom 3:4); Mt 12:37; Lk 10:29; 16:15; 18:14. Clear traces of this legal emphasis are to be found especially in Paul in the eschatological texts (Rom 2:13; 8:33; 1 Cor 4:4), *dikaioun* (to justify) can be understood only in the legal sense. It is probable that with the passage of time "to justify" was used by the Jews in an eschatological sense, and that as a result of this, legal-eschatological justice in Paul is already attributed to man in the present time. He especially is considered as "justified" who is pronounced free in a legal process (in the *krinesthai* [going to law]), who has won (in Rom 3:4 *dikaiōthênai* [to be justified] and *nikan* [to win] are placed in parallel). That is, generally speaking, the innocent party, but not insofar as he *is* innocent but insofar as he is *recognized* as such. In Jesus Christ to be sure—the paradox of grace (Rom 3:23 f.; 5:20) —it is precisely the unjust one who is recognized as just on the basis of his faith, and thus "to justify" now means the same as "to reckon faith as righteousness" (Rom 4; Gal 3:6). For the legal usage of *dikaioun* [to justify] this is likewise the case. The *enōpion autou* (in his sight: Rom 3:20) and *para tô theô* (before God: Gal 3:11; Rom 2:13) used with this word are characteristic court forms. The opposite of *dikaioun* (to justify), that is *katakrinein* (to condemn: Rom 8:33; 1 Cor 4:3–6), is a legal concept. Also the use of *dikaiōsis* (justification) and *dikaiōma* (justification) (precisely in contrast to *katakrima* [condemnation]) is legal. The adjective *dikaios* (just) manifests even in the Septuagint a strong connection with the judgment of God. Man is just when he is recognized as such, that is, when he is declared just or is justified, if this was necessary. Finally, the noun *dikaiosunē* (righteousness) goes considerably beyond the meaning of *dikaioun* (to justify), yet the legal traces are unmistakable even here. These traces are recognizable not only in the Greek moral teaching in Josephus and Philo, not only in the Old Testament, in the Septuagint and the synagogue, but also in the New Testament itself, both in the non-Pauline and especially in the Pauline writings. *Dikaiosunē* (righteousness) as a condition of salvation or also as a fruit of salvation is possessed by man not simply in himself but in the presence of another to whom he is answerable, in the judgment of another who attributes it to him (not as a quality but as a relationship). Nonetheless, precisely in the case of *dikaiosunē* (righteousness) (and also with the adjective *dikaios* [just]) as the union of judgment and *grace,* it becomes particularly clear that in "the act of justifying" (*dikaioun*) and in "justification" there is no question of an act where the judge makes good a debt, but one in which the judge bestows unmerited grace for the salvation of man. The grace-character of justification, in which precisely the *un*just person is acquitted and declared just, shows that *God's* justification can be conceived only analogously as a legal act.

Dikaioun is thus used by Paul almost exclusively for God's judgment, either for the act of God which justifies or for man's acquittal by which he is changed into a *dikaios* (just man) and receives in Christ the divine gift of *dikaiosunē* (righteousness).

The legal character is of fundamental significance for justification. Since it is a question not merely of some physical occurrence in man but of a statement that he is just, a declaration of justice, a court judgment, a nonreckoning of sins, and a reckoning of Christ's justice (imputation: Rom 4; Gal 3:6) through *God*—for that reason the *gravity* of the situation, in contrast to all sinful frivolity, becomes evident: what is involved is *God,* his personal anger, and his personal grace. But precisely for that reason, in opposition to all the faintheartedness and despair of the tormented conscience, the overriding *consolation* of the situation is manifest. It is not I myself who must strive in vain to cast off my burden of guilt. No, it is God himself who lifts it off because he forgives me, whole and entire, through his gracious word. It has been shown elsewhere[2] that Catholic tradition not only does not exclude the legal character of justification, but actually includes it. Catholic tradition, however, lays great stress on this: God's justification must be taken seriously; God does what he says. When God declares a man just, he draws him into the righteousness of God and thus he effects a transformation of man's very being. When God *says* a man is just, since it is *God* who says it, man is simultaneously *made* just. From this it follows that justification includes in itself all the effects which touch the very being of the man who is justified, and his effective transformation, and thus also includes a positive sanctification effected by God. But it remains true that biblical and especially the Pauline act of justifying ("justification") does not say this explicitly.

2. *Sanctification is linked to divine worship.* The stern word *hagios* (holy) is originally a concept connected with worship and is used in speaking of the characteristics of persons and things that are allowed to come into contact with God. It is used in nonbiblical Greek first of all in connection with the sanctuary and takes on an Oriental coloring in the Hellenistic period. It conveys all the inflections of its Hebraic equivalent *qdš*. This in its turn has from the very beginning onward, in noun, adjectival, and verb forms, an intimate connection with the divine worship, whether it is used in speaking of God, man, things, space, or time. *qdš*, (*hagios*, holy), the basic concept of worship, is in actual fact cognate with *ṭhr* (purity, *hagnos*), which is the basic concept of ritual. But both of them have their origin not on the level of human morality but on the level of the divinely numinous. Only in the course of time, in the theology of the prophets, does the concept of worship-sanctification gradually change into the moral concept, so that in postexilic Judaism the stream emphasizing priesthood and worship (predominant in the literature of the Law) joins the stream which stresses prophecy and morality (prevalent in the Psalm poetry). Yet in the postexilic literature, as also later in the rabbinical, the concept of *hagios* (holy) never loses its connection with its origins in a context of worship.

The New Testament concept of holiness rests on that of the Old Testament. The connection between holiness and worship is already expressed in the name of God (Ap 4:8). Although the holiness of the Father is more presupposed than expressed, the deutero-Isaian expression *ho hagios pais* (the holy servant) *'bd yhwh* (the servant of Yahweh) is applied to Christ (Acts 4:27, 30; cf. Mt. 12:18). This, an expression simultaneously of loftiness and lowliness, points— always with an indication of divine origin—to the role destined for the savior in divine worship. Christ offers himself as a holy victim in order to reopen to the sinful people the entrance to the sanctuary (intimated in Acts 3:14; 4:27; then above all in 1 Pt 1:18; Heb 9). Christ appears simultaneously as victim, priest, and temple. But it is in the Holy Spirit of Jesus that the new community of worship is founded (Rom 5:5; 1 Cor 3:16; 6:19; 2 Cor 13:13; Eph 2:20–

22). He dwells in the Christian community (1 Thes 4:8; 2 Tm 1:14) to the degree that it exists in the sanctification of the Spirit (2 Thes 2:13). The holy people is a royal priesthood (1 Pt 2:9), and at the same time a victim sanctified in the Holy Spirit (Rom 15:16), the holy and faultless Church (Eph 5:27), the Church of the saints (1 Cor 14:33). Yet in relation to individual Christians, too, the connection between holiness and worship is obvious: the Christian life as a holy sacrifice well-pleasing to God (Rom 12:1; 15:16), holy and blameless (*amōmos* [without blemish] in the sense of faultlessness for worship or suitability for the rite of worship). Especially pronounced is the worship character of *hagios* (holy) in its application to the flesh of the victim (Mt 7:6), to the sanctuary (Heb 8:2; 9:1, 2, 3, 24, 25; 13:11), to Jerusalem (Mt 4:5; 27:53; Acts 11:2; 21:2, 10; 22:19), to the Temple (Mt 24:15; Acts 6:13; 21:28), to the covenant (Lk 1:72), to the Scriptures (Rom 1:2), to the kiss (Rom 16:16; 1 Cor 16:20; 2 Cor 13:12). The theme of worship which is associated with the concept of *hagios* (holy) is discernible throughout all of the Old and New Testament up to and including their eschatology (Ap 20:9; 22:11).

But what about the words which are used not just to say "holy" or "holiness" (*hagiotēs, hagiosunē*) but to express directly the idea of "sanctification"? *Hagiazein* (to sanctify) which occurs almost exclusively in biblical Greek, already in the Septuagint, as a translation of *qdš,* has a meaning linked to worship. In the New Testament it is used for things which are dedicated to use in worship or which render things suitable for worship (Mt 23:17, 19; 1 Tm 4:5), or for persons upon whom a special fitness for worship was conferred, who, having been drawn into the holy sphere, and for that reason consecrated, are made holy. This happens through Baptism (1 Cor 6:11; Eph 5:26), through the blood of sacrifice (Heb 9:13), through the blood of Christ (Heb 13:12; cf. 2:11; 10:10), through contact with some holy person (1 Cor 7:14). The undercurrent of emphasis on worship is therefore especially tangible in the connection of sanctification with the propitiation sacrifice (Heb 2:14; 10:10, 14, 29; 13:12; Rom 15:16), with purity (Eph 1:4; 5:26; Col 1:22; 1 Tm 4:5; 2 Tm 2:21), and with Baptism (1 Cor 6:11; Eph 5:26). Only with the word *hagiasmos* (consecration, sanctification), which in contrast to the words *hagiotēs* (holiness as the state of being holy: 2 Cor 1:12; Heb 12:10) and *hagiosunē* (holiness as a dynamic, active property: Rom 1:4; 2 Cor 7:1; 1 Thes 3:13; it has its origin in propitiation and thus has an element of worship), means not holiness but sanctification, and that in the active sense, is the stress now clearly placed on the moral element: the exercise of holiness especially through putting aside impurity (*akatharsia*): Rom 6:19,22; 1 Thes 4:3,4,7; 2 Thes 2:13; 1 Tm 2:15; Heb 12:14.

From the original connection of sanctification with ritual worship it becomes clear that the biblical concept of sanctification has a *Sitz in Leben* (life context) different from that of the concept of justification. Here the picture of a trial and judgment never stands in the background. But *qdš* is used to indicate segregation and cutting off, separation and setting apart from all that is profane and impure, being especially chosen for God's service; the pure becomes the holy by being withdrawn from profane use and consecrated by a positive act to God. In the New Testament the physical element in sanctification drops out (Jerusalem, Temple, holy of holies, sacrificial gifts, times of worship, instruments of worship, vestments of worship, etc.: what is alluded to in the New Testament is spoken of in the perspective of the Old Testament), that is, it becomes transformed into something spiritual. (Cf., for example, Rom 12:1 f. where the religious terminology of ritual worship is given a spiritual and ethical meaning.) Sanctification is the action of God which sets life in opposition to sin and lays claim to it for himself: a separation from what is worldly and sinful and a special election for what is divine and sacred. So, according to the New Testament, holiness in the context of ritual worship consists in being snatched out of this world of sin, of darkness and of Satan (Acts 26:18; Eph 2:19; Col 1:12 f.), and consequently in being called to share in the heritage of the saints (Eph 1:18; Col 1:12; 2 Thes 2:13; 1 Pt 1:15). At the same time, this concept of holiness receives a transcendental character and expresses the divine elevation of God above the world, which the saints can share (cf. the expression *pneuma hagion* [holy spirit] as the spirit which goes out from God, or *graphai hagiai* [holy writings] as the writings which are produced by God, or the implantation of believers into divine truth described in Jn 17).

We saw that sanctification is always tied in with justification. We shall go on to see in what way the two are linked. But just as the declaration of justice in the Bible does not explicitly include sanctification, neither does sanctification in the Bible explicitly include declaration of justice.

3. *Justification is directed more to the individual, sanctification to the group.* Even justification is not purely a personal affair of individuals, but it is a concern of the community. Paul himself does not isolate justification as a private event but places it within the over-all salvation-history context of the redemption of *all* men for the Church (Rom 5:18 f.; cf. 5:12–17; 8:32; 11:32; 2 Cor 5:14; 1 Tm 2:6). In Christ's death and Resurrection all are redeemed and justified (Rom 3:21–26; 4:25; 5:9; 8:3; Gal 3:13; 2 Cor 5:18–21; cf. Jn 12:31). The collective, ecclesiological character of justification cannot be overlooked and every individualistic doctrine of justification is a false approach (the questions of the theology of the Church and the sacraments related to the doctrine of justification are excluded from our treatment here).

And yet it is true that justification—in contrast to sanctification—is directed more to the individual (who of course then becomes at once a member of the body of Christ). It is striking that neither *dikaioun* (to justify) nor *dikaiōsis* (justification) is ever met in connection with *ekklēsia* (church) or a corresponding word. A similar observation can be made with regard to the use of *dikaios* (just) and *dikaiosunē* (righteousness). In general, the way community relationships are pushed into the background when dealing with justification is striking, as contrasted with the way sanctification is treated.

When we consider the legal character of justification, this observation is not surprising. It is a matter of God's personal declaration of justice, and so it is definitely the *individual* who is put on trial. It is a matter of God's personal judgment, before which the individual must take a stand, i.e., must submit himself in faith. For this reason the most "objective" statements about God's justice are always the very ones which are linked to faith (cf. Rom 1:17; 3:22,28; 4; 5:1). If faith is to be reckoned as justice (Rom 4:3, 5 f.; 9:11,22; Gal 3:6), then this affair is a matter of personal reckoning for each individual. Hence justification, precisely because of its legal character, though certainly not individualistic, is still determined primarily on an individual basis.

It is different in the case of sanctification. Naturally, the New Testament speaks about individual "saints" (prophets in Lk 1:70; Acts 3:21 ; 2 Pt 3:2; John the Baptist in Mk 6:20; the Apostles in Eph 3:5; Christians in 1 Pt 1:16 and *passim;* cf. the expression *hoi hagioi* [the saints] in Acts 9:13,22; Rom 8:27 and *passim*). How could there be a holy body without holy members? (Eph 4 and *passim*). The individual personal character of sanctification is unmistakable and every collectivistic doctrine of sanctification a false approach.

But the holy members are always seen as a part of the holy community. And it is the idea of ritual worship which makes clear why in sanctification the community aspect stands in the foreground. For a new holy generation has sprung up, a royal priesthood, a holy people (1 Pt 2:9). Christ, the Holy One of God, is the founder of the new worship community. He has sacrificed himself for his Church in order to sanctify it, so that it might be holy and blameless (Eph 5:26 f.). Thus this community has been founded by his death (Rom 5:9 ff.; 2 Cor 5:18 f.); its visible signs are Baptism (Rom 6:3; 1 Cor 12:13; Col 2:12; Ti 3:5), and the Lord's Supper (1 Cor 11:26; 12:13; 2 Cor 5:17). National boundaries are torn down. God's people are no longer only the Israelites but Gentiles as well. They also are God's holy and beloved chosen ones (Col 3:12). They are those sanctified in Christ Jesus (1 Cor 1:2 cf. 6:11), a sacrificial gift, sanctified in the Holy Spirit (Rom 15:16), no more foreigners or strangers, but fellow citizens of the saints and members of God's household (Eph 2:19), made capable of sharing in the inheritance of the saints in light (Col 1:12), in the riches of his glorious heritage in the community of the saints (Eph 1:18). In this way Jew and Gentile—both communities are often designated as the "saints"—form a holy and spotless Church (Eph 5:27) into which the individual churches of the saints (1 Cor 14:33) are incorporated as participating communities. A holy temple in which the believers are the living stones and in which God dwells in the Spirit (Eph 2:21; cf. 1 Cor 3:16; 6:19; Eph 2:20), a community of the Holy Spirit (Rom 5:5; 2 Cor

13:13; 1 Thes 4:8; 2 Tm 1:14), in which Christ himself is priest and victim (Heb 9). Accordingly, Paul views the Christian community of the "saints" (Rom 1:7; 1 Cor 1:2; 14:33; 2 Cor 1:1; Eph 1:1; Phil 1:1; Col 1:2 and *passim*) as a people (Rom 9:25 f.; 11:1 f.; 15:10; 2 Cor 6:16), as Israel (Rom 9:8; Gal 3:29; 4:26 ff.; 6:16; Phil 3:3), as *ekklēsia* (church) (1 Cor 1:2; Eph 1:22; 5:23; Col 1:18 and *passim*), as temple (1 Cor 3:16 f.; 2 Cor 6:16; Eph 2:21), as body (1 Cor 10:16 f.; 12:12 ff.; Eph 1:23 f.; 4:4,12,16; Col 1:18; 3:15 and *passim*), as bride (2 Cor 11:2; Eph 5:26 f.).

Thus in the New Testament and especially with Paul the Christians are regarded as a collectivity, as the continuation of the chosen, holy people of God in the Old Covenant, that is to say, as *ekklēsia* (Church), as the assembly of those summoned through God to holiness, to a participation in his own holiness. The Christian community is holy—not through itself, but through the Spirit who is the sanctifier. The individual Christian is holy in the Holy Spirit (Baptism) through his membership in the holy community. Because he belongs to the holy community, he is set apart from the world and sin, and chosen out for God.

Hence sanctification, precisely because of its worship character, derives its characteristics from a situation which, though not "collectivistic," is nevertheless predominantly collective.

4. *No self-justification.* From the fundamentally legal character of justification a further conclusion naturally follows. It is not works, not moral achievements which count in justification. "We hold that man is justified through faith (alone) without the works of the law" (Rom 3:28). "Only for him who does not perform works, but rather believes in him who justifies the godless, will faith be reckoned as justice" (Rom 4:5). "But since we know that no man is justified by works of the law but through faith in Jesus Christ, we also have believed in Christ Jesus in order to be justified by faith in Christ, and not by the works of the law, because by works of the law no man is justified" (Gal 2:15–16; cf. 3:5–14,24; 5:5; Rom 3:21–27; 4; 5:11; 9:30–32; 10:4–6; 1 Cor 4:7; 2 Cor 12:9; Phil 3:9).

Looking at the problem as he does from an anti-Pharisaical viewpoint, Paul is referring primarily to the works of the Mosaic law, but all other works and moral achievements of man are included. If even the works prescribed by the holy law of Israel do not contribute to justification, then a fortiori other works certainly do not. For it is certainly not true that the works of the law would be evil *in themselves;* certainly they must also be fulfilled by the *believer,* in a new way of course, through love (Rom 3:31; 13:18; Gal 5:14). What is false in the old way is that works, with a view to justification, wanted to provide grounds for man's *kauchasthai* (glorying). Since works want to be somehow one's own achievement, which could mean "glory" for man, they are *for this very reason* radically useless for justification (Rom 3:2 f.). And this is true not only for the works of the Jews whose sinful basic attitude is actually "self-glorification" (Rom 2:17,23), but also for the works of the Gentiles (1 Cor 1:19–31). *No one* may glory before God (1 Cor 1:29) except in the Lord (1 Cor 1:31; 2 Cor 10:17) and in his own frailty (2 Cor 11:30; 12:9; Gal 6:14). Should man praise himself for *any* of his works, he would be forgetting that he has *nothing* which he has not *received* (Cor 1:29). Every justice "of one's own" is to be ruled out (Rom 10:3). Whether it be works of the Mosaic law, whether it be works of general morality—they avail not at all for the justification of man. No one can stand before God in his own strength. We are justified through God's *grace,* and thereby *every* human achievement is excluded when justification is in question (Rom 3:24; 4:14–16; 5:13, 17; 6:14; 11:5 f.; Gal 2:21; 5:4). "But if it is by grace, then it is no longer on the basis of works; otherwise grace would no longer be grace" (Rom 11:6). If by grace, then it will be impossible to speak of a justification given because of *any* obligation.

Every human work, every human achievement, is excluded, but not every human *act,* which does not set itself up as the achievement of some work but rather as renunciation of achievement, which does not desire to force itself through by works, but rather trustfully to abandon itself. This fundamental deed of man, which is supremely active in its extreme passivity, is *faith.* Faith is the radical surrender of *kauchēsis,* of "glorying" (Rom 3:27). This faith, which it at the same time radical obedience (Rom 1:5; Gal 3:2,5), is not justification itself. It is, however, the condition for the subjective reception and for the realization of justification in man (Rom 1:17; 3:22,26,

28,30; 4; 5:1; 9:30,32; 10:6,10; Gal 2:16; 3:6–14,24–27; 5:5; Phil 3:9).

Justification through "faith alone" bespeaks the complete incapacity and incompetence of man for any sort of self-justification. In justification the sinner cannot give anything which he does not receive from grace. The attitude of simple trusting submission under God's gracious judgment is faith, which does not even appeal to its own self, its deed or its attitude, which would only be the craftiest kind of "glorying" (1 Cor 4:7; Rom 4:20). Thus, no work, not even a work of love, justifies man, but only faith, justified through God himself. This faith as a gracious gift of God is not achievement through works, but rather self-surrender to God, an abandonment by grace to the grace of God as a response to the act of God. This basic human act as a reception of the kerygma is simultaneously insight (Rom 5:3; 6:8 f; 2 Cor 1:7; 4:13 f; 5:6) and trust (Gal 3:6; 4:3; 2 Cor 1:9); it is simultaneously recognition, acknowledgment and profession of faith, and includes fear (Rom 11:20–25; 2 Cor 5:11) as well as hope (Rom 4:18; 5:5).

And love? There are works of love, but they too are excluded from justification, although the belief of the justified man must be active in love (Gal 5:6). Still, love itself is not a work. Insofar as it too looks away from itself and surrenders itself unconditionally and entirely to God, it is rather to be classified as faith. There is a dead faith of the demons, which yields only knowledge and not self-surrender (Jas 2:19). Yet this is not the genuine, loving faith for which God justifies the sinner. Faith and love, if they are genuine, are a surrender of the whole man. There is no genuine faith without love, no genuine love without faith. However, in faith the dominant element is trusting (and, of course, loving) self-submission in view of one's own worthlessness; while in love, what dominates is self-forgetting (and, of course, believing) self-effacement in the contemplation of God's lovableness. But neither lives without the other, and each lives from and in the other. It is not without reason that faith and love are named to describe the whole of Christian existence together with hope which expresses the eschatological tension contained in man's gift of himself (1 Cor 13:13; 1 Thes 1:3; 5:8). Without love, faith would be nothing (1 Cor 13:2). Genuine love is rooted in faith, just as true

faith culminates in love. Faith is made living through love, for love
is the gift of the Spirit of life. We are thus not surprised that in the
broader context of justification (Rom 5:1), love also is still spoken
of, the love of God, that is, which is poured out in our hearts through
the Holy Spirit who has been given to us (Rom 5:5). Through the
Spirit the love of God in us becomes the new power of life, so that
we ourselves are capable of perfecting faith in love (1 Cor 13:13).
So also in justification, faith is not present without love in which it
is always God, of course, who justifies, and not either faith or love.

But what is the reason, after all, for the correlation of justification and *faith* which Sacred Scripture clearly intends? Even in Rom
5:5 there is no *direct* connection between justification and love,
quite apart from the fact that in that text there is question not of the
love of man but of the love of God. And the different interpretations
of the exegetes leave it quite uncertain whether Luke 7:47 (cf. also
1 Pt 4:8) treats of justification in the strict sense. Why then does
Sacred Scripture never speak about justification by love and always
speaks emphatically about justification by faith? This too is understandable if we think with the legal character of justification in mind.
Justification is the declaration of justice by God in a court judgment,
and the appropriate human attitude is obedient submission to this
judgment. Justification is the declaration of justice by the *merciful
judge,* and the human attitude appropriate to this is one supported by
fear and above all by trust, the abandonment which affirms one's own
unworthiness before God's grace under the divine judgment of grace.
In short: faith. Certainly a faith of one who loves, and thus a loving
faith, yet not a love which overshadows faith. It is not in accordance
with the situation of the sinner for him to forget his sinfulness and to
lose himself in God's gracious lovableness without regard for his own
pitiable state of sinfulness. Faith in and from love certainly, but—
for the sinner who is still to be justified— a love which is bashful, not
bold. It would be impudent love if the prodigal son, unmindful of his
state, simply fell upon his father's neck with the words: "I love
you"; instead of—in confused love—casting himself down before
him and humbly, trustingly confessing: "Father, I have sinned; I no
longer deserve to be called your son." It would be impudent love if
the sinful woman, forgetting her past, presumed lightheartedly to be

an intimate friend of the merciful Lord, instead of—in ashamed love
—with tears for her sins, kissing his feet from behind in order to beg
his mercy. It would be impudent love if the sinner with embarrassing
misjudgment of the situation should speak of love, instead of—in
ashamed love—accepting in simple faith the merciful forgiveness of
God. As if it were not precisely the love of God of which the sinner
had shown himself unworthy, and thus would first of all have to confess that he was no longer worthy to love the Father, in order once
again to *become* worthy of love. As if justification were the trivial
reconciliation of two lovers who had fallen out and would only have
to throw themselves in one another's arms to be able to sing: "And
everything is fine again, everything!" As if justification were a loving
"reciprocity" on the same level and not rather the merciful *judgment of God upon* the sinner! Confronted with this judgment,
what is appropriate is not an avowal of love, but—precisely because it is love ashamed of itself—a confident submission in faith.
Thus although faith without love is worth nothing, Sacred Scripture
always with good reason speaks of justification through faith. This
faith, however, which excludes all works and merits for justification
itself, desires, once justified, to co-operate actively through works
of love; a faith which proves itself efficacious through love (Gal
5:6). The way in which the *"sola fide"* (by faith alone) must be
established in Catholic tradition (and especially in the Council of
Trent) has been shown elsewhere.[3]

It was Paul who occupied himself expressly with the question of
the "how" of becoming just. Now it is characteristic that in the
specifically Pauline usage of *dikaioun* (to justify), he never speaks of
self-justification by men. *Dikaioun* (to justify) is used either in
speaking of God, who himself justifies (Rom 3:26,30; 4:5; 8:30,33;
Gal 3:8), or of man who does not justify but is *justified* (Rom 2:13;
3:20,24–28; 4:2; 5:1,9; 1 Cor 4:4; 6:11; Gal 2:16 f.; 3:11,24; 5:4;
Ti 3:7). Some instances to be added from the rest of the New Testament, also applied to men in the passive sense, are: Mt 12:37; Lk
18:14; Acts 13:39; Ap 22:11 (the unconditionally preferred reading is, however: *dikaiosunēn poiēsato eti:* the just man ought to continue to advance in the practice of justice); Rom 6:7; and Acts 13:38
(*dikaiōthênai apo:* pronounced free of guilt or sins). Neither do the

following texts express self-justification: Rom 3:4 (so that your justice may be vindicated: said of God), 1 Tm 3:16 (proven just in the
Spirit: said of Christ), Mt 11:19 (wisdom is proven just; cf. Lk
7:35), Lk 7:29 (to acknowledge God's justice). Only two texts in
Luke speak of a self-justification. In Lk 10:29 the question at issue
is not justification in the theological sense, but self-justification in human conversation. Lk 16:15 on the contrary has theological import.
The Pharisees want to declare themselves as just before men, to represent themselves as just. This is rejected decisively by Jesus with an
appeal to God's judgment.

Nor does James speak of self-justification. He always uses
dikaioun (to justify) passively with reference to man. Man *is* justified by God, which James presupposes as completely obvious. To be
sure, this is on the basis of works, as James declares, in explicit opposition to the Pauline thesis (Jas 2:14–26). Yet we observe a
fundamentally different *Problematik*. Both ask themselves: how
does man become just? Paul, however, in his answer is arguing
vigorously against Pharisaical self-righteousness, James against lazy,
literal orthodoxy. For this reason Paul maintains: it is not man with
his works who justifies, but God by faith. But James says: only then
is a man just if his faith bears fruits in works. Yet, although Paul with
his "by faith alone" has no intention of defending Corinthian liber-
tinism, James with his "faith and works" is no less opposed to Pharisaical merit morality. Paul has no more intention of substituting faith
for works than James has of substituting works for faith. Nonetheless, Paul's posing of the question is more comprehensive: he too
emphasizes the necessity of works (which for him represent fruits of
the Spirit, and by which man is judged). Yet, whereas James directs
his polemic only against lazy faith-quietism and thus remains more
on the surface, Paul simultaneously proceeds against the empty
activism of work and poses the question of justification on another
level. Paul penetrates thereby into that ultimate depth where even
every good work of man is questioned—through the grace of Christ,
which strikes the sinner. In this last depth of the grace of God which
justifies the sinner, only one thing is appropriate for sinful man: faith
which trustfully accepts it. Thus Paul's "through faith alone" constitutes the presupposition for James' (and Paul's) "faith and works"

(works as the fruits of the Holy Spirit). One easily perceives that the same thing means something different in Paul and James, respectively: "justice": the ethical agreement of doctrine and life (James), and the gift of God's grace freely promised to the sinner (Paul); "faith": the merely intellectual advertence to a fact, which in itself is dead (James), and the assenting, self-giving of the whole man, confidently ratifying the kerygma, made active in love (Paul); "works": works of piety and love of the neighbor to be practiced by the Christian (James), and works of the law or of general morality preceding justification (Paul). Thus "justification" is taken by James not in the strict sense of Paul, but in a wider sense. The verbal contradictions in this instance are not real contradictions. Difficult as it is to establish an agreement between Paul and James, in any event self-justification is out of the question in James as well.

Thus only once (Mt 16:15) does the New Testament employ *dikaioun* (to justify) for self-justification—in order to reject it sharply. Likewise the term *dikaiōsis* (justification) is never used for a self-justification. In the New Testament, of course, God's justification of sinners means the self-justification of *God* (Rom 3:26), but no way leads from God's justification to the self-justification of *man*.

Certainly the justified sinner has become just and ought to live as a just person, ought to seek righteousness, ought to practice righteousness (Ap 22:11). "Righteousness" operates directly in life, is related to action, more than holiness which—according to the meaning of the word—signifies primarily an enduring condition of consecration to God. But it is not by practicing and seeking after righteousness that man justifies himself. Neither before nor after God's justification ought he to justify himself, nor is he able to do so. Once again this is connected with the legal character of justification. The sinner is pronounced just, and he ought to submit himself in faith to this judgment. It is not up to him to pass a sentence in his own case to his own advantage. As a sinner in need of justification, he is completely and wholly unqualified to do that. But this is true even *after* God's justifying judgment. Without any merit of man, indeed, contrary to his whole sinful being, this judgment becomes an acquittal which brings salvation. Justification purely from the grace of God! How then could he who has been graciously judged and justified by

God subsequently dare to set himself up as a self-justifying judge? As if grace does not *remain* just that—grace!

From the legal nature of justification, we understand why Paul nowhere derives a moral demand from the juridical doctrine itself of justification. Even where it would seem to suggest itself naturally, namely, in the midst of his explanation of the doctrine of justification where he has to answer the libertarian objection, his ethical argument is not based directly on the justifying judgment of God, but on Baptism and burial in Christ (Rom 6:1 ff.). It is not as if the doctrine of justification could be isolated. This was emphasized and will be re-emphasized immediately. Yet, in order not falsely to turn God's work of grace into a grace merited by man's works, it must be asserted with great vigor that God's justification of the sinner may not be allowed to become the self-justification of the sinner.

5. *But "self-sanctification."* Now with sanctification the case is different. God's sanctification impels man to sanctify his own self. "Just as he who calls you is holy, so also ought you to become holy in all your dealings. For it is written: 'Be holy, for I am holy' " (1 Pt 1:15 f.; cf. Lv 11:44). This "self-sanctifying" of man can be very easily misunderstood. It is God who sanctifies; we saw that. God in Jesus Christ. On the Cross, the Holy One of God, rejected by man, sacrificed himself for our sanctification, to be given back to us in the Resurrection: Christ is our sanctification (1 Cor 1:30); his Holy Spirit makes this holiness fruitful in external works (2 Thes 2:13); 1 Pt 2:2). Holiness thus means the state of belonging to God and being dedicated to God, in which man, sharing as a member of the Church in the Holy Spirit, has been called to holy service and holy sacrifice—in Christ. Up to this point, then, there is no self-sanctification of man: no sanctification of man by himself, but only by the unmerited grace of God in Jesus Christ through his Holy Spirit.

But there is a "self-sanctification" of man insofar as man himself —not by himself, but he himself—has to sanctify himself. "This is the will of God, your sanctification" (1 Thes 4:3). God's will is the basis and goal of our continued sanctification. This sanctification means behavior pleasing to God (4:1), which consists in the observance of the commandments (4:2), especially purity of bodily life in refraining from unchastity (4:3), so that even the marriage relationship is fulfilled with sanctification and honor (4:4). "For God has not called us to unchastity, but to sanctification" (4:7). We ought then to dedicate our members to the service of justice for sanctification (Rom 6:9). Thus the fruit of purity is sanctification (Rom 6:22); with modesty we must persevere in it (1 Tm 2:15). We must actively pursue sanctification. Without it, no one will see the Lord (Heb 12:14).

Thus there is such a thing as "self-sanctification," a sanctification in the ethical sense. In the New Testament this is not expressed by the word *hagiazein* (to sanctify). Generally speaking, the meaning of this word is linked to worship, not to ethics. But it is precisely out of the worship character of sanctification that the ethical components arise (cf. the point of contact in Rom 12:1 ff.: the moral life of the Christians as holy sacrifice; cf. Rom 15:16). This judgment of God which justifies has no need of ratification from man. But this sanctifying action of God which segregates man from what is sinful and profane for the service of God peremptorily demands from this chosen man a withdrawal of himself from the world and sin, which is renewed daily. The indicative becomes an imperative, and is its basis: "Let him who is holy sanctify himself still more" (Ap 22:11). In the work of Christ our sanctification is complete and certain, but still it must be continuously fruitful through the power of Christ's Spirit. Sanctification is a pure gift of God, but it must again and again be laid hold of and carried further by man. The initial giving of oneself in faith to God who justifies and sanctifies must be followed by loving obedience to God's commandments. This is a fulfilment of the law which is at the same time free of the law, through love. Against legalism on the right and libertarianism on the left—the freedom of the children of God.

Ethical sanctification is accomplished through good works, which God in his mercy lets us do (2 Cor 9:8; Eph 2:10; Phil 2:12–16); good works are the fruit of the Spirit (Gal 5:22). We are co-workers with God, *synergoi, cooperatores* (1 Cor 3:9). Man is justified without works, by faith alone. But he is judged according to his works of sanctification (Rom 2:6; 2 Cor 5:10; 2 Tm 4:7 f., 14). In these the genuineness of faith proves itself (Ap 2–3). They are works which are done in God (Jn 3:21), works of faith (1 Thes 1:3; 2 Thes 1:11), which is active in love (Gal 5:6).

The ethical sanctification of man is expressed chiefly by the word *hagiasmos* (sanctification) (in complete contrast to the use of the word *dikaiōsis* [justification]). As is clear from the texts cited above, it denotes almost everywhere the moral pattern of life and the moral conduct of man, the practice of holiness and the process of becoming holy. The word *hagiosunē* (holiness: 2 Cor 7:1; 1 Thes 3:13) also, which involves an element of worship rooted in reconciliation, has an ethical character.

But it must always be noticed that there is no autonomous human "self-sanctification." Even where sanctification appears to be man's own doing (1 Pt 1:15–17), it still is rooted in the sanctifying work of redemption of Jesus Christ (1 Pt 2:24). And if Christians ought to keep Christ holy in their hearts (1 Pt 3:15), then it is for the very reason that they are already holy through Christ's grace (1:15 f.; 3:18–22). In this sense the "self-sanctification" of Ap 22:11 can be taken in two ways—in its relation to worship: the holy person should continue to let the sanctification of God act effectively in him; in its relation to ethics: he who is holy should sanctify himself still further. The *hagiazein* (to sanctify) of worship is not to be confused with *hagnizein* (to purify), which carries the idea of ethical "self-sanctification," to render one fit for worship.

The believer, therefore, will never rely on his works, but will always think of himself as a useless servant who has done only what he was obliged to do (Lk 17:9 f.). His own nothingness and his constant dependence on God's grace is only too well known to him. He works out his salvation with fear and trembling with complete confidence in the workings of God's grace alone (Phil 2:13 f.). He is aware of the temptations which threaten him (1 Cor 7:5; 2 Cor 2:11; Gal 6:1; 1 Thes 3:5), and the constant possibility of his rejecting God's grace (1 Cor 10:12; 15:58; 16:13). He examines himself (1 Cor 11:28; 2 Cor 13:5; Gal 6:4), and prays to be preserved in faith (1 Thes 3:13; 5:23). And thus he is aware that Jesus Christ has laid hold of him and that he himself does not yet cling irrevocably to him. He knows that he is altogether imperfect and knows what the perfection is toward which he looks forward in expectation.

It is not as if I had already attained it or had already reached perfection; but I pursue it to see whether I may not lay hold of it, since I have been grasped by Christ Jesus. Dear brethren, I for my part do not consider that I have already made it my own, but one thing I do: I forget what lies behind me, and strain forward towards what lies ahead of me. With the goal placed before my eyes I seek after the prize of victory which God's heavenly call in Christ Jesus sets before me (Phil 3:12–14).

There is no self-justification of man, but there is a "self-sanctification." It is God in Jesus Christ who sanctifies men through his Holy Spirit. But the greatest marvel of God's pure grace is that in the working out of God-given sanctification, man—not by himself, but he himself—may sanctify himself.

6. *From justification to sanctification.* The mere fact that "sanctification" can be expressed by the word *hagiazein* (to sanctify) and *hagiasmos* (sanctification), the first of which suggests religious worship and the second, the ethical dimension, shows that in every discussion of sanctification (and justification) one has to guard against a pernicious ambiguity. To identify God's justification with the ethical sanctification of man is self-reliant Pelagianism. But to separate God's justification from the sanctification (making holy) which takes place in worship and which changes man in his very being, is dead legalism. The justification of God and the sanctification of *man* are to be separated, or better, to be distinguished; to this extent, justification and sanctification are two "steps." God's justification and *God's* sanctification are to be identified; to this extent justification and sanctification are two "sides" of one and the same process. The redemption event in Jesus Christ is a unity, and in him God simultaneously justifies and sanctifies. In justification more is at stake than merely a forgiving declaration of justice; when man is declared just, he is really made just. *Dikaiosune* (righteousness) is not something which will eventually be given. It is already granted; it is already poured into the present (Rom 3:24–26; 5:1,9,17; 8:30; 9:30; 1 Cor 6:11). It is not just an active property of God, but also a *dorea,* a gift (Rom 5:17; cf. Rom 9:30; 10:16; Phil 3:9), received by man, which signifies life in the Spirit (Rom 8:10). Even in the earlier polemic epistles, Romans and Galatians, legal justification can never be separated

from existence in Christ (Gal 2:16–21; 3:22–29; cf. Col 5:21) and from union with the Spirit (Gal 3:2–5; 5:5; cf. 1 Cor 6:11). Still, in the controversy with the Judaizers the legal doctrine of justification was necessarily emphasized by Paul in a more isolated way. (The other themes of the doctrine of redemption are not related harmoniously to it, but rather stand alongside of it: thus Rom 3:4: justification by faith alone; Rom 5: reconciliation with God; Rom 6: incorporation into Christ through Baptism; Rom 8: the fruits of the Spirit, etc.) Later on, the more polemic way of treating the subject, which focuses on a single aspect, may be permitted to yield to a more irenic treatment which places it in its over-all context. An example of this might be Phil 3:7–11; it is especially clear in Ti 3:4–7: "But when the goodness of God our Saviour and his love for man appeared, he saved us, not by works of righteousness which we ourselves had performed, but by his own mercy through the bath of rebirth and renewal in the Holy Spirit, which he poured out abundantly upon us through Jesus Christ, our Saviour, so that we, justified through his grace, might become heirs in hope of eternal life."

But though it is certainly true that God's justification is to be identified with *God's* sanctification, it is no less true that God's justification (and this is the only point which is theologically relevant) is not to be identified with *man's* sanctification. Rather everything depends—precisely in the Pauline way of posing the question—on man's moral sanctification not being justification before God nor being its cause. It is just the other way round: God's justification must *lead to* man's ethical sanctification. For St. Paul it always held good that the justice attained through the justifying decree (God's *dikaiōsis zōês* [justification which brings life]: Rom 5:18), which is linked to the new life (Rom 5:17,21), leads to the sanctification (Rom 6:19) exercised in faithful obedience (Rom 6:16,18), which in its turn again is bound up with all the elements which made up Christ's redemptive action.

Justice does not cling to man in a static way, but, while in man, it is and remains anchored in God's grace. Justice is and remains linked to faith, just as sanctification itself can also be nothing other than an active application and confirmation of the passive receptivity of faith, the constant affirmation proving itself in love, of that which faith receives in justification. Thus the sanctification of man is the fruit of the justification and sanctification of God, perfect if we look to Christ, who is our sanctification (1 Cor 1:30), imperfect if we look at ourselves, who only strive after perfection (Phil 3:12–15; Rom 8:23–25; Gal 5:5), subject to temptation, exposed to struggle, a life of death to self to live for God in Christ. "Let the just man continue to go forward in righteousness, and he who is holy sanctify himself yet more! Behold, I am coming soon . . ." (Ap 22:11 f.).

Translated by Mr. Edward Gilpatric, S.J.

NOTES

A translation of "Rechtfertigung und Heiligung nach dem Neuen Testament," which appeared in *Begegnung der Christen,* ed. by Maximilian Roesle, O.S.B., and Oscar Cullmann. Reprinted and translated by kind permission of the author and the joint publishers, Evangelisches Verlagswerk, Stuttgart, and Verlag Josef Knecht, Frankfurt am Main, 1959.

1. *Bibliography:* Besides Old Testament dictionaries (F. Zorell, Brown Driver Biggs, L. Köhler) and New Testament dictionaries (F. Zorell, W. Bauer), and the Old Testament biblical theologians (P. Heinisch, P. van Imschoot, T. C. Vriezen, G. von Rad, W. Eichrodt, O. Procksch, L. Köhler, E. Jacob) and New Testament biblical theologians (M. Meinerz, J. Bonsirven, F. Prat, A. Wikenhauser, R. Bultmann, E. Stauffer), the following encyclopedia articles are especially important: O. Procksch, K. G. Kuhn, articles on *hagios, hagiazo,* etc., in Kittel's *Theologisches Wörterbuch zum Neuen Testament* (Stuttgart: W. Kohlhammer, 1933), Vol. I, pp. 87–116; G. Quell, G. Schrenk, articles on *dikē, dikaios,* etc., in Kittel's *Theologisches Wörterbuch zum Neuen Testament,* Vol. II, pp. 176–229; A. Descamps, L. Cerfaux, articles on "Justice" and "Justification" in *Supplément au Dictionnaire de la Bible* (Paris, 1949), Vol. IV, pp. 1417–1510; W. Grossouw, article on "Rechtfertigung" in H. Haag, *Bibellexikon* (Einsiedeln, 1951, pp. 1403–1409; article on "Heilig" in H. Haag, *Bibellexikon,* pp. 674–680; in this connection see A. Köberle, *Rechtfertigung und Heiligung* (Leipzig 1930³), and A. Kirchgässner, *Erlösung und Sünde im Neuen Testament* (Freiburg, 1950). Other monographs of Catholic exegetes: E. Tobac, *Le problème de la justification dans St. Paul* (Gembloux, 1908); M. J. Lagrange, *Épître aux Romains:* Note sur la justice de Dieu et la justification, pp. 119–141, Paris, 1931²; S. Lyonnet, "De 'justitia Dei' in Epistola ad Romanos," in

Verbum Domini, Vol. 25 (1947), pp. 23–34, 118–121, 129–144, 193–203, 257–263; A. Rosman, " 'Justificare' est verbum causativum," in *Verbum Domini,* Vol. 21 (1941), pp. 144–147; O. Karrer, "Der Galaterbrief" in *Liturgischbiblische Monatsschrift,* Vol. 9 (1949), pp. 31–35, 92–95, 115–118, 142–144, 164–167, 174–178; B. Bartmann, *St. Paulus und St. Jakobus über die Rechtfertigung* (Freiburg, 1897); E. Tobac, "Le problème de la justification dans St. Paul et dans St. Jacques," in *Revue d'histoire ecclésiastique,* Vol. 22 (1926), pp. 797–805; J. Dillersberger, *Das Heilige im Neuen Testament* (Kufstein, 1926); P. van Imschoot, "La Sainteté de Dieu dans l'Ancien Testament," in *Vie Spirituelle* (1946), pp. 30–44. For Protestant monographs (W. Grundmann, A. W. Heidland, J. Resewski, H. Hofer, T. Preiss, W. Michaelis, H. Braun, F. V. Filson, W. Mundle, R. Gyllenberg, U. Bunzel, J. Hänel, H. Ringgren, E. Gaugler, S. Djukanovič, etc.) see the detailed bibliographical references in Bauer's *Wörterbuch* or in Kittel's *Theologisches Wörterbuch.* Further bibliography on the subject can be found in H. Küng, *Rechtfertigung, die Lehre Karl Barths und eine katholische Besinnung* (Einsiedeln, 1957²), pp. 300–304.

2. Cf. H. Küng, *op. cit.,* pp. 206–218.

3. *Ibid.,* pp. 243–266.

SELECTED READINGS

1. Bouyer, Louis, *The Spirit and Forms of Protestantism.* Westminster, Md.: Newman, 1956. Chaps. 2–5 (pp. 17–115) give an appreciative Catholic description of the Protestant doctrine of justification.

2. Cerfaux, Lucien, and Descamps, A., "Justice, Justification," article in *Dictionnaire de la Bible. Supplement,* Vol. IV, pp. 1417–1510. Two outstanding Catholic scriptural scholars examine the idea of justification in the Old Testament, in St. Paul, and in the rest of the New Testament.

3. Chavaz, E., *Catholicisme romain et protestantisme. Pour la clarté du dialogue.* Tournai: Casterman, 1958. 157 pp. An irenic but straightforward discussion of man's co-operation with God. A response to Professor Leenhardt.

4. The Council of Trent, "Decree on Justification." English translation in *The Church Teaches. Documents of the Church in English Translation.* St. Louis: Herder, 1955, pp. 230–246. Authoritative formulation of the Catholic teaching.

5. Küng, Hans, *Rechtfertigung. Die Lehre Karl Barths und eine katholische Besinnung.* Mit einem Geleitbrief von Karl Barth. Einsiedeln: Johannes Verlag, 1957. 304 pp. The most important recent work by a Catholic on justification. Contains an abundant bibliography.

6. Lagrange, M. J., O.P., *Epître aux romains.* Paris: Gabalda, 1931². The

"Note sur la justice de Dieu et la justification" on pp. 119–141 is a scriptural study with theological reflections by the outstanding Catholic Scripture scholar of the early twentieth century.

7. *Lumière et Vie,* Vol. 9, No. 47 (avril-mai 1960), "La Conversion." 114 pp. Conversion in the Old Testament (Lacan), the Synoptics (Lacan), Acts (Dupont), Paul (Boismard), and John (Mollat).

8. Lyonnet, Stanislaus, "De 'justitia Dei' in Epistola ad Romanos," *Verbum Domini,* Vol. 25 (1947), pp. 23–34; 118–121; 129–144; 193–203; 257–263. By a recognized Pauline exegete of the Pontifical Biblical Institute in Rome.

9. Möhler, Johann Adam, *Symbolism, or Exposition of the Doctrinal Differences Between Catholics and Protestants in Their Symbolical Writings,* trans. by J. B. Robinson. London: Gibbings, 1895. Originally published in Tübingen in 1832. Chap. III, "Opposite Views on the Doctrine of Justification," pp. 83–202. By one of the most stimulating Catholic theologians of the nineteenth century.

10. Newman, John Henry, *Lectures on the Doctrine of Justification.* New York: Scribner, 1874[3]. (First ed., 1838.) 404 pp. Aims to show "that there is little difference but what is verbal in the various views on justification, found whether among Catholic or Protestant divines."

11. Van de Pol, W. H., *The Christian Dilemma. Catholic Church—Reformation.* London: Dent, 1952. The two chapters on "Catholicism and Protestantism" and "The Content of the Faith," pp. 24–104, help to understand the difference between the Catholic and the Protestant approach.

12. Sartory, Thomas, O.S.B., "Von der Rechtfertigung," in *Gespräch zwischen den Konfessionen.* Frankfurt: Fischer, 1959. In pp. 138–143 of this paperback there is a simple explanation of the Catholic teaching on justification. This is the Catholic side of one of sixteen Protestant-Catholic dialogues between Thomas Sartory and Hans Asmussen.

13. Tavard, George, "Grace and Faith," in *Protestantism,* Vol. 137 of *The Twentieth-Century Encyclopedia of Catholicism.* New York: Hawthorn Books, 1959, pp. 19–31. A Catholic view of the Protestant doctrine on justification.

14. Tobac, Édouard, *Le problème de la justification dans Saint Paul. Étude de théologie biblique.* Louvain: J. van Linthout, 1908. 276 pp. A careful doctoral dissertation which after fifty years has still not outlived its usefulness.